Praying and Preying

THE ANTHROPOLOGY OF CHRISTIANITY

Edited by Joel Robbins

Praying and Preying

CHRISTIANITY IN INDIGENOUS AMAZONIA

Aparecida Vilaça

Translated by David Rodgers

UNIVERSITY OF CALIFORNIA PRESS

University of California Press, one of the most distinguished university presses in the United States, enriches lives around the world by advancing scholarship in the humanities, social sciences, and natural sciences. Its activities are supported by the UC Press Foundation and by philanthropic contributions from individuals and institutions. For more information, visit www.ucpress.edu.

University of California Press
Oakland, California

Library of Congress Cataloging-in-Publication Data

Vilaça, Aparecida, 1958- author.
  Praying and preying : Christianity in indigenous Amazonia / Aparecida Vilaça.
    pages cm
  Includes bibliographical references and index.
  ISBN 978-0-520-28913-0 (cloth : alk. paper)—ISBN 0-520-28913-7 (cloth : alk. paper)—ISBN 978-0-520-28914-7 (pbk. : alk. paper)—ISBN 0-520-28914-5 (pbk. : alk. paper)—ISBN 978-0-520-96384-9 (ebook)—ISBN 0-520-96384-9 (ebook)
    1. Indigenous peoples—Amazon River Region—History.
  2. Christianity—Amazon River Region.   3. Pakaasnovos Indians—Religion.   4. Missions, Brazilian—Amazon River Region—History.   5. New Tribes Mission—History.   6. Conversion—Christianity.   I. Title.
    GN560.A53V55 2015
    305.800981′1—dc23   2015034176

25   24   23   22   21   20   19   18   17   16
10   9   8   7   6   5   4   3   2   1

To the Wari' for their capacity to re-create themselves.

To my Wari' family, especially to my father Paletó and to my brother Abrão, for their efforts to make me into a real daughter and sister.

To my sons, Francisco and André, for their companionship in the field and outside of it.

To my father Hélio and to my mother Temis for their never-ending support, comprehension, and love.

To the memory of Claude Lévi-Strauss.

CONTENTS

ILLUSTRATIONS

ACKNOWLEDGMENTS

My field research among the Wari' was funded by FINEP, Faperj (Cientista do Nosso Estado 2012–2014), CNPq (Edital Universal 2011–2013; Produtividade em Pesquisa 2003–2015), the Wenner-Gren Foundation for Anthropological Research (International Collaborative Grant—ICRG 40), and the John Simon Guggenheim Foundation (Latin America and Caribbean Competition 2007). I thank Carlo Bonfigglioli and the Universidad Nacional Autónoma de México, as well as the Centre for Research in the Arts, Social Sciences and Humanities (CRASSH, Cambridge, United Kingdom) for the Visiting Scholarships that enabled me to discuss chapters and arguments from this book, and King's College, Cambridge, for my appointment as a Senior Associate in 2014.

My thanks for the support and intellectual stimulation of my colleagues from the Postgraduate Program in Social Anthropology of the Museu Nacional of the Federal University of Rio de Janeiro, especially Carlos Fausto, Eduardo Viveiros de Castro, Luiz Fernando Dias Duarte, Otávio Velho, and the late Gilberto Velho. And to my translator, David Rodgers, for our second large venture together.

Other colleagues around the world discussed my work on Wari' Christianity with me on numerous occasions, whether in seminars, conversations, or through intense virtual correspondence. I am especially grateful to Anne-Christine Taylor, Cristina Osward, Geoffrey Lloyd, Marilyn Strathern, Mark Mosko, Marshall Sahlins, Naomi Haynes, Peter Gow, Peter Rivière, Philippe Descola, Piers Vitebsky, Rupert Stasch, and Stephen Hugh-Jones. This book would have been impossible without my close collaboration over the years with Joel Robbins and Bambi Schieffelin, who guided me through this new field of studies and into a beautiful friendship. I also thank my editor Reed Malcolm and UCP's anonymous reviewers for their attentive reading of the manuscript and excellent suggestions.

Passages of this book appeared in earlier forms as parts of chapters published in *A Companion to the Anthropology of Religion* (Wiley Blackwell) and *Native Christians* (Ashgate) and as parts of articles published in the journals *Mana: Estudos de Antropologia Social, Journal de la Société des Américanistes, L'Homme, Ethnos, Journal of the Royal Anthropological Institute, Comparative Studies in Society and History, Current Anthropology, Cambridge Anthropology,* and *HAU: Journal of Ethnographic Theory*. I thank the editors for permission to use the revised versions here.

Beth Conklin, a close friend and fellow specialist in the Wari', became three times my *comadre* when, on a boat trip in Wari'land, she baptized the book. Archaeologist Dušan Borić accompanied us on two field trips and in the work of extending the limits of the Rio Negro–Ocaia Indigenous Land.

My students, past and present, have been a constant source of stimulation. I am especially grateful to those working directly on the theme of Christianity and who have contributed their own readings and ideas over the years: Artionka Capiberibe, Oiara Bonilla, Elizabeth Albernaz, Bruno Guimarães, Leonor Valentino de Oliveira, Marilia Lourenço, Rafael Mendes, and Virgínia Amaral. Tainah Leite deserves special acknowledgment for her inspiration, evident in the body of the text.

Current and former employees of FUNAI in Guajará-Mirim contributed in innumerable ways to the success of the research. I especially thank Juscileth Pessoa (Preta) and Francisco das Chagas Araújo. I also thank Dom Geraldo Verdier and Gilles de Catheau, from the Diocese of Guajará-Mirim and CIMI, and above all the missionaries Barbara Kern and Royal Taylor from the New Tribes Mission, for their openness and help.

Without my friends Isabella, Doty, Claudia, Daniel, Bia, Clara, Lazar, Joaquim, Fabienne, Stephen, the two Christines (Langlois and Hugh-Jones), Julie, and Simeran, and without my dear Ruth, I would have been unable to complete this book. Nor without Carlos, his love, comprehension, and companionship.

Introduction

It is well known what confusions and misunderstandings have
arisen in the history of Christianity by translations from one
language into another.

EVANS PRITCHARD,
"The Perils of Translation," 1969

Their misunderstanding of me was not the same as my misunderstanding of them, and thus the difference between our respective
interpretations could not be dismissed on the basis of linguistic
dissimilarity or communicational difficulty.

Wagner on his Fieldwork Among the Daribi,
The Invention of Culture

TWO THOUSAND YEARS AGO, a small sect, just one among the many
seeking to redefine Judaism in opposition to the assimilation of Hellenic
culture that had characterized the followers of the Law of Moses since the
Roman Empire's expansion into their lands, obtained a relative degree of
success. Among other factors this was due to its missionary emphasis and
inclusivity, which broke with the patriarchal and hierarchical structure of the
Jewish tradition (Kee 1993: 47, 52–55). Here inclusivity should be taken to
mean not only an openness to the poor and the marginal but also this new
religion's capacity to constantly redefine itself through the incorporation of
the social, cosmological, and ritual peculiarities of the peoples caught up in
its missionary expansion.

It was a historical accident, though, that transformed this minority
religion, worshipped by a mere 5 to 10 percent of the population (Veyne
2007: 10), into the official religion of the Roman Empire: the conversion of

Emperor Constantine in A.D. 312, following a dream foretelling his victory in a battle fought under the Christian symbol, formed by the first two letters of Christ's name (X and P). Ceasing the harsh treatment inflicted on the church between A.D. 303 and A.D. 311, and using persuasion more than persecution (21, my translation), Constantine gave Christianity a global dimension within the space of ten years. Veyne writes, "Without Constantine, Christianity would have remained simply an avant-garde sect" (13; see also Kee 1993: 63).

But Christianity survived the fall of the Roman Empire, became associated with other empires, survived the new configurations of power, and today remains a dominant religion across a large swath of the planet. As Hefner reminds us in his introduction to a pioneering collection on conversion to Christianity among contemporary native peoples, the world religions are "the longest lasting of civilization's primary institutions" (1993: 3, 34; see also Wood 1993: 306).

A missionary religion, Christianity was carried to the world's most distant corners and isolated peoples, very often accompanying the expansion of the empires associated with it, initially the Roman Empire, later the Spanish and Portuguese Empires, whose religious orders in the sixteenth century took it to places as far away as China and America. In these lands the church's envoys came face-to-face with cultures that were radically different from each other but that posed equally challenging problems. Certain that they were faced with a "civilization" in the fullest sense of the term, the missionaries in China strove to learn the language and traditions of the sages, behaving like them— that is, as emissaries of Western knowledge and science, an approach that meant they were initially well received (Gernet 1982: 27, 29, my translation). Comparing the work of the Christian missionaries in China and the Americas, Gernet writes, "The conditions were very different on the two sides of the Pacific. . . . Among the Indians of America, the question of adaptation to local cultures never arose and conversion relied on the miraculous effects of baptism" (60). As the author reminds us (59), this was combined with authoritarian imposition, made possible in situations where the "Portuguese and Spanish had imposed themselves through the Conquest," but unthinkable in the context of the "scholarly traditions" like those of China and India.

However, there was an even more important reason for not attempting to adapt to local cultures in a similar way, particularly in the lowland Americas: the Portuguese and Spanish did not recognize the illiterate Indians as possessing what today are understood as full-blown cultures, much less civilizations. Although indigenous peoples had been declared descendants of Adam and Eve at the start of the sixteenth century by papal edict, they were labeled barbarians, which, among other things, hindered the work of translation. As Father Manuel da Nóbrega wrote in 1549 concerning the Tupinambá (S. Leite 1954: 112, my translation): "I cannot find a *língua* ['tongue': interpreter] who can tell me, since they are so brutish, they don't have the words."

The difficulty in converting them was, however, very different from that posed by the Chinese. The latter, especially the sages with whom the missionaries tried to dialogue, were interested in what seemed to them to be their Western peers, but they guarded their own knowledge jealously and rejected the exclusivism characteristic of Christianity (Gernet 1982: 51, 92; Jordan 1993: 286), which led to the deterioration of relations when a new wave of Jesuits decided to act in a more arrogant manner.

"Myrtle statues" rather than "marble statues," to cite the expression used by Father Antônio Vieira in 1657 (quoted in Viveiros de Castro 2002: 183–184; 2011: 1–2) to refer to the same Tupinambá of the Brazilian coast, the "Brasis" were easily moldable, since they appeared keen from the outset to adopt the new religion: they learned how to pray, for example, asked to be baptized, and simulated prayer at mass. In the words of Father Manuel da Nóbrega: "They are a people who have no knowledge of God, nor idols, they do everything they are being told to" (S. Leite 1954: 111, my translation). However, just as rapidly as they converted, they abandoned the new faith and returned to their old customs, like cannibalism and warfare, forcing the missionaries to conclude that "the conversions were superficial, at best" (Pollock 1993: 167).

For over five hundred years this type of encounter has been reproduced in the Amazonian rain forest, where many indigenous groups once lived in a relative degree of isolation. On this temporal scale, the events that I wish to examine here happened just recently. In 1956, after years of attempts, a group of Evangelical missionaries from the U.S.-based New Tribes Mission (NTM), accompanied by agents from the Brazilian government, achieved the first peaceful contact with a group of warlike Indians who had become infamous in the region: the Wari', at the time known as the Pacaás Novos owing to their habitation of the river of the same name, located in the present-day Brazilian state of Rondônia.

Until then the Wari' had been totally averse to any kind of contact, and even with other indigenous groups of the region their only relation was one of warfare. Hostilities with the whites were then at their most intense, provoked by the invasion of their lands by armed rubber-tappers, who machine-gunned entire villages in surprise attacks, usually at dawn (Vilaça 2010: 83–88, 197).

Unlike other indigenous groups who had been in contact with Christianity via neighboring groups with whom they exchanged, the Wari' had never heard of this religion; and while the first words heard by them from the mouths of the whites probably included the word *God*, they certainly would have been unable to differentiate it amid the meaningless babble emitted by these strange enemies.

Just like the sixteenth-century Catholic missionaries, the American Evangelicals offered presents, communicated through gestures and founded village settlements, where they began to live on a daily basis for years on end. Immediately after arriving, they began to study the language. As in the sixteenth century too, devastating epidemics, an outcome of contact, decimated two-thirds of the Wari' population. In contrast to diverse cases from the past, though, these epidemics were not associated by the Wari' with the sorcery of the whites (or with the baptismal water, as in the case of some Tupinambá groups), who, on the contrary, were able to act as curers with the aid of medicines, which they associated with the name of God.

With or without medicines, however, the impact of the presence of the missionaries and their goods was little different in spite of the four centuries separating the arrival of the Jesuits on the Brazilian coast from the first contacts with the Wari'. Neither was the reaction to this show of power different: the Wari' set themselves to imitating the missionaries, although this did not include—given the different religious practices involved—the simulation of masses and baptisms as occurred in the past.

Around ten years later, in 1969, when some of the missionaries were already fairly fluent in the Wari' language and able to preach God's word, by then in the process of being translated, something occurred that both the missionaries and the Wari' describe as a wave of conversion, spreading through different villages. The Wari' presented themselves to the missionaries, saying that they "believed" (*howa,* "to trust") in God. They abandoned their rituals in favor of collective meals, attended church services, and no longer saw any sense in eating their dead. The shamans ceased to cure, in part because their actions had proven ineffective against the epidemics. People confessed publicly to killings in the past and to adultery and also abandoned their food taboos, assuming the right given to them by God to subjugate all of creation.

Albeit not as quickly as appears to have happened with some Tupinambá groups, about ten years later the Wari', too, reverted to their "bad customs," except for warfare and cannibalism, leading the missionaries to complain of the superficiality of their conversion in similar fashion.

They had not resumed their old practices out of choice, the Wari' told me, but because the fights—usually between husbands and wives—proved inevitable, provoking anger, the name given to sin, which escalated into collective club fights involving entire communities. The shamans resumed their activities, reapproaching their animal partners, previously shunned in order to "accompany Jesus." Present again, the animals started causing diseases among the Wari' once more, attracting the latter to join them. The chicha festivals were revived, bringing together different Wari' subgroups to become drunk together.

FACING CHRISTIANITY

In 1986, when I arrived for the first time, the Negro River village, in the Brazilian state of Rondônia, situated between six and twenty hours by boat from the city of Guajará-Mirim (depending on outboard motor size and river level), was inhabited by 350 agriculturists, hunters and gatherers with little access to manufactured goods. Although a health worker, a teacher, an agent of the National Indian Foundation, and a missionary couple from the New Tribes Mission were also living among them, they seemed to be living, we could say, a fairly traditional life. They told me that they had been Christians throughout the 1970s, but had "abandoned God" at the start of the 1980s. At the time four shamans were active there, curing people attacked by animal spirits and traveling to the subaquatic world where the dead lived.

Christianity remained a minor theme in our conversations and, in my view, in the everyday lives of the Wari', despite the continued presence of missionaries in the villages. Aside from the missionaries' work as teachers and nurses, any explicit catechism during the periods I was there, between 1986 and 1990, and between 1992 and 1996, was limited to discreet meetings, first in a small village house used as a church and then in the missionaries' house with a small group of people who had stayed Christian. In these meetings they read translated fragments of the Bible and prayed.

Understandably the Wari' seemed to have had difficulties comprehending the universe of biblical events. On a visit to the Lage village, in 1993, where a missionary couple also lived, I was able to witness an open-air lesson about figures from the Old Testament in which the missionary Royal Taylor, equipped with a poster, tried to explain to a small group of people what a king, a pharaoh, and a sheep were. On this occasion he complained of the inconstancy of the Wari's faith and their problems in understanding

FIGURE 1. Negro River village, 1987. (Photo by Beto Barcellos.)

the Christian message, especially the question of sin and salvation by Christ.

Inspired by Royal's remarks, I talked to the Wari' about their Christian past and noted that some people appeared nostalgic about that experience, associating it with abundant game and the absence of internal conflicts. At that time my grasp of this past experience was guided by these observations, which I associated with the Wari' attempt to eclipse affinity within the group and thus avoid the tensions and conflicts associated with these relations. As mentioned above, in their accounts of why Christianity was abandoned in the 1980s, they attributed it precisely to the conflicts between affines, manifested in the form of club fights and sorcery (see Vilaça 1996, 1997, 2002b).

With the Wari' uninterested in or disillusioned with Christianity, it was understandably not a topic of our conversations during that period. Moreover, having been mistaken for a missionary when I first arrived, owing to a similar interest in learning the Wari' language, being white-skinned, and coming from afar, I needed to invest heavily in explanations and acts that differentiated myself from them. The topics that initially interested me—cannibalism, warfare, rituals, and mythology—seemed diametrically opposed to Christian themes (see Vilaça 1992). Later, when I studied the first encounters between the Wari' and the whites, the relation with the missionaries became central, though Christianity itself was little present in the narratives on these initial contacts (Vilaça 2006, 2010).

This situation was transformed at the turn of the twenty-first century when a revival occurred, accompanied by a new wave of conversions. According to some, the principal reason for the collective conversion was the fear that the world would end because of the United States' response to the September 11 attacks, an event the Wari' had been able to watch on the community television. When I arrived in January 2002, after almost six years away, apart from a brief visit in July 2001, I was surprised by the changes and indeed experienced a kind of reverse culture shock: the Wari' now appeared much like Christian Brazilians. As in the past, a house had been transformed into a church, where various services were held each week. People came up to ask me whether the war had already reached Rio de Janeiro, my hometown, and were eager for international news of the conflict. They said that if the end of the world caught them unprepared, still non-Christians, they would go directly to hell, where they would spend eternity roasting like game animals.

The Wari' quickly perceived my mixture of surprise and disappointment, since they knew my interest in the histories of the ancient people and in shamanism, as well as my disposition to take part in maize beer festivals. Paletó, one of the people to whom I am closest, and who I call father, hid his Christian activities from me as soon as I arrived, sneaking out at night to attend the services without my knowledge.

Informed about what was happening in the village, and always interested in the life of the Wari', I began to attend the services with them. At first this was not easy for me. For three hours, while sitting on one of the church's wooden benches, I would listen to them read the catechism books in the Wari' language. My children, who accompanied me on this trip, and whom I encouraged to participate in the everyday life of the village, attended the village church service with me but then refused to repeat the experience. The oldest, Francisco, then aged eleven, had witnessed various traditional rituals and shamanic cures with me when younger and apparently preferred them to the services. Even so, Francisco learned Christian hymns with friends of his age, and André, then four years old, learned how to pray.

As well as leaving me nostalgic for the vibrant ritual life of the past, frequenting the church services placed me in an ethical dilemma: the act by itself would signal to them my approval of the choice that they had made and of the missionary work as a whole. Each time a Wari' pastor saw me in church, he would announce to everyone: "Finally God has spoken in the heart of our older sister." Once after we had talked in the afternoon about biblical stories, the pastor Awo Kamip, during the Sunday evening service, said to everyone: "Look, the stories of our ancient people were definitely no good. Our older sister, Aparecida, doesn't want to hear them anymore, only the Bible stories."

I tried to get round the problem by always explaining in our private conversations, or on propitious collective occasions, that my attendance at the church services and my interest in the new stories derived simply from my interest in their life, not from any intention on my part to become Christian. This caused some problems, especially for my close kin, and particularly my father Paletó, who said he was sad to ponder my future in hell, from where I would beg him for water and he, in heaven, would have to decline. He asked me to put myself in his place, obliged to refuse a daughter such an urgent request. On the other hand, every time he saw me enter church, he swelled with pride, the same way that parents today display their pleasure when a child announces that he or she is Christian.

Although I have been unable to make my father happy in this way, ever since then I have sought to comprehend the Wari' experience of Christianity and turn it into an intellectually stimulating project, which would have been impossible without their tolerance of my bewilderment concerning their new practices. Neither would it have been possible without a long journey through some of the literature on Christianity, previously unknown to me. I needed more than ten years exploring this literature, an iceberg of which I know merely a tip, as well as many discussions with other scholars of the theme, before I felt able to describe this experience. If the Wari' reinvented themselves as Christians, I have also reinvented myself in the process of writing a third book about these people whom I have accompanied for thirty years with great admiration, looking at them now from a different angle. The Wari' today declare themselves Christians, and this is the starting point of this book.

A "REPUGNANT OTHER"

My initial bewilderment was perhaps unsurprising, however, given that until a couple of decades ago anthropologists had usually tended to view Christianity as a kind of "repugnant other" (Harding 1991), something best ignored whenever possible or minimized in favor of the idea of a resistant indigenous culture (Barker 1992). Various reasons can be suggested for this attitude. Authors looking to explain anthropology's general disinterest have pointed to the Malinowskian model of the primeval savage and the historical rivalry between anthropologists and missionaries (Robbins 2004; Van der Geest 1990; Harding 1991). In the case of Christianity, the situation is further complicated by its position as the predominant faith in most of the countries from which anthropologists originate: the interest in the exotic is thus incompatible with studying Christianized natives (Robbins 2007b; Cannel 2006: 8; see also Gow 2009). Moreover, the theoretical tools of our discipline, particularly the culture concept, are founded on the idea of permanence and stability (see Sahlins 1997a: 51; 1997b: 137; Viveiros de Castro 2002: 191–196; 2011: 13; and Wagner 1975: 20–34). Robbins (2007b: 7) notes that these premises of cultural continuity directly conflict with Christian ideas "organized around the plausibility of radical discontinuities in personal lives and cultural histories." The outcome, he adds, is a notion of culture split between form and content, which inevitably assigns Christianity the place of form.

Various changes within the discipline enabled Christianity to move from being a "repugnant other" to being an object of study capable of intellectual stimulation. Fundamental to this shift were a series of critiques within anthropology since the mid-1980s concerning its theoretical and ethnographic foundations (Clifford and Marcus 1986; Clifford 1988; Strathern 1988; Schneider [1968] 1980, 1984; Sahlins 1981, 1985; Wagner 1975). This process led to the formation in this century of the subdiscipline called the anthropology of Christianity (see Cannell 2006; and Robbins 2004), which enabled a more coherent dialogue with the other subdisciplines concerned with religion and collaboration between researchers from different disciplines, as well as an expanding conversation between ethnographers of widely different regions (Hefner 1993; Cannell 2006; Lambek 2013), from which I have personally benefited enormously (Vilaça and Wright 2009; Vilaça 2013a, 2013b, 2014a, 2014b; Robbins, Schieffelin, and Vilaça 2014).

We cannot ignore the role of the natives themselves in this theoretical-ethnographic turn, since they began to insist on the new religion being recognized by those with whom they live. Some of them, indeed, colliding with anthropology's interest in continuity, postulated a radical cultural rupture by defining Christianity as something completely new, unknown, and without parallel with the native religion, in a clear appropriation of the classic model of Pauline conversion as an abrupt break with the past (see Meyer 1999: 139; Xavier 2013; Wright 2004: 13).

Moreover, native peoples have begun to describe themselves as more Christian than ourselves. Marilyn Strathern (1998: 109; 1999: 89) describes how she was approached by a Lutheran pastor from Hagen with a message he wished to transmit to England: "Observing that Papua New Guinea is now one of the most Christian countries of the world, the pastor said I [the anthropologist] must return to England where he knew there were few believers and bring people back to God."

It should be remembered, though, that this view of cultural continuity in response to the adoption of Christianity by indigenous communities cannot be attributed merely to the intellectual, moral, and conceptual difficulties of anthropologists ever keen to seek out primeval savages and reject Christianity. We need to take into account the very plasticity of Christianity, which, as I observed above, is an inclusive and missionary religion, characterized from its very beginnings by its capacity to absorb cultural aspects of the peoples it touches.

This question takes us to a long-standing discussion between anthropologists on one hand, and theologians, historians of religion, and missionaries on the other. According to diverse anthropological analyses, especially those emphasizing the resistance of native cultures, Christianity is an amalgam of practices and ideas that can be adopted independently, depending on how suited they are to indigenous categories, values, and interests. For the other group, though, it is an integrated and cohesive whole, recognizable as such.

Attempting to mediate this debate, Hefner (1993: 18) reminds us that although Christianity has indeed adapted to local settings, and that the idea of a monolithic Christianity is unsustainable, we cannot make the reverse error of an extreme particularism, since the continuities of Christianity (and other so-called world religions) are evident in time and space (5).

What do these continuities consist of? Evidently any perception of continuity varies significantly according to the focus of the authors concerned. To stick with the sociological analyses, and simplifying them enormously, these turn around two main axes: the cosmological and the identificatory or relational. According to the first group of authors, world religions such as Christianity offer a more universalist and rational doctrine suited to dealing with a new lived world arising from the expansion of the perceived universe through contact and globalization (see Weber 1956, 1987; Bellah 1964; Geertz 1973; Horton 1975; also see Hefner 1993; and Pollock 1993, for critical comments). For other authors, among whom I include Mauss ([1950] 1999),

Dumont (1983), Leenhardt ([1947] 1971), and more recent authors like Robbins (2004), as well as specialists in lowland South America like Pollock (1993), Taylor (1981), and Rivière (1981), Christianity is characterized by a specific morality and an individualized conception of personhood, both with direct effects on the indigenous relational universe.

I think that the transformations experienced by the Wari' with Christianity derive primarily from the latter two characteristics attributed to this religion—that is, morality and the conception of the person—meaning that my analysis situates itself principally alongside the second group of authors. However, I also recognize that these two axes, the cosmological-intellectual and the relational, are indissociable, not because Christianity introduces a more rational and universalizing cosmology, but because it establishes—at least among the Wari'—the very notion of the universe, no longer as a variable outcome of the relational context, as we shall see below in discussing the notion of perspectivism, but as a fixed nature created by God.

However, these different approaches cannot be attributed merely to the different authors involved and their particular lines of work, or to the peculiarities of Christianized cultures: rather, they are constitutive of a historical religion that, in its peregrination through time, has experienced all kinds of reconfigurations, sometimes emphasizing one aspect, sometimes another (see Kee 1993: 55, 61–63; and Pollock 1993: 172). Over time, especially after the Protestant Reform, for example, the focus of conversion went from practicing rituals to the inner individual, accompanied by notions of belief and sincerity (see Mauss [1950] 1999: 333–364; Dumont 1983; Keane 2002, 2007; Robbins 2001a, 2007c; Robbins and Rumsey 2008; Schieffelin 2007).

But variations in focus have occurred not only over time. As we shall see below, various authors argue that the Christian message is intrinsically ambiguous and paradoxical, even though, like other "moderns," Euro-American missionaries and religious agents tend to deny and mask the profusion of hybrids produced by Christianity (see Latour 1993: 133; and Keane 2007). In the specific case of Amazonian cultures, we can also add factors such as their intrinsic plasticity and transformability, which make it difficult to establish any dividing line between the new and the traditional. If continuity and change constitute two indissociable sides of the encounter with each and every kind of alterity, including Christianity, we are presented with an especially complex case.

The models analyzing the Christian experience of native peoples oscillate between the poles of cultural resistance and complete change (which, as we saw above, may match not only the view of the missionaries but also that of the natives themselves). Between these poles we find all kinds of mixtures, usually labeled *hybridism* or *syncretism,* a response that ends up merely juxtaposing the Christian and non-Christian elements without proposing a model for how they are related.[1]

Two models, situated away from the extremes, stand out from the others and are particularly interesting in terms of our present case. The first was developed by Robbins (2004) in his study of the Urapmin of Papua New Guinea, and it proposes a specific organization of Christian experience with respect to tradition. No longer a mixture of mutually diverse aspects, randomly juxtaposed or mixed, at the mercy of their compatibilities, but a structured experience in which the moral domain, objectified in the different values of the two cultures (6), constitutes the central organizing principle.

Robbins's model elegantly combines two models of cultural change of structuralist inspiration: those of Sahlins (1981, 1985, and [1992] 2005) and Dumont (1983). The initial phases of the encounter of the Urapmin with Christianity are explained by the categories of "assimilation" and "structural transformation," considered by Sahlins to be phases subsequent to the encounter between cultures, but which for Robbins are similar as the native culture's attempts to reproduce itself in the new environment. If changes occur, they are in a certain sense involuntary, according to the famous proposition that "the more things remained the same, the more they changed" (Sahlins 1985: 144).

Everything transformed following the Urapmin revival in 1977, when, unlike what had happened two decades earlier, they already had a good knowledge of the content of the Christian message and had experienced a process of cultural humiliation on seeing their culture from the critical viewpoint of the colonizers. This was when they decided to adopt the new, Christian "culture" as a whole (Robbins 2004: 3).

Robbins's attention was drawn to this process after reading a little-known article by Sahlins ([1992] 2005) in which the latter examines the phenomenon of humiliation and proposes the idea of the substitution of one culture for another as a solution to this crisis. However, as Robbins (2004: 9) notes, Sahlins's approach to modernization was "suggestive rather than systematic";

and looking to systemize his analysis, Robbins turns to Dumont's model of hierarchical encompassment, which enables transformation to be conceived no longer as substitution but as "adoption," recognizing the fact that diverse aspects of traditional culture, specifically its values, are not simply eliminated but remain active within the Christianized context. These traditional values relate to Christian values not casually, at the whim of events, but in a structured way, in the form of their hierarchical encompassment.

It is this focus on the sphere of values, Robbins argues, that differentiates Dumont's model from Sahlins's, making it particularly well suited to exploring the transformations arising from Christianity, whose central axis is formed by morality and personhood. In other words, Christianity imposes itself on the organization of the everyday life of the Urapmin, but the latter's traditional values, incompatible with it, continue to regulate diverse spheres of life, albeit those considered less central.

The second model proposing systematic interconnections between the native and Christian universes resonates directly with the questions explored by the ethnology of the South American lowlands (or Amazonian ethnology), especially the idea of transformation as a mode of alteration, a becoming other, reversible as a matter of principle, as we shall see. This model proposes an organization of Christianity and tradition based on the alternation, or oscillation, between them, in terms of both their global and their particular aspects. In the former case, the global, the alternation occurs through the spatial separation of Christian and traditional quotidian lives, taking the form of two "practico-moral-environments," to evoke Barker's pioneering analysis of Maisin Christianity (1993: 200; see also Robbins 2004: 324–325). According to Barker, the arrival of the missionaries and the creation of a "mission station," located at a certain distance from the village, prompted the Maisin to divide their everyday life between the world of the mission, where they went to school, spoke English, dressed in Western clothing, and attended church services, and the world of the village, where they lived in a way similar to how they had before the arrival of Christianity (see also Keesing 1982). Another example of alternation would be the switching between collective Christian and non-Christian phases, as happened among the Wari' in the recent past, and among various other Amazonian groups who, as we have seen, were said to have undergone a superficial form of conversion.[2]

It is worth noting that a very similar model of cultural change was proposed by Strathern (1998: 118; 1995: 7–8; 1999: ch. 5). According to the author, in Hagen, Papua New Guinea, the insertion in the Western world is perceived not as a progressive development but in an episodic and nonevolutionist way, as the shift from one type of sociality to another, as happened with the alternation between everyday and ritual socialities, or domestic and political, and so on. In her words: "If persons also afford a perspective on one another, and thus occupy alternating positions, then each person seemingly has within themselves the capacity to act in either an old or a new way" (Strathern 1998: 118; 1999: 98; see also Andrello 2006: 279). The resonances with Amazonian perspectivism, which we shall see later, are clear.

Among the models that explore Christianization in the form of alternation, some do not refer to Christian experience as a whole, but select one of its aspects—namely, the notion of the person. This is considered—in the same way as Robbins's model of encompassment, where morality and person are intertwined—as the crucial point of Christianity and thus the place where we need to consider transformation properly speaking. For Werbner (2011: 198–199), for example, in his analysis of the Christian experience of Apostolic Charismatics in Botswana, the Christian experience is objectified in the form of an "alternating personhood" (see, too, Mosko 2010).

The divergent notions of personhood evoked in both Robbins's model of encompassment and those that propose alternation as a model are identified either as relationalism and individualism (Robbins) or as dividualism and individualism (the latter cases). To quickly summarize, *relationalism* is a term coined by Robbins (1994; 2004: 13) to describe the prevalence of relations over persons, differentiating this configuration from holism, which serves as the opposite to individualism in Dumont's analysis (1983), and in which culture as a whole, rather than relations, is the primary value. Dividualism (Mosko 2010; Werbner 2011; Daswani 2011) is a term coined by Marriot (1976) in relation to the South Asian context but disseminated more widely through its use in Melanesian ethnology, especially in the work of Strathern (1988).[3] The dividual is a person doubly constituted, by two or more opposed aspects, such as male and female, one of them being either eclipsed or revealed through a dynamic based on the relation between two persons (or groups). As in Strathern's analysis (1988), for example, a person's gender is defined through the encounter between two composite persons, two dividuals, when one of whom eclipses that person's male aspect and the other his or her female aspect, producing a new dual configuration no longer internal to one person but constitutive of a pair. The encounter corresponds to what Strathern calls a process of "individuation," in no sense related to the individualization characteristic of urban Euro-American systems, especially since it involves a momentary relational configuration, which will later give way again to internally constituted dividuals, and so on successively.

This relational model has many resonances with those proposed in Amazonian ethnology, especially the notions of an "opening to the Other" and "dualism in perpetual disequilibrium" advanced by Lévi-Strauss (1991: 16, 316; also see [1958] 1991). The content of the dividual person is, however, distinct from the Melanesian context since its focus is not on gender but on the human and nonhuman, or animal, poles, more significant in a cultural environment in which humanity is the main position at stake.

We shall return to this point in the book, but I would quickly point out that in most of the analytic models of Christianization employing the notion of the dividual, the oppositional dynamic of pairs that characterizes it tends to disappear in favor of a notion of the relationally constituted multiple person, one that ends up differing little from the notion of relationalism (Robbins 2015; see also Vilaça 2015a). In Daswani's analysis of the Ghanaian Pentecostals, for example, the opposites are defined as "individual desires for rupture" and "dividual affective relations" (2011: 257; see also Meyer 1998). Likewise, individualism either emerges in its stronger version in the form of the self-contained individual, conceived independently of relations, that populates the urban Euro-American universe, or in its weaker version, restricted to a conception of the secret interior self. The latter, as we shall see, applies to the Wari' case.

In contrast to Robbins's model of encompassment, the models based on alternation, though they emphasize tension (Daswani 2011: 257), do not recognize any moral conflict, since each configuration of the person is associated with a particular relational context, possessing a specific morality. At any rate, in the conclusion to his monograph and in a recent article, Robbins (2004, 2015), by emphasizing the persistence of traditional values and the transcendent character of Christian individualism, which poses difficulties to its realization in everyday life, allows an approximation between his model and the model of alternation presented here—although for Robbins this involves not an alternation or oscillation but a "hybrid situation" as "one in which two cultures operate among the same people without in key aspects being synthesized" (2004: 332). This provokes a series of "contradictions and confusions" (182–183) that convinces the Urapmin of their condition as sinners, which they attempt to resolve through the elaboration of new rituals in which the different values become momentarily reconciled.

Returning to the question of the Christian message's ambiguity, some of the models proposed in the literature, especially those developed in the analyses by Cannell (2006) and Mosko (2010), relativize the problem of the conflict between Christianity and particular native cultures by recalling that Christianity itself is compatible with an idea of the multiple person, objectified in, for instance, the notion of the Trinity and the dual constitution of the human person in its opposed components, body and soul. Cannell stresses the "paradoxical" nature of Christianity (43), defining it as a "chimerical" religion (6), meaning that the message transmitted by it will never be univocal. These paradoxical aspects have been emphasized by historians like Peter Brown (1988) and anthropologists like Mary Douglas (1995: 20–21) and later reexamined by Werbner (2011: 197) in his evocation of the Renaissance theological debate found in the work of Cusanus, exploring the concept of the *coincidentia oppositorum*—that is, the idea of the "implied tension at the heart of Christian theology" (197; also see Keane 2007; and Orta 2004: 106).

In the case of peoples among whom Christianity was introduced by American fundamentalist missionaries, like the Wari', these factors are compounded by the conflict between the life experiences of the missionaries, educated in an environment in which individualism is undeniably a key value, and the message contained in the Bible, a set of texts written and stabilized in a single book around two thousand years ago, when, as we know, individualism was not a dominant ideology. As Assman (2010: 10) says, the Hebrew Bible resembles a "picture puzzle," related to "two quite different forms of religion—one polytheistic, the other monotheistic; one turned towards the world, the other turned away from it."

Unlike some Charismatics who receive the Christian message directly from the Holy Spirit and have little direct contact with the Bible, even going as far as to reject it—as in the Ghanaian case studied by Daswani (2011) and the Zimbabwean case studied by Engelke (2007)—for the Wari' the Bible is the only means of forming a relationship to God, its message being mediated by lower-middle-class fundamentalist missionaries from urban North America whose own belief requires them to translate the text literally.

In the case of the Wari', as among the Hageners described by Strathern (1999), the model of transformation based on the idea of alternation long preceded Christianization and was immediately employed in the encounter between the Wari' and the missionaries, as we shall see in chapters 2, 3, and 5. I conclude this section by observing that the Wari'—to borrow Gershon's description of another context (2007: 147)—were "no innocents to the experience of conversion," and that, as Sahlins wrote (1997b: 133) in his analysis of cultural transformations in diverse ethnographic contexts, "imperialism is not dealing with amateurs in this business of constructing alterities or producing identities."

I turn now to a brief presentation of the questions of Amazonian ethnology that make the model of alternation of interest in my own analysis of the Wari' case.

AMAZONIA: BODY, INSTABILITY, AND ALTER-A[C]TION

Until the first anthropological monographs on Amazonian peoples began to emerge in the 1960s (with some earlier exceptions), this ethnographic province was identified as "the least known continent" (Lyon 1974; Jackson 1975; Rivière 1993).[4] Moreover, in a curious parallel with the sixteenth-century missionary observations, the region's cultures were defined in negative terms, through the idiom of lack, as we find in Lowie's remarks (1948: 1) in the first paragraph of a book that for many years served as the reference point for Americanists: "The Tropical Forest complex is marked off from the higher Andean civilizations by lacking architectural and metallurgical refinements."

The monographs produced around this time and a decade later (Maybury-Lewis 1967; Rivière 1969; Overing Kaplan 1975; C. Hugh-Jones 1979; S. Hugh-Jones 1979; Seeger 1981) revealed the existence of distinct organization principles in the region, whose difference from the main characteristics of those peoples whose ethnographies served as the basis for producing the concepts then in fashion in anthropology, such as those of the Pacific and Africa, accounted for the amorphous and disorganized appearance of Amazonian systems.

Hence, for example, in the place of corporate descent groups, Amerindians displayed, in the words of Seeger (1980: 130), "corporeal descent groups," understood as groups of people related by substances, such as blood, semen, and food. So while classical anthropology supplied us with a notion of social structure as a system of relations between groups, Amerindians presented structural principles based on a system of relations between bodies (Seeger, Da Matta, and Viveiros de Castro 1979: 14), or, to quote the succinct formula of these authors, "indigenous socio-logics is based on a physio-logics" (13). Moreover, rather than an exchange economy alive with objects and commodities capable of mediating relations and standing for people, the Amazonian region (with some exceptions, including the Xingu region and northwestern Amazonia, where exchange is an important dimension) revealed values that were directly inscribed in bodies via specific forms of visual and verbal display (Turner 1995: 147). The publication of the four-volume *Mythologiques* by Lévi-Strauss (1964, 1966, 1968, and 1971), which revealed the importance of the "categories of the sensible" to the thought and classificatory systems of the Americas, resonated with the recently produced ethnographic data and had a marked influence on the new conceptualization.

Subsequently, notions of the body and the exchange of substances began to be explored in a more consistent fashion in ethnographic works, enabling theoretical elaborations that, somewhat surprisingly, ended up being limited to a debate between local specialists. Though influenced by the boom of discussions on corporeality in anthropology in the 1990s, especially by the notion of embodiment (Csordas 1990), the latter for their part dialogued little with the Amazonian material, even the material published by Anglophone authors (see Vilaça 2005, 2009a).

It was the revival of the notion of the body through the elaboration of the concept of perspectivism (Viveiros de Castro 1996, 1998; Lima 1996, 1999) that led to a change in the flow of these dialogues, when the categories of Amazonian thought began to exert a clear influence on anthropological thought as a whole, and to inspire the ethnographic research conducted in other regions (Venkatesan 2010; Holbraad 2010; Costa and Fausto 2010; Brightman, Grotti, and Ulturgasheva 2012; Willerslev 2004; Willerslev and Pedersen 2009; also see Strathern 1999).[5]

According to Viveiros de Castro's groundbreaking definition, *perspectivism,* like its correlate *animism,* is defined as an ontology founded on extending humanity to other types of beings with which social relations are established, the opposite of Western naturalism, therefore, where humans and animals differ radically in terms of their cultural attributes (1998: 472–473; see also Descola 1992). In animism and perspectivism, the difference between the many types of humans is given by their bodily characteristics—that is, by their "nature," in opposition to the underlying "cultural" continuity.

However an important difference in relation to animism was formulated by Viveiros de Castro (1998: 474) on the basis of the following question, grounded in Amazonian ethnographic data: "If animals are people, then why do they not see us as people? Why, to be precise, the perspectivism?" (also see 484n10). In contrast to animism, therefore, perspectivism is based on the "perspectival quality" of humanity, which far from being a fixed attribute depends on the relational context. This "perspectival quality" applies not only to other beings but also to the world as a whole, which varies according to the subject's perspective. So rather than a fixed nature perceived differently by each culture, as in our own cultural relativism, whose corollary is universalism, in perspectivism the variable is precisely "nature," determined by perspectives that differ according to the body. The nature/culture poles of naturalist ontologies are thereby inverted (Descola 1992, 2005; Viveiros de Castro 1996, 1998). As Viveiros de Castro observes (2002: 384; 2012a: 110), and as we shall see in chapter 2, in perspectivism persons and objects are similar to kinship terms, since they exist not a priori but as the result of a particular relational configuration: a woman is the sister of one man and the wife of another, an animal is a fish to the living and a corpse to the dead (Århem 1993; Lima 2002: 15–17).

With perspectivism the focus shifts from processes of constructing the body to those related to its transformation. While in both approaches the body is defined in opposition to the Western genetic model, emphasizing instead its fabricated and relational character, perspectivism accentuates the focus on the body's mutability and above all its instability, enabling a clearer differentiation from preceding models, especially the paradigm of embodiment that had until then remained a source of inspiration in studies of corporeality (Vilaça 2005, 2009a; see also Strathern 2012). What we find throughout much of Amazonia are not only bodies fabricated through relations of care and exchanges of body substances and food, as well as through adornments and designs (Seeger 1981; Turner 1995; McCallum 1996), but also unstable, transformational bodies, sometimes person, other times jaguar; sometimes consanguine, other times affine; sometimes Indian, other times white.

Paying attention to this specific aspect of Amerindian corporeality allows us to approach another central theme in the Amazonian literature—namely, the "opening to the Other," an expression coined by Lévi-Strauss (1991: 16) to characterize the region's systems in his analysis of mythology, and which has been present for a long time in the ethnographies produced on a wide range of groups living in the region (Viveiros de Castro 1992b; Overing Kaplan 1975; 1976). As these authors have shown, local systems show a constitutive incompleteness to be filled by whatever is exterior to them: enemies, spirits, gods. In the words of Viveiros de Castro (2002: 195; 2011: 16) in analyzing the place of warfare for the sixteenth-century Tupinambá: "There, the other was not merely good to think—the other was necessary for thinking" (also see Carneiro da Cunha and Viveiros de Castro 1985; and Overing and Passes 2000: 20–22).

In his analysis of a set of myths dealing with the relations between Indians and whites, Lévi-Strauss (1991: ch. 19) associates this openness with the dualist character of Amerindian thought, analyzed by himself decades earlier (Lévi-Strauss [1958] 1991) but here receiving a dynamic and transformational twist. In this set of myths, things and beings are organized through a series of bipartitions where one term demands its opposite, generating a state of "perpetual disequilibrium" (1991: 316). Consequently, the author continues, "the creation of the Indians by the demiurge necessitated as well the creation of non-Indians" (1991: 90), which explains, he argues, the interest with which the invaders were initially greeted by the inhabitants of the New World and quickly absorbed into their mythology.

Not merely an opposite, though: the other is above all a "destiny" (Viveiros de Castro 1992b; 2004: 220; 2011), since relating to the other implies transforming into the other, adopting their perspective and thus mobilizing their powers, which explains, at least in part, the mimetic behavior, taken by Christian missionaries past and present as superficial and meaningless. As Viveiros de Castro (1996: 139n20; 1998: 485n14) has previously observed, and as we shall discover over the course of this book, bodily transformation is the indigenous correlate of the notion of conversion underlying the Christian vision. Given that this transformation, like shamanic transformations, is essentially reversible, the difficulty resides in comprehending this mode of becoming other through a logic alien to our own (Viveiros de Castro 2002: 195–196, 2011: 17; see also Clifford 1988: 344). The alternation or "inconstancy" (Viveiros de Castro 2002, 2011) is a constitutive part of this system in "disequilibrium."

But these bodily transformations cannot always be controlled. The instability inherent in bodies inevitably implies the possibility of unexpected transformations, present not only in the mythic world (in which, according to Lévi-Strauss and Eribon [1988: 193] and Viveiros de Castro [1996: 136n6], men and animals were undifferentiated from each other) but also in the everyday life of groups who, like the Wari', were until recently haunted by attacks from humanized animals who wanted to take people with them, transforming their captives into beings like them. As a position rather than a fixed attribute given at birth, humanity was essentially unstable. It is precisely this instability that accounts for one of the primary interests of the Wari' in the Christian message. As we shall see in chapter 5, Christianity, especially the Book of Genesis, was taken by them as an effective way of stabilizing bodies and perspectives, since divine creation allowed them to fix themselves in the position of humans, associated with predators. In a sense we could say that they pray in order to prey.

Considering that in this world where all beings are human, and people may not be what they seem, the specter of metamorphosis replaces our fear of solipsism (Viveiros de Castro 1996: 132; Taylor 1996). The problem ceases to be knowing whether a certain person has a soul-subjectivity, since all beings do, but is instead determining what kind of body is involved—that of a jaguar, a human, or another animal. The consequences of any equivocation can be fatal, meaning that the principal everyday investment resides in ensuring oneself the position of human.

THE WARI' AND THE MISSIONARIES

As well as the conceptual dialogue between Amazonian ethnology and the anthropology of Christianity, another parallelism features strongly in the book, one related to the ethnographic approach adopted. Here Christianization is examined as the outcome of the encounter of two specific groups: the Wari' and the missionaries of the New Tribes Mission, allowing a dialogue between the concepts, worldviews, and theories of action of each of these parties.

I should make clear that the symmetric approach sought here has a number of clear ethnographic limits, given that my field research over these thirty years has been centered on the perspective of the Wari' rather than that of the missionaries, and especially given that during its most intense phase—in the 1980s and 1990s, when I was working toward my master's degree and doctorate—the Wari', as I have already observed, did not call themselves Christian. On the other hand, when I began my research on Christianity, there were no longer any missionaries living in the Negro River settlement, my base village. In addition, the missionaries, though usually polite during our day-to-day life in the village, avoided talking to me about the Wari', especially about the experience of catechism and conversion. Sometimes, indeed, my attempts at contact and dialogue were explicitly rejected. The exceptions, just two of them, should be named: Royal Taylor, an American missionary, granted me a long interview in 1994, and Barbara Kern, also American, one of the leading specialists in the Wari' language and also one of the missionaries who remained among them the longest, kindly agreed to enter into an online dialogue with me in 2011, during which we discussed some of the episodes from the initial periods of the missionary presence and especially the questions of translating some key terms, like *God* and *devil*.

This lacuna in the ethnographic data obtained from direct experience was filled by the written production of the NTM missionaries, including diaries, biographies, catechism guides, and articles published in newspapers and journals, some of them already analyzed in anthropological works (Almeida 2002; Gallois and Grupioni 1999). Although only one missionary (F. Scharf) who worked among the Wari' has written a small book of memoirs, home printed, the uniformity of this literature as a whole allowed me to use other accounts to comprehend the perspective grounding missionary activities among the Wari'. More important for the present work, however, was the set of materials produced in the Wari' language for the purpose of catechism, such as the NTM's lesson books, as well as the course books and hymn sheets, which contain not only literal biblical translations that can be compared with the original version but also the exegeses of the missionaries.

EQUIVOCATION AND CHANGE

Among the diverse theoretical perspectives on the changes resulting from the encounter between native and Western peoples, I focus on those that highlight the equivocations resulting from the encounter between distinct thoughts and cultures, especially since the notion of equivocation is central to the Wari' understanding of the world, as noted earlier and as we shall see in chapter 2. I should point out that the notion of equivocation is used here not just in the sense of a misunderstanding, an involuntary error arising from the incomprehension of one of the parties, but as a concept in itself, defining a mode of knowledge intrinsic to perspectivist ontologies, as proposed by Viveiros de Castro (2004), in which the difference between perspectives is not merely acknowledged but taken to be a positive tool able to be used to guide the action of the agents involved. As we shall see, taken as a mode of knowledge, the equivocation acquires a number of agentive and productive dimensions.

In my earlier book where I explored the first contacts between the Wari' and the whites (Vilaça 2010), the question of equivocation was already present, having been examined in the light of Sahlins's theory (1981, 1985). The ethnographic material examined there, however, led me to focus on the Wari' perspective of the encounter rather than that of the whites, which, given their diversity, could be determined only in outline.

The analysis of the Christian experience, though initially taking us back to the context of these first encounters, is fairly distinct in ethnographic terms since the perspective of the missionaries can be determined in considerable detail. Moreover, it is always made explicit, a procedure essential to catechism.

The possibility of obtaining a better grasp of the kind of equivocation involved in the encounter with the missionaries led me to combine Sahlins's approach with Wagner's theory of cultural invention (1975), whose resonances with the questions of Amerindian perspectivism are clear. While both authors think of transformation as the result of the extension of native concepts, taking the form of a "semantic stretch" (Lloyd 2011: ch. 4; see Wagner 1975: 37–38; Sahlins 1985: 149), Wagner allows us to understand that this process does not occur in identical fashion on both sides of the encounter. Instead of two groups whose cultures are equivalent to each other as cultures, for Wagner (1975: 22–30) it is the very notion of culture that is at stake, a fact that generates distinct equivocations. We are dealing, therefore, with the encounter between one group that thinks of itself in terms of culture and another that does not see itself in these terms—in other words, that does not conceive its actions to be intended to create rules, laws, and documents to be preserved. On one hand we have those whose inventive movement is called "conventionalizing" by Wagner (1975: 41–50), who look to adapt the Indians to their conventions and who perceive the unexpected outcomes of the encounter (the superficiality of conversion, for instance) as the resistance of indigenous "culture" (see Kelly 2011b), and on the other hand the so-called differentiating peoples whose interest resides in differentiating themselves from themselves, turning into others, rather than adapting others to themselves.

The apparent coincidence of the outcomes sought by one and the other (mutual similarity) in itself constitutes one of these equivocations under analysis, since it is the outcome of actions based on completely different motivations. This makes all the difference, since it implies, among other things, the reversibility that characterized the indigenous movement. For Wagner (1975: 116) this reflects a crucial difference between societies that consciously conventionalize and those that differentiate. The first "pattern their thought and action on a model of consistent, rational and systematic articulation, stressing the avoidance of paradox and contradiction." Here the fundamentalist Christian message of the missionaries in contact with the Wari' provides a paradigmatic example; in the words of one New Tribes missionary and author of a highly influential catechism manual: "What we announce here is precisely what happened literally in time and space. It is real, it is a fact, it is history" (McIlwain 2003: 39, my translation). Groups that differentiate, however, are "dialectical societies" who "play out the dialectical and motivational contradictions consciously in their management of roles, rituals and situations" (Wagner 1975: 116). Wagner adds, "It is a 'world as hypothesis' that need never suffer the stringencies of final 'proof' or legitimation" (108).[6] One of the central equivocations resides, therefore, in the confrontation between alternation, on one hand, and linearity, on the other.

This difference becomes clear in Viveiros de Castro's analysis of equivocation as a fundamental element of perspectival epistemology (2004), which in turn takes us back to the theme of the place of alterity in Amerindian thought discussed earlier. Hence, while for urban Euro-Americans the equivocation manifests as noise, a communication problem to be solved, one frequently attributed to the inferiority of the natives and their incapacity to comprehend, the latter turned equivocation into a form of knowledge, classification, and understanding of the world (see Keane 2007: 76–82).

The theme of equivocation is explored at length in chapter 2, which focuses on the different conceptions of translation informing the actions of the missionaries on one hand, and the Wari' on the other. While the former, from their universalist standpoint, assumed that the Wari' language must contain words that could indicate the same Christian meanings, the Wari', equally interested in translation, conceived it very differently. Perspectivists, they took translation to be made between distinct worlds, signified by the same words, derived from the Wari' language. As we shall see, it was necessary to know what the jaguar referred to when it spoke words in Wari', since the referents were certainly not the same things that people meant. The word *tokwa* (*chicha*), for example, designates blood for the jaguar, rather than a drink made from maize, as it implies for the Wari'.

The question of translation, a central aspect of the missionaries' work, pervades the entire book, spanning from the first moments of the encounter, marked by mimetism, considered a translation via the body, to the biblical translations properly speaking, produced in collaboration with Wari' assistants, closely analyzed in chapters 4, 6, 7, and 9. I show the interest of the Wari' in preserving the ways in which they differ from the whites, allowing themselves to be led by the latter into a different world, drawn by words coming from their own vocabulary. The "radical innovations" (Sahlins 1985: ix–x; also see Gernet 1982: 70) in relation to the former meanings of their words not only are the result of the involuntary risks to which these are subjected in the encounter with the other but also are actively sought by the

Wari'. Hence, for example, as we shall see in chapter 9, the missionaries' idea of differentiating the synonymous components of the term *jamixi'/ tamataraxi'*, both of which are used to designate a person's double, into two radically distinct terms was swiftly accepted by the Wari' since it allowed them to inhabit the world of the missionaries and their God, leaving open the possibility of a return to their innate universe of extended humanity. Thus one of the terms, *tamataraxi'*, came to signify the Christian soul, whose attribute as a corporal component was totally alien to the Wari', while the other, *jamixi'*, kept its original meaning as a principle of transformation.[7]

It remains for us to ask what effects these equivocations have for the Wari', or more precisely, how this encounter might affect their alternating mode of reproduction. Could this alternation be reproduced independently of the context that sustains it? Is every kind of becoming other the same?

As I shall show over the course of the book, this is not the case. The Christianity taken to the Wari' by the missionaries, though appropriated by them in line with their traditional alternating mode of reproduction, has proven irreducible to it, leading to alterations in their conceptions of the world, humanity, and the person. Unlike the animal doubles and enemies who inhabited their world, and who shared their perspectivist ontology, the missionaries—like their fellow Euro-Americans—are universalists, in the sense of recognizing a single nature created by God, and conventionalists, in the Wagnerian sense. In terms of their conventionalizing capacity, they are far above the other colonizers who more readily made use of violence, since they can turn to sophisticated techniques of conventionalization, tested and perfected over centuries in every kind of setting. One of these techniques is the introduction of new rituals, especially those Foucault (1990, 1997) called "technologies of the self," which among the Wari' ended up replacing the traditional rites, among them shamanism, essential to the reconstitution of their innate world.

We are not faced, however, with a linear process toward "full-blown conversion" or modernity. The Wari' continue to accept the possibility of living alternate socialities, as we shall see over the course of the book, especially in examining the choices made by them as assistants in the work of translation, as exemplified by the differentiation between the terms *jamixi'* and *tamataraxi'*. Just like the search for new and strange meanings, the preservation of traditional meanings was voluntary, the result of Wari' agency. However, the new meanings ended up imposing equally new concepts on their world, such as those of incorporeality, omnipresence, omniscience, and inner self, incompatible with their perspectivist ontology and with consequent effects on both their conception of humanity and their relational world. Their thirst for the new has now led them to an unknown world whose dimensions can no longer be grasped by their traditional tools of capture and domestication.

It is worth adding that although the missionaries were the first whites to arrive among the Wari', just like those who arrived among many other Amazonian groups (Pollock 1993) they did not come alone. As well as being accompanied from the outset by representatives of the Brazilian state and by Catholic priests, they paved the way for many other kinds of persons and institutions, who brought with them not only their own ideas but also Christianity itself, since a fair number of these people in direct contact with them are Christian, many Evangelical. Likewise, radio and more recently television have also brought Evangelical programs and music to the Wari'. As can be expected, therefore, they are living through a new phase of Christian life, different from the phase experienced in the 1970s (see Maxwell 2007) and one that might not be succeeded by a new phase of pagan life, as happened in the past.

Given that they are surrounded by Christians on all sides, it is somewhat surprising then that the Wari' are still keen to preserve their own world and that they do so in order to enable the Christian life that equally interests them, a desire that requires them to engage in complex procedures to make this composition possible. The aim of this book is precisely to analyze these procedures, revealing their limits as well as their surprising forms of success.

OUTLINE OF THE BOOK

The book is composed of nine chapters. The first five chapters explore what we could call the conversion process, analyzing the historical context of the encounter between the Wari' and the NTM missionaries and the dissonance between their distinct perspectives concerning translation. The second part of the book examines the Christian experience per se, focusing on the Wari' apprehension of Christian figures, on the complexity involved in translating key terms like *God, body, soul,* and *heart,* on the new ritual life, and on the transformations arising over the course of this process.

Chapter 1 forms an introduction to the history and ideology of the New Tribes Mission, setting out from the literature produced by the missionaries, anthropological works about them, and the lesson books in Wari' language prepared for catechism. The objective here is to analyze the concepts of culture, religion, and catechism guiding their work among native peoples.

Chapter 2 analyzes the two distinct concepts of translation at work in the encounter between the Wari' and the missionaries, and the equivocations stemming from this difference. While the missionaries conceive translation as a process of converting meanings between languages, conceived as linguistic codes that exist independently of culture, for the Wari', in consonance with their perspectivist ontology, it is not language that differentiates beings but their bodies, given that those with similar bodies can, as a matter of principle, communicate with each other verbally. Translation is realized through the bodily metamorphosis objectified by mimetism and making kin, shamans being the translators par excellence, capable of circulating between distinct universes and providing the Wari' with a dictionary-like lexicon that allows them to act in the context of dangerous encounters between humans and animals. Since all beings with humanity by definition speak the Wari' language, the shamanic dictionary is not formed of correspondences between words with distinct meanings, like the one produced by the missionaries, but between distinct empirical referents designated by the same words.

Chapter 3 provides a quick overview of Wari' life before the first peaceful contacts with the whites. Since these encounters formed the central topic of an earlier book (Vilaça 2010), they are described here in a summarized form, emphasizing the action of the NTM missionaries, including the specific missionaries involved in the encounters, their backgrounds, and the relation between them and their activities among the Wari' during this initial phase, as well as the response of the Wari' to them.

Although Catholic missionaries were directly involved in one of the "pacification" expeditions, and a small portion of the Wari' population has lived in a village run by the Catholic Church since the end of the 1960s, this relation is not analyzed in the present book. The main reason for the omission of this topic, tackled by myself elsewhere (Vilaça 2002b, 2014a; Robbins, Schieffelin, and Vilaça 2014), is that catechism per se was never pursued by the Catholics. Initially interested exclusively in the introduction of civilizing practices, they found their work was soon altered by the shift in the church's orientation following the Second Vatican Council (1962–1965), leading to the contrary movement—namely, the preservation and valorization of indigenous culture.

Chapter 4 is devoted to the analysis of the first translations produced by the Wari', in which they imitated the missionaries and tried to make them and the God presented by them into kin. Here I look to comprehend Wari' conversion through body language. The chapter also examines the mythic references used initially by the Wari' to translate the Christian figures, which reveal a conception of the primordial world marked by alterity and enmity, in opposition to the Christian world of equality and siblinghood. It also introduces again the notion of equivocation that permeates the missionary encounter.

Chapter 5 continues the analysis of a properly Wari' notion of conversion, turning here to the notion of an opening to the other (Lévi-Strauss 1991: 16) and the interest in adopting the other's perspective. The foray into myth reveals the opening of Wari' thought to this perspectivist notion of conversion, characterized by the possibility of reversal, given that the original perspective is not eliminated, only eclipsed. The persistence of the primordial world marked by alterity and differentiation, taken in the Wagnerian sense of a direction of human action, is explored in this chapter.

Chapter 6 discusses the equivocations involved during a second phase of Christian translation, this time focused on the search by the missionaries and their Wari' assistants for native terms to designate the central concepts and figures of the Christian universe: body, soul, God, Jesus, and the devil. I look to show that while, unbeknown to the missionaries, the Wari' perspective guided this translation, notions foreign to the Wari' universe, such as that of omnipresence, have effects on their world. The chapter also explores how the Melanesian notion of the dividual can help us comprehend the Wari' notion of personhood and its realization in the Christian context through the figure of the devil.

Chapter 7 provides an ethnography of the ritual life of the Wari' Christians, focusing on the church services, holy supper, and baptisms. It examines the guidelines for choosing pastors and deacons, the way in which the services are structured and unfold, and the interpretations of the biblical texts made by pastors and "preachers" through their reading of the lesson books, including the parallels drawn between biblical episodes and Wari' contemporary life. I observe the efforts made to achieve kinship with God by ingesting his words, a topic already explored in chapter 4, and the emphasis on the Book of Genesis and the separation between humans and animals characteristic of the divine perspective.

Chapter 8 explores the moral transformations associated with Christian life, especially with the new rituals, examined here through Foucault's notion of "technologies of the self" (1990, 1997) and its reworking by Robbins

(2004). Two other rituals, confession and the conferences, are discussed as modes of constituting an inner self, an idea alien to the Wari', and of producing the notion of a generalized fraternity, respectively.

Chapter 9 returns to the question of personhood and its transformations through an analysis of the translation of the terms for soul and body, which makes clear that the new meanings for the Wari' terms stem not from uncontrolled noise but from an active interest on the part of the Wari' in inhabiting another world through the Christian experience, as well as in preserving the original meanings, thereby enabling the oscillation that interests them. As in the analysis of the Wari' term for God, however, we shall see that the new meanings refer to a specific kind of unknown world, given the incompatibilities with the Wari' universe. The transformation of the notion of heart and its implications for the emergence of the idea of an inner self are central here. The Wari' conception of heaven, with which I end the chapter, sheds light on the difference between this emerging self and the concept of the bounded individual, which the Wari' can recognize clearly but which is incompatible with their everyday life.

In the conclusion I develop a hypothesis that explains the process experienced by the Wari', recognizing in Christianity a powerful other whose transformative influence cannot be overstated, situating it, as other authors have done, in the notion of the person, which in the Amazonian cases cannot be dissociated from the relations between humans and animals, thereby implying a new conception of humanity and the innate world.

ONE

————————

The New Tribes Mission

"Why go out there and risk your lives on those Indians? They are not worth going out after. They're just animals."

"It is because the name of Jesus is not known here, and **must be made known at any cost** . . . that we are going to the savages."

Dialogue between "Bolivian government men" and an
NTM missionary, reproduced from *Brown Gold*,
January 1944; bold in the original text

In getting information for the anthropological paper, we had to ask about all their miserable customs and superstitions and stories, but we explained that God's Book spoke differently and that His book is true.

ROBERT HAWKINS, *Bob's Diary: Four
Months in the Forests of North Brazil*, 1954

THE HISTORY OF THE NTM READS LIKE A THRILLER, its happy ending a reward for surviving an unbelievable series of accidents and misfortunes, with the added peculiarity of the script being written by God. The ordeals sent by the Lord to test the faith and perseverance of the missionaries included the killing by arrows of the entire first group of missionaries in Bolivia; the disappearance of the mission's first airplane, filled with missionaries; and the collision of the second airplane with a mountain, when once again all those aboard died. The missionaries remained steadfast in overcoming what were taken to be trials set for them by God: the mission prospered and spread across the world. Let's examine this story in more detail.

According to the main "native" reference work on the NTM's history, Kenneth Johnston's book *The Story of the New Tribes Mission,* published in 1985 and based on his personal experience, interviews with missionaries, and compilations of articles published in the magazine *Brown Gold,* the mission was created by a young Californian, Paul Fleming, the son of Swedish Protestants. At the age of twenty-seven, enchanted by a pastor's account of worldwide evangelization in a sermon, Paul, by now married, set off to British

Malaya as a missionary affiliated to the Christian and Missionary Alliance. After Paul had spent three years suffering repeated bouts of malaria, his health took a turn for the worse following a strenuous trip to the interior, and the couple were forced to return to the United States (Johnston 1985: 18–19). Paul then traveled the country with the 35-millimeter films recorded during the mission, showing the reality of the Malay peoples to audiences in churches, conventions, and seminars, where "many hearts were deeply moved and responded to the call of missions" (22).

The mission was founded some years later, in 1942, after Paul met the missionary couple Cecil and Dorothy Dye and other people interested in going to the "mission field" and "becom[ing] effective channels in God's hands" (Johnston 1985: 26). This initial group included Joe Moreno, who would later take part in the first contacts with the Wari'. At first, Fleming wrote, "we had no funds, no organization behind us: we were just a group of fellows who desired honestly to give our lives for Jesus Christ" (Johnston 1985: 29). In the first version of the mission's basic principles, it was established that missionary candidates "shall be chosen, not necessarily on scholastic acquirements, but upon evidence that they have a consistent passion for souls, are soul-winners at home," and that the mission was "directed toward those fields where no other missionary effort is being made and where no witness of the Gospel has yet reached" (29). It was also established that the central and most important objective was "reaching the last unevangelized tribe in our generation" (33).[1]

For linguistic training, part of the initial group went to a training center at the University of Oklahoma run by the already established Summer Institute of Linguistics (SIL), an offshoot of the Wycliffe Bible Translators, a "faith mission" created by William Cameron Townsend in Texas in 1934, also dedicated exclusively to missionary work and unconnected to any national churches (see Stoll 1982; Gow 2006: 216–217; and Fernandes 1980: 146). As early as 1943 the NTM created their own training center in Chicago, and in 1944 the first boot camp was held in California, inspired by army training centers. Already in 1942, the year of NTM's foundation, the decision was taken to send the first group of missionaries, including men, women, and children, to Bolivia. Among them were Joe Moreno and his three children. After many prayers and with an unshakeable faith, Johnston reiterates, they eventually obtained money for the boat tickets and other travel costs, their passports (which during the war period were not readily granted to young men), and even, at the last minute, the vaccines and certificates that might be necessary. Once in the country, and having contacted missionaries from the Bolivian Indian Mission, they decided to head to Robore in the interior and try to contact "the Ayoré, known to the civilized as *bárbaros* [barbarians] who had never had a chance to hear of the love of Christ" (1985: 44). Part of the group entered deeper and deeper into the "Green Hell," experiencing numerous problems, which led representatives of the Bolivian government to ask them, as already noted in the chapter epigraph: "Why go out there and risk your lives on those Indians? They are not worth going out after. They're just animals" (45).

In the chapter "A Living Sacrifice," Johnston reports the disappearance of five male missionaries who, at the end of 1943, had continued to journey farther into the forest, unarmed and seeking to meet the Ayoré. After establishing the first peaceful contact with the group, the search teams discovered that the men had been killed by arrows and buried in a swidden. The book later written about this episode, *God Planted Five Seeds* by Jean Dye Johnston (1966: 64), reveals that the sad incident was later construed as a divine challenge and stimulus, since it ended up generating additional support for the mission back in the United States and a surge in the number of volunteers (Fernandes 1980: 155).[2] As I mentioned already, new incidents occurred, also interpreted as divine trials: in 1946 a blaze destroyed the dormitories at the boot camp, killing a baby; and in June 1950, the first airplane bought by the mission, the *Tribesman,* packed with missionaries, disappeared en route to Venezuela. The mission immediately received donations for the purchase of another airplane—as well as thousands of letters from volunteers. On the new plane's first voyage, also in 1950, it collided with a mountain, killing various missionaries, including the founder, Paul Fleming (156). After each disaster or obstacle encountered by the mission, new prayers were made to the Lord, who never failed to offer quick and miraculous solutions.[3]

TRAINING

As I mentioned earlier, the missionaries are trained to survive in harsh physical conditions at training centers called boot camps or jungle camps, where they spend around six months learning to trek in the forest, chop down trees, build shelters, make fires, plant swiddens, and "a thousand-and-one other things that they would need to know out in the jungles" (Johnston 1985: 73, 123). This is a full-time activity, one that obliges the missionary to save money for training "or look to the Lord to supply his needs." Although these practical preparations for their work are emphasized, they are clearly subordinate to spiritual questions, the real determining factors in a mission's success. Johnston writes, "All the practical training in the world could never replace faith in God" (123), and individual failures to complete training are frequently blamed on the devil's work. A fine example of this view is the account by missionary Millie Dawson (2000), who worked among the Yanomami of Venezuela. The motif of her book, which describes the life of the couple and their children among the Indians, is overcoming endless difficulties through prayer and divine help.[4]

Linguistic training, initially provided by SIL, was later organized by the mission itself, first at its boot camp and, after 1955, at the New Tribes Mission Language and Linguistics Institute. From the outset all missionary candidates would receive—along with their jungle survival training, which included medical, dentistry, and nursing courses—"a smattering of phonetics, phonemics, syntax and morphology," as well as lessons in "literacy, Bible translation, and culture" (Johnston 1985: 183). Sixteen years later, more specialized linguistic training, lasting one or more semesters, was introduced for some missionaries, although the first semester of basic learning was maintained for everyone. The specialized trainees were selected "by testing (somewhat as the Army does) which specific students were of an analytical or detective bent in regard to language. . . . The specialist is a person who can pick up the language almost like a child" and thereby "'feed' phrases to the linguist and cut down the time it takes to break down a language" (217–218). Hence each team of missionaries going to an unknown tribe would contain just one or a few members who would devote themselves to studying the native language and translating the Bible, supervised or advised by linguists outside the field. These specialized team members would also be responsible for providing basic instruction to the other missionaries, enabling them to catechize the population.[5]

"STATEMENT OF FAITH"

For a clearer idea of the NTM's ideology, I provide a very brief presentation of its "Statement of Faith," as published on the mission website (www.ntm .org, accessed April 2010). The following list of principles reveals three central aspects of the fundamentalist doctrine: the literal reading of the Bible, the eschatological emphasis (the end of the world and Christ's Second Coming), and the idea of salvation through faith, linked to individual conversion, modeled on the conversion of the apostle Paul through a divine revelation that led him to exchange his life of sin for a life devoted to missionary work.[6]

We believe:

1. In the word-by-word inspiration and divine authority of the Holy Scriptures.

2. In one true God, eternally existing in three persons: Father, Son and Holy Spirit.

3. In the virgin birth of the Lord Jesus Christ, true God and true man, sinless. In His vicarious death, His bodily resurrection, His present advocacy and His physical and premillennial return.

4. In the fall of man, resulting in his complete and universal separation from God and his need for salvation.

5. In the voluntary and substitutionary death of Christ as a sacrifice for the sins of the whole world.

6. In eternal salvation through Grace as a gift from God, entirely apart of works; that each person is responsible alone for accepting or rejecting salvation through faith in the Lord Jesus Christ, and that a soul once saved can never be lost.

7. In the Holy Spirit, which regenerates the believer with divine life through faith.

8. In the bodily resurrection of both believers and non-believers. Eternal joy with Christ for the saved and eternal torment for the unsaved.

9. In the responsibility of believers to obey the Word of God and be witness to all concerning the saving grace of Christ. Although non-denominational [sic], the Mission is not Ecumenical, Charismatic or neo-Evangelical.

BIBLICAL LITERALISM

Biblical literalism is the distinguishing trait of fundamentalists within the Protestant tradition.[7] They attribute an objective, universal reality to the biblical narratives, taking them to refer to events that occurred in humanity's history. This history, and the moral principles embedded within it, can and must be transmitted to any people or individual through the use of translation. From this fact stems the centrality of translation in missionary work.

According to one NTM missionary, the author of a catechism teaching manual, the Bible is more than simply the real history of humanity. It "is the narration of ancient history, seen from God's perspective. It is God recounting the historical events occurring since the beginning of history" (McIlwain 2003: 104, my translation), a narrative mediated by the prophets to whom God "gave the messages that He wished to be written. Sometimes God spoke to them audibly, sometimes through visions, at other times God merely placed the message directly in their minds. God made the prophets write precisely what He said to them" (107). "Saving faith is based on Biblical facts that are objective and historical" (22). The words of the missionary Ronaldo Lindoro (2011: 135, my translation) dispense with the need for further examples: "The content of the Gospel is non-negotiable."[8]

The Bible is not only the divine narrative of worldly events but also a plan, since everything that happens to humans is designed by him like a "Master Builder in the construction of His Church. . . . He is always in total control of all His works. Everything was created according to a perfect plan. . . . God leaves nothing to chance" (McIlwain 2003: 3). Filled with this certainty, but unsure about the true comprehension of the Christian message of natives of a "remote island in the Philippines," the missionary Trevor McIlwain obtained a divine response to his prayers, showing him, whose mind had been "limited to the traditional methods of Biblical teaching, . . . the teaching principles that He has used in all His words" (4). It became clear to him that the teaching of the Gospel, the starting point of missionary catechism until then, required firm foundations. The "historical sections of the Old Testament form the basis for a clear understanding of the coming of Christ to the world and the necessity of His death, burial and resurrection" (6). The Bible is therefore more than the history of humanity produced by God and narrated by him: it is a didactic book for humans: "God designed the Bible with a teaching plan already included" (5).

Thus began the "chronological teaching of the Bible," "beginning with Genesis and ending with Christ's ascension" (5), an idea enthusiastically approved in 1980 in seminars held in various countries where the NTM was active, and which still today constitutes the NTM's institutional method for evangelizing tribal peoples.[9] McIlwain himself systemized his teaching method in the book *Building on Firm Foundations* (1988). I was unable to consult the original work in English, but its Portuguese translation (2003) is a didactic book for catechist teachers that instructs them on how to produce lesson books chapter by chapter, with very clear moral and behavioral guidelines on the attitudes to be adopted in classrooms and during course preparation. Above all the teacher must read the lesson exhaustively and "pray daily for his students. He asks the Lord to help him to understand and teach His word clearly" (93). McIlwain emphasizes that this involves a "panoramic" rather than in-depth study of the Bible.

Since the work of translating the Bible into Wari' had started shortly after contact, as soon as the missionaries were able to communicate with them (see chapter 4), there was not yet an institutional policy to apply McIlwain's "chronological principle." According to Barbara Kern (email message to author, 2011, my translation), the person most responsible for translating the Wari' Bible, this work occurred in the following order:

> First was the Gospel of Mark, then Acts, then 1 Timothy, all separate booklets. After that we translated 1 and 2 Thessalonians in a booklet, followed by Matthew 5–7 (The Sermon on the Mount) and some of Paul's epistles (Ephesians, Philippians, Colossians, Philemon) and John (1, 2, 3 John), all in one booklet. Then, if I am not mistaken, we translated more or less one-half of Genesis and Exodus, plus other sections of the Old Testament to accompany the chronological lessons. Afterward we translated sections of the Gospels to accompany these lessons too. And after that we turned to the rest of the New Testament. Everything is "translated" apart from the Gospel of Luke—in quote marks as we have to revise most of these books still, especially those we translated years ago. Those books that are "ready" (i.e., that have been checked by the consultant or are ready to be checked) are: Matthew, Romans, Ephesians, 1 Corinthians. I am working now on the Gospel of Mark and John they are almost ready to be checked.[10]

This order differs from that given by the pastor Awo Kamip, a man of about sixty, who worked for many years as a translation assistant. One day in 2007 we were talking about the Bible books and I asked him which book he had translated first.

> AWO: Genesis. It's the very beginning. Only Adam and Eve existed. Afterward the people of Adam appear. . . . It ends. Then Noah comes, Noah, Noah. Noah ends. Genesis up to Noah. No, after Noah. Then comes Exodus, Exodus, Exodus, Exodus. Exodus ends. Then comes the work of God, Jesus. Jesus was born, Jesus worked. Until he died. Those who helped Jesus appear: Peter, John, Andrew, Phillip. Only now the Romans arrived. Romans, up to Romans [was translated], it's the end. Exodus, Thessalonians, Timothy, Mark, the book of Mark. That's it. Acts came too, the book of Acts. That's it. I had Acts, but it fell from a canoe. It was lost. It fell in the water. There are the Bible course books [he begins to show me the written material].

APARECIDA: Is *Our Course in Tanajura* [a booklet prepared for a specific conference meeting held in Tanajura village] new?

AWO: [Yes, it's] new. Here's Ribeirão [showing me the booklet *Our Course in Ribeirão,* dated 2000]. Here's Sotério. This here is really good. Acts. Lesson number 5. This one is really good.

APARECIDA: Who wrote these small books [called "courses"]? A missionary?

AWO: [Yes,] a missionary [he shows me all the books]. . . . We sent Romans back to Barbara. We corrected it and sent it.

APARECIDA: Who helps Barbara?

AWO: She learnt the Wari' language completely. She can work alone now. You would be the same if only you didn't stay just a short time with us and then leave. As soon as you hear a bit of the Wari' language, you're off. You should record us and then take your recorder to listen. That's what the missionaries do. In your home, in Rio de Janeiro, you should listen to the recordings. Get it to work in your home. That's what Barbara does.

The divergence in the order of translating the books probably stems from the fact that preaching, as we shall see in chapter 4, began before formal translation and focused on presenting God as the Creator. Moreover, as we shall see in chapter 5, divine creation constituted from the outset—and even today—the focal point of Wari' interest in the Christian message.

Returning to the translation procedure itself, both Barbara and Awo comment on the final stage of native "consultants" checking the translation.[11] This is standard procedure, as Johnston (1985: 222) indicates in his step-by-step description of the stages involved in translating the New Testament to the Trinatario language, spoken by the Chimane of Bolivia.

In terms of the lesson books proposed by McIlwain and mentioned by Kern (the "chronological lessons"), six books have been produced since 1998, each of which contains the following inscription: "This is a book of Biblical studies in the Pacaas Novos language. It contains [#] lessons on [theme]. These lessons are based on the series *Building on Firm Foundations* by Trevor McIlwain and translated into Portuguese under the title *Construindo Sobre Alicerces Firmes.*"

In 2008, the date of my latest field trip to the Wari' (before a brief visit in 2014), I was able to consult the latest lesson book, dedicated to the study of the Book of Romans. Immediately after the standard foreword reproduced above, the following appears: "The Biblical sections are taken from the New Testament, translated (albeit in provisional and incomplete form) into the

Pacaas Novos language." The theme of each of the books and the organization of the chapters follows McIlwain's 2003 instructions almost verbatim. Thus book 1 is about Genesis, beginning with an explanation about God, his powers, his incorporeality, the Holy Trinity and the devil; book 2 is about Exodus and Numbers. Book 3 shifts to the New Testament, beginning with the announcement of Jesus's coming, his birth, miracles, persecutions, the Last Supper, death, and resurrection, with sections taken from all the gospels. Book 4—called *Teaching the New Believers: from Genesis to Acts* in the manual and "Lessons of God's word for those who have started to believe [*howa,* 'to trust']" in Wari'—mixes the earlier volumes with a focus on church formation. According to the manual, the objective of book 5 is to "present the order in which the epistles should be taught" (McIlwain 2003: 72), and it contains parts of Romans and Ephesians. For the Wari', therefore, book 5 covers "Acts, Matthew and John," while book 6 is entirely dedicated to Romans and is titled *Lessons from Romans.*

Hence from book 5 onward the volumes prepared for the Wari' apparently cease to follow the manual verbatim, though they do retain the same structure as the earlier books. Each lesson from a particular volume has a highlighted title and is divided into topics, highlighted in bold and generally followed by a Bible verse, also in bold. Explanations from the missionaries then follow. Each of the lessons or chapters terminates with a series of about ten questions on the studied theme, each followed by the correct reply.

To take an example: lesson 6 from book 1 is called (in Wari'), "Of When God on Being So Powerful Saw Everything and Made Everything." This is immediately followed by item 1, with the following title: "In Ancient Times It Was Always Night on Earth: [The Earth] Was Not Right Yet." And then: "Let us see Genesis 1:1, 2." The text that follows is considered a literal translation and is treated as biblical text, marked in bold, with additional highlighting in italics: "1. There was no sky in the past. There was no earth either. There was none, none at all, so God made it. 2. He made the earth for no reason. It was not right. It lacked parts/pieces. It was just water. The center [chest/heart] of the water was completely dark. It was never day. The God's spirit [*tamatarakon Iri'Jam,* the Holy Spirit] flew in the heart of the water" (lesson 6, book 1, p. 23).

This is immediately followed by three paragraphs of teachings by the missionaries on Creation, which differ from the Bible verses by being displayed in normal type. The paragraphs state,

Look at the sun and moon. They shine. If they did not shine, if the sun did not illuminate the day, if the moon did not illuminate the night, would it be beautiful? Would it not be ugly/bad for us if the sun and moon did not shine? Would it be ugly? Yes. . . . And if there were no resin [which they use as lighting] for us, would it be beautiful? Would it not be ugly? It would be ugly. We would not see the paths on which we walk, we would not see each other, we would not see the fish for us to kill, we would not see the game for us to kill, the women would not see the swiddens for them to plant. (lesson 6, book 1, p. 23)

The text continues to repeat the fact that in the ancient past everything was dark, there was just water and no land, the entire firmament was water. Next we pass to item 2: "God's spirit already existed completely. He created everything." Then, in bold, the verse Genesis 1:2 is repeated, the same as transcribed above. The missionary text follows, in two paragraphs: "There were no animals before. There were no people, there was nothing. But God's spirit already existed. He already existed on earth. He already existed completely. I shall create all things, he said. God is one, but not exactly. There are three who live in him. All of them are God. God his father, God his son, God his spirit. It was this God that has three living in him that made all things. He made all things, God who is three living in him" (lesson 6, book 1, p. 23).

A number of questions are also included at the end of this lesson 6. The question section is called "We Speak among Ourselves So That We Can Understand Each Other." This contains a series of questions and replies:

1. What was the earth like when God had yet to make it right?

REPLY: It was no good. There were no parts, there was just water, the center of the water was black, black.

2. Why did God make everything? Did he make all things [with his hands]?

REPLY: No, he made all things exist with his words.

. . .

6. Why did God make the water? Why did he make the fruits?

REPLY: If he was not content with us. . . . He does not dislike us, he feels sorry for us. He made the water for us. For you to drink, he told us. He made all the fruits for us. So you can eat them, he told us. He made all the animals in our lands for us. (lesson 6, book 1, p. 30)

The entire text is written in the Wari' language and the church services are structured around these lesson books. Each service involves a reading of one of the lessons by a pastor—who, while reading, makes no distinction between the biblical text and the missionary text—interspersed with explanations and repetitions by the pastor himself. At the end he reads the questions for the congregation to reply to out loud. We return to the question of the written material and the structure of the church services in chapters 4 and 7.

THE ESCHATOLOGICAL EMPHASIS

The urgency behind this work of transmitting the truth stems from the eschatology foreseeing the imminent end of the world as it currently exists. The central reference point for it is the Book of Revelation, though it is also announced in the Gospels of Matthew and Mark, in 1 and 2 Thessalonians, and in 2 Peter.[12] This moment will occur without warning, or will be announced by signs to be carefully interpreted and which refer to the domination of the world by the antichrist, or the devil, one sign of which is the outbreak of many wars in different parts of the world. As we already know, among the Wari' the fall of the World Trade Center, which they were able watch on television, was, according to some people, the cause of the collective conversion associated with this idea of the imminent end of the world. Robbins (2004: 157–158) writes that the Urapmin of Papua New Guinea were always on the lookout for potential signs of war, which was expected to begin in the large urban centers, and constantly questioned the anthropologist about his knowledge of these signals. Likewise the Wari' asked me continually in 2002 who the Taliban were and whether they had already reached Rio de Janeiro. The end of the world will be preceded by the Second Coming of Christ, who will take all the true believers with him to heaven, including the dead, who will be resuscitated with their bodies intact. According to the pretribulationist eschatological viewpoint, the others will remain in the earth in constant suffering in a world now ruled entirely by the devil. In the Wari' case, as we shall see, this suffering entails being fixed in the prey position, since the Wari' will be pursued and eaten by jaguars. This same position characterizes the suffering of the dead in hell. According to the premillennialist version of this eschatology, after the period of great suffering Christ will return to earth, imprison the devil and his earthly retinue, and reign here for a thousand years with all the saved who accompanied him in heaven. After this thousand-year period, the devil will be released and then destroyed once and for all.[13]

It is important to note that this eschatological vision is closely related to literalism, grounded in the idea of a chronological sequence of eras or phases, known as dispensationalism, as set out in the biblical texts. As we shall see later, like these eschatological conceptions, biblical literalism equally founds the missionaries' vision of culture, allowing us to reaffirm the central role of this "statement of faith."[14]

OPPOSITION TO THE OTHER
DENOMINATIONS AND SECTS

Going back to the "Statement of Faith," the objective of item 9 is to differentiate the faith mission clearly from other Protestant groups: ecumenical, pentecostal, neo-pentecostal (also classified as "neo-charismatic" or "neo-evangelical"), and the denominational missions. The missionaries among the Wari' emphasize this difference both in their oral preaching and in written materials produced for divulgation. At a conference held in July 2009, a Brazilian missionary explained the need to create a Wari' Christian association so that they could collect money for a common fund, but also so that, as a legal entity, they could take legal action to prevent the entry of missionaries from other creeds into the villages. In the course booklet *Our Course in Ribeirão,* the last chapter (chapter 11), "The Whites Who Believe Differently to Us," is an explicit exhortation against other variants of Protestant Christianity, named one by one. The introduction states the following:

> There are whites who believe [*howa,* "to trust"] differently to us. They do not understand the word of God well." "Jehovah's Witnesses. They do not understand anything. They believe wrongly. For them Jesus is not God, Universal [referring to the Universal Church]. They are very wrong. They do not believe in the truth of God's word. They become excited about the "money" to be able to purchase things for themselves.... Adventists. They do not understand properly either. They only concur with what Moses wrote. They say: God does not like us to eat peccaries, capuchin monkeys, pacas.... Assembly of God. There are lots of Assemblies of God, where they believe more or less. Look at what they do not understand. This is what they think: if we become angry when we have already once been believers, we will not escape. (*Our Course in Ribeirão,* p. 27)

The text goes on to explain that if these other believers wish to enter "our church," they should be sent away and warned never to return.[15] They should not be allowed to preach, and should be told clearly that they (the Wari') already have their own church and their pastors. And here the text cites Romans 15:20, where Paul teaches that one should not preach to those "who have already heard the name of Christ" (p. 29).

The Wari' pastor Awo Kamip once told me the following while we were discussing the different denominations:

> The Universal Church is wrong: it asks for money and distributes it for the pastor to become rich. Baptists don't ask for money. They only call on people to hear the word of God, to know that Jesus died in our place. Baptists [the church that the missionaries attend, along with the Presbyterian church, when in the neighboring city of Guajará-Mirim] cannot steal, become angry, smoke or drink alcohol. Adventists don't eat meat, only greens. They only eat red brocket deer. During the time of the Pharisees [people] could not eat paca meat because it looks upwards to God. Deer don't look upwards. The Assembly of God is no good either. They built a church in Deolinda [a Wari' village]. They wanted to build one in Ribeirão, but when Barbara and Manfredo [NTM missionaries] came, they gave up because Manfredo said that if they preached in Portuguese the elders would not understand them.

All of which coincides with the words of McIlwain (2003: 39): "There is just one historical and real religion and that is the religion of the Bible. . . . All the other religions are false and the treacherous work of Satan."

THE NOTION OF CULTURE

Separate from nature, culture is conceived by the missionaries—Christians in general and the fundamentalists in particular—as a set of practices and beliefs, not along functionalist lines in which these elements constitute an indissociable organic whole, but in accordance with an evolutionist conception that presumes both the mutual independence of the constitutive aspects of a culture and the localization of this whole within a particular evolutionary scale, whose apex would be Euro-American civilization.[16] This view is expressed in value statements concerning indigenous beliefs and practices, deemed to be "wrong," that justify the sense of urgency in the missionary action needed to eradicate them.[17]

I turn back to the booklet produced by the Wari' in 2000, *Our Course in Ribeirão,* because of its clarity and didacticism. Chapter 9 is titled "What Our Ancestors Believed In." The topics are itemized as follows:

There were those who believed that the spirit ["double," *jami*] of the animals gave us diseases.

There were those who dreamed of animals, the white-lipped peccary, the spirit of the peccary caught me, it walks beside me.

There were those who dreamed of foreigners and said: they will kill us.

There were those who did not believe the doctor from Guajará [the nearby city], what he said about disease. They thought: no, this is a Wari' disease, it is an animal spirit, my disease came from the forest....

There were also those who thought thus about diseases: the foreigner poisoned me, I shall die.

There were those who thought wrongly that the snake had shot them with arrows. Ah, the spirit of the snake entered me, it's eating me from within.

There were those who misunderstood the death of a relative. Maybe the doctor from Guajará was right: it wasn't like that, it was the damned mosquito, that's why he died [said the doctor]. They didn't believe it. They thought no, he was attacked by sorcery. (p. 22)

These are followed by exhortations: "Our ancestors believed these things long ago. If only they had known the word of God! They only knew the devil's things. It was the devil who gave them all those things. Liar. Our ancestors were forced to hear many lies in the distant past."

I should make clear that this is a conviction of the missionaries themselves, made explicit by Scharf (2010: 57) in his description of a Wari' shaman acting as a white-lipped peccary. This text reveals that Scharf believed that a "transcendental journey" took place that gave the shaman an abnormal force and made leaves "materialize" in his mouth, which he later spat out. The information concerning the localization of a band of white-lipped peccaries passed on by the shaman to the others was subsequently confirmed by the hunters. Scharf concludes, "This act of trance and Maxün Korain's entire procedure, relaying all the guidance he received from the spirits concerning the hunt and the successful outcome of the latter, very clearly shows how these Indians are influenced, guided and dominated by such spirits and demons" (58, my translation). He subsequently cites the First Epistle to the Corinthians 10:19–22: "What I am saying is that what is sacrificed on the Pagan altars is offered to demons and not to God. And I do not want you to take part in the things of demons" (59).[18] If moral errors are the work of the devil, what we could call historical errors are associated by the missionaries (and, as we shall see later, by the Wari') with illiteracy. We shall return to this question in chapter 4.

Concomitantly with the classical, valorative, and hierarchizing component in the evolutionist conception of culture held by the missionaries, Almeida (2002) calls attention to the more immediate influence of North American cultural anthropology (its determinist school inspired by evolutionism) on the missionary training courses. In his words: "The missions consider culture to be a dynamic totality composed of cultural traits, which are classified as positive and negative. . . . The aspects considered negative (drunkenness, adultery, violence, etc.) must be abandoned and replaced by more appropriate conduct. The positives, for their part, must be maintained and *revealed* within each society, such as the consciousness of guilt and the idea of a supernatural and saving God" (Almeida 2002: 126, my translation).

According to a paper presented by SIL missionaries at the International Congress of Americanists (1977):

> As a human being, the anthropologist, linguist or other field researcher must admit the existence of good and evil. He or she must recognize the presence of negative aspects in all cultures. . . .
>
> Negative traits are considered those that lead to the self-destruction of the culture and/or the physical or psychosocial suffering of its people, or that lead to injustices against individuals within or outside this culture. . . . Injustices are defined in general by universally recognized values, such as those stated in the United Nations Universal Declaration of Human Rights. . . . Positive traits are those that are not negative. They cover the entire range of a people's social, physical and spiritual reality: marriage patterns, family structure, kinship system, . . . language, . . . art, music, clothing." (Wise et al. 1977: 507, 503, cited in Gallois and Grupioni 1999: 107, my translation)

Like everything else, the missionary view of culture is subordinate to the idea of faith as knowledge of God and his word. The words of the missionary Royal Taylor, in an interview given to me, illustrate this conception perfectly. We were talking about the funerary cannibalism practiced by the Wari' until at least the start of the 1960s, when pacification occurred. I asked Royal how the missionaries stood in relation to this practice, and he replied by recounting an event that had taken place at the Lage Velho Indigenous Post in 1962, a year after the establishment of peaceful contact with Wari' subgroups that lived there:

Paton died, and so a woman came to ask us: could we eat old Paton? We are extremely sensitive to the indigenous culture. What matters is when we teach the word of God concerning the spiritual world, which differs from their spiritual world. They learn that God is the one who controls, not the spirits. At that time [1962] we had not taught them the word of God, and we replied to the woman: "As far as we are concerned, you could eat him because we know it is important. But you know that the SPI [the government's Indian Protection Service] personnel don't like it." We knew that we were subordinated to the SPI. They ended up burying the man. (Royal Taylor, pers. comm., 1994, my translation)

The submission of "culture" to faith was clearly expressed by the same man: "We were not that interested in their development in civilizational terms. We wanted to learn the language so we could communicate God's word" (Royal Taylor, pers. comm., 1994).

To return to the idea of indigenous culture as a set of traits with differentiated values (good and bad): the missionary conception asserts that these values are shared by the Indians, who find themselves imprisoned by cultural practices that keep them in a "regime of terror" (Gallois and Grupioni 1999: 106–110).

In the words of Royal on the Wari': "When the first [Wari'] accepted the message of the gospel, especially the spiritual liberation offered to them through the gospel, they lost their fear of many things, such as the animal spirits that caused diseases. They knew that the dominant spirit was God, and they lost their fear of wraiths, of animal spirits. They freed themselves from enslavement. They could wander outside at night, they could eat everything" (pers. comm., 1994).

In his memoirs, Scharf (2010: 59, my translation) discusses the fears of the Wari' at some length: "They go from one error to another, all because they fear these spirits tremendously. . . . Who can liberate them from these errors and fears? From these demons and malign spirits that force them to live in this way and to sacrifice themselves to them?"[19] It is worth mentioning again that the missionaries share with the Wari' the idea of the concrete existence of the spirits (animal doubles in the Wari' case), thereby reserving a place for them in the Christian cosmology. The difference in their conceptions clearly resides in the type of relation established with these spirits in the Wari' and in the Christian contexts.

The lengthy debate between missionaries and those they classify as "defenders of indigenous culture"—a group that includes above all anthropologists but also activists from nongovernmental organizations, Catholic priests defending the practice of "enculturation," and, at various moments, government agents—amply illustrates the missionary view of culture and its transformation. The response of the missionaries to accusations by such defenders centers on the premise that the indigenous viewpoint of their own culture coincides with that of the missionaries, as I observed earlier. Johnston (1985: 272, 273), in a chapter called "Happy as They Are . . . Now!" cites native declarations to argue that the idea that they are satisfied and comfortable with their "traditional" culture is pure fiction. Hearing this idea expressed, a young Yanomami man responded as follows: "Then they don't know much about my people and their old ways. When someone in our village would die (even a natural death), they always got mad and blamed it on other Yanomamö. Therefore, the death had to be revenged. . . . We lived in fear! . . . No, we were not happy!" This is followed by a statement from a Bisorio man from Papua New Guinea: "Just look at us. We have long pieces of sticks through our noses, and our hair is long and matted and full of lice. . . . We are roaming in the jungle like a bunch of wild pigs. . . . We need someone to live with us and teach us. Will you stay with us here in our village?" (275).[20]

In an issue dedicated to the debate on the expulsion of the NTM from the Zo'e Indians' territory by the government's National Indian Foundation (which in 1967 replaced the SPI), the magazine *Eclésia* (2000) cites the arguments of some anthropologists, who argue against missionary interference among indigenous peoples as a whole: "For thousands of years they lived in their own way, and very well, before the introduction of the colonizers. Why is the God of the whites better than their own?" The magazine's publishers, in their counterargument, like that of Johnston, resort to what they argue to be the indigenous viewpoint: "The fact is that the biggest stakeholders in this issue, the Indians themselves, are not always heard. 'They want to decide for us without knowing what we want,' protests the President of the National Council of Evangelical Pastors and Leaders (CONPLEI), Carlos Terena, 45 years old" (*Eclésia* 2000: 29, my translation).

In his article on the mission website, titled "The Indian: A Brazilian without Citizenship," Silas de Lima, a "Linguistic Consultant for the NTM," argues,

> Even though our Magna Carta assures the right of citizenship to all Brazilians, the legitimate Brazilians of pre-Colombian origin do not enjoy this right in full; it is apartheid in a democratic country. . . . Here I cite just one of the rights

denied them: Every change appears acceptable and indeed a greater participation of indigenous communities in the entire process of acculturation is encouraged. The Indian may become a farmer, a logger, a prospector, a politician, a capitalist, etc. and continue to be seen as indigenous. However he is criticized when he assimilates Christian values. This has led some Indians to respond: "Do they think that I've ceased to be an Indian because I'm a Christian?" The right to religious choice is being monitored, controlled and denied to Brazil's indigenous peoples. (www.mntb.org, accessed in 2010, my translation)

These views are shared by SIL's missionaries. According to Stoll (1982: 16), "Translators customarily indict anthropologists for wanting to preserve Indians as cultural specimens, like animals in a zoo, rather than helping them to adjust to change as SIL says it does. . . . Since SIL refrains from all coercion by simply offering an alternative, it respects the rights of native people to choose their own future."

However, this discussion is intended for an outside public rather than the missionaries themselves. For the latter, cultural integrity or change is clearly a secondary issue, as the statement by the missionary Royal on Wari' cannibalism reveals. As in all other spheres or questions, the "true" core and objective of missionary action rises above everything else. Again Johnston (1985: 275) makes this clear in commenting precisely on this debate concerning missionary interference in indigenous culture: "One warning, however, is that whether or not people are 'happy as they are,' God's command to 'GO' has not changed. Scripture does not say 'Go ye, therefore, and tell the unhappy ones . . .' but 'Go ye, therefore, and teach all nations' (Matthew 28:19)."

Whether the Indians are happy or not, the NTM missionaries, unlike the sixteenth-century Jesuits in Brazil mentioned in the introduction, do not doubt that the Indians have a "culture." The missionaries see this culture as a set of premises—mistaken premises owing to involution or pure ignorance—that is projected onto a single nature and history, which constitute "reality," since they were created and orchestrated by God, in accordance with their literal approach to the Bible. The missionaries attempt to adapt native cultures to this reality, a task achievable only through knowledge of the word of God, which must therefore be translated.[21]

The conception of language underlying this translation, which I explore in the next chapter, is constitutive of this same notion of culture. It also radically opposes the conceptions of the Wari', for whom, as we shall see, the invariant is not "nature" (of science or God) but precisely what we call "culture," which is held in common by all the different types of humans.

TWO

Versions versus Bodies

TRANSLATIONS IN CONTACT

"The question is," said Alice, "whether you can make words
mean so many different things." "The question is," said Humpty-
Dumpty, "which is to be the master—that's all."

LEWIS CARROLL

IN THE PREVIOUS CHAPTER I EXAMINED THE ESCHATOLOGICAL
and ontological principles that inform Evangelical missionary work and concluded by presenting, very briefly, the conception of culture held by the missionaries. As we shall see, this conception is replicated in their notions of
language and translation, which I contrast here with the equivalent notions
among the Wari'.[1]

THE PLACE OF THE NATIVE IDIOM

From its earliest moments, Christian missionary activity was intrinsically
related to the work of learning the native language, taken as the condition of
possibility for transmitting the divine message. In his analysis of the activities
of Catholic missionaries among the Tagalog of the Philippines, Rafael (1993)
shows that as early as 1603 the Spanish king issued a decree requiring that all
missionaries in the islands learn the indigenous language. According to one
seventeenth-century Franciscan cited by Rafael: "Nothing can be done in the
ministry if the religious do not learn the language of the natives" (19).[2]

The same policy was adopted in the American colonies, both in
Mesoamerica and in the Andes, with the difference that in Spanish America,
in contrast to the Philippines where no supralocal organization existed con-
necting the different tribes, the domination of the Incas and Aztecs enabled
Quechua and Nahuatl to be used as lingua francas by the Spanish (Rafael
1988: 18), facilitating the work of translation.[3] In Portuguese America,

although there was no dominant structure of this type, the fact that colonization and Christianization had begun on the Brazilian coast, where groups speaking Tupi languages predominated, led the missionaries to use the Tupian-related dialects as the basis for developing a lingua franca, Nheengatu. This would later spread to distant regions unoccupied by Tupian peoples, such as northwestern Amazonia, mostly inhabited by speakers of Tukano and Arawak languages. However, as shown by numerous documents produced by missionaries from the many different Catholic orders that arrived in Brazil later, the lingua franca did not simply expand everywhere as new indigenous groups were contacted. Even where it became known, Nheengatu existed alongside diverse other languages, which the missionaries believed needed to be learned for effective communication with the natives.

This does not mean, though, that the Catholics at that time believed it possible to translate the Bible into just any language, since they considered Latin to stand in "a close relation to God's own language" (Rafael 1993: 28). The first translation of the Bible into Castilian dates from the end of the seventeenth century, and until the first half of the twentieth century Latin remained the universal language of the Catholic Church.

As Rafael (1993: 28) observes, the Catholic interest in native languages was an explicit response to the tendency toward vernacularization propagated by the Protestant Reform. The first German version of the New Testament, printed in 1522, had been produced during Luther's forced exile between 1521 and 1522. Over the centuries, and following the global expansion of Protestantism, which culminated in the faith missions created as part of the revivalist movements in nineteenth-century Europe and North America (among them the New Tribes Mission), translations were made into the idioms of native peoples around the world.[4]

MISSIONARY CONCEPTIONS OF TRANSLATION

As we saw in chapter 1, for the fundamentalist missionaries, preaching in the native language forms the core of their activity: "The missionaries have concluded that for the spiritual truths to penetrate their hearts, to be understood and move them, they must be transmitted in the maternal language, even though some [Indians] know how to express themselves in Portuguese."[5] With this objective in mind, and as we have already seen, from its outset the NTM's missionary training included studies of language and literacy, which would later focus exclusively on those trainees demonstrating more aptitude for linguistics. In the words of Shapiro (1981: 147), "They are, as it were, in the service of God's Central Intelligence Agency, learning to intercept messages in a foreign code so that they can use that same code to transmit messages of their own."

Schieffelin (2007: 144) argues that the idea of language as a code separable from cultural practices has been a recurring Western conceit which presumes that the vernacular can be modified to express foreign ideas while nonetheless remaining the same. Schieffelin adds that the author directly inspiring many evangelical Protestant missionaries, including those of the Unevangelized Field Mission working among the Bosavi of Papua New Guinea, is missionary-linguist Eugene Nida. In particular she cites his work from 1964, where he developed the "dynamic or functional equivalence model of translation," which centers on the practical search for "close functional equivalents to words" (144, 145).[6] The aim is to achieve translations that will thereby "stay very close to the literal meanings of the 'original Bible text'" (147).

Although personally disinterested in the native culture, conceived to be little more than an array of errors, the missionaries need to understand at least some of its basic premises, especially those relating to the "religious" universe, since this is where many of the key terms to be translated are sought, including words for God, the devil, good, evil, and sin. In his missionary training manual, McIlwain (2003: 20, my translation) writes, "Missionaries must have a good knowledge of the culture of the people they are instructing. Jesus and his apostle Paul presented the Gospel within the cultural context of their listeners. Likewise missionaries must use appropriate cultural illustrations and idiomatic expressions to communicate effectively in the cultural context of their listeners."

In the words of the missionary Silas de Lima, a NTM "linguistic consultant": "We make annotations in cultural databases. We record, transcribe a large volume of narratives, audio tapes with testimonies. This provides the basis for our research into their cosmovision, the way in which they conceive the invisible and visible world. The work provides a map of the religious phenomenological system" (Almeida 2002: 119, my translation).

No consensus exists over the translation of the key biblical terms mentioned above. Many missionaries past and present have opted to keep at least some of these terms in the original language—Spanish, Portuguese, and so on—to prevent contamination by cosmologies incompatible with the

Christian universe. According to Rafael (1993: 6, 7, 29), missionaries working among the Tagalog considered various of these keywords impossible to translate, retaining them in the original language as *Dios, Maria, Espíritu Santo, Cruz,* and so forth, which coincided with the symbolic value attributed by the native people to foreign words.[7]

The question of whether to keep the original language or look for a native equivalent seems to surface primarily in relation to the term for God (and the Trinity), since the ethnographies indicate that the missionaries can fairly easily encounter an equivalent for *Satan* or *devil* in the native language, or even for *soul* and *sin.* The devil typically receives the name of native spirits, thereby generating a large series of equivocations, not only by attributing malevolence to some benevolent spirits who act as shamanic auxiliaries—as occurred among the Amazonian Marubo (Cesarino 2011), Trio (Rivière 1981: 8), and Kulina (Pollock 1993: 189)—but also by reserving a central place for native entities in the Christian cosmos, contrary to the intention of the missionaries, thereby retaining them as part of the daily life of worshippers, as shown by Meyer's analysis of the Christian experience of the Ewe of Ghana (1999: 65–66).[8]

In Amazonia, in some cases, such as among the Piro/Yine in Peru (Opas 2008) and the Marubo (Cesarino 2011) and Paumari (Bonilla 2009: 136) in Brazil, the name for God was kept in the original European language (Spanish or Portuguese, respectively). Among the Marubo, however, and unknown to the missionaries, the Christian deity was associated with the demiurge Kana Voã, which immediately attributed to God an ontological multiplicity irreducible to the Christian conception of a unity subjacent to the Holy Trinity (Cesarino 2011: 165–166). Among the Yanomami, the reverse situation is found: the initial association of God with the demiurge Omama was eventually rejected, given the impotence of the Christian God, who began to be called Teosi (a corruption of *Deus*) and was later associated by the shaman Davi Kopenawa with Yoase, a mythical trickster figure (Kopenawa and Albert 2010: 582).

Among the Wari' the term for God was initially from Portuguese—a choice probably related to the fact that there had been no figure of a demiurge or any kind of divinity among the Wari'—and was replaced by a neologism in the native language, Iri' Jam, created by the missionaries and which, according to them, signified "true spirit." However, until about ten years ago, as we shall see in chapter 4, the Christian God was also often associated by some people with Pinom, the only Wari' mythic figure to inhabit the sky (*pawin*), a place with little significance in the Wari' lived world.

According to Rafael, as we have seen, the untranslatability of the biblical keywords derives from the missionaries' presupposition that Latin or Castilian Spanish is better at communicating the word of God, or in other words, the notion of the superiority of one language over another. Hence, their use of *Dios,* instead of the Tagalog term *bathala,* presumed "the perfect fit between the Spanish word and the Christian referent in a way that would be unlikely to occur were the Tagalog word used instead" (Rafael 1993: 29).[9]

The mythic reference point for the hierarchy of languages—and of peoples and cultures—is the episode of the Tower of Babel (Genesis 11:1–9), in which the different peoples refused to spread out across the earth as God wanted, so that "the whole world had one language and a common speech" (Genesis 11:1). They then decided to build a high tower to reach the heavens. God perceived himself under threat and thwarted their project by imposing linguistic incommunicability, saying, "Come, let us go down and confuse their language so they will not understand each other" (Genesis 11:7), thereby causing the peoples to separate. Meyer (1999: 57) writes that the hierarchy arose from the fact that the descendants of Ham, accursed son of Noah, were identified as the main proponents of the tower's construction and were punished by being forced to live the farthest away from God. According to the author (58), the African peoples, among them the Ewe studied by herself, are described as descendants of these people, whose customs and languages degenerated after the separation.[10]

LITERACY

As we saw in chapter 1, the degeneration of "customs" associated with a single original culture whose true history is told in the Bible is explicitly associated with orality. As Silas de Lima observes in relation to the Wayãpi tradition (a Tupi group from northern Brazil), this tradition "was 'incomplete,' because it was orally transmitted" (Gallois and Grupioni 1999: 111). The account of the missionary Carlos Carvalho concerning the Zo'e (another Tupi-speaking people) makes explicit the relation between nonliteracy and falsity: "There were errors in what was orally transmitted. What is here [in the written document] is fact and cannot be altered. It has never changed and never will change, it's fact, it's written here, it cannot be changed. You will revise that which you once believed in. . . . It is in the nature of the thing to be false" (Gallois and Grupioni 1999: 112, my translation).

According to Silas de Lima in an interview with Almeida (2002: 124): "You teach them [the Indians] the unknown through the known. In that way we make a correlation. But the unknown is already part of their culture. . . . There are many parallels with the Bible in their culture. I would call these fragments of parts of God's special truth incorporated in orality, in their oral culture, passed from father to son. So many Biblical traditions are there. The story of the Fall is found in their culture. Various versions of this factual event exist."

The first chapter of lesson book 1, written in the Wari' language, introduces the idea of translation and the relation between biblical writing and truth. I reproduce a few excerpts below:

> The Bible is the name of God's speech [*kapijakon*] in writing. . . . When God's speech was being narrated [*pijim*], nobody was yet speaking our language [*kapijaxi'*, *we* inclusive, referring to the narratives of the Wari']. Not all the languages of all the Indians [*wari'*] were spoken. No. Only the true language of God. They did not know the language of God. Our ancestors were unaware of it. Their thought/heart [*ximikokon*] went astray/was lost. . . . Our ancestors spoke aimlessly. No, the ancestors came from the rocks [referring to a Wari' mythic segment in which the enemies with whom the survivors of the flood married to recompose Wari' society lived in rocks]. There was Pinom [the mythic figure who stole fire from the Wari'], they climbed up high with Pinom. It was Pinom who gave us fire. There is Cowo', and Wirin [mythic figures], this is what the ancestors spoke about aimlessly. Had they known. Had they spoken the truth. . . . Only God knows where we came from. Only God knows about our death. Only God speaks the truth. (p. 1)

> The ancient ones who wrote the speech of God were Jewish. There was just one who was not Jewish. . . . Israel was the name of the land of the Jews. They didn't come from the United States, they didn't come from Germany, they didn't come from Brazil. No. They came from Israel. . . . The ancient ones who wrote the speech of God did not know Portuguese. They did not write in Portuguese. They wrote in their true language [*iri' kapijakokon*], they wrote imitating/repeating. After a long time they went to see the foreigners who spoke another language [*xijein topak*]. They lived far from Israel and spoke differently. They came to speak of God and write, they wrote in their true language, they wrote imitating/repeating. They went on and on and various other people wrote in their language. Today the speech of God appears in many different languages. Many. (p. 3)

It is interesting to note that the term chosen by the Wari' to express the idea of translation, the passage from one language to another, is *to imitate/repeat*, revealing a particular conception of language and translation in which the change of language does not comprise any obstacle to the integrity of the message. I shall return to this point.

Here we can understand the central importance for the missionaries of teaching the natives to read and write, which not only was intended to solve the problem of the correct transmission of the "true" facts but also was related to a basic practical contingency: making the Bible available in the native idiom only makes sense if there are readers. Johnston (1985: 218–224), in the chapter on linguistic training in his book recounting the history of the NTM, devotes five pages to the subject of literacy and, in line with the Protestant tradition, states that the starting point for catechizing the Indians has to be their direct access to the biblical text: "Missionaries . . . have suddenly found that they had to teach reading before they could really have a functioning New Testament church" (219). Consequently the first endeavor had to be to cultivate in the Indians an "interest in the miracle of the written word." The account of a missionary couple among the Yanomami in Venezuela offers an objective example of this procedure: first, they repeated the names of people from the group written down on paper, in the form and order in which they had been dictated, and "word soon spread that 'paper talks.'" Later, when preaching about the sin of extramarital relations, the indigenous women asked the couple: "Well, how do you know we were . . . (giggle) . . . flirting with other men?" The missionary, who initially said that he lacked this specific knowledge, realized that he had almost lost "a golden opportunity" and, inspired by God ("the Lord jogged my memory"), modified his response: "No, no one said anything. We saw it on the paper. The paper says that people who don't know the Lord are like that" (Johnston 1985: 220). This confirms the power of paper: "The paper knows! And the people know that the paper knows. It's been somewhat of a turning point that the people are now willing to consider what the written Word of God says" (221).

The attribution of human agency to paper was also commonly found among other groups. Gow (2001: 208–213) presents an interesting account of a man called Sangama from the Piro/Yine people (an Arawak-speaking group from Peruvian Amazonia), whose capacity to read was linked to shamanic powers that allowed him to see the paper as a woman with whom he conversed: "I always see this paper. She has red lips with which she speaks. She has a body, with a red mouth, a painted mouth" (Gow 2001: 209). As a consequence, he taught another man to read through the shamanic procedure of blowing on the top of his head and his back.[11]

A clear association between shamanic vision and writing was made by a young Mbya (Guarani) man: "What the shaman sees in the *petÿgua* [pipe], the pastor sees in the Bible" (Mendes 2013, my translation). The same was observed by Orta (2004: 179) on the relation between the reading of the Bible by the Aymara Catholic catechists and coca leaves by the traditional ritual specialists, and by Keane (2007: 192) on the Sumbanese, for whom reading of animal intestines is equated with reading books (the theme of literacy is further explored in chapter 4).

DIVINE INSPIRATION

As well as the act of finding equivalents to words per se, there is something else that overdetermines the entire translation process: divine inspiration. Just as the writing of the Bible was divinely inspired,[12] so is the work of translating the book into the native language, undertaken by the missionaries with their indigenous assistants. In other words, just as the physical and intellectual preparation of the missionary is secondary to divine providence, as we saw in chapter 1, the latter also determines the success of translation and conversion as a whole.

For the Catholic missionaries of the seventeenth century, Rafael (1993: 32) writes, the capacity to learn the native language was considered not an ability but a divine gift, one that generated a debt to be paid through oral dissemination of the word of God among the natives. As a result, he adds, translation acquires a ritual aspect in which the missionary, just like the disciples enlightened by the fire of Pentecost, speaks a "pure language," the image of "God's Word" acting "directly on the bodies of priests and converts." For Meyer (1999: 57), the place of Pentecost in the missionary imaginary forms the bridge between this event and the Tower of Babel. Pentecost (see Acts 2:1–6) represents the inversion of the situation of linguistic incommunicability generated in the episode of the Tower. The disciples interpreted their capacity to speak all languages simultaneously as a sign from God for them to learn all the world's languages so they could preach his word and thus unite the peoples once again.

In the specific case of the NTM, Johnston (1985: 221–224), in a section of his book titled "Translation Notes," states that the work of translation involves the participation of the missionary, called "the translator," and "his native helpers, and secretaries." And, owing to its difficulty, it requires "much prayer for alertness" so that he or she "can **feel** [original emphasis] with them [the natives] as to how they will relate the new *truth* [my emphasis] to their culture" (222).

The religiosity of the missionaries is considered a positive differential factor when the latter are compared to other agents, such as anthropologists, giving them a greater capacity to understand indigenous culture and translate it. Here we return to the dispute between missionaries and anthropologists briefly mentioned in chapter 1, and specifically to the article by the missionary-ethnologist Van der Geest (1990: 591) on the topic. In accusing anthropologists of being just as fundamentalist as the missionaries, the author ends up siding with the missionaries, claiming that, unlike anthropologists, they can understand a religious experience "from within," while for the anthropologists "religion thus becomes 'ritual', 'social control', 'a survival strategy', 'an etiology', 'a philosophy.'" Everything reduces down to metaphors, as in the anthropological interpretation of the famous assertion by the Kwakiutl that they are salmon, which, Van der Geest (592) asserts, is reduced to the perception that they "organize their world in such a way that they regard themselves as belonging to the same category as salmon." Here the author cites Sandor's observations concerning this kind of interpretation, which condemns anthropologists "who are not prepared to take the Kwakiutl's world literally. Their metaphoric interpretation ... violates Kwakiutl reality" (1986: 593). According to Sandor, "Seeing metaphors everywhere means assimilating other worlds to a particular world: it is ethnocentric" (101).

It is notable, though, that Sandor's alternative explanation, taken by Van der Geest to be respectful of the native point of view or its "reality," is also unable to recognize the fact that a person can really be a salmon, a type of supposition that abounds not only in the Native American mythological universe, as Lévi-Strauss attested (1964, 1966, 1968, 1971), but also in descriptions of the everyday experience of Amazonian peoples, as we shall see in the Wari' case. Van der Geest (1990: 593), citing Sandor, compares this affirmation to the (scientific) continuity between the caterpillar and the butterfly, the same insect in different phases: "Salmon and Kwakiutl presuppose one another and are part of a greater whole which may not be empirically verifiable but is real nevertheless."

Once again the universality of the material world, and an exclusivist conception of humanity that does not include other beings beyond those that we ourselves conceive as human, is very distinct from that of the Wari' and other Amazonian peoples, and certainly from the Kwakiutl too. While linguistic translation for the missionaries is the condition of possibility for communication between people from distinct cultural universes, for the Wari' this communication is based on premises other than language. In a certain sense, we could say that the Wari' are more faithful to the possibility of a single language, given the biblical episode of Pentecost cited above, since, while for the missionaries there are two (or more) languages, requiring the passage from one to the other, for the Wari' there is just one language through which people who live together could immediately communicate, irrespective of whether this is Wari', Portuguese, or a mixture of both.

THE WARI' PERSPECTIVE

The Wari' term for "language" is the same for "mouth" and "tongue," *kapijaxi'* (our [inclusive] mouth/tongue), which designates not only this part of the body, but also the voice, lexicon, prosody, and the oral tradition as a whole, including the histories told by parents and grandparents, and myths, considered histories of ancestors who are not personally known. The term can also signify the mouth of any animal species and the sounds emitted by them, such as *kapijakon jowin* (the mouth/voice of the capuchin monkey), as well as the rim of an object such as a basket or pan. Like other Wari' substantives, the term for the first person singular is also the verb *kapija,* which designates a gossipy person. Also like some other substantives, there is a free, nonpossessed form, *topak,* meaning "talk."

Until pacification, which took place between 1956 and 1961, the Wari' had no peaceful contact with any other ethnic group. Consequently, unlike those groups living in multiethnic complexes such as the one situated in the Upper Xingu River area (Franchetto and Heckenberger 2001), in the Upper Rio Negro area (Andrello 2006; S. Hugh-Jones 1979; C. Hugh-Jones 1979; Lasmar 2005), and in the Upper Ucayali River area (Gow 1991, 2001, 2009), where people live on a day-to-day basis with completely distinct languages, the Wari' were not exposed to any other language. The only differences in speech identified by them refer to prosody and to elements from the lexicon of foreigners, members of other Wari' subgroups, inhabitants from neighboring territories, and speakers of the same language, in the broad sense, who maintain ritual and marriage relations.[13]

These differences are more or less marked, depending on geographic distance and the relation between subgroups. Until contact there were three territorial clusters: the OroWaram, OroWaramXijein, and OroMon on one side; the OroNao', OroEo, and OroAt on the other; and the OroNao' on the left shore of the Pacaás Novos River, who, as we shall see in the next chapter, had remained isolated from the rest for fifty years owing to historical contingencies. Within each of these clusters the variations are less perceptible, given the more regular contact and the more frequent marriages, although it is always possible to pick out one or another particularity of an outsider's speech, as the OroNao' do in relation to the very distinct accent of the OroEo, for example, designating their dialect *kapijakon OroEo*. This, it should be noted, refers not just to variations in their speech itself but also in their histories, musical elements, and mythic accounts, which are differentiated within the wider set usually referred to simply as *kapijaxi'* or *kapijakon wari'* (people talk).[14]

The differences in dialect and oral tradition are associated with habits and practices. As we shall see in the next chapter, the origin myth of the subgroups itself attributes the division of Wari' society into these units to their distinct habits, with each group going to inhabit different spaces. The Wari' projected the difference between the subgroups on those that they began to perceive among the whites, classifying their different "ethnic groups" as *oroboliviano, oroamericano, orofrancês*.

The Wari' associate these differences with bodily peculiarities by saying of them: "That's what the body of the OroNao' is like'" (*je kwerekun* OroNao'), or, in the case of whites, "That's what the body of the Americans is like," for example. It is worth observing that "body," *kwerexi'*, for the Wari' is what characterizes the person and refers not only to physical substance, flesh, but also to habits, affects, and memory. It explains why a person acts in a particular way; for example, the Wari' would say of a quiet woman: *Je kwerekem* (That's what her body is like).

Internal differentiation occurs mainly on the dividing line between consanguines and affines, which partly coincides with the divide between coresidents and outsiders. Hence, within the supposedly uniform group, people who consider each other close kin, *iri' nari*—a category that may include coresident real affines, consubstantialized by commensality and daily care—share a single perspective: in other words, they see everyone as kin. Outsiders in general, and kin with whom one has not lived for many years, are all designated "distant kin" (*nari pira, nari paxi*) or "other people" (*xukun wari'*) and are treated as affines, especially in ritual contexts, where until recently they were subject to various kinds of symbolic aggression, such as "killing" through the offering of excessive amounts of chicha. Foreigners are the potential sorcerers—that is, those who may treat the Wari' as though they were nonhuman prey. In the case of actual coresident affines, the initial difference may rematerialize on certain occasions, as in fights between spouses, which involve not just the two families but the entire group; and in the past, it rematerialized during funerals, when real affines joined distant kin as eaters of the deceased, no longer perceiving him or her as human and thereby differentiating themselves, through their point of view, from close kin.[15] Generally, though, the differences between persons and between the members of subgroups are, just as occurs with speech, usually eclipsed by the general term *kwerexi'* (our body) or *kwerekun wari'* (Wari' body), which considers the unity of the Wari', especially in relation to others, such as the whites.

HUMANS AND ANIMALS

Although from the viewpoint of the Wari' they themselves are the only humans, *wari'*, they know that enemies, *wijam,* other indigenous peoples, and whites, as well as animals of diverse kinds, including fish, various types of birds, snakes, and mammals like jaguars, peccaries, tapirs, capuchin monkeys, pacas, cutias, and armadillos, all of which can be killed and eaten by the Wari', see themselves as humans and may act as such, preying on the Wari' (which manifests as sickness and death). The subject imposing itself as a predator is considered human, *wari'*, causing the other to occupy the position of prey, *karawa,* associated with nonhumanity. *Wari'* and *karawa* are positions, therefore, that define the difference within a wide relational universe in which all beings are human.

Although both animals and enemies can occupy the position of humans, animals were the only ones, at least until contact, with whom the Wari' had social relations properly speaking, through their shamans. Through them, they know that animals speak the same language as themselves, *kapijakon wari'* (people language), although they can be comprehended only by those who can "hear" (*taraju pa'*) what they say, a capacity that depends exclusively on the social relations established between them, especially living and eating together. The Wari' concept of translation, as the possibility of communication between different types of people, therefore involves the shift from one collective of humans to another and occurs through a bodily transformation

FIGURE 2. Preying, Negro River village, February 1987. (Photo by Beto Barcellos.)

enabled by new foods, the proximity to other bodies, and the new relations of sociality as a whole. The person thereby begins to inhabit another world, the automatic consequence of which is the capacity for verbal communication with these new people.

In no case of encounters with humanized animals, whether mythic or historic, do the Wari' mention language as an obstacle to communication. To them it seems obvious that those who perceive each other as human, as companions, automatically share the same language. Wagner observed (1975: 107,

114), based on his experience among the Daribi of Papua New Guinea, that while language for us is a product of history, evolved to describe a world of facts, for several native peoples it is a given, just like morality. It is manifested in a person's actions but cannot be used consciously. Thus, for example, a child says "Mummy" when he or she recognizes the filial bond with a particular woman, the consequence of living and eating together, initiated with breast feeding. This is why the Daribi said to Wagner, just as the Wari' told me, that he would learn their language by eating their food. According to Taylor (2007: 162–163n16), among the Amazonian Achuar the "recognition of a shared field of communication also implies recognition of kinship: kin are defined as people who talk in the same language."[16] The first Wari' bilinguists were precisely the young men and women who lived more intensely with the whites and therefore ate their food and shared their habits. As we shall see later, these were the essential attributes required by the missionary assistants in order to translate the Bible and by the missionaries themselves to learn the Wari' language.

Given the "transparency" of language and its determination by coresidency, it is understandable that the Wari' do not share the same concept of translation as the missionaries, although they do elaborate this topic in minute detail, as we shall see.

TRANSLATION THROUGH BODY METAMORPHOSIS

I turn to the account of an abduction by jaguar, very common among the Wari' until the recent past, which provides a clear illustration of their concern with translation. The event was told to me in Sagarana village in July 2005, and the narrator and victim was A'ain Tot, a woman of about sixty at the time we spoke. Various other local inhabitants were present. When the episode happened, close to Kojain, a village located on an affluent of the Laje River, A'ain Tot was about five years old. One day the adults had sent the children to the stream to fetch water. A'ain Tot's mother then appeared and called her to come and catch some fish somewhere else. So she went along. She had no idea it was a jaguar, since it looked exactly like her mother. On the way, they came across *nao'* fruits (from a type of palm), much relished by the Wari', and her mother took maize from the basket she was carrying to eat with the fruit. Soon after a thorn pierced the child's foot, which her jaguar mother removed (at this point the listeners laughed in surprise). After walking for a while, they stopped to sleep. Milk was seeping from the breast of her mother, who was breast feeding one of A'ain Tot's brothers at that time. When the girl was almost asleep, she noticed a man approach, who lay down on top of her mother to have sex. The girl asked, "Who is this man?" So the mother smacked the girl's bottom lightly, as the Wari' do to put a child to sleep (again the listeners laughed, very surprised, and asked for more details about this moment). They had no fire. The next day they ate some *nao'* fruit and continued walking, until the girl heard the voice of her older brother (or mother's brother, both called *aji'*), who was shouting to her. At this point the supposed mother said that she was going to defecate and disappeared into the forest. Her kin then approached. A'ain Tot's body was covered in jaguar fur, which they cleaned off. At the end of the narrative I asked whether she had not seen any trace of jaguar in the supposed mother, a bit of her tail or something similar (which appeared in other accounts), and she replied, "Nothing. It was truly my mother."[17]

According to the Wari', the cases of abduction by jaguars were frequent in the past, but, they said, the jaguars had a "heart"—that is, thought—and the jaguar would take pity and release the captive when his or her kin arrived. This did not occur with tapirs, who, after abducting someone, would never let the victim return. Paletó and To'o Xak Wa testified to a rare case of a young man who was captured by tapirs and returned. His name was Tokorom Xiao, and he lived in Terem Matam. According to Paletó's account, one day the young man was out hunting with other men and vanished. When they went searching for him, they found his footprints following in the tracks of a tapir and concluded that the tapir had taken him. His kin wept and after some days gave up searching for him. A long time later, some men saw him while trekking in the forest. He had a human appearance but the knees and hands of a tapir. His body was covered in large tapir ticks, and he scratched himself the whole time. They removed all the ticks and he got better. But, just like To'o Xak Wa's mother, as we shall see in the following account, he began to act strangely. He would eat leaves. One time he brought home a bunch of *karapan* fruits (which the Wari' do not eat) saying that they were *xiraki* (a fruit that the Wari' do eat). They blew maize smoke on him and, it seems, he recovered. "Only his knees were like a tapir's," concluded Paletó.

Just how much of a problem translation is for the Wari' becomes evident in comments made by the listeners at a specific point in the jaguar account, when the narrator said that they stopped to eat *nao'* fruit. "What was it? A fruit [*memem*]?" someone asked. To'o Xak Wa (whose mother had been abducted by a jaguar) suggested, "Seven-banded armadillo" (*kwari*). Paletó, her husband, retorted, "Tail of six-banded armadillo" (*kahwerein pikot*). To'o Xak Wa pondered, "Perhaps it was paca [*mikop*]." "I don't know," the narrator said, and To'o Xak Wa immediately corrected herself: "That's it, papaya is paca [*makujam na mikop*]!"—meaning, for the jaguar.[18]

In the case of the tapir abduction, the issue focused on the boy-tapir's equivocation concerning the fruit that he was eating, which he called by the same name as a fruit classified as edible by the Wari' (*xiraki*) but indicating a different empirical referent: a fruit that the Wari' do not eat (*karapakan*). This case is also interesting because the young man objectified his two humanities in his body (with the tapir knees) and his dietary preference (his liking of leaves), which are like the short circuits sometimes experienced by shamans, as I shall discuss shortly.

It is as though the listeners had Wari'-jaguar and Wari'-tapir dictionaries in their minds that they used to translate what the narrator said in the first case, and what the young man ate in the second. As can be seen, the problem is not in finding equivalents in the Wari' language to words spoken by the jaguar. It is presumed that the jaguar, to the ears of the girl who saw it as her mother, spoke the Wari' language—that is, a "people language," comprehensible to all humans. The problem resided in identifying the world of the jaguar—the empirical equivalents to the words uttered by the animal. What is the *nao'* fruit for the jaguar? As a jaguar, it cannot be the same thing as for the Wari' who, in contrast to the girl who saw the animal as her mother, did not share its point of view.

PERSPECTIVISM, SHAMANISM, AND TRANSLATION

This is a clear example of what Viveiros de Castro has called "perspectivist translation," highlighting the difference between the standard Western conception and the native concept:

> The problem for indigenous perspectivism is not therefore one of discovering the common referent (say, the planet Venus) to two different representations (say, "Morning Star" and "Evening Star"). On the contrary it is one of making explicit the equivocation implied in imagining that when the jaguar says "manioc beer" he is referring to the same thing as us (i.e., a tasty, nutritious and heady brew)[,] ... the same representations and other objects, a single meaning and multiple referents.... The aim is to avoid losing sight of the

difference concealed within equivocal "homonyms" between our language and that of other species, since we and they are never talking about the same things. (Viveiros de Castro 2004: 6)[19]

As the author observes in the same article, the capacity to translate is typical to the shaman, who, through an experience of bodily transformation, can circulate through more than one of these "discordant exteriorities," returning to tell the Indians what they saw and heard. It is the shaman, therefore, who constitutes the "lexicon" of the Wari'-jaguar dictionary to which my Wari' friends resorted when they heard the abduction narrative. Given that each shaman has a unique experience, it makes sense that this dictionary has different "entries" for the same referent, which explains the oscillation and conjectures of the listeners concerning the relations between two referents (rather than between two words).

The verb meaning "to transform" is *jamu,* understood as the actualization of a (new) body, one that is equally human since it is seen as such by the new companions in another relational context. This capacity is not limited to shamans, who differ by being able to control the process, but is common to all beings deemed human, *wari',* which includes diverse animals, as attested by the jaguar episode described above. It is the capacity of some beings to transform themselves, *jamu,* which leads to the attribution of a "double," *jam-,* to them.[20] I have decided not to translate the term as "spirit," except where referring to missionary translations, in order to avoid evoking the idea of a component of the person, something like a vital principle. The Wari' notion in fact resists any essentialization.[21] The attribution of a double results from the capacity to transform, not the contrary. Nobody, under normal conditions, has a double.

Shamans, generally men, are like chronically sick people who, assailed by animals of a particular species, have not been cured but have turned into their companions. The Wari' often say that animals prey on the Wari' (whom they see as enemies or as prey animals) with the eventual aim of turning them into kin, the outcome of which is death for the victim, who goes to live forever on the side of the animals. In such cases, the person's Wari' body disappears (traditionally ingested in funerary cannibalism), and what goes to live among the animals is, from the Wari' viewpoint, the person's double. In the case of shamans, the animals (the Wari' would say "the animal's double," *jamikon/jaminain karawa*) decide to cure him by bathing his body in apparently boiling water (simulating a cooking process) after which his body is reconstituted.

Next the animals insert annatto and babassu into his body, both plant substances used in body painting and which will be used during shamanic cures. They also insert some of their typical foods, such as particular fruits. One of the animals will become the shaman's father-in-law, offering him daughters in marriage, children still, as was the custom among the Wari'. Henceforth the shaman's double will be continually activated, implying the coexistence of two bodies, one of them living among the Wari', whom he perceives as human and kin, and the other among the animals, which he also sees as human, but as affines rather than kin.[22] The Wari' typically say that the shaman "accompanies [jaja] the animal" or the "animal's double" (jami karawa).

The consummation of the marriage with the animal brides through sex leads to the definitive death of the shaman's Wari' body.[23] Hence, he tries to delay this outcome, which becomes increasingly difficult when the animal-girls reach maturity. The shaman very often ignores their attempts at seduction, as well as the usually explicit request from his father-in-law to consummate the marriage. The shaman Orowam, for example, already elderly, used to tell me that his jaguar-brides were beautiful and seductive, and that he would be unable to delay marrying them for very much longer. The death of the shaman, like that of any person, is the beginning of life in another human collective.

Some shamans complain about the difficulties of their experience, always called upon by their animal affines and always tired of running through the forest with them. The traditional solution to put an end to this is fumigation with maize smoke, which, when successful, impregnates the shaman's body with a smell so redolent of Wari' humanity—where maize consumption is central—that it repels the animal for good. This was the procedure used with the tapir-boy and, as we shall see later, in the case of a jaguar-woman.

With this double body, the shaman acquires a double perspective, that of the Wari' and that of the animal species that he accompanies, which gives him access to animals as a whole, since, as they would explain to me, they do not differentiate a deer from a collared peccary or a jaguar: all are seen as people, and it is common for a shaman to change his animal companions (and body) simply by accompanying and eating with other species. This "strange" vision (kirik xirak, "to see strange") is precisely what allows him to act as a translator of perspectives. One time I was watching a group of Wari' children having a lot of fun using an injured vulture as a football. Seeing what was happening, a shaman yelled that the vultures were people and would take revenge. Moreover what the children thought was the football pitch was actually water—that is, the abode of the dead (their subaquatic world) and other human animals, such as fish. They had to be careful not to be captured by this world.

In the case of animal-caused diseases, the shaman removes the traces of the animal from the body of the sick person, including fur, food, and sometimes annatto and babassu, which indicates that the animal plans to turn the victim into a shaman. In one example I saw, a child was attacked by a capuchin monkey (*jowin*), and the shamans—who usually worked in pairs and relied on the help of their animal companions—told the kin of the sick boy that they had seen him among the capuchin monkeys, acting like one of them. Meantime they examined the semi-inert Wari' body in front of them and removed bits of monkey fur as well as some of the fruits on which these animals feed. I heard one shaman say that he had seen tiny monkeys walking across the sick child's body. While removing traces of the animal from his body, a shaman talked with the monkeys and asked them to leave the boy alone, since he had kin who wanted him to stay with them, in the Wari' universe. The Wari' say that both the child and the capuchin monkey transformed, *jamu*, which can be expressed in two ways: by saying either that the child accompanies the double of the capuchin monkey (*jaja non jamikon jowin pije*), or that his double accompanies the capuchin monkey (*jaja non jowin jamikon pije*). The fact that these two phrases are considered equivalent is evidence that the process of transformation is a whole that involves both sides—or both types of people—simultaneously.[24] This also highlights the fact that what is a body, *kwerexi'*, or a double, *jamixi'*, always depends on the perspective: the Wari' body that lives among animals is a double to the Wari', but it is a body to the animals. In the account of the jaguar abduction described above, what the girl saw from the Wari' viewpoint was the jaguar's double (*jamikon kopakao'*), since this appeared to the girl transformed into a human form. What the others saw, though, was the body of the jaguar, since it looked to them like an animal.[25]

Given his continuously transformed state, the shaman is a being who circulates through distinct relational universes, living with different types of humans and learning about their language—that is, about the distinct referents to which the same words from "people language" apply. Sometimes the two perspectives merge in a kind of short-circuit, and the shaman may see his Wari' coresidents as animals and attack them. This almost happened to me once in the presence of the shaman-jaguar Orowam, who was preparing to attack myself and his grandson. The latter, realizing what was happening—while I remained entirely oblivious to the fact—defused the situation by calling him grandfather and kindly including me in his kinship network.

It is the distinction between bodies that makes the shaman a translator, since from the moment when they identify with each other, the shaman becomes a common sick person, subjected to the animal's perspective. A translator, in the Wari' sense, is not an equal but someone who contains difference within him or herself. The girl abducted by the jaguar was not, therefore, a translator, because she was totally identified with the animal. In the words of Viveiros de Castro (2004: 20): "Translation becomes an operation of differentiation—a production of difference—that connects the two discourses to the precise extent to which they are *not* saying the same thing, in so far as they point to discordant exteriorities beyond the equivocal homonyms between them."[26]

Since the shaman's capacity to transit across different worlds is a pan-Amazonian phenomenon, the relation between shamanism and translation is a common theme in the region's ethnological literature.[27] Carneiro da Cunha (1998), in an article subtitled "Shamanism and Translation," based primarily on the ethnographic literature on the Pano groups of southern Amazonia, explores the question in terms of a geographic "code" through which shamans are defined as persons who combine the local and global, the upriver and downriver viewpoints, giving them the capacity of synthesis definitive of translation.

What is particularly pertinent to our discussion of translation is the notion of the "twisted words" mentioned by Carneiro da Cunha (1998: 12–13) based on an analysis of Yaminawa shamanism by Townsley (1993: 460). These are words from everyday language applied to distinct objects—a fish may be called a peccary, for example—the mode encountered by the shaman to solve the dilemma of interpreting the unusual that becomes objectified through his perception.

For the notion of "twisted words" to be applicable to the discourse of the Wari' shaman, or indeed to the discourse of anyone in a state of transformation, it must be emphasized that this does not refer to metaphors, at least in the substitutionist notion of this figure of speech, founded on the distinction between literal and figurative, or true and false.[28] Overing's analysis of Piaroa shamanism concerns precisely this point and coincides with the perspective of Viveiros de Castro cited above:

Uncertainty about identity was a daily ontological puzzle for the Piaroa....
But such "problems" of identity ... were certainly not those of "metaphor,"
for the Piaroa are obviously worrying about factual identity: "Is that wild pig
a human or a vegetable?" "Is that jaguar an animal, a human sorcerer or a god
from the "before time"? ... If they got it wrong, it was their understanding
that the literal consequences could be grim—the individual could become
subject to a predator attack. It was the *ruwang* [shaman] who was able to solve
such mysteries of identity.... A metaphysics very different from our own.
(Overing Kaplan 1990: 610)[29]

The same type of critique of this standard Western acceptation of metaphor is made by Cesarino (2011) in his study of the shamanic chants of the
Pano-speaking Marubo. There the use of uncommon terms to describe
visions or actions is related to the duality between bodies/carcasses and
doubles, both those of the shamans and those of the spirits that inhabit
them. So, for example, when a spirit speaks through a shaman (who acts as a
reproducer, a "radio"), who chants "along the wrinkles of the sun embira
tree / along the wrinkles I descend / I descend crawling" (141, my translation),
this involves not a metaphor for movement as we would conceive it but
a reference to the activity of the spirit's caterpillar body. In the author's
words (pers. comm., 2012): "The spirit speaks of something that all the
Marubo know and do: move along a path. But it speaks in a distorted way
through its body-mode, that of an embira caterpillar that crawls down the
tree trunk."

As Viveiros de Castro (2002: 384; 2012a: 110) comments apropos Casevitz's
analysis of Matsiguenga cosmology, what happens in Amerindian perspectivism is that substances named by substantives are used as if they were "relational pointers." These substantives can be compared to kinship terms: "You
are a father only because there is another person whose father you are: father-
hood is a relation.... Something would be 'fish' only by virtue of someone
else whose fish it is." Hence propositions like "people are monkeys to jaguars,"
examples of which abound in Amazonian ethnographies, are "of the same
nature as a proposition such as: 'my uncle is grandfather to my son'" (Lima
2002: 15). So, "if I am alive, a peacock bass is a fish; if I am dead, a peacock
bass is a corpse. If I am a woman, the brother of my mother is grandfather to
my children; if I am a man, he is a cousin to my children" (17, my translation).
And this, of course, is precisely what perspectivism is all about. There is no
pregiven natural or objective universe. Things, like persons, are constituted
within relations, as the outcome of the latter.

The Wari' work of translation may also involve another level, no longer related to an oral manifestation of distinct referents designated by homonyms, as the shaman does through his use of "twisted words," and as the listeners did in response to A'ain Tot's account of abduction. The following narrative shows that, more than a capacity arising from bodily transformation, translation itself may be achieved by the body.

In July 2005, in Sagarana, To'o Xak Wa, a woman of around sixty-five, wife of my Wari' father Paletó who I call mother, narrated some events witnessed by herself when she was a child and involving her mother, A'ain Tain. The account was recorded by myself in the Wari' language. What follows is a summarized version.

When To'o was around five years old, she lived with her family at I Pa' Wijam, located on the shores of a small affluent of the Santo André River (We Turu), itself a right-shore affluent of the Pacaás Novos River. One morning, after a discussion with her older sister,[30] her mother went to the river and was invited by a young man, her nephew, the son of her younger sister, who called her "mother," to go fishing at a spot farther on, where, he claimed, there was a lot of fish. The young man carried her on his back for a stretch of the path. After a while, A'ain Tain began to hear voices calling her: "It's an animal that called you! It's not Wari'! Look, here is your daughter! She's crying a lot." And her true nephew shouted to the figure who was pretending to be him, whom everyone except A'ain Tain was seeing as a jaguar: "Put my mother down on the ground." This was when A'ain Tain realized that the supposed nephew was licking leaves as they trekked along the path, just as jaguars do. She looked carefully and saw a glimpse of tail. Hearing the insistent calls from her kin, the jaguar left her behind and departed. According to To'o, the mother was covered in jaguar fur from being carried. When I asked whether the mother had been scared of the jaguar, To'o replied, "She wasn't scared. It was *wari'* [a person]."

A short time after they went to a festival at Hwijimain Xitot, farther up the same creek. To'o's father killed a woodpecker and gave it to her mother for her to cook. A'ain Tain accidentally touched her mouth with bloody fingers, ingesting the blood (which turned her into a commensal of the jaguars, who eat meat raw). At night, A'ain was at home, sleeping on the stilt palm platform with her daughter To'o Xak Wa in one arm and Wem Parawan, her

FIGURE 3. Paletó (*right*) and To'o Xak Wa, Sagarana village, July 2005. (Photo by the author.)

older brother's son, in the other (Wari' houses were open and wall-less, and people did not use hammocks to sleep) when a jaguar leapt on her and dragged her into the forest, until it bumped into a trunk and fled, pursued by the Wari'. A'ain was bleeding heavily. They took care of her and blew maize smoke over her body, a technique used by the Wari' to repel animal doubles. Her injuries healed.

One day sometime later, close to Pin Karam, To'o's father killed a lot of capuchin monkeys in the forest. According to To'o, her mother acted as though she already knew that her father had killed game and went into the forest to meet him. Seeing the prey, she put the monkeys in her mouth, still raw, and drank a lot of blood. She then spat out the liquid and To'o and other people saw that what emerged from her mouth was not blood but bits of maize chicha drink (*xikari tokwa;* here we should recall that the jaguar's chicha is blood).

Afterward, according to To'o's descriptions, her mother's body turned into a kind of living dictionary that transformed one object into another, a consequence of her double identity. One time she called her daughters to go bathing with her in the river. There they saw many tiny fish that the Wari' call *wam* (red wolf fish, *Erythrinus erythrinus*). The mother told the girls, "I'm going to fetch insect larvae [*orojat*]. Wrap some leaves together [in which to enclose the larvae] for us to roast them." Meanwhile the mother caught the little fish. When she showed them to her daughters, they were no longer fish but insect larvae. To'o, narrating the event to me, exclaimed, *"Orojat pin na wam,"* "The fish turned completely into larvae." On another occasion, To'o went into the forest with her mother and older sister. They made a woven basket and, on the river, caught many catfish (*opa, Pimelodella* sp.). Her mother swallowed the fish raw and spat out bits of peach-palm chicha (*xikari tarawan*). On seeing this, people exclaimed, *"Opa ira! Tarawan pin na!"* "It was *opa!* It turned completely into peach-palm!" During this period, To'o's mother began to cure sick people, becoming one of the few women to act as a shaman.

The efficacy of the body as a medium of translation, like a three-dimensional Google Translate,[31] emerges here in its extreme and almost caricatural form, when the metamorphosis of the person is objectified as a metamorphosis of the things surrounding him or her. The duality of the person's body, invisible to the Wari', is expressed as a duality of things transmuted as they traverse the body. Those who observed To'o's mother therefore had the opportunity to live in two distinct worlds simultaneously: the world of the jaguar and that of the Wari'.

But the idea of translation by the body is not limited to specific and rare cases like the one narrated above. Isn't the mimicry of whites, common in the first contacts of native peoples around the world, an example of perspectivist translation too? Let us turn to some examples.

MIMETISM AND TRANSLATION

Viveiros de Castro, in his essay on the Christianization of the Tupinambá, cites various proofs of the interest of the latter in mimicking the ritual actions of the missionaries, one of them taken from Nóbrega's First Brazilian Letter (1549: I, III, cited in Viveiros de Castro 2002: 196; 2011: 19):

> All those who talk to us say that they want to be like us. . . . If they hear the sound of the Mass, they awaken right away, and whatever they see us do, they do in its entirety: they kneel, they beat their chests, they lift their hands to the sky; and one of their leaders is learning to read and takes lessons each day with great care, and in two days knew the full ABC, and we taught him the sign of the cross, taking all with much desire. He says he wants to be a Christian.

Writing about the Guarani of Paraguay, Chamorro remarks that at the mission village (*reducción*) of San Ignacio de Ipaumbucú, the chief and shaman Miguel de Atiguaje, considered by Montoya a "true minister of the demon," "pretended to be a priest" and "simulated that he was saying mass. He put some cloths over a table and on top of them a manioc tart and a heavily painted vase with maize wine and, speaking through his teeth, conducted many ceremonies, showing the tart and the wine like the priests and finally eating and drinking everything. With this his vassals venerated him as though he were a priest" (Montoya 1985: 57, in Chamorro 1998: 63, my translation).[32]

Santos-Granero (2009: 118) describes the mimetic behavior of the Peruvian Yanesha priestly leaders in relation to Franciscan missionaries, including one who spent a year in the mission attending mass and catechism before going on to replicate the acts of the Catholic liturgy. "The most important of these acts was the solemn 'reading' of a book made of feathers, which undoubtedly replicated the Bible."

The impressions of the missionary Friedrich Scharf on his first visit to the Wari' (a short time after contact) reveal the same kind of mimetic behavior; unlike the examples cited above, however, this imitation did not refer to the religious ritual per se: "While we were on the river shore washing ourselves, the Indians were on the bank watching us and trying to imitate our gestures. . . . One of our missionaries used false teeth and when he removed them from his mouth to wash them—imagine this—two of the Indians also tried to remove their natural teeth from their mouth in order to imitate the cleaning gesture" (Scharf 2010: 32, my translation). The information from the missionary Royal on the initial period of contact at Tanajura points in the same direction: "The Indians, at their own initiative, dressed in clothes when they arrived at the post: they liked to imitate civilized people" (Royal Taylor, person. comm., 1994, my translation).

The replication of this mimetism five centuries later is obviously not unique to the Wari' and will be familiar to any Americanist. According to Taylor (1981: 672), for example, many Achuar, especially the great men, imitate the behavior of the missionaries, praying, singing hymns, and simulating the mastery of reading in an attempt to control the symbolic techniques that they understand to be the key to reproducing the material wealth of the whites. This type of action, the author states, is consistent with the Achuar idea that producing anything, including the plants obtained from their swiddens, depends on the appropriate ritual acts.

Mimesis involves more than simply the assimilation of specific techniques. The descriptions of the mimetic behavior of native peoples indicate the central place reserved for the body and for bodily transformations in this process of apprehending another perspective. For Taussig (1993: 46), mimesis is "an alternative science" based on a "sensuous transformation." As Viveiros de Castro (1998: 482) notes in his article on Amerindian perspectivism, ritual paraphernalia, like clothes, masks and adornments, are instruments, not costumes, with the power to conjure metaphysical transformations. Among various examples, we have the Yagua of Venezuela, whose shamans utilize "clothing" that allows their transformation into animals (Chaumeil 1983: 51, 66, 125).[33] Likewise, as I have sought to show elsewhere (Vilaça 2007, 2010), the Wari' use of white people's clothing and the consumption of their food are both effective modes of transforming into whites that, like shamanism, do not imply a fixed identity and, far from being a process without return, are founded precisely on this oscillation of positions.

Lattas (1998: 43–46), in his work on Melanesian cargo cults linked to the arrival of the whites, analyzes the detailed process of imitation undertaken by the natives, who copied not only the body postures, gestures, and etiquettes of the whites but also their bureaucratic structures, organizing police forces, cricket clubs, and banks, behavior that would be no surprise to an Amazonian specialist. Just like the Amazonian notion of ritual efficacy, in Melanesia it was "a way of capturing those secret magical acts that would deliver the European existence they copied" (44).[34]

At the end of his book, Lattas (1998: 45) highlights a point that, to me, seems crucial: imitation is never perfect, and it leads to transformation, or metamorphosis. What is involved, therefore, is not imitation but translation, in the sense I have been discussing.[35] Santos-Granero (2007: 58–62), discussing the Yanesha, draws attention to the fact that mimetism, when conceived within historical time, involves not only transformation but also appropriation. In other words, over time people forget the external origin of a given practice or object, such that mimetism and selective memory constitute ways of reversing inequality and power differences.[36] As we shall see, this is not the case of the Wari', who insist on preserving the external origin of practices, ideas, and objects, thereby maintaining the power derived from their exteriority.

It is important to observe, too, that, as I discuss later (see chapter 5), metamorphosis is not a one-way process. As Kelly (2011b: 74–84), inspired by Wagner's symbolism, has shown in relation to the Yanomami, metamorphosis into whites cannot be dissociated from adopting and socializing them.

Unaware, the missionaries with their commitment to living among the Wari', including eating with them (out of choice or the lack of any alternative) and "imitating" their language, offered the Wari' the return in kind that made the translation they desired possible. The matching of words encountered the matching of bodies, except that in the latter case the difference crucial to the Wari' conception of translation was kept. The Wari' did not want to become completely white (just as they do not want to turn whites completely into Wari', keeping their transformative agency active); they wanted to maintain the double identity characteristic of their professional translators, the shamans, as part of their transformation.[37]

Before turning to the practical experience of this encounter and its equivocations, I wish to return to a specific point that strikes me as interesting. The biblical episode of the Tower of Babel suggests a coincidence between the Wari' notion of culture as a set of practices shared by all types of humans (all make houses, hold the same kind of festivals, drink chicha, and so on) and the notion held by the missionaries, which supposes an original similarity followed by a later involution of some peoples. Both notions are opposed to our mainstream relativist conception, though they differ on one crucial point: for the missionaries, this same original culture, and the differences found today, all refer to the same world created by God (for lay Westerners, the equivalent of the nature explored by science). For the Wari', cultural similarity is based on radical material discontinuities and relates to a present fact rather than to something from the past.

Let us examine what happened during these first encounters between the Wari' and the missionaries. Having presented in the first chapter the motives that took the missionaries to the indigenous people, next I analyze the questions involved in the Wari' approaching these whites for the first time.

THREE

The Encounter with the Missionaries

Approximately fifty years ago the MNTB [New Tribes Mission of Brazil] initiated contact with the Pacaas Novos people through their missionaries, some of whom are already with the Lord. And through their testimonies, this people saw the light of Christ's love shine in their lives.

... The Wari' People, as they like to be called, were in the past a people who engaged in cannibal practices; in other words, they also ate human flesh. As God so loved this people that He gave Jesus to pay the price of their sins, He sent some missionaries who gave their life for them to know the infinite love of Our Father.

"The Light Still Shines," by Maria Tereza Montovani,
missionary among the Pacaas Novos people, New
Tribes Mission of Brazil

IN THE PREVIOUS CHAPTER we examined the metaphysical questions surrounding the concepts of translation held by the missionaries and the Wari', and saw that very distinct notions of culture, language, and communication were at play in this encounter. On one hand, we observed a search for an equivalence of words based on the existence of a single universe, in which cultures and languages that had become different through involution following the Tower of Babel could reestablish communication (albeit on hierarchical bases). On the other hand, we found multinaturalism—that is, the supposition of a multiple universe, inhabited by beings with equivalent cultures and distinct bodies, speaking the same language, the "language of people," implying a notion of translation based on bodily metamorphosis.

Before returning to the question of translation, I wish to explore the first scenes of this encounter in order to explain what led the Wari', who until that moment had no peaceful relations with any other group, to become interested in the missionaries. Given that just like all the other whites seen before them, the missionaries were classified and treated as enemies (*wijam*), I begin with an analysis of this latter category, comparing it to other positions of alterity—namely, animals (*karawa*) and foreigners (*tatirim*)—and revisiting some of the questions discussed in the previous chapter.

PEOPLE, ANIMALS, ENEMIES, AND FOREIGNERS

As we have seen in chapter 2, from the Wari' point of view the enemies, *wijam*, are nonhumans, associated with beings from the *karawa* category (animals, prey). Having myself been classified by the Wari' as an "enemy," in the same way as whites in general still are today, on various occasions I experienced an explicit identification of enemies with animals. One time I was chatting with a woman whom I called "older sister" (*we*) when her small daughter approached and, surprised to see me, exclaimed, "Hey, there is a *wijam* [enemy] here!" The mother was clearly embarrassed by this observation and admonished the child: "Is she walking on all fours? Is that what you see? She's not a *karawa*! She's *wari'*!"

Paletó made a similar observation when I told him, after he had stayed with my family in Rio, that my mother liked him: "She is *wari'*! She isn't a white-lipped or collared peccary! She is *wari'*." On another occasion, a child again compared me to animals, but from the other way around: while watching some cattle grazing, he referred to the animals as *wijam*. His grandparents, who called me "daughter" (*arain*), were highly embarrassed and pointed out his classificatory mistake, explaining that the cattle were *karawa*.

An analogous association was made by an adult woman, To'o Orowak, when I jokingly called some Wari' young men *wijam* when they were talking playfully in Portuguese: "If we had tails! We are *wari'*. Only what we speak [in this case, what the young men had spoken] is different." More recently, another example was prompted by my youngest son, seven years old at the time. Disheartened by the difficulty he felt communicating in Wari', he exclaimed in Portuguese: "I'm white, I'll never manage to speak like you." My Wari' sister immediately responded in Wari', consoling him: "You're a person (*wari'*), you just speak strangely, but you're a person!" suggesting that with time he would naturally learn the language.

These examples are interesting not only because they clearly make explicit the identification between *wijam* and *karawa*, but also because they indicate a peculiar aspect of the enemies: unlike animals, which were simply killed and eaten, never adopted (an exception being made for the relation between the shaman and his animal affines),[1] enemies could be incorporated into Wari' society, shifting from *karawa* to *wari'* through a process of kinship production that involves living and eating together. This was the process that my children and I had experienced, though neither they nor the Wari' children were aware of this fact. And as we shall see, it was also the same process to which the missionaries had been subjected.

This possibility of incorporation by living together, though uncommon during historical time, is prefigured in myth (myths are considered histories of the ancestors), which establishes that the enemies originated from Wari' society, implying that they could become part of it again. The two myths describing the origin of enemies are attributed to a conflict within a group of Wari' kin (between brothers in one of the myths and between grandfather and grandchildren in the other), which led to their separation. As time passed, they no longer recognized or communicated with each other (which takes us back to the biblical theme of the Tower of Babel, mentioned in chapter 2) and began to attack each other with arrows and, later, firearms. In some versions of the myth of Oropixi', in which the enemies originated from a pair of brothers, this movement is reversed and the dissident and his family are reincorporated into Wari' society.[2]

And not only the enemies originated in Wari' society: the contemporary Wari' are themselves descendants of enemies. Unlike origin myths of some other Amazonian groups, the origin myth of Wari' society describes not the emergence of humans out of an initially chaotic mixture of human and animals forms and affects, but the reconfiguration of society, almost totally destroyed by a deluge, following the encounter with enemies. The myth tells of an old woman, the rain spirit, who appears in a village and provokes a huge flood when she leaves. Only a father, widowed by the disaster, and his daughters survive. Determined to encounter new men who could become his sons-in-law, this father, Nanananana, comes across an unknown group of people, whom the narrators always classify as enemies, *wijam*. The father goes to meet them, recounting what happened and asking for single men to marry his daughters (note that communication via language is not a problem). The marriages take place, and after a while the different families disperse and lose day-to-day contact. In the sporadic encounters that followed, one group begins to note strange aspects of the others, which provide the basis for the various names by which these groups became known, eventually forming the Wari' subgroups introduced in the previous chapter.[3] The myths make clear that the foreigners, *tatirim,* members of other subgroups, are like halfway enemies, and that the ritual in which they make each other drunk with sour maize chicha is a domesticated form of warfare.

The foreigner category clearly reveals that the *wari'* and *wijam* positions are located on opposite poles of a continuum. *Wari'* are the people with whom one lives and who therefore share the same language, the same habits, and the same kin group. As we briefly saw in chapter 2, the Wari' say that they are all kin to each other, although they conceive this kinship as a gradient differentiating close, true kin (*iri' nari*) from those who are more or less distant and "more or less" kin (*nari paxi, ma pam nari, nari ximao*). Close kin are those with whom one maintains day-to-day relations, which includes real affines who, though not genealogically close (the Wari' have a Crow-Omaha kinship terminology and marriage is prohibited between close kin), are consubstantialized by living and eating together. In everyday life the use of affinal terms is avoided, and people try to find a consanguineal term, or teknonym, for everyone, which allows a brother-in-law, for example, to be called "brother" or "father of my nephews."

In this kinship gradient, foreigners as a whole are found at the most distant pole and, interestingly enough, were addressed directly by affinal terms in the chicha rituals. As among other Amazonian groups (Viveiros de Castro 1993), the Wari' differentiate real from prototypical affines, relations with whom are marked by tension and rivalry, and marriage avoided. Although they occur with a certain frequency, marriages between people from different subgroups—when the children were affiliated to the group of the mother or father—are not thought desirable, since, given the intrinsic alterity of the foreigners, objectified in the strangeness of their customs, they were seen to be doomed to fail.

It is precisely the constitutive difference of foreigners that makes them the way out—and way in—to Wari' society. Hence, all foreigners are undoubtedly classified as *wari'* (people), but, over the course of history and in the mythic universe, foreigners can become enemies, *wijam,* thereby becoming associated with the *karawa* category: prey, food. And it is in this position that they constitute the object of war.

I should emphasize that we are not dealing here with a relational dynamic of a kind widespread in the South American lowlands, such as among the Yanomami (Albert 1985) and other peoples from the so-called Guiana complex (Rivière 1984), who classify local populations from the same ethnic group either as kin/affines, or as enemies, in a constant fluctuation of the relational geography, depending on the success or failure of exchange and intermarriage, as well as more random events, such as diseases attributed to sorcery cast by people from a particular group. The Wari' relational context did not oscillate in this way and, normally speaking, over the course of a person's life an enemy would always be an enemy, a non-*wari'*.

The equation between enemies and animals implies a continuity between warfare and hunting. This continuity is made explicit by the Wari' when they describe the predatory action of animals as either hunting or warfare. At some moments, they say, the animals—humans beings from their own point of view—see the Wari' as enemies, *wijam,* and attack them as in war. In other occasions, the Wari' are seen as animals, *karawa.* In both cases, the beings located in the position of prey are ideally roasted and eaten. This was the fate of hunted animals, and of enemies in the context of warfare (see Vilaça 1992, 2000, 2010). Given that humanity is a position occupied by those who act as predators, warfare and hunting are the means available to the Wari' to appropriate this position.

However, the equation between hunting and warfare contains a number of asymmetries, such as the fact, mentioned above, that only enemies can be adopted. Likewise the actions of animals and the Wari' as agents of predation differ, insofar as animals prey on the Wari' not only because they perceive themselves as human and, therefore, as predators, but also to extend their families, turning the victims into kin, the fate of all those killed or captured by animals. In this sense, the Wari' are mortal: that is, once preyed upon, they never return to their own kind. This contrasts with the animals who, after being eaten, return to their houses as though nothing has happened (see Vilaça 1998).

WAR

According to Wari' memory, they were always warriors. At least until the start of the twentieth century, they warred with neighboring groups, including the Tupian Karipuna and Uru-Eu-Wau-Wau. With the arrival of the colonizers, who caused the flight or extermination of various groups, the traditional enemies of the Wari' turned scarce and the whites became their primary enemies. The latter were killed and eaten just like the other enemies, the only difference being that they were easier prey since many whites lived alone in isolated houses in the forest.

A killer never ate an enemy whom he killed, since he had the latter's blood (*kikon*), or blood double (*jamikikon*), inside his (the killer's) body, which, when digested during reclusion, transformed the enemy into a kind of child that would accompany him through life and, after, in the posthumous world. Another product of this digestion was the killer's semen, which, offered to women during sex, made their bellies swell, either with fat or with babies (who were not considered enemy children but the Wari' father's; see Conklin [2001a, 2001b]).

The enemy's roasted flesh could be eaten by everyone but the killer: the men, women, and children who had stayed in the village (the exception being those children who had shot arrows at the displayed body parts). The Wari' ate discreetly, albeit angrily. According to the Wari', only the anger of the eaters differentiated this meal from the flesh of animal prey, which, like the flesh of the Wari' dead, was eaten with restraint—in the case of the latter, delicately and sadly too. The anger felt for enemies, the Wari' say, was a given and did not depend on the experience of mourning the dead killed by them.

Save for a mythic episode and an exceptional historical one, which is discussed in chapter 5, the Wari' did not bring back live enemies to be incorporated into the group, a widespread practice among other native groups of the Americas. Neither did they appropriate items from enemy "culture," like names, rites, and songs.

The Wari' disinterest in living enemies, including their objects and techniques, is quite striking. For example, although the Tupi neighbors with whom they warred very probably knew how to produce fire, the Wari' claim they have never known the technique, that they originally captured fire from the jaguar and have kept it alight ever since. Similarly, during their first contacts with the whites, they were interested in nothing related to them, including food and other objects (with the exception of metal tools), alleging that white things had a strong, unpleasant smell.

I should add that, for the Wari', war is not a means of appropriating what Viveiros de Castro (1992a) calls an "enemy position." Among the Tupian Araweté studied by the author, the killers became enemies to the group during their period of reclusion, threatening them periodically with outbursts of anger and armed attacks. Among the Wari' this alteration was an attribute of shamans who, acting like animals, could see their coinhabitants as animals or as enemies, as we saw in the previous chapter. In war itself, although the enemy's blood, incorporated by the killer, made them consubstantial for the time of reclusion (meaning that the killer could not eat the enemy's flesh), and although the killer represented the properly human (wari') aspect of the enemy,[4] it did not make him into an enemy. On the contrary, this blood—

only after its digestion, it should be stressed—made the killer fully Wari', beautiful, fat and potent.

War and cannibalism were devices for differentiation, not identification (see Strathern [2012] on the Wari'). Given that humanity is a highly unstable position for the Wari' the problem was to secure it: eating the enemy was a way of making themselves the predator and thus human.

Let us see what happened at the moment when the Wari' accepted the idea of peaceful contact with the whites.

ENCOUNTERING THE WHITES

The importance of historical determination and the causality of events in the classification of Europeans was brilliantly analyzed by Sahlins (1981, 1985) in his works on Pacific societies, particularly in his study of Captain Cook's welcome by Hawaiians. Just as for many peoples of the Americas—like the Aztecs, Mayans, Incas, and Tupi, who served as examples of an "opening to the Other" for Lévi-Strauss (1991: 16)—the arrival of the Europeans was anticipated in indigenous mythology: the gods, temporarily absent, could return, and both Captain Cook and the Spanish and Portuguese sailors matched these prophecies perfectly (even if temporarily). Among the Aztecs and the Mayans, people spoke of white-skinned and bearded gods who would one day arrive by sea. This, according to Lévi-Strauss (293–294), explained the welcome given by the Aztecs to Cortez, who venerated him and adorned him in sacred garments, or the response of the Incas, when thousands of warriors were paralyzed before a little over one hundred armed Spaniards.

We should consider that in these episodes, unlike in the Wari' case, the arrival of the Europeans took the form of spectacular events. As Schieffelin and Crittenden (1991: 285–287) have shown regarding Papua New Guinea, the place and form in which the Europeans arrived among the different peoples was essential to determining how they were classified.

Although both Sahlins and Lévi-Strauss link the fascination with Europeans to myth, each author explores different aspects of this association. For Sahlins (1985: 78) the starting point is the theme of the "stranger king," which provides the basis for the political system of diverse Pacific Island peoples: the new king is always a stranger who arrives from across the ocean and usurps the throne by marrying a local woman. In a more recent article, Sahlins (2010: 109) identifies this same political system in other parts of the world, both in Africa and among some peoples of the Americas, which enables the idea of power associated with the outside to be generalized by the author.

Lévi-Strauss, for his part, focuses in particular on the ontological aspects involved in this question. For him the determining factor is the dualistic nature of indigenous thought, which classifies the world through pairs of opposites in perpetual disequilibrium, leading to the continual proliferation of dichotomies. Hence, given this dichotomous principle "that at each stage forces the terms to become double[,] . . . the creation of the Indians by the demiurge necessitated as well the creation of non-Indians" (1991: 292). The place of the whites was, therefore, in Lévi-Strauss's words, a "hollow space" in native thought, anticipated in the form of a radical alterity to which Europeans could easily conform.

Certainly for the Wari' the enemy always represented this radical alterity; although, in contrast to what seems to have happened among indigenous people at the start of European conquest, it was attributed not to their extraordinary capacities but rather to a quality that seems to be the exact opposite: their nonhumanity, determined by the prey position that enemies were supposed to assume. This is what really interested them: the possibility afforded by the encounter with the enemy for realizing their capacity to make themselves human. And while this also applied to animal prey, enemies— because of their mythic origin as Wari', a certain human appearance visible to everyone (and not just shamans, as in the case of animals), and their incorporation through blood by killers—amplified the evidence of this capacity.

The first whites encountered were not, in the eyes of the Wari', very different from the other enemies, at least in terms of material wealth. They were poor rubber tappers living in isolation in the forest, and the Wari' indeed considered them defenseless, incapable of using bows and also unfamiliar with firearms.[5] It is worth adding that the Wari' did not have gods or demiurges of any sort, capable of inspiring prophecies about the return of these powerful beings. The realization of the extraordinary capacities of the whites, immediately visible to some other peoples, occurred only much later, when, as we shall see, the whites proved to be both an inexhaustible source of goods of every kind and powerful curers. It was then that the Wari' became interested in sharing the "enemy's point of view" (Viveiros de Castro 1992a).

We do know, though, that the Wari' mythology prefigured the possibility of another type of relation with the enemies who, originally part of Wari' society, could return to it. Generally speaking, the foreigner category, *tatirim*, constituted a kind of communicating door between the Wari' and their enemies. It was with this model in mind that the Wari' first approached the whites.

THE WARI' BEFORE CONTACT

Just before the whites began to penetrate their territory more intensively, around the start of the twentieth century, eight Wari' subgroups—OroNao', OroAt, OroEo, OroWaram, OroWaramXijein, OroMon, OroKao'OroWaji, OroJowin—occupied a vast geographic area in the northwest of the present-day Brazilian state of Rondônia, close to the border with Bolivia, all on the right side of the Madeira, Mamoré, and Pacaás Novos Rivers. With the exception of the OroJowin and the OroKao'OroWaji, of whom just a few remain who identify themselves as such, the subgroups still exist today, though their spatial distribution has undergone alterations following pacification.

The Wari' occupation of affluents flowing into the left side of the Pacaás Novos, especially the Dois Irmãos River, took place during the first decade of the twentieth century, when families from the OroNao' subgroup (with a few OroEo and OroAt individuals) decided to settle in locations they had sporadically visited during hunting and gathering expeditions. According to the Wari', as soon as they settled there the circulation of whites on the Pacaás Novos River suddenly intensified, which coincided with the rubber boom. This activity isolated the group of migrants from the other Wari', since the fear of being attacked by the whites prevented them from crossing the Pacaás Novos. Instead they moved to regions farther and farther away from the shores of the main river.[6] The situation of total isolation between the two groups was maintained for almost fifty years, and contact was reestablished only by the pacification teams, when the isolated group became the first to take an interest in making peaceful contact with the whites.

The Wari' villages were relatively small. Each village, comprising twenty to thirty people on average, was usually formed by a group of brothers and their wives, sometimes themselves a group of sisters, as well as the parents of the men and any widowed aunts and uncles. These groups were not fixed over time but recomposed annually after each change in settlement location, when new swiddens were cleared to plant maize, their main crop. Hence, one particular year one of the brothers might go to live with the parents of one of his wives, or the brother of one of the women might go to live with his sister,

FIGURE 4. Wari' reservation areas in Brazil, 1996.

accompanied by his wives, one of them probably a genealogical relative of one of these men, and their children. Various arrangements were possible and were indeed realized over time.

The construction of the Madeira-Mamoré railway between 1905 and 1911, which cut across the borders of the Wari' territory, worsened the conflicts already initiated with the penetration of rubber tappers. Along with the deaths on both sides, these clashes began to involve the capture of Indians, some of them taken to the city to be displayed, many of whom died.

With the success of the rubber plantations in Malaysia beginning in 1910, interest in Brazilian rubber faded, and though some of the rubber tappers decided to stay, many returned to the Brazilian northeast, where they had originated. The relations between those who remained and the Wari' contin-ued to be exclusively bellicose, even though some of invaders, according to the

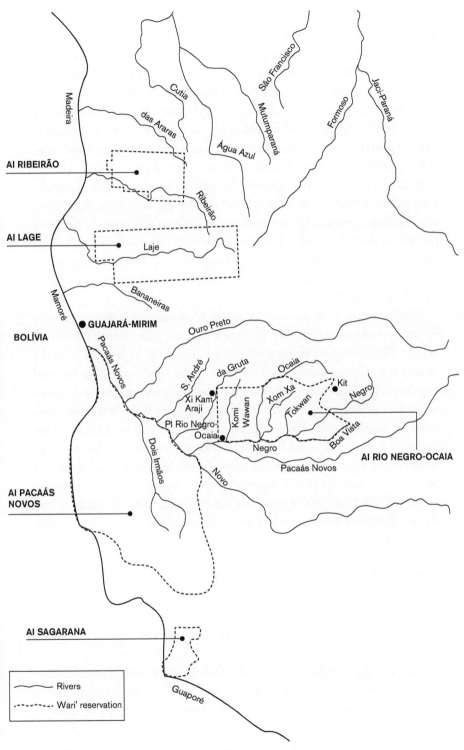

FIGURE 5. Wari' reservations, 1996.

memories of the oldest, had tried to make peaceful contact with seemingly good intentions and presents. Some new diseases were introduced during this period but did not cause epidemic outbreaks, and were very often attributed to the sorcery of members of another Wari' subgroup after a ritual encounter.

This situation of relative equilibrium underwent a sudden change at the start of the 1940s with the occupation of Malaysia by Japanese forces during the Second World War. This provoked to a new rubber boom in Amazonia and the penetration of a new wave of rubber tappers into more isolated areas, reaching the smaller rivers farther upstream, favored by the Wari' as settlement locations. The Wari', frightened by the mass attacks on their villages by men armed with machine guns, who attacked while they slept, decimating entire villages, ceased actively searching for enemies and began to flee from the whites instead, taking refuge ever farther upriver. As Paletó said to me one time: "It was as though we were game, peccaries." The Wari' thus began to live in even more acute form the problem of unstable humanity that already haunted them.

The first attempts at "pacification" of the Wari' were organized in the 1930s by the government agency assigned this purpose, the Indian Protection Service (SPI). The government was motivated especially by pressure from the traders and rubber plantation owners and by the shock caused to the local population at the discovery of corpses of rubber tappers found on the outskirts of Guajará-Mirim without heads, arms, and legs (which the Wari' had taken home to roast and eat). The SPI strategy involved choosing locations where evidence of the Indians had been discovered and leaving presents in situ to attract them, especially metal tools. Each of these locations, called attraction posts, was occupied by an SPI officer, who would wait for the "wild" Indians.[7]

At first the Wari' would approach these locations and, thinking it very strange that the enemies would leave tools out in the open and accessible, would take them, sometimes shooting arrows at the SPI house. No other kind of contact was established. When the conflicts worsened in the 1940s, expeditions began to be organized in search of the "anthropophagic" Indians.

MEETING THE MISSIONARIES

As mentioned in chapter 1, the decisive factor in establishing peaceful contacts with the Wari' was the work of missionaries from the New Tribes Mission, in collaboration with the SPI. These missionaries had recently arrived in the region and were well trained for the tasks at hand. According to the U.S. missionary Royal Taylor (interviewed in 1994), the base of the mission in the city of Guajará-Mirim had been built by Virgil Sharp between 1946 and 1948,[8] but the first wave of missionaries did not arrive in the city until 1950. These included Royal, still single at the time, and Thomas Moreno, son of the Mexican Joe Moreno, who had taken part in the fateful expedition to the Ayoré of Bolivia. According to Royal, other missionaries who arrived in this wave headed to "Boca do Acre," in what was then the territory of Acre, where "there were rumors of Indians." On this occasion, he and Thomas Moreno traveled up the Guaporé River toward the city of Cafetal, "looking for a tribe," and during the voyage encountered the Moré Indians on the Bolivian side, speakers of a language from the same family as the Wari', the Txapakura. The Moré already had considerable experience of living with whites in the Moré Indigenous Nucleus (Leigue Castedo 1957). I do not know for sure whether this encounter was planned, but according to Royal, between this voyage and 1957, when he returned from holiday, his colleagues had already returned to the Moré another time and collected a small vocabulary for use in studying the Wari' language.

Between 1951 and 1952, and by now married to Joan, Royal conducted expeditions with Abraham Koop in the headwater region of the Mutum-Paraná River, where rumors of Indians had been heard from rubber tappers. These Indians were only later identified as Wari', probably members of the OroWaram, OroWaramXijein, and OroMon subgroups, who would trek there from the Laje River in search of metal tools. They did not find the Indians or even traces of them.

Abraham Koop was married to Delores Koop, both Canadian. I have been unable to establish the exact dates when the other missionaries arrived, but according to information from Delores Koop (pers. comm. to Barbara Kern, 2011),[9] Abraham was accompanied by Joe Moreno and Richard Sollis (married to Rose Sollis, daughter of Joe and sister of Thomas Moreno) during the first expeditions, between 1954 and the start of 1956. In accordance with Brazilian law, the team always worked in the company of SPI agents. This information is confirmed by Johnston (1985: 249), who wrote, "Dick Sollis, along with Joe Moreno (his father-in-law) and Abe Koop—had spent more than two-and-one-half years of extremely dangerous contact work with [the] cannibalistic Pacaas Novas tribe of Brazil."

On that occasion the missionaries used an old rubber-tapper house as the base for their expeditions into the Pacaás Novos River area. Named Tanajura, it was located on the left shore of the river, an area used by the isolated OroNao'. According to Royal, "The first step was to clear the forest to a distance further than an arrow could be shot." Afterward they cleared paths in the forest in the direction of the *malocas* (houses), along which they hung up presents, like machetes, axes, and pans. The Wari' initially took the presents and fled without making direct contact, repeating what had happened during previous attempts in other areas.[10]

Over time, the presents were left ever closer to the missionary base. In May 1956 a group of Indians peacefully approached the mission house in Tanajura and, standing on the edge of the clearing, began to shout for the whites to come out. The missionary Joe Moreno and SPI agent(s) walked to the middle of the clearing, stuck two poles in the ground and hung presents from them. They went back to the house and waited. They emerged again, this time unarmed and their arms held high. They took the presents from the poles and waited for the Indians to approach in order to hand them the items personally. Afterward, the Wari' returned various times, receiving presents, spending the day there, and returning to Pitop village to sleep.

According to Royal and documents from the SPI,[11] as well as to the accounts of the Wari' themselves, between 1956 and 1959 the Indians came and went, contracting diseases such as influenza, chicken pox, and malaria, which killed many of them. Some of these diseases were brought by people from Guajará-Mirim, who came to meet "the famous Indians" and give them presents.

It was only in 1959 that some Wari' families settled near to the Tanajura base. According to Delores Koop,[12] living in Tanajura in 1957 were Abraham and Delores, Royal and Joan Taylor (who had returned from holiday), the recently arrived LeRoy and Lillie Smith, and Friedrich (a São Paulo resident of Swiss descent) and Gisela Sharp. Until 1959 they were accompanied by Seila Soeiro, a Brazilian woman who worked for the Koops as a housekeeper, and who, after two years of training at the Peniel Bible Institute in Jacutinga, Minas Gerais, Brazil, returned in 1961 as a missionary, living in Tanajura at least until the end of the 1990s, when she retired.

By around 1959, Richard and Joe were apparently no longer a fixed part of the Tanajura team, since they had begun work with Friedrich Scharf and SPI agents, by then accompanied by a number of Wari' men, organizing expeditions to contact the isolated Wari', those living in the region of the Laje River and the affluents of the right shore of the Pacaás Novos. Royal confirms this fact: "After contact was firmly established, Moreno left. He was a contact man. Ricardo [Richard] also went away."[13]

The names of Moreno, Richard, Friedrich, and Royal himself are mentioned in the Wari' accounts of these expeditions. These men headed to areas where information existed on an indigenous presence, most of the time related to the death of whites from arrow attacks.[14] There are records of expeditions undertaken to the Laje in 1959 and 1960, when they encountered no more than signs of the Wari', who fled as soon as they saw the whites arrive, but who returned to collect the tools left behind. In mid-1960, they also undertook one or two expeditions to the Negro River region, an area where the OroEo, OroAt, and OroNao' lived at that time. Again they were unsuccessful in encountering the Indians.[15]

As I discussed in a previous book (Vilaça 2010), it is noteworthy that only the contact attempts undertaken in the Tanajura region, an area inhabited by the isolated OroNao', proved successful, even though earlier expeditions in the Laje and Ribeirão River areas had been organized exactly in the same way, including the participation of the NTM missionaries. The Wari' accounts of the event, which parallel a number of mythic narratives, reveal that the isolation in which they were living—which prevented them from performing their rituals, all of which involve the relation between different subgroups enacting the roles of hosts and guests—was the determining factor in their decision to contact the whites peacefully. According to their accounts, they even tried dividing into two groups to perform their rituals, but it was not the same thing. They had enemies with whom they could war, since the whites were living in the surrounding region, but lacked the foreigners needed to complete their social life.

The arrival of the well-meaning whites was initially taken as a chance to incorporate them as one more subgroup, which explains why they immediately attempted to reciprocate the objects given to them, offering the whites objects like baskets, maize cake, and bows and arrows. But the whites were unsuited to this position. Instead of acting as ritual partners, they were disposed to live there and establish relations with specific people, especially those who became their first translators. These relations, a mixture of close collaboration and commensality, actualized another possibility also prefigured in myth, and which I discuss in chapter 5: the incorporation of the enemy as adoptive kin.

The interest that the OroNao' of the left shore had in encountering foreigners was evident in their keenness to take part in the expeditions organized some years later to contact the other Wari' subgroups. When, in 1961, they finally met the Wari' of the OroWaram subgroup, who inhabited the region of the Laje River, and who had not been seen for at least fifty years, they acted very similarly to the protagonist of the flood myth mentioned above: isolated with his family, he sets out in search of people, *wari'*, and encounters members of an enemy group, whom he insists on transforming into affines. Isolated for such a long time, the OroNao' who arrived with the whites were taken by the other Wari' to be enemies, *wijam* (even though they spoke a comprehensible language), and were aware that they were seen likewise, again indicating the positional nature of the *wari'* and *wijam* categories. Those who first spoke to the recently arrived Wari' and carried the news to other villages said, "The enemies are crazy: now they say they are OroNao'." The others replied, "So, let's shoot them."

A short while later, though, those Wari' who arrived offered to assume the role of guests of a *huroroin'*, the most complex festival performed among Wari' subgroups, and thereby changed from enemies to foreigners, just as they desired. Although the missionaries Abraham, Richard, and Royal did not work on the front line, leaving the Wari' to undertake the initial approaches, they took part in this episode.

A last expedition, which set out from Guajará-Mirim on May 20, 1961, established the first peaceful contact on the Negro River on June 25, the same year. This expedition differed by involving the partnership and initiative of the Catholic Church, represented by Dom Roberto Arruda (at the time Father Roberto), who was accompanied by SPI employees coming directly from the head office in Brasilia. Evangelical missionaries were excluded. This provoked a strong reaction from the latter, and Joe Moreno, accompanied by an SPI inspector, even went to the Negro River to meet them and stop them from going farther. His attempt was unsuccessful. However, months later, the NTM missionaries LeRoy Smith and Gabriela were already in Koxain, the Wari' village closest to the attraction post situated on the shores of the Negro River, near to the mouth of the Ocaia, a site that became known as Barracão Velho.

Since the first contacts, therefore, missionaries had settled next to almost all the so-called attraction posts, local SPI bases, and, later, National Indian Foundation (FUNAI) posts, around which the Wari' themselves gradually came to live. At first the missionaries moved relatively frequently, going where they believed themselves to be needed most. We can take the case of Barbara Kern as an example.

Born Barbara Louise Brown in National City, California, she arrived in Guajará-Mirim in November 1962, the same year that she graduated from Biola University, situated on the outskirts of Los Angeles and geared toward missionary training.[16] In December of the same year, she left for the Negro River, where she lived until mid-April 1963. From there Barbara headed to the Lage Post along with the recently arrived Brazilian woman Ester Cavalcanti da Silva. There they met Royal and Joan (Royal had taken part in the first contact in the region), along with Abraham and Delores Koop. The two young unmarried women stayed on the Laje River until mid-1964, when they moved to Tanajura, where they stayed for a year and a half. From there Barbara returned to the Laje River, where she lived until the end of 1966. This was when Manfred Kern, a missionary of German extraction, arrived in Guajará-Mirim and they married. The couple then relocated to Tanajura, where they stayed until the transference of the post by the FUNAI to the traditional Wari' site of Pitop, deeper into the forest, in 1968. There they remained for ten years, before returning to Tanajura in 1978, accompanying the Wari' from Pitop.[17] They stayed in Tanajura (where I met them in 1986) until 1993, when they accompanied some of the inhabitants from there and Santo André, who were transferred to the new post opened by FUNAI on the Sotério River, an affluent of the Mamoré. Manfred and Barbara left the Sotério Post in 2003 for medical treatment. Since her arrival in 1962, Barbara had been the person responsible for coordinating studies of the native language, begun, it would seem, by Royal Taylor, Richard Sollis, and Friedrich Scharf (Scharf 2010: 77).[18]

We can observe, therefore, that two years after the contact with the isolated groups, around 1963, the Evangelical missionaries abandoned their pattern of high mobility and began to settle at the different posts—or to accompany the inhabitants of the latter when they moved site—remaining at each of them for several years. For example, the Brazilian couple Assis and Maria Eli lived on the Negro River between 1963 and 1966,[19] followed by Royal and Joan Taylor between 1966 and 1967 and another Brazilian couple, Basílio and Carmelita, between 1968 and 1976. They were succeeded by Abílio and Ester, who lived there for more than a decade. After various other movements, the missionaries were found in 2009 in just three Wari' villages/posts: the Brazilian couple Valmir and Fátima in Ribeirão; Tereza, a Brazilian woman, at Lage Velho; and finally Royal Taylor's American nephew Thomas and his Brazilian wife, Claudeliz, at Santo André.

Although the Wari' considered the prolonged stays of the missionaries to be a factor differentiating them from other whites,[20] some employees from the SPI (and later FUNAI) would remain with them for many years, among them Antônio Costa, Josias Batista, Pedro Azzi, and later Walter Stozek. The latter, who lived at the Negro River Post between 1971 and 1976, told me (pers. comm., March 2011) that he initially had a number of conflicts with the missionaries Basílio and Carmelita, with whom he lived on the Negro River, but that over time he came to admire their work and began to attend some of the Evangelical services, despite being unable to understand Wari', the language used in the services. Other whites also began to be catechized by the missionaries. Given the lack of resources from FUNAI, which at the time failed to provide Stozek even with a boat in which to travel, the goodwill and relative abundance of material items from the missionaries proved indispensable. It was the missionaries' boat, for example, that was used to take seriously ill employees to Guajará-Mirim for hospital treatment.[21]

Contrary to what happened in Tanajura, where the contacts happened progressively, the contacts in the Laje and Negro River areas were followed by violent epidemics: many of the two-thirds of the Wari' population who died during this period lived there.[22] The situation on the Negro River was made even worse by the fact that some of the recently contacted inhabitants of the Laje River region, who had been asked to take part in the expedition, were already ill themselves. The Wari' accounts of this moment are striking: of people watching as their mothers, fathers, and siblings died almost simultaneously, and of being too weak to give them a proper funeral.

Even with this situation, and despite some groups of people moving away and living in isolation for years, most of the Wari' insisted on staying close to these enemies, making it clear that they perceived something special in them, something they could appropriate to resolve questions inherent to their existence, just as they aimed to do by incorporating them as foreigners. The relation with the new whites, including the missionaries, therefore reveals a sudden change in attitudes, only then similar to those observed by travelers, missionaries, and others during the first contacts of indigenous peoples with the whites: they wanted to imitate their gestures, eat their food, and wear their clothes, displaying a kind of mimetic "fever" that surprised the whites, as we saw in chapter 2.

THE POWER OF THE MISSIONARIES

A fact always recalled by the Wari' whenever they wish to emphasize the special capacities of the missionaries is the incident when the missionaries, coming across the Wari' as they traveled up the Dois Irmãos River, escaped unscathed from a volley of arrows. Like the missionaries themselves, the Wari' today attribute this invulnerability to divine protection, as shown in the account given by Oroiram, one of the men in the group who shot the arrows.

> OROIRAM: Maxun Kworain tried to shoot them but missed. [Noise of motor leaving.] "You're a woman!" they said to Maxun Kworain when he missed the target. Had they not been Christians [*crentes* in Portuguese].[23] They only struck trees, they felled no one. They [the whites] left tools there.
>
> APARECIDA: Why did the arrows miss the Christians?
>
> OROIRAM: God helps them. (Oroiram, conversation with the author, 1993)

Friedrich Scharf (2010: 82, my translation), who took part in the Laje River expeditions and the contact attempts on the Negro River, also described the event: "But the powerful and protective hand of God shielded us from being struck by the arrows or ambushes. Truly the Angel of the Lord camped next to us and protected us from the dangerous arrows."

In their sermons the missionaries told the Wari' all about this power, in which they themselves believed. On the same Negro River, during what seems to have been a rapid visit soon after contact, Royal Taylor, in the middle of a sermon in the native language, had explained why the missionaries had arrived. As Paletó recalled in 2009, when visiting me in Rio de Janeiro, the missionary said, "We came from far away. God told me to come to you. That's why I saved you from being killed by guns. That's what God told me, my brothers" (Paletó, conversation with the author, 2009). A prayer by Rosenio, a OroWaram pastor, during a Christian conference in 2009 reaffirms that power: "You made Noah escape, made Lo escape, made Moses as a child escape. You will do the same for us at the present, when you come back" (Lage conference, 2009).[24]

Not only was the power of the missionaries' effective over weapons, but it also gave them abundant resources, very often contrasted with the scarcity of the SPI's resources. As Paletó told me in 2009: "The people of God have rice, beans, medicines. We only had maize" (Paletó, conversation with the author, 2009).

One fact that seems to have been decisive in awakening Wari' interest in the missionaries was the effort they put into caring for the sick, when they used words and gestures to directly associate the curing capacity of the medicines with the divine power mediated by themselves.

Friedrich Scharf provides a harrowing account of the outbreaks of malaria and influenza in the Tanajura and Dois Irmãos region, along with the untiring work of the missionaries, recognized and requested by the Wari', who themselves sent the missionaries to the sick.[25] One of these accounts refers to the attempt to cure an old woman suffering from malaria and, it appears, close to death. Scharf later said that, after giving her injections of Aralen (an antimalarial drug) and Plasil (an antiemetic), and finding it difficult to transport her, he believed that "the only recourse was to pray once again and ask for help from the Lord. So I prayed with my hands laid on her" (Scharf 2010: 66). The woman was cured.[26]

In the words of Tem We in 1994, a man from the first group to be contacted: "The Christians said: 'Believe in God.... So that you don't become sick.'" In Tanajura, said Tem We, the missionaries went to speak in the houses: "God exists. Believe in him. It is God who makes us strong.'" Over time, news of the curing power of God spread among them As Paletó explained in 1995: "The OroNao' [of Tanajura] said [to the people of the Negro River]: 'Become Christians. It's good to be a Christian. The Christians help us. When we are sick, we speak to God and we get better.' 'Okay.' And all the Wari' believed" (Paletó, conversation with the author, 1995).

The association between the curing power of the medicines and the missionaries' capacities was common in various parts of the Americas, especially because, for diverse native groups from the region, the missionaries were the first whites with whom they had contact and were responsible for introducing new pathogenic agents.[27] One result was that in many cases the missionaries were taken to be powerful shamans, both in positive terms, as people able to cure, and negative, as sorcerers.[28] Consequently, and given the impotence of the indigenous shamans' auxiliary spirits in the face of new diseases, some shamans tried to communicate directly with this God, just as they did with their auxiliary spirits. According to Hugh-Jones (1994: 48), the Tukano shamans claimed that "in visions they ascended to heaven and had direct communication with the dead, with spirits, with the saints, and with the Christian God and various indigenous figures . . . that are often identified with him. The shamans-prophets claimed to be Christ, and some of their followers took on the names of the saints—Santa Maria, São Lourenço, and Padre Santo."

In some situations, such as the case of the seventeenth-century Tupi-Guarani groups and the Inuit of Canada (Laugrand 1997; Laugrand and Oosten 2009), among many others, both the missionaries and the shamans explored the advantages of their association, although they acted on the basis of completely different premises. The missionary appropriation of shamanic language and actions was strategic and intended to lead people to the "truth." The shamans, on the other hand, as we saw in the discussion of mimetism in the previous chapter, used Christian symbols and elaborated discourses similar to those of the missionaries in order to appropriate signs of alterity capable of transforming themselves, thereby acquiring a power that, though just as strategic, was based not on the notion of deception but on a traditional conception of ritual efficacy and translation.[29]

Generally speaking, the associations were based on experiments rather than beliefs.[30] While the success of prayers and the use of Christian symbols in rituals to obtain cures and good harvests reinforced the power attributed to the missionaries, failure was very often sufficient reason to reject both them and Christianity, even if just temporarily.

In more recent times, the availability or absence of medicines during epidemic outbreaks was a determining factor for some groups. The shaman Davi Kopenawa (Kopenawa and Albert 2010: 281, 285) tells that Yanomami shamans were unable to see the Teosi (Deus, God), whom the missionaries of the same New Tribes Mission spoke so much about. Even so, trusting the words of the missionaries and fearful of divine punishment, the shamans attempted to establish the same relations of exchange and trust with him that they maintained with the *xapiri* spirits, not through dialogue, music, and offerings of the hallucinogen yakoana, but through prayer. A particularly important event recalled by Davi Kopenawa was the sudden death of a man after an intense prayer vigil performed by his brother-in-law, an important local shaman, who had broken the relation with his auxiliary spirits to rely on the superior efficacy of the Christian God. This and other deaths during a virulent measles epidemic, precisely at a time when they were living as Christians, led them to realize the ineffectiveness of the prayers, and the incapacity and "laziness" of the Christian God, who failed to answer the intense prayers of the Indians (275–276). Teosi had not given them what they most needed, a cure for the sick, and part of the Yanomami population abandoned this relation, resuming their exchanges with the effective and loyal *xapiri* spirits.[31] In other cases, in line with the highly ambiguous nature of Amazonian shamans in general, the missionaries were taken to be the agents causing the epidemics. A classic example is the association between baptism and epidemics among the Tupi-Guarani of the Brazilian coast after the conquest and the ritual actions of the local shamans who tried to "debaptize" and rename the population.[32]

Although, as in the cases mentioned above, the Wari' associated the curing power of medicines with the action of the missionaries, they never took the latter to be shamans, and the latter did not appropriate the Christian discourse and symbols for their own practices. As we have seen, though, shamanism was also the key to translation among the Wari' via a mimetism defined above all by its collective dimension: as we shall see, understanding the Christian message meant establishing consubstantial relations between the missionaries and the Wari' as a whole.

FOUR

Eating God's Words

KINSHIP AND CONVERSION

Jesus doesn't dislike you, you, and you.

> *Hymn 90 of Oro Tamara': Hinos e coros em Pacaas*
> *Novos e Português* (Missão Novas Tribos do Brasil)

IN THE PREVIOUS CHAPTER we examined the first encounters between the Wari' and the missionaries and the questions involved therein. We have seen that a specific historical context, which led to the isolation of part of the Wari' population, prompted their initial interest in establishing peaceful relations with a group of enemies, with the idea, soon abandoned, of transforming them into ritual partners. Though without historical precedent, this possibility was anticipated in their mythology, where enemies, having originally been members of Wari' society, could be reincorporated into it. The purely random coincidence between the attitudes of the whites—peaceful and generous, which was unusual for a group of enemies—and the expectations of the Wari' enabled the approximation between them. The coexistence allowed them to observe the special capacities of these enemies, bearers of numerous objects and abundant food, who proved to be powerful curers in the epidemic outbreaks that followed contact.

We also need to consider the dramatic situation in which the Wari' had found themselves since the 1940s with the increasing penetration of whites into their territory and the new waves of armed attacks that wiped out entire villages. The successful warfare of the Wari' in earlier years, when they were able to attack the houses of isolated rubber-tappers without being immediately pursued by the tappers' comrades, underwent a sudden reversal. From predators they turned into prey. This was combined with the painful experience of the innumerable deaths caused by the epidemics, which, given the equation that the Wari' made between the diseases and animal attacks or sorcery, also made them prey and equated them with animals. Hence, while the first group approached the missionaries out of an interest in ritual affines, the critical situation quickly made them realize that the special capacities of the missionaries provided an effective means of reinverting the balance of power of humanity. What the Wari' wanted above all—and still want— was to live, and for this they had to reappropriate the position of humans.

But while their initial interest in the missionaries was not an interest in the Christian message per se—since they would have been unable to comprehend the whites during this initial period—neither was it merely an interest in the material goods provided by the missionaries, for which the natives were described in the literature under the label of "rice Christians" (Robbins 2004: 85), since, as we have seen, it involved particular conceptions of mimetism, metamorphosis, and ritual efficacy. With time and proximity they became capable of "hearing" the missionaries, who began the process of learning the native language, teaching Christian doctrine, and translating biblical texts.

FIRST MOVES

Faced with a completely monolingual group, the missionaries, in their study of the Wari' language, began with some fairly unsystematic attempts to collect material. According to Johnston (1985: 249): "The difficult and frustrating task of language work" began soon after the first contacts with the Wari'. Richard ("Dick") Sollis was part of the "Research and Planning" sector of the NTM and, it seems, was the first to study the language. Johnston observes, "The tribe was completely monolingual. They spoke no language but their own, and no one but they understood their language" (249). A message from Dick, sent to the mission, is reproduced in its entirety by Johnston: "Signs, gesticulations, and charades were not sufficient. For example, to try to get the tribal word for 'frog,' we might point at a frog sitting on a lily pad. The tribal person might respond, 'That's a frog,' or 'That's a lily,' or 'What are you pointing at?' or whatever. We would try to write down their response, even though we have very little idea of its meaning. What we most needed to learn at this stage were language-learning questions: What do you call this? What do you call that? What am I doing? What is he doing? Etc." (taped message, Language School Fall Conference, 1983, in Johnston 1985: 249).

In a personal communication in 1994, the missionary Royal told me, "We began—perhaps as early as 1957—to record tapes in their language of them telling histories. . . . We tried to get informants who taught us the language, but they didn't have much patience."

As we have seen, according to Royal, the missionaries had already met the Moré before their first contacts with the Wari' and had collected a series of words from them. Following the contact established in the regions of the Laje and Negro Rivers in 1961, the possibilities for learning multiplied as the Wari' came to visit the whites. In the case of the Negro River, some Wari' men from the region went to work on rubber plantations soon after contact, or in the plantation owners' houses in the city, returning months or sometimes years later with some knowledge of Portuguese, which they learned living closely with their employers' families, who, according to those young men, would treat them like adopted sons. Some of these men, in their work as translators for the missionaries, would join the first Wari' contacted.

Obviously, no teaching of doctrine was undertaken during this initial period, though as we saw in the previous chapter, the prayers offered for the sick, combined with the antibiotics and antimalarial drugs, even though incomprehensible, proved to be a highly effective means of transmitting the message of God's power. Among other Amazonian peoples, the existence of the so-called buffer groups, who had longer contact with the missionaries, and who spoke a language from the same family as the recently contacted people, constituted an important resource for evangelization. This had been the case for the Waiwai and the Trio, speakers of Carib languages, who, once evangelized, began to act as propagators of the Christian message to neighboring peoples.[1]

TRANSLATION AND ADOPTION

An important precondition for missionary work is, as we know, the long periods spent living among the natives. The pastor Awo Kamip (pers. comm., 2005) cites the time spent living with them as one of the factors differentiating the missionaries, and he associates it with learning the language: "They stayed. They knew the names of kin, the names of things." Hence, although, as I remarked in chapter 3, other white people also lived with them, including government agents, nurses, teachers, and anthropologists, save for the latter, none of the others showed any interest in their way of life or their language, sometimes openly criticizing both.[2]

Taking into account that, for the Wari'—as we saw in the case of the boy with a sickness caused by a monkey—metamorphosis (*ka jamu wa*) is a two-way process, it is relevant to consider the fact that the missionaries were the only whites to imitate them, and that learning the language was one of the missionaries' primary means. Because they very often arrived in the indigenous areas alone (or as a childless couple), they were taken to be stray orphans, ready to be adopted. The missionary Assis, who arrived with his wife, explained his mission to Awo Kamip, associating it with leaving behind his house and goods: "We have a house, a car, we have a store where food is sold. The mission president said to us: 'Go to other lands. There are Indians [*wari'*] on the borders of Brazil.' . . . They told other missionaries too: go to other tribes [here he uses the term *tribos* in Portuguese]. They spread out and reached all the Indians. They taught them the words. Go to Rondônia, they said to me" (Awo Kamip, conversation with the author, Negro River village, 2007).

Some people were important mediators in this process, especially those who became particularly close to the missionaries. The testimony of a current Wari' pastor, from the first group to be contacted, shows that the state of abandonment does not characterize just the Wari' perspective of the missionaries;[3] it also characterizes the Wari' perspective of themselves: "I was young still and was alone. My mother had died and so I stayed with my sister. There was a fight with my brother-in-law, so my brother began to look after me. Soon after, my brother sent me to help the missionary Abraão, so I fished and fetched firewood for him" (Rubens/Jimon Maram, quoted in *Revista Confins da Terra,* no. 125, my translation, http://issuu.com/digital-anapolis /docs/125_-_revista_confins_da_terra, accessed August 2009).

Some of these collaborators became translators. According to Paletó, soon after contact, around 1962, they were visited on the Negro River by Orowao Toko Jai, an OroNao' man from Tanajura, the first group to be contacted, who told them how he had been taken by the missionaries to Manaus, where they talked to him about Jesus. Another important translator was Manim, an OroJowin man, now deceased, who lived on the Dois Irmãos River, also from the first group contacted. According to Scharf (2010: 55), he was called *te,* father, by the missionaries. As Awo Kamip (person. comm., 2005) said, "Manim was the leader [*waximakon*] with the missionaries. He traveled to Manaus."

Another translator who worked for the missionaries was Awo Kamip himself, an OroNao' man from the Negro River region, today aged around sixty and one of the oldest active pastors on the Negro River. On returning to the latter area after a trip to Guajará-Mirim with various other Wari' soon after contact (in 1962), when he was still a boy and had lost his father, he was called by the rubber boss Manoel Lucindo to work on his plantation on the upper Pacaás Novos River: "'Come with me, you're going to live with me, you'll kill game in my plantation.' 'Okay,' I said." He worked for Lucindo for about a year and a half, calling him father, but, missing his Wari' kin, he decided to return to the Negro River, which was fairly close to the plantation.[4]

Arriving there around 1963–1964, Awo encountered the NTM missionaries Assis and Maria Eli, recently arrived. The period spent on the plantation, living with white people in a family context, had allowed him to learn a little Portuguese, knowledge that made him a valuable tool for the linguistic studies of these missionaries who, unlike Royal, did not yet speak Wari': "We're going to talk to you. None of the Wari' understand us," they said to him. Awo was hired by them to "saw wood"; he worked during the day and at night met with them in the mission house.

He explained to me his work as a translator for these and, later, other missionaries:

AWO: "Awo Kamip!" [the missionaries called him] "Okay." I arrived at their house in Guajará, and they talked and talked and talked with me. . . .

APARECIDA: Did they write?

AWO: Royal had a tape recorder in Guajará. An old tape recorder, it's not flat, it's long. . . . Royal said [in Portuguese]: "I'm going to read first and explain to you. He read, read, and read. "Did you understand?" [Royal asked]. "Yes, I understood you." "How do you say that then?" [Royal asked]. "You say it like this" [Awo spoke in Wari']. "Okay," [Royal said]. He wrote it down. "How do you say this?" [Royal asked]. "It's like this in our language," [Awo replied]. "Really?" He wrote it down. "And how do you say this?" It grew and grew [what Royal knew].

APARECIDA: Was there anyone else who did the same as you?

AWO: There was just one man from Santo André [where the inhabitants of the Dois Irmãos River, from the first contacted group, had moved] like me. Jimon Maram, who did the same as me, teaching the Wari' language. Another from Tanajura, Hwerein Kat Wa. . . . Barbara [Kern] wrote, Manfredo's wife, and Royal wrote. . . . Royal paid me to work in our language. I would travel to Guajará and receive my pay: "Here is your money. Buy some small things for yourself," [Royal would say]. I would return [to the Negro River]. . . . "Do you have any food, Awo Kamip?" [Royal would ask]. "No, I don't." "Take some frozen meat and your wife can cook it for you." The milk for the children to drink would run out, and I took milk. It meant I didn't have to leave [looking for food]. He wanted me to stay there. "You taught me much of your language, which is very extensive," [Royal said].[5]

I would go to the mission house in Guajará. I would teach. Every morning, afternoon, morning, afternoon. Just me. Every morning, afternoon, morning, afternoon. Their book was finished. (Awo Kamip, conversation with the author, 2007, Negro River)

Awo Kamip's knowledge of Portuguese began with his period spent living with the family of the rubber boss, though this did not involve any systematic learning of the language. Awo directly associated this with the process of becoming kin. Likewise in his relation with the missionaries: physical proximity and living together, especially the commensality that, for the Wari', implies bodily transformation, stand out in Awo's account of his work as a translator. Even so, it is notable that the presence of tape recorders and the insistent questions from the missionaries undoubtedly transformed this informal learning context, forcing the Wari' to reflect on the meaning of concepts expressed in their language and in the extensions and transformations proposed by the missionaries. We could note that Awo uses the expression "to teach the language" instead of "to imitate," which was used before. We return to this question in chapter 6.

Just as Awo was fundamental to spreading the Christian message, the heavy circulation of the Wari' between the posts during the initial period, especially between the Negro River on one side, and the Tanajura and Dois Irmãos Rivers on the other, where the people with the longest contact with the missionaries lived, allowed them as a whole to serve as transmitters of Christian teaching. The Wari' of the Negro River recall that a key moment in their conversion was the visit made by Maxun Hat and Jamain Xok Tain, the sons of Wan e', a man from the Negro River who had moved to the Dois Irmãos in 1964 with his family and lived there for many years. Calling themselves believers, the young men, whom the Wari' from the Negro River saw and treated as kin, apparently convinced the others to convert.[6]

Once, after hearing one of Paletó's diverse narratives on the puzzled reaction of the Wari' to the first sermons given by the missionaries, I asked him directly:

FIGURE 6. Pastor Awo Kamip trekking, July 2007. (Photo by Dušan Borić.)

APARECIDA: Where did your being Christians come from?

PALETÓ: It came from the Dois Irmãos [where the OroNao' of the left shore live]. Jamain Xok Tain and Maxun Hat, sons of Wan e', came from the Dois Irmãos and said, "Be Christians!" [he uses the word *crentes*, "Christians" or "believers," in Portuguese]. It's good to be a Christian," said Maxun Hat, who is no longer a Christian. The Wari' of the Negro River disliked this business of believing [*howa*—"to trust"]. Jamain and Maxun Hat arrived: "Be Christians, be Christians, believe." So the Wari' of the Negro River believed. . . . Like a gale. Everyone believed. (Paletó, conversation with the author, 2009, Rio de Janeiro)

From the outset, the conversion to Christianity was a collective enterprise, strongly associated with kinship. As soon as the first people converted, they turned to their kin both near and distant (which ultimately includes the Wari' as a whole) to take them along. Similarly, the abandonment of Christianity around a decade later also occurred collectively.[7]

The life history of Paletó, today aged about eighty, illustrates the very particular way in which Christianity was propagated among the Wari', as well as the initial reluctance expressed by some. It also shows that, given their complexity, the events that followed contact, involving other agents besides the Evangelical missionaries, such as government employees and Catholic priests, meant a constant series of relocations. Among the most radical was the move of part of the population to Sagarana village, an area acquired by the Catholic Church for the establishment of an "agricultural colony" in 1965 on the shores of the Guaporé River, a region never before visited by the Wari' (see Vilaça 2002b). Among those who moved there was Paletó, coming from the very distant Negro River. One day, in 1973 or 1974, some of their Negro River coinhabitants whom they had not seen in years arrived at Sagarana. They told the news to those living there, who had lived for little time with the missionaries before the move:

> Our late Severino arrived, Hwerein Tamanain [Severino's Wari' name]: [he said,] "We are complete Christians. We believe in God [Iri' Jam]." "There is a spirit [double] called "true spirit" [the translation of *Iri' Jam,* according to the missionaries]," Royal told us. "All our people believe completely," [said Severino]. (Paletó, conversation with the author, 2009, Rio de Janeiro)

> Late afternoon they called us: "Come all of you, come and hear God's word," Wem Parawan said, very convinced. We sat down, and they said, "The Christians turned us into Christians. Don't smoke, don't have sex with other women, don't steal. All your former coinhabitants are Christians. Don't steal anymore." The foreigners also arrived [Wari' from other subgroups who lived in Sagarana] and heard. They [from the Negro River] said, "That's how we sing." I was angry: "Why are you Christians pointlessly? Go to your houses, your women are there! These ones saying that they're Christians must be there having sex with your wives," [Paletó told them]. They sang, "Let's follow Jesus to heaven." I said, "Why are you Christians pointlessly? The whites lie. Look how we're not Christians here." "The priest who lives here with you believes in stone. He sculpts the stone and says that it is your God. The true Christians do not believe in stone," Wem Parawan said. (Paletó, conversation with the author, 1993, Rio de Janeiro)[8]

Two things stand out in this account: the emphasis on behavioral and moral questions linked to the Christian experience of the already converted, and what seems to be a total lack of knowledge of this same message on the part of Paletó. This is explained by the fact that the Catholic Church's investment among the Wari' at that time (and even today) was almost completely focused on civilizing the Indians rather than catechizing them, save for the sporadic masses performed by the priests during their visits, since they did not live there. The Wari' say that they understood nothing of these celebrations: "We sat down and we also sang in Sagarana. I didn't understand the name of the music. I just stayed there with my eyes closed. Afterward, 'Amen'" (Paletó, conversation with the author, 1993, Rio de Janeiro).

Sometime later (probably around 1975), Paletó returned to the Negro River to see his kin again, especially his older daughter, who had returned to the region and was now married; people said she had been beaten by her husband. Paletó hitched a ride to Guajará with a worker from Sagarana called Paulo, and from there he was taken to the Negro River in the boat of the missionary Abílio.

Meeting his son-in-law, Paletó had the following conversation with him:

PALETÓ: I came because of your anger [because he had beaten Paletó's daughter].

SON-IN-LAW: No. I am a Christian. We have been Christians for many years.

PALETÓ: Why do you believe in God? You believe pointlessly. If at least you could see God. . . .

SON-IN-LAW: No. "If it wasn't for him, we would not exist," Royal told us.
(Paletó, conversation with the author, 2009, Rio de Janeiro)

Royal went to see Paletó, speaking his language fluently and calling him "brother": "Royal came up to me. 'You arrived, younger brother?' he said to me. 'I arrived.' 'This is our son?' [Royal asked referring to Abrão, Paletó's son]. 'Yes it's him. He's called Wem Xain.' . . . 'You can't give a name pointlessly. Our son will be called Abrão. The one who very long ago believed in God, our grandfather,' [Royal told him]. 'I don't know about you. I don't know about this,' [Paletó said]. He ended up being called Abrão" (Paletó, conversation with the author, 2009, Rio de Janeiro).

GENERALIZED FRATERNITY

The Christian notion that the faithful constitute a community of siblings led the missionaries, purely by chance, to replicate the Wari' practice of treating all coinhabitants by consanguineal terms, thereby avoiding the tensions inherent to relations between affines and reinforcing the ties of consubstantiality produced in the community by sharing food and care.[9] The missionaries called themselves siblings of the Wari' (older siblings, because they had been Christian for longer); they claimed that they were all siblings to one another, and they stressed the immorality of acts that the Wari' related to affinity, such as usury, conjugal betrayal, physical aggressions, and sorcery.

This aspect immediately interested the Wari', since generalized fraternity, enabling the masking of affinity, was an ideal always pursued by them and only experienced in posthumous life. The missionaries presented them with an effective way of actualizing this ideal, suggesting large-scale rituals of commensality, as the testimonies below show—probably referring to the similar collective rituals realized today, called conferences (see chapter 8)—and which came to substitute for the traditional chicha festivals, where the focus was precisely on the opposition between affines through a symbolic cannibalism realized through the offering of fermented chicha.[10] They addressed each other through sibling terms. The foreigners (*tatirim*) were called younger sibling (*xa'*) or older brother (*aji'*). In the words of one man: "With Jesus the OroNao,' the OroMon, the enemies ended. We are all siblings. We are completely kin to each other."

Paletó, an OroNao' man, recalls that on visiting the OroWaram soon after they had turned into Christians, he arrived there and said, "I've arrived, my siblings" (*maki ina ta, xere*). They replied, "Our younger brother has arrived" (*maki na koxa'ri*).

It was precisely this fraternal behavior that was recalled nostalgically by the Wari' during the period when they abandoned Christianity in the 1980s and 1990s:

> If the OroNao' [from the left shore] were to arrive here, we would invite them to eat, and we would all of us eat together happily. We would sing God's music. We would sing and sing until all of us would go to eat together. If Xijam had food, he would call everyone to eat at his house. Everyone would eat. They would eat happily. (OroNao' man, aged around seventy, inhabitant of the Negro River, conversation with the author, Negro River village, 1992)

> The war club fights ended. Anger ended. They ate happily with God. All of them were Christians. There were no angry persons. Everyone was a Christian. (Xi Waram, OroEo, Negro River village 1992, conversation with the author)

CONVERTING, DECONVERTING,
AND RECONVERTING

Even today, the conversion to Christianity as an effective means of controlling anger—associated with "sin," *ka karakat wa,* derived from the verb *kat,* "break"—and of controlling conflicts in general is mentioned frequently by the Wari', as in the remark by pastor Rubens/Jimon Maram: "Anger makes us want to fight the others. And then I read the gospel and the urge passes" (pers. comm., February 1987).[11]

The Christian ideal of generalized siblinghood is a core aspect of the Wari' experience of Christianity, and so its dissolution is cited in almost all the explanations given by them for abandoning Christian practices. The case of one of the first people from the Negro River to convert to Christianity, the late pastor Xin Xoi, is fairly representative. When, at the start of the 1990s, I asked his wife whether he was a believer, she responded, "He left God."[12] She explained to me that his son-in-law, who lives in Santo André, had beaten their grandchild, causing the child's belly to swell. Xin Xoi and various other men went there and beat the assailant and his family. Sometime later, Xin Xoi's nephew, also living in Santo André, hit his wife, and the OroNao' of Santo André beat him. Xin Xoi went there once again to fight using a war club, which left him with various marks on his body. Some years went by and Xin Xoi became a Christian once more.

Paletó once explained to me why he had stopped being a Christian: "Tokorom Mao Te struck Xiemain on the head. A'am Tara hit Orowam, and Moroxin went there and hit A'am Tara." These fights would eventually involve entire communities and the Wari' as a whole, leading to a collective abandonment of Christian practice for a variable period. It can be presumed that this movement of deconversion had a strong impact on the missionaries. As Cannel reminds us (2006: 38): The "assumption of [a] nonreversible event may be the most disturbing when it is contradicted."

After living as believers throughout the 1970s, many of the Wari' ceased being Christians in the 1980s, but converted again for a while in the mid-1990s. In 2001, they converted once again and, since then, have remained Christians. These two moments of collective conversion are related to events that suggested the end of the world and the posthumous fate of non-Christians: hell and the separation from one's own kin.

In 1994, a small earthquake shook the region near to the Ribeirão Post and led the inhabitants—who, like the rest of the Wari', were in a pagan phase—to reconvert immediately. When I arrived in the region around six months after the event, I heard diverse accounts of the tremor and people's reactions. According to one woman living at the Lage Post, around an hour's drive by car from the Ribeirão, the earth shook there too, in the late afternoon, causing pans to fall from the shelves. Alarmed, some people ran to the house of the missionary Tereza, who told them about the end of the world and the return of Jesus.

Some years later a different episode produced the same outcome. According to Orowam, as the Wari' were watching the attack on the World Trade Center on the community TV, they concluded from the exegeses of the pastors that a world war was about to erupt, itself a sign that the end of the world was looming. When I arrived on the Negro River in January 2002, I found that many people had reconverted, and various residents asked me for news of the war, keen to know whether the Taliban had already reached Rio de Janeiro.[13]

A conversation I once had with an OroWaramXijein man during the pagan phase illustrates the eminently collective character of conversion. He told me of the nostalgia he had for the time during which he was a Christian, when, on leaving on a hunting trip, he would ask God for help, praying, "My father God, you who made the animals, give me game so that I can eat enough." And the prey then became abundant. At the time of my visit, though, when they were no longer Christians, the hunting trips were disappointing, he said. I asked him why he did not simply continue to offer the same prayer, and he replied that praying was no use. His wife and children would have to become Christians too. The church services held on Saturdays and Sundays, in which he talked and sang, would have to be resumed. And then, on Mondays, if he went hunting and had prayed beforehand, then there would be game.

Some of the reasons for the return to Christianity also relate to kinship ties: people are afraid that when Christ comes at the end of the world to take Christians with him to heaven, they will be left behind, separated from their kin. What finally led Paletó to declare himself a Christian was, according to him, the fear of the end of the world—more specifically the fear of being abandoned by his coinhabitants and kin who, as Christians, would be going to heaven. Below I provide two accounts concerning the same moment:

> I returned [from Sagarana] and stayed on the Negro River. Royal was still there. He called us to sing music. I entered the church and sat down. Royal said, "If you don't believe, you're going to stay on the earth and the jaguar will eat you. All kinds of animal doubles will appear. An enormous cricket will

eat the Wari'. An enormous cricket sent from heaven. God will send it to eat the people who do not believe." . . . I went hunting with Abrão [Paletó's son] and heard thunder. I became scared. The believers go to heaven. We were very scared. This was when Abrão was young. When I slept I dreamt: everyone will drown. (Paletó, conversation with the author, 2005, Linha 29 village)

After a long time living on the Negro River, I went fishing. It's not known what day God will arrive. "They're going to leave me here," [he thought]. A huge rainstorm fell with wind and thunder. "All the believers must have left already." I was afraid. (Paletó, conversation with the author, 2009, Rio de Janeiro)

On returning home, he said to To'o, his wife, that he wanted to be a Christian: "I'm going to be a *crente* [using the Portuguese term]." At first she disliked the idea, but after a while she decided to accompany her husband, and both went to the pastor's house to inform him of their decision. On the day of the church service, they told everyone, and sometime later they were baptized.

Some years later, owing to his involvement in club fights, Paletó, like the majority of the Wari', abandoned Christian practice ("I abandoned God"), and then, as an elderly man, went back to being a Christian in 2001. He told me in 2005: "I returned to God. Today I believe [*howa*, 'to trust'] truly. I'm old. Old people don't live much. 'Be a Christian so that your double [*jamum*] stays well. Your wife too,' they said to me."

As we shall see in the next chapter, the fear that propels conversions is related not only to the separation from kin but also to the idea of hell as a posthumous destiny, the characteristics of which refer us to one of the central interests of the Christian message for the Wari': the possibility to put an end to metamorphosis and, consequently, to stabilize themselves in the position of humans.

But kinship through commensality does not apply solely to the relations of the Wari' among themselves and with the missionaries, since it constitutes an intrinsic aspect of their relations with God.

EATING GOD'S WORDS

When the late Wao Tokori, a man of about seventy, told me that people write all the time in heaven, and that nobody worries about food, I asked him what they actually eat and I received a surprising response: "This is what they eat.

They eat paper. They get a satiated stomach from their writing." Once when Paletó was talking with me about heaven, he made a similar assertion:

APARECIDA: What do people do in heaven?

PALETÓ: They write a lot.

APARECIDA: What do they write?

PALETÓ: I don't know, I think it's the word of God [*oro kapijakon Deus*]. That's what leaves them satiated.[14]

The association between the word of God and food is frequent in the church services, as shown in the two examples below:

This is what makes our spirit satiated. It's as though they eat the word of God. (Xin Xoi, Negro River village, January 27, 2002, filmed church service)

It's like food [*karawa*]. Look at the animals that we eat. If we eat animals, all the animals that we kill, we become very satiated, very strong. If we don't have food to eat, if we go two days without killing fish, there will be nothing for us to eat. We become weak, we become sad. We become soft. It's the same thing with the word of God today. That's why we are always falling. We don't eat the word of God. We carry with us the word of God pointlessly. We don't eat it. (Awo Tot, Negro River village, January 27, 2002, filmed church service)

As we know, this is not an original association per se, since the Bible and missionary doctrine are full of allegories of this kind: the word of God feeds, satiates (see Matthew 4:4 and John 6:35). Robbins (2004: 264), in his research among the Urapmin of Papua New Guinea, observed that, for them—who, unlike the Wari', are Pentecostal—"only with the Holy Spirit's help can he [the pastor] give a sermon that 'feeds' the people."[15]

In the first lesson book produced by the missionaries for the Wari', lesson number 1, totally dedicated to translation, explains this relation: "That's what the word of God is like as well, like the food [*karawa*] that we eat. If we hear the word of God a lot, we can become strong and we know all the things that he wants us to know. The word of God is very good. It helps us a lot" (p. 4).

Even taking into account that the Wari' did not invent the association between the word of God and food, and although the dialogues reproduced above suggest that this association is taken in metaphoric terms through the use of the conjunction "as" ("as though we eat the word"), it seems clear that the missionaries' conception fell on fertile soil. It situated itself in continuity with nonmetaphoric material processes, given that, for the Wari', food and the act of eating are fundamental mediators of relations, constituting them and defining them.[16] Some specific acts of the missionaries, which seem to have been common, corroborate this association. In a statement to the missionaries mentioned above, the current pastor, Rubens/Jimon Maram, recalled that in the initial phase: "At eating time, Mr. Abraão [the missionary] picked up the Bible and read verses, I don't remember which" (Rubens/ Jimon Maram, quoted in *Revista Confins da Terra*, no. 125, my translation, http://issuu.com/digital-anapolis/docs/125_-_revista_confins_da_terra, accessed August 2009).

And not only because words are directly equated to food. As we shall see in analyzing the Holy Supper ritual in chapter 7, a kind of generalized commensality takes place, both between those participating and between Jesus and the Wari', who share the same foods (they lack the idea of transubstantiation). In addition, the blood of Jesus also constituted a way of producing kinship with the divinity, penetrating their bodies in the same way that the dead enemy's blood penetrates the killer, making them consubstantial for the period of reclusion. In the words of the pastor Awo Tot in a prayer given during a Holy Supper ritual in 2002 (Negro River village): "Jesus who died in our place [*ko mi' pin kaho na pari*] a long time ago. He washes our heart completely. The blood of Jesus washes my heart. Jesus Christ is with me."

According to the late pastor Xin Xoi, the blood of Jesus allows us to escape: "'It pays' [*paga* in Portuguese] for our anger too. If there were something else able to pay for our anger. . . . That's what Jesus is like. He pays for our anger with his blood. It's his blood that dispels our anger. As if it unbinds us. What unbinds our anger? The blood of Jesus" (Xin Xoi, January 27, 2002, Negro River village, filmed church service). Sometimes they also say that our anger was *comprada* ("bought" in Portuguese) by Jesus, as did the pastor Rubens/Jimon Maram (July 2002, Santo André, filmed church service), while the preacher Antônio said during a sermon that Jesus paid dearly for our sins, and that the blood of Jesus is like the "shirt we wear" (Antônio, Negro River village, July 2007, Sunday morning church service filmed by author).

When I asked the late Hwerein Pe e' whether Jesus had bought our sins with money, he answered, "No, with his blood! [*Om na. Kikon!*] God told him to descend and with his blood erase and sweep away sins." The question of blood takes us back to the war context analyzed in the previous chapter. As we saw, the relation between the Wari' and the enemy group was mediated by the killer / dead enemy pair through blood, in the same way that the relation between God and the Wari' takes place through, among other means, the death of his son—more specifically by the blood spilled by him, which penetrates the body of the Wari'.[17]

It is important to note here an inversion in relation to the effects of warfare, which was an operation of differentiation, rather than identification, of the enemy group. In warfare it was the temporary identity established between the killer and enemy, making ingestion impossible, that enabled the differentiation of the two groups as a whole. It is as though, in the case of Jesus's death, the Wari' believers placed themselves collectively in the position of killers, precisely equivalent to the position of humans, in a singular interpretation of the missionary idea of the redemption of sins through the death of Christ.

Here, we can examine more closely the initial association of God and Jesus with enemy affines in order to clearly establish where the starting point in the production of kinship is located for the Wari'.

MAKING KIN OUT OF OTHERS

Based on accounts of Bible translation in other regions, as well as the Wari' recollections of the first sermons, God was probably the first Christian concept that the missionaries attempted to introduce.

According to the missionary-linguist Barbara Kern (pers. comm., 2011), they initially decided to keep the word for God, *Deus,* in Portuguese—perhaps they did so because they had observed the absence among the Wari' of any demiurge who could be immediately associated with God. To the missionaries' disappointment, however, the Wari' soon began to associate the Christian characters with mythic figures with incompatible characteristics, including, according to Barbara, Pinom and Oropixi'. This was when the missionaries decided to create a neologism that could designate this new entity for the Wari': *Iri' Jam,* which, according to the missionaries, means "true spirit." We return to this topic in chapter 6. Here I wish to examine the first associations—those founded in myth, which were gradually abandoned over time—and the transformation of the relations enabled by living and eating together and by physical evidence of divine presence.

Pinom, a man-vine, is the protagonist of the Wari' myth describing the origin of fire and the origin of funerary cannibalism. During the initial period of contact with the missionaries and in some narratives collected by myself in the 1980s, Pinom was associated with the Christian God, which, some of my Wari' interlocutors said, arose from the fact that Pinom was the only Wari' figure to inhabit the sky. However it seems that this association relates mainly to the enemy-affine character of this early God.

The myth begins with the actions of an old woman with jaguar traits. She is the only person to possess fire, forcing the Wari' to obtain it from her by offering game or fish in return. When they try to take it without exchanging anything, the old jaguar-woman attacks a child and eats her or him raw. One day, the Wari', tired of her behavior, decide to flee to the sky (*pawin*), climbing up using a monkey ladder vine (*Bauhinia glabra*), called *pinom* in Wari'. In some versions, the vine is the penis of a man called Pinom, who lives in the sky. Taking the fire to the sky, the Wari' abandon the jaguar-woman, cutting the vine when she tries to climb up. The sky at this time is inhabited by fish— apparently the form taken by the Wari' when they ascended to the sky—and Pinom invites each of the fish to cut the vine with its teeth. The task is eventually accepted by the piranha. In some versions, Pinom is identified with the piranha that cuts the vine. Falling from the vine, the jaguar-woman explodes in a bonfire alight on the ground below. From her body emerge diverse types of jaguars and venomous animals that, consequently, now inhabit the earth. The Wari' begin to feel hungry and decide to climb down to eat the ripe fruits. To do so, each one decides which animal he or she wishes to "imitate" (*an xiho'*), and subsequently they all transform their bodies into those of different animal species, as though decorating themselves, by painting their mouths and bodies, making tails, and imitating the animal's sounds.

The Wari' jump onto the tree canopies and, reaching the ground, the majority once again acquire human form. The exceptions are those who decide to remain animals, since they want to separate from their spouses after a fight. In some cases the animal spouses are subsequently preyed upon. (Some narrators have described this as an animal origin myth, although we can note that the game animals are present from the outset.) Arriving back on the ground, the Wari' realize that they have left the fire in the sky and ask two youths still up there to climb down with it. The youths transform into *uru* birds, swallow the fire, and carry it down inside them. At this moment, though, Pinom, who had been hiding from the others, appears once again and kills the two birds. He opens their chests, removes the fire, and swallows it for his own selfish use, defecating on the firewood every time he wants to cook. He does so always out of sight of the Wari', vehemently denying that he possesses fire. The Wari' one day decide to spy on him, waiting until he is distracted. They grab some embers, taking them to their house and lighting the fire, which is then shared by everyone. Discovering the theft, Pinom and his wife yell angrily, condemning the Wari' to be roasted over a fire when they die, to which the latter reply that the same will happen to the bodies of Pinom and his wife.[18]

Pinom was not just a myth about funerary cannibalism, in which the Wari' are condemned by Pinom to eat their dead, but also, according to some versions, a myth about the very origin of death (although at the myth's beginning children had already died from jaguar attacks), which reinforces the association between God and Pinom when we recall that Genesis 3 also refers to the origin of mortality or the end of immortality. This is made explicit in lesson book 1, page 82, in the Wari' translation of Genesis 3:22: "God said to them. The Wari' is going to imitate us now. We saw him being good and we saw him acting wrongly. We are going to be usurious with the fruit that would make him live and live. If he takes it [from the tree], if he eats it. His [the Wari'] life would never end."

In different versions of the myth, Pinom is called a wife-taking brother-in-law (*nem*) by the Wari'. He is an ambiguous figure: at the same time that he himself makes the sky-earth connection in the form of the vine, he behaves like a typical brother-in-law, acting in an avaricious and aggressive way, representing, in the second part of the myth, a role equivalent to the one played by a predatory old jaguar-woman in the first part.

Regarding the aggressive side of God, an observation made by João (who trained to become a pastor in 2005) is interesting since it describes the divine punishments inflicted by the same kind of sorcery procedures typically enacted by affines: "If we do not believe properly, he kills our double. He does not kill our body, but our double." "As in sorcery attacks?" I asked. "Yes. The double of God [or the Holy Spirit] strikes our double very hard with a stick and we die. That's why we fear God."[19]

Oropixi', mentioned by the missionary Barbara as one of the mythic figures wrongly associated with God, is, according to my own experience, more commonly associated with Jesus, or Jesu, as he is called today by the Wari'. I noted Oropixi' briefly in the previous chapter. While still a baby Oropixi', is blamed by his older brother for having sex with the latter's wife and, enraged, Oropixi' severely castigates the Wari' by taking away all the existing water, leaving them with none. Later, after appearing to his mother as an adult, he leaves once again, transforming into the first white person (see Vilaça 2010:

135–138). According to the Wari', the association with Jesus stems from the fact that he was a magical baby who grew rapidly when he so wished (related in the myth to a strong sexual desire).

Like the association between God and Pinom, the consanguineal relations defining the contexts of the Christian figures of God (Iri' Jam, also called *kotere,* "our father") and Jesus/Jesu (also called *kwaji'ri,* "our older brother") were initially taken as relations of affinity, or more specifically as "brother-in-lawness." I should point out that despite being a brother, Oropixi' acts like a brother-in-law, taking his brother's wife as his own, something he would be prohibited from doing, and he later acts like an enemy, originating the first settlement of whites seen by the Wari'. In addition, Jesus was born among the distant whites, as becomes clear in the correction made by one man to his own account after initially naming the city of São Paulo as Jesus's birthplace: "It wasn't in São Paulo, it was in the land of the Americans."[20]

The initial association of God and Jesus with brothers-in-law/enemies amounts to a typically Amazonian twist, seeing that in this region the vertical and horizontal relations of consanguinity are encompassed by those of affinity (Viveiros de Castro 2000: 17; 2001: 25–26) in terms of their sociological meaning. The most significant other is the brother-in-law, rather than the brother or father, with relations of consanguinity, founded on identity, produced from relations of affinity, founded on difference.[21] Among the Wari', consanguine kin are produced "out of others" through a continuous process of differentiation from animals and, at a later moment, from affines through commensality and mutual care.

The direction of this process becomes clear when we note the absence of the verb "to love" among the Wari'. The feeling is expressed as "to not dislike" (*om ka nok wa,* where *om* is "not," and *ka nok wa* is "dislike"). Love for a person is conceived as the suppression of indifference and anger, precisely what people feel for brothers-in-law who have not been consubstantialized, or even for those who have when they act improperly.

One episode I witnessed firsthand, during the visit of Paletó and Abrão to my home city in December 2012, seems to illustrate this idea perfectly. An artist from Rio de Janeiro offered us a red heart sculpted in wood, and I suggested to Abrão that he give it to his wife as a souvenir of his visit to Rio. The next day he came to show me that he had written, with a Pilot pen, in the middle of the heart, the following phrase: "I don't dislike you at all, Tem Xao'" (*om ca' noc ca'main xim' Tem Xao'*).[22] This was Abrão's translation of the expression "I love you" (*eu te amo*) written on hearts he saw depicted in magazines.

It is interesting to observe the implications of this absence of a term for "love" in the translation of Christian hymns and biblical texts. Although they sometimes use the verb "appreciate," *ka param wa*—which the Wari' use in reference to objects, food, behaviors (he likes peccary, he likes bathing, for example), or "to be content with someone," *ka kirik te wa*—most of the time "divine love" is translated as "not dislike." The texts of lessons, such as the one on page 34 of lesson book 1, makes clear that God appreciates (*param*) those who "do not dislike" him. The text continues thus: "He doesn't dislike us, he is probably content [*kirik te*] in relation to us."

The verb "dislike" is present even in the speeches of the missionaries, as we find in a translation into Wari' by the missionary Thomas of a discourse by the missionary Hélio, who came from Manaus in 2009, and who said in Portuguese: "I am very happy to be with you. We have come from Manaus and we are the New Tribes Mission of Brazil. It would be good if I could speak your language. My heart loves you." This last phrase was translated by Thomas as: "I don't dislike you with my heart" (*om ka nok xuhu pain xumu ka*) (conference meeting, 2009, Lage, audiotaped by Abrão).

Another interesting illustration is hymn 90 ("Om ca noc cacam Jesu," from the hymn book *Oro Tamara': Hinos e coros em Pacaas Novos e Português*, edited by Missão Novas Tribos do Brasil, n.d.), which, in its Portuguese version, states that "Jesus loves each one"; this is translated into Wari' as: "Jesus doesn't dislike you, you, and you" (see also hymns 40 and 52 in the same book). Note, too, the absence of a term for "each one" in the Wari' language, referring to a world peopled by bounded individuals unknown to the Wari' but known by the American Christians who composed the hymns.

The opposition between siblings and siblings-in-law directly evokes one of the examples used by Viveiros de Castro (2004) to speak of the "translatable equivocations" inherent to the contact between Indians and whites. This concerns the visit of a famous Brazilian singer to the Cashinahua Indians of Acre. The singer and his collaborators were convinced that the term *txai*, by which the singer was called during the visit, meant "brother," when in fact it means "brother-in-law." Viveiros de Castro (2004: 16–17) observes that this did not involve an error, or an equivocation in a purely negative sense, but a "perspectivist" equivocation: the brother, for us, is the ideal other, a similar, while for the Cashinahua (and other Amazonian Indians) the ideal or generic other is the brother-in-law. In contrast to the relation between brothers, the brother-in-law relation is based precisely on the difference of perspectives: the woman whom I see as a sister is seen by my brother-in-law as a wife. It is this difference that needs to be kept constantly in mind when dealing with the other, as the Wari' indicated when listening to the narrative of the woman abducted by the jaguar related in chapter 2. When the jaguar says "palm fruit," what is it referring to? An armadillo?

Divine alterity was especially marked during the initial period of contact with the missionaries, as well as in the narratives about these first experiences, where the emphasis constantly falls on God's anger with those who disobeyed him—a central aspect of the Old Testament. Orowao Toko Jai once told me that after they became believers, he would go at night to see if his brother, Orowam, was still breathing, afraid that God had killed him for his sins. Paletó recollects wondering whether, if they did not obey God, the whites would kill their children.[23]

Paletó's surprise over the first sermons by the missionaries reveals the alterity of the missionaries and their God, and the state of suspicion in which the Wari' lived:

> We went to meet Royal [the missionary] and entered. He took his paper and began to play the guitar. He sang and sang and sang. It was something like: "Let's go to heaven, let's go to heaven with God." We heard wrong [without understanding].
>
> We did not understand properly what they said: "You won't drink water." To which the Wari' replied, "What's this story of the whites that we won't drink water?" [The missionaries continued:] "When we die we shall go to heaven and drink water. If we die without believing in our father, we shall go to the sky and we shall feel ashamed for not believing him." The Wari' asked, "What business is this with Royal? He is cursing us." "Those who believe drink water, and those who don't believe will go to the fire." The Wari' asked, "Why will they go to the fire?" "I don't know. Do you OroNao' know [they asked the OroNao' of left shore present there, who had already known the missionaries for some time]? "We don't know." (Paletó, conversation with the author, 1993, Rio de Janeiro)

> [Royal said,] "God made the snakes. Eve became angry, the snake came into existence. Let's go to heaven, let's go there. He made us, he made our neck, our language so we could speak." The Wari' replied, "What business is this?" He sang in the Wari' language: "Let's follow Jesus without coming back." And the Wari' replied, "What business is this?" "I don't know," [some said to the others]. "Let's go to heaven and return. We shall resuscitate." We didn't understand well; we thought that Royal had said that he himself had died

and come back to life. We thought, "He's a ghost!" He limped. One shoe was normal and the other strange. He had undergone surgery. The Wari' spread the news: "The white man said that he revived!" "Which white man?" "The one called Royal." "Wow!" (Paletó, conversation with the author, 1993, Rio de Janeiro)

No. We laughed at the Christians. They prayed pointlessly. The white man is crazy! ... We disliked God. (Paletó, conversation with the author, March 1995, Guajará-Mirim)

Over time, living in close proximity with the missionaries, and thereby learning new concepts of personhood and morality by reading and practicing Christian doctrine and rituals, enabled the Wari' to engage in a process of transforming the relation of affinity and enmity with God and Jesus into one of filiation and siblinghood. As we shall see, however, the very incompleteness of this process is a constitutive part of it. The resistance of their innate world coincides with the intrinsic ambiguity of the Christian God, also constitutive of the missionary version, as well as with the ambiguity of the missionaries themselves, who, while they made kin out of everyone, also acted in an incompatible, ungenerous way by refusing the requests of the Wari' for objects, demanding forest produce in exchange rather than simply giving them.

This allows us to return to the question of the equivocation involved in the relation between the Wari' and the missionaries. The apparent coincidence between the perspectives of each demands that we accentuate their dissonance, and here the translation of the verb "to love" discussed above offers a paradigmatic example. In their mutual work, the missionaries and the Wari' seem to have reached an agreement on the suitability of the term "to not dislike" as the translation of the verb "to love." Indeed "to not dislike" is "to love," which is clearly expressed by the text written by Abrão on the wooden heart offered to his wife. However, in contrast to the missionary conception of love as the natural basis for the relation between God and humans, and as what good Christians should feel for each and every person (to the point of turning "the other cheek" when attacked), the notion of love as "not dislike" reveals an entirely distinct starting point, a world of anger and enmity on which human agency acts with a transformative capacity.[24] We are presented, then, with a radical difference in what is conceived as the innate universe and as the direction of human agency. For the Wari', kinship and love must be produced by themselves, and the incompleteness of this process is conceived as resistance—that is, as the imposition of this innate world, which entices them back. This attraction is what they identify as the devil and sin. For the missionaries, human agency is historically situated in the opposite direction, producing sin and hate from the paradise constituted by God for Adam and Eve (see Sahlins [1996] 2005: 528–520; [1992] 2005: 39).

Lesson book 1, which presents God and Creation, explains that everything created by God, from the forest to the animals, was initially good: "God's things were very good in the past, just after he created them, in the beginning. Everything was entirely good. There were no bad animals, there was no bad forest. There were no thorns.... He didn't know how to make bad things" (p. 26). Evil first arose from the greed of Lucifer and his followers. Lucifer, who was created by God to be his assistant, attempted to take God's place instead and was expelled from heaven as a consequence. Later, evil came too with the foolishness of Adam and Eve, who ate the prohibited fruit, allowing them to discern good and evil, even after being advised by God not to do so. Their punishment was the loss of immortality and expulsion from paradise.

Hence, although the present Christian world is one of (original) sin, which makes it similar to the innate world of the Wari', it does not involve, for the missionaries, the true original world but its "fallen," or corrupted, version. Christian practice is intended precisely to overcome this state of sin and reconstitute the paradisiacal world created by God, where Christians will live at the end of time. In the words of the missionary Royal Taylor:

> But sin always separates us from God. We have to pay for our sins. God resolved the problem of sin through his son. Once men have got used to sinning, there is no way they will abandon it. If you have done evil things, you will go to hell. It was because Christ gave himself in sacrifice that the punishment for my sin fell on him. If I am connected to Christ, God will not punish me further, because he will not punish me twice. It is not conduct that saves you, but the belief in Christ that changes your conduct. Because you are saved, and not because you want to be saved. Jamain [a *wari'* Christian] is concerned more with conduct. There is this mystery of mental belief and spiritual belief. Mentally, everyone knows. Knowing Christ died is one thing, but throwing oneself on him for salvation, depending desperately on him for salvation.... The only thing that erases our sins is the death of Jesus. You have to reach the point of saying: Thank you, Jesus, for having died for me. I depend only on you: were it not for you I would go to hell for my sins. (Royal Taylor, pers. comm., 1994, my translation)

As can be seen, there is an important difference, though not one immediately visible, that provokes the illusion that we are facing coinciding visions of personhood and moral action. The missionaries, observing the interest of the Wari' in suppressing anger, believed that the indigenous people recognized their corrupted state and wished to act in the same way as other Christians to overcome their state of original sin. The Wari', for their part, through the differentiation afforded to them by the missionary presence, looked to maximize their kinship-producing process, appropriating new ways of consubstantializing affines and differentiating themselves from animals, as we shall see in the next chapter.

The equivocity involved in the apparent coincidence of these movements accounts for the missionaries' disappointment at the deconversion of the Wari' and what seemed to them to be the main Wari' misunderstanding: that salvation would be based on actions, rather than on any recognition of original sin. The Wari' observation of this misunderstanding occurs in other ways: the animals insist on making themselves present in human form through the figure of the devil, an idea offered to them by the missionaries themselves. As a result, the Wari' see themselves as dehumanized and angry, not because of any feeling of guilt for their actions, since they strive to act correctly, but because of the resistance posed to their actions by this innate world of mixture between humans and animals.

FIVE

Praying and Preying

"Eat all these animals, I was the one who made them," Royal told
us God had said. . . . The Wari' ate and did not become ill.

PALETÓ, 2001

My father God, you who made the animals, give me game so that
I can eat enough.

PRAYER BY A WARI' MAN, 2001

Le christianisme s'est imposé parce qu'il offrait quelque chose de
different et de neuf.

PAUL VEYNE, Quand notre monde est
devenu chrétien (312–394), 2007

IN THE PREVIOUS CHAPTER WE SAW that the establishment of kinship
relations with the missionaries, combined with the activation of ties of consubstantiality internal to the group, were essential for the Wari' to begin to
understand what the missionaries were saying. Christianity was initially
conceived by the Wari' as an actualization of the native ideal of masking
affinity—a relation associated with anger, conflicts, and sorcery—by adopting the Christian principle of universal fraternity. In this sense it was an
eminently collective experience, as attested by the movements of mass conversion and deconversion, the latter prompted by disputes related to affinity.
As we saw, the adoption of the missionaries, and their adaptation (albeit partial) to Wari' conventions, took place concomitantly with the differentiation
of the Wari'—that is, the metamorphosis engendered by mimetism, physical
proximity, and commensality.

In this chapter I return to the theme of conversion via the notion of
a change in perspectives, showing, through the recourse to myth, that a
collective transformation of this kind was not alien to Wari' thought.
Having identified their interest in the fraternity intrinsic to Christianity,
reading conversion in the light of myth allows us to locate another properly

"intellectual" point of interest in the Christian message (Robbins 2004): the dehumanization of animals implied in the act of divine creation narrated in Genesis, which would enable the Wari' to stabilize themselves in the position of humanity.

As we have already seen, these two focal points of interest are intimately related insofar as affines—whose prototypical representatives are foreigners, sources of disputes and sorcery—constitute internal and domesticated versions of enemies and animals.[1] The consubstantialization achieved through the rituals of commensality performed during the early years of Christianity, the effect of which combined with the suspension of the traditional rites involving the inebriation of affines and their symbolic killing, led to a movement in the same direction as the widespread suppression of the agency of animals. Both of these movements offered the Wari' ways to solve their main problem: the unstable condition of humanity, which had become acute during the intensification of the massacres before contact and the epidemics that followed the latter.

THEY WERE "NO INNOCENTS TO THE EXPERIENCE OF CONVERSION"

Here I turn to the narrative of a myth that I consider to be about conversion, though not about Christianity.[2] My interest resides precisely in showing the points in common between this narrative and conversion to Christianity, with an emphasis on the adoption of the enemy's perspective and the transformation of humans into predators of animals.[3]

The Lizard Myth

They only ate lizard, which they called white-lipped peccary. People said, "Let's eat peccary!" They killed them. They whistled [as they arrived with the game]. "We killed peccary!" "Oh, really?" They roasted it. When the meat was cooked they distributed it to the others.

The child knew. A Wari' child. "Why are you eating lizard? I don't want it! The peccary my father used to kill was different. Lizard is one thing, peccary another." The child refused to eat it.

[Was the child kidnapped by the Wari'? I asked, recalling the emphasis on that detail in other versions.]

They took him from his house and raised him. He grew. He saw and said, "You didn't see the peccary my father killed. That's lizard." But the Wari' insisted, "This is peccary." He grew and grew. He made arrows. He wandered the forests. One day an agouti was on the path. He killed the agouti, a real one, and carried it back. The others said, "Release that damned jaguar! Put it down! It's a jaguar!" But he retorted, "No, it's not. It's an agouti. My father used to kill agouti for their teeth." They fell silent. He washed it. "Leave him alone," said the woman who had raised him [his adoptive mother]. Its innards were cooked. "Give me maize pudding, mother." "Okay." And he ate it.

[Was he the only one to eat the agouti? Were the others scared? I asked.]

They were scared. For them, it was a jaguar. When the meat was cooked, he said to everyone, "Come to eat! Eat, lads." "Don't eat," people said. "This is going to make you sick." "It's not jaguar," he said. "Jaguar has spots. What you are all eating is lizard. You eat anything. What you eat are large lizards."

The Wari' said, "There are some peccary over there! Let's go, let's go!" And the Wari' went after them. Shot them and killed them.

"No, that's lizard!" he said. "I'm going to hunt." He went alone. He killed a capuchin monkey. He carried it back. "That boy has killed a jaguar, he killed a jaguar" [people said on seeing him].

[Did it look like a jaguar? I asked.]

It was a jaguar. The ancient ones did not see well [kirik pin, "recognize"]. The person who saw well was the child who ate proper food. The ancient ones, including their children and wives, would eat anything. They were the ones who ate lizard.

He whistled [on arriving back home with a monkey]. "Cook the monkey!" "Okay," said the woman who had raised him. His mother and father saw properly and ate. "Ah, this is real game, son!" They ate. His brothers ate. The other Wari' didn't want any, though; they ate their lizards.

His father ate well.

"I want to eat game, father. Let's go hunting!" "Let's go!" So they went and saw a jaguar. They [the ancient Wari'] called white-lipped peccary jaguar, collared peccary jaguar, spider monkey jaguar, guan jaguar, tinamou jaguar. The ancient ones were truly strange.

The father had never seen a jaguar. So the father ran away from the jaguar and the boy went to find him. "This is a jaguar, father. I killed it! White-lipped peccary, agouti, collared peccary, they are all different. This is the true jaguar, father. Come and look. It's dead." "Okay," he said. He looked. "I think the jaguar is beautiful, son. Are you going to leave it there?"

"No. I'm going to take it, so they can see it." "Okay, go ahead then. You know the way. Carry it." "Okay!"

They carried it all the way back. "Go ahead and let them know, so they won't run off." "Okay." The father arrived and announced, "My son killed a jaguar. You called everything jaguar when it was really collared peccary, deer, agouti. You've never seen one before. It has spots. Its teeth are very big. That's what the jaguar is like. Come and see the jaguar. You called every kind of animal jaguar. Spider monkey, capuchin monkey, saki monkey, guan, curassow.

You called them all jaguar. Look what a real jaguar is like." They arrived. They all looked. They didn't like it. They cut it up. They burnt the fur. They divided it. They [the others] didn't eat it. Just them, the father, the brothers, ate it.

They ate everything, just a little bit was left. Some Wari' killed game while others still ate lizard. They [those who hunted] learned. They stopped eating lizards. In other villages they still ate them. Like those from here [the Negro River village] to Guajará [the nearest town, six to twenty hours away by boat].

The ancient ones did not see [recognize] the animals properly. They only recognized their lizards. Those they ate. They did not see [recognize] all the forest animals properly. It was he, the Wari' boy, who taught us to eat properly. (Hwerein Pe e' (OroEo), conversation with author, January 25, 2002, Negro River)[4]

Paletó told me about what seems to be a historical event, one that interests us here because it can be related to the myth with the association between the adopted enemy and God: according to Paletó , the OroNao', except for the elders, used to avoid eating some animals. The OroWaram (another Wari' subgroup), who moved to live near them, taught them to eat tapir, sloths, and toucans. "Anteater became true prey [iri' karawa, 'edible']. So the OroNao' began to eat, even the women: 'They [the OroWaram] became our coresidents.'" Paletó then laughed and said, "Perhaps they were God."

There is another myth, one that is the symmetrical inverse of the captured-boy myth, about a Wari' girl, named Piro, abducted and consubstantialized by enemies. One day the girl's vision is altered by a bird, making her see the people she called kin (her father, mother, and siblings) as enemies, something they had indeed originally been. She decides to run away and returns to her family of origin, teaching them the correct way to perform various practices learned from the enemies. This includes showing the Wari' that their way of mourning the dead is shameful, since they say things like: "My husband, who used to have sex with me." She teaches them the correct way to mourn, where the dead person is always addressed with a consanguineal term, and where the mourners refer only to acts that characterize kinship, as in this example: "My older brother, who hunted for me." Piro explains, "If your husband is your grandfather [jeo'], say 'grandfather'; if he is your older brother [aji'], say 'older brother.'" Among other things, she also taught them to make maize chicha, since previously they had drunk a thick, unsweetened maize porridge, claiming it was chicha.

In both myths the main figures are adopted—that is, they are foreign people who, by living intimately among their past enemies, eventually become kin. This is the condition for the change of perspectives: between the boy of the myth and his adoptive Wari' kin, and between Piro and the enemy group who had abducted her and, later, between her and the Wari'.

Some of the commentaries made by the narrators (such as: "They called white-lipped peccary jaguar, collared peccary jaguar, spider monkey jaguar, guan jaguar, tinamou jaguar. The ancient ones were truly strange") clearly recall those made by the listeners to the narratives on jaguar abductions (chapter 2). Those listeners tried to discover what the jaguar was referring to when pronouncing the name of the *nao'* fruit, and concluded that it was not paca, as they had thought, since "papaya is paca" (for the jaguar). Once again, what varies is not the words but the material referents. The interesting point to observe here is that, while in the case of jaguar abduction, the mistaken material referent is attributed to the jaguar (and to the girl who identified with the animal), in the case of the myths cited in this chapter the equivocation is associated with the Wari', and the correct perspective is attributed to enemies.[5] The narrators here are translators, just like the listeners to the abduction narratives and like the shamans were in everyday life until recently. By revealing the perspective of the ancestors, the narrators can show the difference between the perspectives of the former and the present-day Wari', who adopted their (correct) view of the world directly from the enemies.

There are some very clear similarities between the process of adopting the enemy's perspective described in the myths and adopting the perspective of the missionaries by the Wari', narrated in the previous chapter. In the case of the enemy boy and Piro, the change of perspective takes place through mediators, who are initially their closest kin, and who eventually include their more distant kin, who had previously viewed the new message, or the new world, with considerable distrust, just as occurred with the arrival of Christianity.

For the Wari' this change of perspectives is the primary meaning of what we could call conversion.[6] Consequently, on encountering the Evangelical missionaries, the Wari' were, in the words of Gershon concerning the same phenomenon among the Samoans, "no innocents to the experience of conversion" (2007: 147).[7] One example of the naturalness with which change is treated was given to me by the pastor Awo Kamip in 2005, when, after hearing my concern about him failing to recall the Wari' myths, he exclaimed, "I can't remember because my head is filled with God's speech. I forgot, I forgot. It's gone. No problem."

And not just the mode of propagation: the message of the enemy boy also exposed a crucial problem for the Wari'—namely, the instability of the human condition, which is solved by positioning diverse animals as prey. As we shall see later, the same is achieved by God in his act of creation. First, though, we need to examine the idea of instability more closely.

CHRONICALLY UNSTABLE BODIES

Like other Amazonian peoples, the Wari' have an extended notion of humanity, which includes not only themselves but also a series of animals, as well as other indigenous peoples, their traditional enemies. However this does not mean that these all see each other as humans or people, *wari'*.[8] The Wari' know that the animals see themselves as people, but that they see them (the Wari') as *wijam*, "enemies," or *karawa*, "prey" or "food," positions that, as I have already noted, are closely associated. The human/nonhuman, or *wari'/karawa*, relation is determined by predation; the first term is associated with predators and the second with prey. This position is established at each encounter and may be reversed on the next occasion.

As I observed earlier, the difference between beings (whether between different "kinds," between consanguines and affines, or between individuals) is determined by the body, *kwerexi'* (our body). In its narrower acceptation, the term designates "meat" or "substance," such as when one says, for example, that the body of the white-lipped peccary or other game is tasty. In its broader acceptation, however, *body* refers to a way of being, a perspective, which implies a particular way of seeing and acting on the world. The Wari' may say, for example, that a certain man is angry because "his body is like that," or the peccary wanders in bands because "the body of the peccaries is like that."[9] And not only the Wari' and animals: all things have a body that determines their actions: the wind blows strongly because "the wind's body is like that," just as the rain falls usually in the afternoon because "the rain's body is like that."

The consequence of this extended notion of humanity and the location of difference in bodies that are continually being produced is that the Wari' and other Amazonian worlds are haunted by the dangers of metamorphosis (Viveiros de Castro 2002: 391)—an outcome of the relation with other types of subjectivities, especially animals that prey on people to incorporate them as members of their own group. The outcome of this capture is the transformation of the victim into an animal of the same "kind." This metamorphosis applies not just to them but to animals as well: *jamu* is a capacity possessed by all human beings, and it means that people are continually at risk of perceiving any animal as human—as in the case of abductions by jaguars and tapirs—and being captured by them.

The most effective form of avoiding metamorphosis in Amazonia is the continuous assimilation of human bodies within the sphere of kinship relations, especially through commensality, speech, physical proximity, and other day-to-day interactions.[10] Consequently, this wider universe of subjectivities forms the background to the production of kin through the fabrication of bodies, meaning that humanity is conceived to be produced out of others (see Viveiros de Castro 2001: 23, and Vilaça 2002a), a category that includes enemies and affines, as we saw in chapter 4 when analyzing the consubstantialization of God and Jesus through commensality and blood.

In the words of Viveiros de Castro ([1977] 1987: 32), the fabrication of the human body is based on a negation of the nonhuman body (also see Descola 2001: 108). The Trio Indians encapsulate this idea perfectly in the expression used to describe the mother's raising of a child: "to undo the spider monkey" (Grotti 2009: 115n15).

Certain practices common to indigenous Amazonian worlds also make this point clear. As I have shown elsewhere (Vilaça 2002a: 349), among many different groups the fact that parents are humans is no guarantee of the child's own humanity. Writing about the Piro/Yine, Gow (1997: 48) tells us that the baby is inspected at birth to determine whether or not it is human: it might be a fish, a tortoise, or another animal. Among some groups, such as the Ge-speaking Panará (Ewart 2013: 184) and the Tupi-Guarani-speaking Araweté (Viveiros de Castro 1986: 442; 1992b), Guayaki (Clastres 1972: 16), and Parakanã (Fausto 2001: 396; 2012: 214), the body of a child is literally molded by hand after birth to differentiate it from the bodies of animals.[11]

The couvade and other abstinence rituals that follow birth clearly show that even this process of directly molding bodies fails to guarantee their human form. Though heavily marked during the postnatal period, this ambivalence in identity occurs at various other times during a person's life. Infancy as a whole and even various periods of adult life—especially initiation, first menstruation, warfare reclusion, and illness—are marked as times of high susceptibility, frequently taken to involve the potential loss of a properly human identity. Writing about the Suyá, Seeger (1981: 24) concludes that "severe illness, death, weakness, and sexuality are also transformations of the social human beings into more animal-like beings."[12]

The question of humanity is central to many Amazonian socialities, and the human/nonhuman (or predator/prey) opposition ends up encompassing all others—including gender relations, which have a similar centrality in Melanesian social worlds—making it the key idiom for expressing difference in general.[13] The concept of the dividual developed by Strathern (1988) via Marriot (1976), in the context of Melanesian ethnography, provides an interesting formula for conceptualizing the dynamics of Wari' personhood where identity is the provisional outcome of a relationship based on oppositional difference. Put succinctly (we shall return to this question in chapter 9), in the Wari' case we could say that the person is a dividual made up of two components, *wari'* and *karawa,* which have the double sense of "human" and "animal," "predator" and "prey." The production of kinship via the flux of elements conceived as constituent parts of their bodies (*kwerexi'*), including semen, sweat, speech, care, affection, and the sharing of food, is ultimately determined by the relation between the Wari' and animals, both of which are internally constituted as *wari'* and *karawa.* The Wari' are produced as humans by differentiating themselves from animals/prey, who are produced as animals/prey in their confrontation with the Wari' when their human component is eclipsed (see Vilaça 2011 and 2015a).

The dividual *wari'-karawa* pair ceases to be *intrinsic* to one person and instead characterizes the Wari'-animal pair, along the same lines as in the Melanesian model. It is important to add that the end result of any confrontation may be precisely the opposite: the animal preys on the Wari', assuming the predator position, *wari',* and turning its victim into a *karawa.* That person's posthumous destiny will be to live among the animals, acquiring a body like theirs and forming a new family among them. This helps explain, then, the Wari' interest in the desubjectivization of animals enabled by conversion to Christianity. I now turn to the translations of various sections of the first chapter of Genesis by the missionaries with the help of Wari' interpreters. Like the actions of the captured boy, these texts imply the establishment of a new relation between humans and animals.

As we shall see in chapter 7, the Book of Genesis, especially the first chapter, plays a central role in Wari' church services. Along with commenting regularly on divine creation in their sermons and prayers, Wari' pastors also display posters on the church walls with verses taken from Genesis and translated into the Wari' language, such as the following:

Genesis 1.1. There was no heaven in the past. There was no earth in the past. There was nothing, nothing, nothing, so God made [them] in the past. [Bible text in English:[14] "In the beginning God created the heavens and the earth."]

Genesis 1. 24. He said too. All the animals stayed on the earth. All the animals, the strange animals [which they do not eat], the true animals [which they do eat], all the strange animals who crawl on the earth. And so they came to exist. [Bible text in English: "Then God said, 'Let the earth bring forth the living creature according to its kind: cattle and creeping thing and beast of the earth, each according to its kind'; and it was so."]

Genesis 1. 26. He also said: Let's make people. Who are similar to us. He will be the leader [*taramaxikon*] of all the fish and birds and all the strange animals. He will be the leader of all of the earth too. He will be the leader of all the strange animals who crawl across the earth. This is what he said. [Bible text in English: "Then God said, 'Let Us make man in Our image, according to Our likeness; let them have dominion over the fish of the sea, over the birds of the air, and over the cattle, over all the earth and over every creeping thing that creeps on the earth.'"]

Genesis 1. 28. He spoke contentedly. Reproduce yourselves many times.... Spread across all the other lands. Be leaders. Be leaders of the fish, the birds, and all animals. [Bible text in English: "Then God blessed them, and God said to them, 'Be fruitful and multiply; fill the earth and subdue it; have dominion over the fish of the sea, over the birds of the air, and over every living thing that moves on the earth.'"][15]

Genesis 1: 30. Eat all the animals, all the birds, and all the strange animals that crawl across the earth too. [Bible text in English: "Also, to every beast of the earth, to every bird of the air, and to everything that creeps on the earth, in which there is life, I have given every green herb for food'; and it was so."]

Although a number of observations can immediately be made by comparing the Wari' and English versions, these differences become still more evident if we add a third comparative axis—namely, the oral version of Genesis narrated by an old Inuit man and analyzed by Laugrand (1999). Like the Wari', the Inuit are a hunting people (though not horticulturists) for whom the notion of subjectivity extends beyond the human species to various types of animals, including their preferred prey. Although Laugrand was working with an oral account, while here I am using a widely distributed written translation produced by missionaries with the help of Wari' interpreters, it is clear that, just as in the Inuit case (94), elements of Wari' cosmology affected the interpretation of the biblical text, though these may have gone unnoticed by the missionaries.

First, we can note that, unlike the English version, the Wari' translation of the first verse has to emphasize an original void for the act of creation to become possible. As their perplexity during the initial period of catechism showed, the idea of creation is foreign to the Wari'. For them, things, animals, and people always existed in the world. The Inuit, for their part, emphasize the indifferentiation of the primordial world where humans and animals looked alike and lived together. Hence, in their version of Genesis, the primordial world emerges "very smoky" and dark until God creates light (Laugrand 1999: 95–96). In contrast to the Wari', therefore, the notion of creation through words was not strange to them: the Inuit have a myth telling how light was created by the word of crow, tired of crashing against the cliffs as he searched for his nest, thereby outwitting the word of fox, who, as a nocturnal hunter, did not want light (95).[16]

We can also note that the difference between wild and domestic animals found in the "original" biblical text makes no sense to them whatsoever. The Wari' replaced this difference with the opposition between edible and inedible animals, while the Inuit replaced it with the difference between land animals and those of the sea, a central dimension of their experience (Laugrand 1999: 97). Nonetheless, Laugrand highlights a point that contains an important difference between the Inuit and Wari' versions: in the Inuit narrative, the section referring to the submission of all animals to human control is omitted entirely, since, the author writes, this would imply a radical transformation of the status of animals for the Inuit, a "complete transformation of the ontological and cosmological systems" (98). In the Wari' version, the relationship with animals is indeed modified, since men become leaders of all animals, whether edible or inedible (the "strange" animals to which the Wari' refer). This leadership was made explicit in a prayer by pastor Rosenio, a OroWaram man, during a conference meeting at Lage in 2009. After listing God's creations, like the sun and moon, animals, fish, and fruits, he added that God finally created Adam in order for him to be the leader in breeding the animals.

This comparative discussion refers us to another complex of myths about creation that, though not Christian, indicate the paramount importance given to the resolution of the problem of instability in Amazonia, allowing us to establish direct parallels with the biblical Genesis.

AN AMAZONIAN GENESIS

The traditional mythology of the Yanomami, inhabitants of northern Amazonia, includes two distinct sets of myths on the origin of humanity, whose contradictory aspect was first noted by Albert (Albert and Kopenawa 2003: 76n35; Kopenawa and Albert 2010: 682) and recently further explored by Leite (2013). The first of these sets includes narratives describing how the ancestors lost their humanity, against the background of a primordial world in which diverse beings share not only the human condition and culture but also the instability of bodily form (Leite 2013: 79, 82).

The second set of myths concerns the creation of a distinct Yanomami humanity by a demiurge. In this narrative, the fall of the sky provokes the transformation of the ancestors into animals. A small group of ancestors survives inside the stem of a palm tree in the form of eggs and is transformed by the demiurge Omama into the true Yanomami, each person attributed with specific social functions. As Leite (2013: 81) emphasizes, the principal characteristic of this second mythological set is precisely "the end of transformability" that typified the first humans. In the words of a Yanomami man:

> Omamë caused the people to become Yanomam; he made the world stop transforming; he put an end to the transformations. He made the Yanomam speak the way we speak today; *he made the people stop becoming others.* ... He made us think straight.... When he was not yet there the people were very ignorant. *The forest was unstable, and the people were constantly changing form.* They used to turn into tapirs, armadillos, and red brockets; Teremë cut them into pieces.... Finally Omamë created us as a new people after those first Yanomam fell underground. We are different Yanomam. (Wilbert and Simoneau 1990: 42–43, my italics, cited in Leite 2013: 81–82, my translation)[17]

Considering that other Amazonian groups possess the same kind of creation mythology, where a demiurge acts to stabilize humanity—for example, the Piaroa (Overing Kaplan 1985a, 1990), Yekuana (De Civrieux 1980; Kelly 2011a), Tukano (Hugh-Jones 2009: 55), and Baniwa/Koripako (Hill 1993; Journet 1995; Xavier 2013: 71–74, 411)—its absence among the Wari' helps explain the focus of their interest in Christianity.[18]

Given that the Wari' experience humanity as an unstable position, a consequence of the mythical continuity between humans and animals, it seems plausible to claim that there was a kind of hollow space (Lévi-Strauss 1991) in their cosmology ready to accept the biblical myth of Genesis, allowing the introduction of the figure of a demiurge previously absent from their mythology and an end to involuntary metamorphosis.[19] Their adoption of the Book of Genesis as an origin myth is related to their interest in the story of divine creation, focused on the separation between humans and animals in the form of predators and prey.

Leite's observations concerning the actions of Omama among the Yanomami reveals the demiurge's similarity to the Christian creator God, since in both cases diet is a key factor separating humans from animals, making this opposition equivalent to one between predators and prey: "With the demiurge's intervention the body of animals ceases to be a human body— potentially dangerous because invested with 'souls,' an enemy body—to become merely and definitively a source of food that can be consumed by the Yanomami without risk of eating one of their own, or becoming merged with what is eaten" (2010: 37; see also 2013: 83, my translation).[20]

I turn now to Wari' comments about divine creation.

SURPRISED BY CREATION

The surprise expressed by the Wari' in response to the idea of creation during the initial phase of catechism becomes evident in their comments regarding this period of contact with the missionaries. Paletó describes their astonishment as follows:

> Royal [the missionary] was singing. The Wari' wondered, "What is he singing?" We just stared at him. He said, "It was our father who made us." The Wari' remarked, "What's he on about?" The OroNao' of the whites [the first Wari' subgroup to have contact with the missionaries and with the whites in general] did not understand this story of God either. And Royal said, "Our father made us. He made you, myself too, my wife, your women, the fish, frogs and ants and all the animals. God made the snakes. He made our throat

and our tongue so we could speak." And the Wari' continued to ask themselves, "What on earth is this about?" (Paletó, conversation with the author, 1992, Rio de Janeiro)

As Paletó explained to me on another occasion: "We don't know from where our ancestors came. The oldest ancestors did not know from where they came. When the youngsters asked the elders, 'Where did we come from?' 'I've no idea.' 'Who made us?' 'Nobody made us. We exist for no reason.' … We never thought about God. We never thought: does God exist? No, never." And his daughter Orowao Karaxu added, "In the past nobody knew that it was God who had created everything. We met the whites and learned about him. For the elders, the animals always wandered around pointlessly. There was no reason for the animals' existence, they thought."

Today, around fifty years after missionization began, the constant affirmation of divine creation in the church services, as we shall see in chapter 7, shows how the idea of creation remains foreign to the Wari', meaning that they must continually reaffirm this idea, especially in the prayers spoken aloud at the start of the services. The three examples below come from three different people in the same service in 2002:

Had there been a *wari'* [person] who knew how to make … all the fruits, all the fish, all the birds. The stars in the sky, the sun as well.

We are very happy with your word. All the animals that you made on earth. The elders didn't know. This is why we eat. Were it not for the animals that you made.

Who was the person [*wari'*] who made things? Why does honey exist? We admire God for this. This is his work.

During the same service, the preacher in his final prayer declared, "My father God. We adore you for all the animals that you made on earth. All the animals that we eat, all the fish that we eat, all the fruit that we eat."

Like the prayers, various hymns sung in the Wari' language also mention Creation, such as hymn 87, which states that God made the sun, day, night, moon, jaguar, dog, chicken, macaw, parrot, flowers, forest, streams, and rain for us, along with "my father, my mother, and me too," which is why he is very good. Likewise in hymn 89, the stanza "Look at the animals. Who made them? Was it the Wari'? It was God" is repeated with the replacement of the term "animals" with "forest," "fish," "birds," "streams," and "moon."[21]

Finally, while chatting with me one day, Paletó remarked, "It was God who made us speak. He is the one who makes babies in the womb. The Wari' don't know how to sculpt with clay. It was God who knew how to make us."

The fact of creation in itself implies the imposition of the perspective of the creator, God, who made men the masters of animals—that is, predators. The Wari' enthusiastically recount the moment when they began to eat various animals once prohibited. In the words of Paletó: "They used to avoid armadillo, coati. When we encountered the whites, the Christians told us to eat all animals since it was God who had made them. They didn't cause sickness. Pregnant women eat armadillo, eagle. The latter animal became a true bird [prey] for us. They eat electric eel and nothing happens. Why? 'I created the animals,' said God. 'Oh, so that's how things are, then!' we said."

Several other analogous comments made by the same man are worth citing here: "Today the animals have turned into true animals" (*Pain xokori, iri' karawa na karawa*). "Today the animals are animals. We are no longer afraid of animals. Their doubles have vanished" (*Pain xokori, karawa pin na karawa. Om ka jin ma xine karawa. Om pin na jaminain*). "It's only now that the coati has become an animal for us" (*Xo' karawa na parut hota*). "'Eat all these animals, I was the one who made them,' [said God], Royal told us." Paletó concludes, "The Wari' ate and didn't become ill."[22] In a church service, João, speaking from the pulpit, stated that the Wari' before had been just like those who believed in Moses, who avoided animals, who thought that animals caused diseases. Today they hear the word of God and no longer avoid animals. Before, though, the animals had caused diseases and killed them.

Like God, the enemy boy in the myth created animals for the Wari' by altering their vision so that they could see the animals properly. In Abrão's words: "Before, in the forest, the Wari' sight was like television. Now it is another kind of sight." God creates the world by fixing the Wari' in the position of predators, in the same way that the captured enemy adjusts the viewpoint of the Wari', transforming them from prey (when all the animals were jaguars) into predators.[23]

A clear example of the centrality of predation for the Christian Wari' can be seen by comparing the Portuguese (original) and Wari' versions of hymn 15. In Portuguese: "God is good, God is our father, God is love. The rain falls, falls, falls. The sun shines in all its brilliance. God is good, God is a father,

FIGURE 7. Preying, Negro River village, July 2014. (Photo by the author.)

God is love." In Wari': "Our father God is good. Our father God is good. He gives us lots of game [*karawa*] to eat. Our father God is good."

The same applies to a prayer whose theme was very common, at least until 2008: "My father God. We admire you for all the animals that you created on earth. All the animals that we eat, all the fish that we eat, all the fruit that we eat" (church service 2002, Negro River village, final prayer).[24]

The description given by the missionary Royal Taylor (pers. comm., 1994, my translation) of the Wari' conversion is illuminating: "When they first accepted the message of the gospel, especially the spiritual liberation offered by the gospel, they lost their fear of many things, including the animals that cause disease. They learned that the dominant spirit was God, and they lost their fear of specters of the dead [*jama*] and of animals. They freed themselves from slavery. They could wander freely at night, and eat everything. And with the morality that comes from the word of God, they ceased the thefts and infidelities."

The concern to differentiate themselves from animals also explains one of the aspects most cited by the Wari' to explain their adoption of Christianity, which combines with the fear of becoming separated from their kin at the end of the world, as discussed in the previous chapter—namely, the fear of hell.

In line with the eschatological approach that, as we saw in chapter 1, is central to the NTM's ideology, the missionaries' presentation of the word of God to the Wari' gave considerable emphasis to divine punishment and hell. The missionaries dwell on the existence of a huge fire that consumes nonbelievers and, indeed, wrote about this in diverse texts, one of them a "course book" in the Wari' language, produced after discussions at a conference held in Ribeirão village in 2000 (*Curso nexi pain Ribeirão*). In chapter 8 of the twenty-nine-page booklet, titled *All the People Who Lie to Us,* the missionaries warn the Wari' about those people who say that they should not believe in white people's things because they have their own things to believe in. The text continues: "These people who say those kinds of things are lying. The word of God says as follows: the person [*wari'*] who does not believe in Jesus will probably go to a large fire, that's what God's word says. . . . What God wants for us is for us to escape" (19).[25]

That kind of proselytizing also happened among other groups. There are indigenous accounts of hell in so-called autobiographical works, in which "Christianized savages" testify to the missionaries of the radical change that occurred in their lives after they had understood the divine word. In the words of Tariri, a Candoshi man (Jivaro, Peru) in contact with missionaries from the SIL: "He [God] will put those who kill into darkness. . . . It's like walking in a fog. . . . You will always be falling. It is terrible to be lost like that. That is where people who do not love God will live" (Tariri and Wallis 1965: 70). Among the Waiwai the emphasis on suffering in hell with its eternal fire provoked the following episode, observed by the missionaries: "As Hawkins and Leavitt made their way back to the mission at Kanaxen, they encountered hastily abandoned houses and panicked families who were fleeing from the rumored flames and heading for the mission, which they thought would be spared. This sudden influx of people seeking the Lord's Word delighted the missionaries and exceeded the fondest hopes" (Howard 2001: 64).[26]

For the Wari', hell, situated next to heaven in the sky, is frightening, not only because it implies the separation from kin, a point always recalled by them, but especially because of the fire, emphasized in all those accounts of their fear of hell as a posthumous destiny.[27]

> I am afraid. If only there were no fire [of hell]. . . . God is very strong. (Manim, Santo André village 1993)

The double of someone who believes in God goes to heaven. Someone who does not believe goes to the fire. Christians rise to heaven with their own body, they don't suffer. Those who don't believe suffer greatly. (Xijam, Negro River village, 2002)

I believe in God to avoid going to the fire. I'm really scared of the fire. That's what all the whites fear. (Jamain Tamanain, Negro River village, 2002)

If we do something wrong, God strikes us. We are afraid of the fire that will burn our double. (Hwerein Pe e', Negro River village, 2002)

God says, "If you die, the good will go to heaven. When those of you who are bad die, they will go to the sky and will not be able to drink water." They will arrive in God's house and will plead to him: "Give me water, I am thirsty!" "No! You will not drink water. You were bad, you took things, you stole people's chickens, you illicitly ate all kinds of food. You will go to the fire." He arrives at the fire and stays there. He dances without reason. "Give me water, I'm thirsty!" "No! Stay right there!" His eyes become dry. He is thirsty. The worms find their way into his body. His flesh becomes soft, rotten. His rotten remains dance without reason. That's what happens to the bad Wari'. We are afraid of God. When we were not Christians, in the past, we thought God didn't exist. We heard that we should believe in God. (Paletó, Rio de Janeiro, 1992).

I want to believe in God so my double escapes. (Topa', Negro River village, 2002)

Juxtaposing these testimonies with those referring to the end of the world, we can deduce that the fire's significance for the Wari' derives from the equation made between roasting and the prey position, something they strive intensely to avoid. Orowao Toko Jai told me in 1993, "The Wari' were afraid. The Christians would say that God would arrive the next day. 'Believe in God or you will go to the fire. Those who believe will be gathered. Those who do not believe will stay and will be eaten by animals.'"

The testimonies are surprisingly similar over a twenty-year period, as can be seen in the two different narratives given by Paletó, separated by an interval of ten years, some of which he lived as a pagan and the other as a Christian:

[The missionaries said,] "Believe in God so that he doesn't come to kill you." Like this past, summer [when there had been an earth tremor in Rondônia]: "God will come to destroy the earth. Everyone in all the cities will die. Everyone will die. There will be a lot of water. There will be no land for us to stay. The Christians will go to heaven," say the Christians. "Those who do not believe in God will be left behind. You may well be left. A jaguar will come and eat you on the earth." They talked nonsense: "An enormous cricket will eat you. God will come. If he comes, he'll see you. You'll be moaning. The earth may burn," they told us in our house. . . . The earth will burn, like Sodom, maybe. "We will burn, we will burn," said the Wari'. (Paletó, conversation with author, 1995, Ji-Paraná, Rondônia, as a non-Christian)

I returned [from Sagarana] and stayed on the Negro River. Royal was still living there. He called us to sing music. I entered the church and sat down. Royal said, "If you don't believe, you will stay on the earth and the jaguar will eat you. There will be all kinds of animal doubles. An enormous cricket will eat the Wari'. An enormous cricket sent from heaven. God will send it to eat people who do not believe." (Paletó, conversation with author, 2005, Linha 29 village, as a Christian)

What we can note is that the fate of unbelievers—whether an individual fate, at death, or a collective fate at the end of the world—is to become prey for eternity. In hell they are condemned to exposure to a fire that never completes the roasting process, unlike cooking fire and the funeral fire, which, by making the corpse disappear, released the double for a new existence in the subaquatic world of the dead, where the person was revived young and beautiful (see chapter 6). In hell, on the contrary, the non-Christians become prey forever. The same position is assumed by those who remain on earth after the end of the world, as becomes clear in the reference to the animals, jaguars, or a giant cricket, who will eat the non-Christians.

We can conclude, therefore, that the indigenous interest in Genesis. and the fear of hell, two central aspects of Christianity for the Wari' and the missionaries alike, stemmed from a single issue, one soon identified by the missionaries (as by Royal in the quotation above), who attributed it to the Wari' belief in spirits (taken to be incarnations of the devil): the Wari' were haunted by the fear of metamorphosis and occupying the place of prey.

By conceiving humanity and animality to be essentially reversible positions—given that both the Wari' and their preferred prey can occupy the position of humans (*wari'*), defined as predators, or the position of animals (*karawa*), defined as prey—the Wari' experience life as a continual struggle to define themselves as human and remain as such. Consequently the establishment of predation as a one-way process coincides with what the Wari' seek in their everyday life, a movement analogous to the universal fraternity, or "de-affinization," also sought by Christianity. By constituting themselves as a consanguine group, the Wari' differentiate themselves as a collectivity distinct from animals. Through a comparison with Wari' mythology, we can propose that this redefinition of predation is conceived by them as a change of perspective, starting with an act of enemy origin, and concretized in the production of kinship with the missionaries and with God.

THE PERSISTENCE OF THE ENEMY

Interestingly, although the missionaries—and some other white people, such as the FUNAI officers and anthropologists—who live at the posts in close proximity with the Wari', share their food (some more than others), share their quotidian life, and are very often called by kinship terms, they are also simultaneously classified as enemies, *wijam,* as I showed in chapter 3 in relation to Wari' children's observations about myself and my youngest son.

There are two dimensions to be explored here. First, neither anthropologists nor missionaries have proven particularly well suited to the Wari' project of adoption, since, as for shamans, total incorporation can only happen with marriage. Additionally the missionaries have always imposed clear restrictions on the approximation of the Wari' as a whole, with the exception of their closer collaborators—who, as we saw in chapter 3, are the only ones allowed to frequent their houses and eat their food. While the missionaries call everyone "sibling" in the church, they do not treat them as such outside this context. On the contrary, they refuse to meet their demands for goods, proposing instead that the solicited objects be exchanged for produce from the swiddens, game or fish, or some kind of manual labor.

Contrary to what such evidence might suggest, as far as the Wari' are concerned, it is not the missionaries, anthropologists, and others who are uninterested in marriage, but the Wari' themselves. The few marriages that have taken place, mostly between Wari' women and manual laborers or rubber tappers, have been highly criticized, and indeed most of them seem to be riven by tension and fights. In addition—as happened with the marriages to the OroWin, their ancient enemies who came to live at the Negro River village—these spouses ended up "becoming Wari," adopting their customs and, in the case of the OroWin, even their own language. There are a few recent cases of young Wari' women who have gone to live in the city with their husbands, and I am unable to say whether, like the figure of Piro in the myth, they will return one day to teach the Wari' new things.

The ambiguous behavior of the missionaries, and that of other whites, seems to coincide with a movement among the Wari' to preserve the double character of these new enemies, enabling the Wari' to maintain the powers associated with their alterity. By calling us "enemies," the Wari' retain a degree of distance that allows them to shift between two distinct perspectives, just as their shamans do, thereby maintaining the dividual character of the person. The interest in preserving difference is related to the "opening to the other" (Lévi-Strauss 1991: 16), discussed in chapter 3, that is objectified in the attribution of a maximum alterity to the missionaries and Christianity. The Wari' constantly emphasize the distant origin of the missionaries, observing that they are foreigners from the United States (the *OroAmericanos*) and Germany (*OroAlemão*, when referring to the missionary Manfred Kern).

The interest in the alterity of the missionaries and Christianity is amply described in the literature. Taylor, in the previously cited work on the Christianization of the Achuar, writes that "a crucial aspect of trade relations among the Achuar is the tremendous value attached to goods from 'outside': . . . the more 'exotic', the more highly valued. Moreover, the prestige attributed to 'foreignness' applies equally to material and symbolic values" (1981: 656).[28]

Among the Ewe of Ghana, Meyer (1999: 139) tells us, the Pentecostals "understand Christianity as a religion which has nothing in common with 'heathendom' and which separates its adherents from the past. Indeed, for the Pentecostals, the attraction of Christianity lies in the fact that it is a new and strange religion opposed to African religion and culture."

In Indonesia, too, Christianity was appropriated as a source of alterity. According to Rutherford's analysis of the Christianization of the Biak of Indonesia, the Bible provided them with "an experience of haunting, an encounter with the powers of alien lands," and conversion is recounted as a history of capture: they did not know what was involved, but coming from the foreigners it had to be good (2006: 244, 251). Rutherford adds, "The early evangelists provided Biaks and other Papuan visitors with a place to capture the foreign. . . . The very strangeness of the evangelists' word was what gave them their potential and appeal" (259).[29]

In the same way that the missionaries remained enemies, the external origins of the captured boy in the lizard myth—in contrast to what happens to adopted children among the Wari', usually treated just like biological children—are recalled by the narrators, who refer to his mother not as "mother," as happens with adopted children, but as "the one who raised him."

The enemy must always carry alterity with him or her as a mark or potential. The adoption of the perspective of divine creation is conceived as a "turning into an enemy," as Paletó made clear: "The animal doubles vanished. We ourselves turned into enemies [wijam]." This does not imply a total, and much less an irreversible, transformation, and indeed this kind of affirmation alternates with others where they say that they are entirely Wari', as we shall see in the conclusion.

It should be added that the external origin of the perspective does not entirely explain the interest it provokes.[30] Just as the boy's teachings in the myth would have proved unsuccessful had the new prey not been tasty and had it not satiated their appetite, the word of God would not have attracted them had it not promised the same possibility: to eat more of everything, without fear. In fact we could say that, in a certain sense, conversion, for the Wari', was a liberation not of the soul but of the stomach.[31]

The interest in maintaining difference not only applies to enemies: it is also clearly apparent in terms of internal relations. Just as enemies are kept as enemies while being incorporated, the division into subgroups—which founds the existence of prototypical affines, irreducible to consanguinization—is maintained even today. This is particularly evident when we consider the abrupt reduction in the population after contact and the reorganization of spatial occupation. In other words, given the chance to unite into a single group—whether because of the sudden decline in number or because the spatial distribution of the subgroups had been disorganized by the movements and unprecedented groupings of people from different subgroups—the Wari' maintained their divisions. Today they still present themselves as members of the traditional subgroups and associate these with the different FUNAI posts/villages around which each subgroup ended up living. This active interest in maintaining their prototypical affines is also clear in the episode narrated in chapter 3, where the OroNao', living in isolation, without any foreigners with whom they could hold chicha festivals, decided to embark on the first contacts with whites. The initial movement toward the latter was motivated by the possibility of incorporating them as one more subgroup. Later, realizing this was impossible, the OroNao' proved keen to meet the request of the missionaries and the government agents to contact other subgroups who were still avoiding the attempts by the whites to approach them.

This discussion brings us to another point—namely, the divergence between the conceptions of the Wari' and whites concerning the place of difference, as well as the place of paradox in these systems, a topic to which we return along the course of the book.

Kelly's model of the same kind of relation between the Yanomami and the whites, whom they also call "enemies," *nape,* provides an interesting angle on the Wari' case (2005b, 2011b), returning us to the *wari'/karawa* model of the dividual explored above. Kelly argues for a kind of axis of transformation into whites, with the position occupied by each person on this axis always relative: someone is more or less white depending on this position, which itself is given by the relational context. Hence, even the Yanomami with more contact with the whites act and are seen as Indians, Yanomami, when in the city. But when these same people find themselves farther upriver, in villages with little contact with whites, they are like whites to their Yanomami hosts. This axis of transformation is two-way, since it also involves the domestication of white people—that is, their transformation into Yanomami, equally relative and contextual, analogous to what I have been showing in the Wari' case. An important point to emphasize here is that this process cannot always be controlled: in other words, you may be seen as Indian when you wish to be seen as white, which results from a process of "counterinvention" (Wagner 1975: 45), in which the innate or conventional world returns, a moment intrinsic to all inventive movement, in this case a movement of differentiation of the conventional indigenous world through identification (or mimetism, kinship, or other means) with the whites.

And more than just counterinvention or resistance is involved. As various Americanist authors have shown, especially following the works of Viveiros de Castro (1986; 1992a) on the Araweté and Overing Kaplan (1986) on the Piaroa, the "outside," where the gods, spirits, and enemies are located, is central to the reproduction of Amazonian collectives.[32] While difference may be reintroduced in an uncontrolled form in the case of disease—conceived as involuntary metamorphosis—in the context of ritual and shamanism difference is purposely reintroduced in the form of an inversion of the direction of the inventive movement in order to reconstitute the innate or given that serves as the starting point for these chains of differentiations (see Wagner 1975 and Viveiros de Castro 2001).

This is precisely one of the problems introduced by Christianity, as we shall see in chapter 8: the end of traditional rituals and shamanism suppresses this channel of controlled and voluntary production of difference, replaced by rituals that look to produce identity among a group of humans who perceive themselves to be separate from animals. In this context the translation of Christian concepts into the Wari' idiom becomes an important channel for the preservation of this innate world, owing not only to the fact that the words in Wari' resist the new meanings at the same time that they point to a new world, but also to the fact that the Wari' themselves engage in a voluntary movement to maintain the difference of meanings, as in the case of the not-dislike/love pair examined in the previous chapter, and in the terms for *body* and *soul,* to be explored in chapters 6 and 9.

I conclude this chapter with a clear illustration of the value of alterity in indigenous Amazonia, which in turn takes us back to the questions concerning translation explored in chapter 2. The Yanomami shaman and leader Davi Kopenawa, describing how he prepares his talks for white audiences, argues that the interest of the latter must be related to the same principle motivating the native interest: novelty and the impact caused by incomprehension.[33] "[Speaking to white people,] I am always searching for other words; words they do not know yet. I want them to be surprised and to open their ears" (Kopenawa and Albert 2010: 465, my translation). At the end he clearly summarizes the differences concerning difference: "[The whites] sleep only seeing in their dreams what surrounds them during the day. . . . Sure they have lots of satellite dishes and radios in their cities, but they only serve for them to listen to themselves. . . . The words of the shamans are different. They come from very far away and speak about things unknown to ordinary people" (497).

We can proceed now to examine how duality and alternation assume an objective form in the work of translating biblical concepts and texts.

SIX

Strange Creator

The shamans say that they search and search but see nothing in
the sky. They say that they do not know where the house of God
is located. Does God exist, Aparecida?

ARIRAM, 1993

IN THE PRECEDING CHAPTERS I have examined the reasons why the
Wari' approached the missionaries and the Christian message, and why that
led them, after about a decade, to declare themselves Christians, telling the
missionaries that they "believed" (*howa*, "to trust") in God. As we have seen,
the Wari' saw that, from these powerful enemies—different from those with
whom they had previously warred, and who had capacities that they themselves attributed to their God—they might acquire additional means of
resolving issues that had always tormented them, perturbing their ideal of a
life spent among kin and provoking ruptures, anger, diseases, and death, arising largely from the immoral acts of affines and the aggressions of animals
and affines. Paradoxically they preserved the constitutive difference of the
enemies, as well as of the foreigners, the same people who presented them
with the image of affinity that they so keenly wished to suppress.

In this chapter I explore the questions involved in the invention of the two
key figures from the Christian world: God, in his three persons, and the
devil. The analysis of the process of translating God into the Wari' language
reveals the limits imposed on perspectivist translation by the characteristics
of this divinity. Thus when the Wari' decided to accept the new term chosen
by the missionaries—after initially associating God with the mythic figure of
Pinom (an affine-enemy, as we saw in chapter 4)—this led them to a strange
world by means of familiar concepts (such as invisibility), and they were
obliged to deal with notions incompatible with their perspectivist universe
(such as omnipresence). The notion of the devil, on the other hand, was
quickly placed in the service of their conventional world owing to the latter's
resistance to the differentiation (its "counterinvention"; Wagner 1975: 75)

desired by the Wari' through Christianization. By entering the bodies of the animals and giving them back the agency supressed by God, the devil restored the dividual Wari' person and led the Wari' back to the world of metamorphosis.

GOD

As I remarked earlier, the missionaries initially designated God by the Portuguese term *Deus*. Given the absence of a demiurge or gods of any kind among the Wari', the possibility of finding parallel figures in their cosmology was excluded from the outset. On perceiving that the Wari' associated God and Jesus with mythic figures, the missionaries, according to the missionary Barbara Kern, decided to adopt another strategy, seeking a term for God in the Wari' language, though the name *Jesus* was maintained in Portuguese.

Barbara Kern explains that the missionaries found a term for God as follows: on hearing the expression *kaxikon jam,* which they understood to refer to an "evil spirit," and which ended up being used to designate the devil, it occurred to them to name God using a neologism with a meaning opposite to *kaxikon* (evil): *iri',* which means "true, good." The expression *Iri' Jam* immediately "stuck," Barbara says. "It seems that a light shone in their minds, and they began to understand God's character better" (pers. comm., March 17, 2011, my translation).[1]

Before turning to the meaning of *jam,* it is worth noting that, as far as I can tell, the adjective *kaji* or *kaxi/kaxikon/kaxikam* does not always have the connotation of "evil": most of the time it signifies "strange, different, or unusual."[2] Hence, *kaxi karawa* means "inedible animals," in contrast to the *iri' karawa,* the "edible animals," though these too may be called *kaxi karawa* when, acting as humans, they attack the Wari'. Animals introduced by the whites are also qualified in this way, such that the domestic pig is *kaji mijak,* where *mijak* means white-lipped peccary. Thus, the *kaji/kaxi* and *iri'* pair do not define fixed categories but instead indicate contrasting and alternating positions—very different, therefore, from the binary conception that served as the starting point for the missionary translation.[3]

In relation to the term *jam,* Barbara had suggested in one of her email messages that *jam* is the free form of *jamixi'* (our double). Here she recalled that substantives frequently appear in two forms in Wari' grammar: a possessed form, with the suffix *–xi',* which indicates the first person plural inclusive (our), and a free form. For example, the terms *xirixi'* and *xirim* refer to the object "house," *winaxi'* and *waji* to the head, and *ximixi'* and *xim* to the heart.

Although this explanation is entirely consistent, my ethnographic data presents a number of problems in terms of asserting a complete equivalence between *jam* and *jamixi'*. As I remarked to Barbara, since the start of my research in 1986 I had heard the term *jam* used in only a few specific contexts, none of which coincided with *jamixi'*, the main such context being the reference to a deceased person, when that person's personal name, or the appropriate kin term, was preceded by *jam*. The second context is that of the already mentioned expression *kaxikon jam*, where *jam* refers to animals acting in an unusual way, designating a nonidentified group of animals. As soon as they are identified by shamans during cures, they are named—for example, as *jamikon jowin* (capuchin monkey double) or *jamikon min* (tapir double).[4]

The final context is a myth to which more than one person directly referred when I asked how the neologism *Iri' Jam* had come about. The myth begins with an episode of stinginess, when a man classified as a grandfather (*jeo'*) fails to offer tapir meat to his grandchildren from another village who had come to visit him. One of the grandfather's fellow villagers heard them comment on the grandfather's stinginess and told him. Enraged, he invited them to drink fermented chicha. They initially refused. One group decided to accept the renewed invitation, however, and went. Those who fell unconscious from the heavy chicha drinking and vomiting were killed by the grandfather. He beheaded them and used their arm bones to beat the tree trunk drums played by the hosts during these festivals.[5] A boy in hiding watched what happened and then told his kin, who were still dancing and drinking, allowing them to escape and recount to those who had stayed at home what had happened. Deciding to exact revenge on the old grandfather, from here on called an enemy, *wijam,* they prepared for a war expedition in an unusual form, by covering themselves with animal skins, like those of jaguars and tapirs. This enabled them to act like the animals themselves and made them invulnerable to arrows. One man, though, had the idea of suspending a hammock on a path and sleeping there alone. In the middle of the night he felt the specter of a dead person (*jama*) approach and let it touch his entire body from toe to head.[6] When the specter's hands reached his mouth, the man bit down hard and tore off one of the fingers, which he kept. During the night other specters appeared, and the man did the same thing, eventually ending up with various fingers. When he returned home in the morning, he chewed the fingers, mixed the liquid with babassu palm oil and rubbed it over his entire body, immediately making himself invisible. Everything he held would float in the air, including his bow and arrows. He became visible again only when he sweated (sweat, according to the Wari', frightens away specters). Disguised or transformed in this way, they left for the village of the grandfather-enemy, killing many of the inhabitants. As they returned home, they left their animal skins along the path, except for the invisible man, who remained invisible. This is attested by the observation, made by the narrators of the myth, that the pot from which he drank the chicha offered to killers (*napiri*) seemed to float when it was handed to him. The Wari' refer to this figure simply as *jam* when narrating the myth, making clear the relation between this term and invisibility, the main characteristic of this mythic persona. According to Paletó, when the missionaries spoke to them about God, immediately the Wari' associated God with this invisible man.

What all these contexts share in common is the idea of invisibility, referring to bodies that for one reason or other cannot be seen. This became clear to me when a man, explaining how killers emerged with long hair after reclusion, compared them to my own formerly long hair, referring to it as *jam tenenem* (where *tenenem* means "your hair"). On another occasion, people referred to the train that used to run on the Madeira-Mamoré railway as *jam* train. Talking to my Wari' brother Abrão about this recently, I learned that they commonly use this kind of expression to refer to things that are no longer there, like an item of clothing that a person no longer has.

Over the course of our correspondence, Barbara said that she had found a detail in her field notebooks that corroborated my conclusions concerning the relation between *jam* and the idea of invisibility: the Wari' began to refer to the missionary Abraham, who had returned to the United States, as "*jam* Abraham." As Barbara wrote, "He was still alive [and they knew so], but for them he was absent, they no longer saw him. So he was *jam* Abraham" (pers. comm., April 6, 2011).

Jam always refers to a body, therefore, of a person or object that exists somewhere but cannot be seen. From the viewpoint of speakers, it indicates an ex-body. The dead, for instance, have bodies like our own in the world of the dead: when a shaman sees a deceased relative in the animal form assumed when the dead climb from the subaquatic world to the earth's surface, he refers to it not as *jam*-X (ex- or invisible-X) but as *jamikon jam*-X, which we could translate as the "double of the ex- or invisible-X." So while, grammatically speaking, the free form of *jamixi'* is also *jam,* we could be dealing here with a homonym, an adjective with a specific connotation of constitutive invisibility.

As I mentioned briefly in the introduction, the word *jamixi'* has a synonym, *tamataraxi'*. When asked directly about the terms, the Wari' say that they are interchangeable, such that one says *tamatarakon min* (tapir double) or *tamatarain mijak* (peccary double) to designate the human agency of these animals. A number of times I heard duplicated expressions suggesting the equivalence between the two terms, such as: *mao'na jamikon tamatarakon mijak* (where *mao'* is the verb "to go," *na* is the third person singular pronoun, *kon* is the male suffix, and *mijak* is "white-lipped peccary"), referring, for example, to the actions of a shaman whose double accompanies the double of the peccaries. Jamain Tamanain, a Christian, once said to me of posthumous life in the sky: "*Kirik te tamana na tamataraxi' jamixi'*" (where *kirik te* is "content," *tamana* is "very," and *na* is the third person singular pronoun). I am unfamiliar, however, with the existence of any verb derived from *tamataraxi'* equivalent to *jamu,* signifying interspecies transformation. In my experience the preferential contexts for applying these terms are somewhat distinct, though, with *tamataraxi'* used more to designate the double in dreams, where it normally appears in its human form, as a Wari' body, while *jamixi'* refers to the transformed body of animals and shamans alike.[7]

The distinct use contexts of *tamataraxi'* and *jamixi'* noted by myself were also observed by the missionaries, although equivocally in my view. According to the missionary linguist Barbara Kern in our correspondence, *tamataraxi'* refers to the "spirit" of a living person, while *jamixi'* refers to the "spirit" of someone now dead. She added that when the missionaries noted the difference and concluded that they had made a mistake in their translation of the term *God,* associating God with a "dead spirit," it was too late since the term *Iri' Jam* for God was already a success and the Wari' refused to accept any other.[8]

Consequently the missionaries chose *tamataraxi'* to translate "soul." In every biblical text referring to the soul, therefore, the Wari' term is usually *tamataraxi'*. The translation for Holy Spirit is *Tamatarakon Iri' Jam* (double of God). This does not mean that *jamixi'* had disappeared in the Christian context, since it came to designate everything related to the danger of transformation, the devil, and evil, while *tamataraxi'* acquired the connotation of an immortal component of the person, identified with the heart as the center of moral conscience. Jamain Tamanain once told me, "Iri' Jam does not have a *jamikon*. Nobody says *jamikon Iri' Jam,* only *tamatarakon*. He doesn't *jamu* [transform]."[9] Practically overlapping in the past, these two terms acquired divergent meanings and opposite values through the process of translation, and only *jamixi'* retained the corporal component that characterizes the Wari' double.

Returning to the term for God, *jam* as much as *jamixi'* and *tamataraxi'* originally comprised indices (Gell 1998: ch. 7) of bodies, as aspects indissociably related to the latter: while the first term designates something that was once visible but is no longer, an ex-body, the latter two terms indicate the body transformed, or actualized in another way. In the Wari' universe, bodiless beings are inconceivable; even the wind has a specific affection-body, which people refer to as *kwerein hotowa*, the "wind's way of being."

Invisibility is not incorporeality, therefore, in part because although invisibility is conceivable by the Wari', it has a temporal and relational limit: something can always be seen by someone at some moment. The man who became invisible in the myth mentioned above was already known by all the other figures and, as we have seen, became visible again whenever he sweated. The ex-bodies of the dead, and those of animal spirits, are occasionally visible to the shamans, taking the form of a specific body to their eyes.

For the missionaries, however, incorporeality is a constitutive aspect of God, as explained in lesson book 1, dated 1998, in which they present God, the devil, the angels, and Creation. Item 1 of lesson 3 (p. 11), titled "Jam na Iri' Jam," continues from lesson 2, which explains how God was the first being to have existed, even before the things of the universe, people, animals, and the devil (*kaxikon jam*). It closely follows the indications set out in the manual (McIlwain 2003) and states as follows:

> There does not need to be an earth [*makan*] for me to reside, God said. No, he does not need ["groan for"; *jain jain*] earth, he does not need a house, he does not need food [*karawa*] to eat. Had he a body [*kwerekun*, "his body"]. He does not imitate us [*an xiho'*], he has no body. He has no bones, he does not imitate our *wari'*ness [*pain ka wari'nexi ka*]. Neither does he imitate animals or birds, he has no flesh/body [*kwerekun*] on his bones.... God is *jam*. (lesson book 1, p. 11)

At the end of lesson 7, one of the questions from the list for the pastor to pose to the congregation, followed in the book by the correct responses, is: "Does God have a body? Does he imitate us by having flesh/body on his bones? No, God is *jam*."

However, the Wari' lexicon does not allow the description of the attributes of a being or object without using the notion of body, which produces various contradictions in the translated texts. So, for example, a section from lesson 7 of lesson book 1, which seeks to explain God's way of being, insists on the fact that he possesses a heart, *ximikon* (the *locus* of thought, seated in the body; see chapter 9), just like us and, therefore, also feels love, sadness, joy, and anger. It adds, "That is what the body of Iri' Jam is like (*Je kwerekun Iri' Jam*), he appreciates us when we do not dislike him" (p. 34). Or as one man said while praying out loud to God during a service: "Your double [*tamataram*] is good, your body is good, your son is good. Your son's blood is strong."[10]

"A PROBLEM OF PRESENCE"

The initial period of catechism was marked by the problem posed by God's insistent invisibility for an indigenous worldview that equates knowledge with vision.[11] The fact that shamanic practices were centered on visual capacity prevented any kind of dialogue between the Wari' shamans and missionaries at the beginning of their encounter: the shamans were unable to see God or signs of his existence, such as his house, for example, during their journeys to the sky. As we shall see later, this problem afflicts the Wari' even today. In 1993, Ariram, a woman from Sagarana, the single Wari' village run, until recently, by Catholic priests, asked me, "The shamans say that they search and search but see nothing in the sky. They say that they do not know where the house of God is located. Does God exist, Aparecida?" She repeated this question to me, formulated in exactly the same way, twelve years later in 2005 on another of my visits to Sagarana.[12]

The "problem of presence" is not confined to the Wari' or other native groups, however, since it constitutes the very foundation of Christianity's central tenet: God incarnated himself in his son, a person like any other, possessing a body made of blood and bone, revealing another of the ambiguities intrinsic to the Christian message.[13] As the pastor Xijam said during one church service, in January 2003: "God is *jam*, which is why nobody ever saw him. Jesus was *wari'*, which is why he was seen."

The book of catechism *Curso nexi pain Rio Negro,* which tells of Jesus's life, explains that Jesus came to earth when God made himself *wari'* (*Ka wari' pin ka Iri' Jam*). Lesson 43, the first of lesson book 3, which begins the teachings of the New Testament, explains the human character of Jesus. In the Annunciation the angel (*jam:* see below) tells Mary (*Maria*): "Your son will be a true person [*wari'*, here meaning "kin"] of Iri' Jam, Mary. A true person of Iri' Jam, who will take the place of the Wari' so they can escape [*witan*]" (p. 6). Earlier, the book states,

> Why did Iri' Jam, in the past, want to be *wari'*? Remember what we have already studied, he lives in three [3 *ka e'nukun*]. Iri' Jam seems to be one but he is not. He lives in three. There is his father [*kote ka*], there is his son. Finally there is his spirit [*Tamatarakon*]. They are all Iri' Jam. There are simply three who live in him. Iri' Jam is *jam*. He has no body. He is not like us who possess a body. He has no body. His father had no body. His son had no body. His *tamatarakon* had no body. He is pure *jam*. . . . To be able to take our place so that we can escape, he needed a body. "So I can take the place of the Wari' I shall need a body, perhaps," he said. "I must imitate the Wari'. . . . I shall not imitate them by becoming angry, I shall imitate them only by possessing a body," he said. . . . He became completely *wari'*, he imitated all the Wari', he was born as a baby. (p. 5)

This quotation illustrates the ambiguity of the Christian missionary message concerning God's body, given that it alternately insists on its peculiarity, differentiating God from Jesus, and merges both in expressions of the type "three who live in him," pointing to a notion of the multiple and complex person that contains parallels with the Wari' concept. The second stanza of the Wari' translation of hymn 4 says, "Iri Jam' was not born in the sky. He already existed when there was still no earth. He, the father, his son through his spirit [which here, exceptionally, is called *jamikon*]. He is not various. He is also just one."

JESUS

At any rate, when the topic is specifically the body, the emphasis falls on the distinctiveness of Jesus, who the Wari' also called *aji'* (older brother), as in hymn 2. On page 126 of lesson book 6 (titled *Romans*), citing Romans 6:11, Jesus is spoken of as someone who "has a body just like mine [*win kwere*]." This was emphasized during a church service when a pastor observed, in 2005, that "Jesus was afraid of dying because he was not *jam; wari', wijam!*" [he was simultaneously Wari' and an enemy/white].

We can understand, therefore, why it is Jesus, Jesu, rather than God who appears in dreams that serve as a turning point for the conversion of some people, attesting to his important role as a mediator between God and the Wari', something that we have already seen in the parallels with warfare discussed in chapter 4. This was the case of one of the oldest pastors from the Negro River, Awo Kamip, the same person who, as mentioned in the previous chapter, worked for the missionaries over many years as a translator. In his dream he sees Jesus in the same way that shamans see animal doubles (though he was not a shaman), and he immediately equates Jesus with God, as do the missionaries:

[After a long time understanding nothing that the missionaries said,] I eventually understood. I slept at night and dreamt of *jam,* God's double [*jamikon Iri' Jam*]. I saw him in the sky. . . . I saw Jesus in my dream. I saw Jesus's double [*jamikon*]. [He shows me a DVD cover] Jesus, just like this [image] here. Jesus showed the nail in his hand and foot. He spoke to me.
What did he say? I asked.
"Look, I really am Jesus." . . . I dreamt a lot. I told Assis [the missionary]: "God [Iri' Jam] spoke to me, Assis. I spoke to him in the dream." (Awo Kamip, conversation with the author, Negro River village, 2005)

Jesus's mediating position becomes clear in an observation made by Paletó, who once told me that when you die, you do not go to God's heaven but to the middle (*ximijain*), where Jesus resides, because "you cannot see God, if you do, you die. It's like a lightning bolt."

Another observation concerning Jesus, this time from João, a preacher, is interesting since it clearly situates translation in the body. Telling his congregation that the Bible was written by people who heard or dreamt the voice of God, he concluded, "But it was Jesus who translated the word of God completely."

Despite Jesus's importance as a mediator—recognized by the Wari' in the frequent references, in their prayers and church services, to him spilling his own blood to extirpate their sins—they very often treat him as a minor component of the Trinity, just like the Holy Spirit, following the guidance of the missionaries. An example of this hierarchy is found in the catechism booklet titled *Our Course in Ribeirão,* dated 2000, which on page 5 shows a graph formed by a circle with the name *Iri' Jam* in the middle in uppercase letters. Circling this name in lowercase are the words *Kote ka* (father) above and *Panxika* (his son) and *Tamatarakon* (his double) below.

Generally speaking, Wari' prayers address Iri' Jam directly in compliance with the advice set out in the same catechism booklet. When Jesus's name is mentioned, it generally emerges at the end as a complement to God's name, such as the end of the following prayer by the pastor Awo Kamip addressed to God: "Your talk is very good too. That is why all your things are good. Had you not been the first to be good! That is why you are God. We speak with much joy with you at night. Jesus Christ, amen" (church service, January 20, 2002, Negro River village).[14]

It is God the creator who has the power. As a young preacher said, "Nobody wins against God, no white person, or the devil, or the president." God possesses important knowledge, as the same young man reminded me, citing the end of the world as described in Mark 13:32: "But of that day and hour no one knows, not even the angels in heaven, nor the Son, but only the Father" (New King James Bible).

As with Jesus, prayers are addressed not to the "Holy Spirit" but to God, asking him to send his "double" to them, the Holy Spirit, who, lodged in their hearts, will enable them to comprehend the divine words. Earlier in the same prayer, Awo Kamip beseeches God: "Help us with your speech, Father, help us with the parts we don't understand. Your double/spirit [*tamataram*] does this. So we can comprehend all the things Jesus said in the past."

AUDIOVISUAL RESOURCES

Concerning "the problem of presence," the audiovisual resources offered by the missionaries made a strong impression on the Wari',[15] for whom images, like the voice, can originate only in beings who actually exist and who therefore possess bodies. As Xatoji told me in 1987: "On the radio one hears the true voice of God, in the house of Abílio [a missionary]. And [we] also [see] the true photo of him crucified: it's like real people!" The pastor Awo Kamip explained this:

> AWO KAMIP: We thought they were lying, but we heard through the radio and the boys picked up the Bible in Portuguese and saw. The prophets of the whites. There was a photo of them [*jamikokon*, "their double"]. All of them, Daniel, Ezekiel, Zechariah. Then we fully understood. "Ah! It's not a lie, this about Iri' Jam. He made earth, he made everything." . . .
>
> APARECIDA: Why didn't you know?

AWO KAMIP: Had he written for us.... We weren't aware of the cinema. You invented the cinema, translated the Bible into the Wari' language. The boys could see and say, "It's true what they say. It's on paper. We didn't come [exist] for nothing." (Awo Kamip, conversation with the author, 2003)

Even today, the oldest of the Wari', accustomed to photographs, CDs, television, and DVDs, treat the diverse images of biblical scenes that cover the walls of the Negro River church (and of the churches of the other villages) as if they are photos, and more than once they invited me to peruse them so I could comprehend that the biblical stories told by them during the service had actually happened. It is worth noting that all the prints have captions in English, and the images range from Adam and Eve to Christ's resurrection.

The same applies to the biblical films sent by the missionaries or bought directly in the city. The Wari' think that the people in them, like everything shown on television, are real, and that they are not acting but simply living their lives. Various times I tried to explain to them the meaning of an acted scene and about the work of actors and television script writers. But always in vain. Once we were watching a scene from a soap opera on the community television featuring a pregnant woman. In the previous day's episode she had appeared with a small belly, but this time it was enormous, as though she were about to give birth. I tried to argue my point one more time: "Look, how can a belly grow like that in real life, from one day to the next?" A woman immediately replied, "Do you think we don't know that you whites have medicines for everything? Of course you have a medicine for the belly to grow rapidly."[16]

The problem of invisibility was also eclipsed by the evidence of divine creation. The Wari' frequently use the verb *in ak* (to admire) when they address God directly, referring to their admiration for his power/force (*ka hwara' opa' wa*) and for everything that he created. This appears, for instance, in hymn 7, sung in the Wari' language at the beginning of a church service, called "Admiration":

We admire [*in ak*] you for your strength
For making [*kep*] all the animals
For making the sun, stars, and moon in the past
All the things that exist on earth.
I sing happily to God
Who is very strong.
... We are content with God
He gave us the means to live.

The question of writing (*ka xirao' wa,* design, as applied to the Wari' body paintings), cited as evidence of divine presence in some of the aforementioned narratives, is more complex. The activity is paradigmatic of the missionaries, distinguishing them at the outset. In his book of memoirs, Scharf (2010: 77, my translation) remarks that the Wari' identified the missionaries as those who "make designs on strange leaves." He continues: "Royal [the missionary] had the habit of always sticking a pencil behind his ear and a piece of paper or notepad in his shirt pocket to scribble down new words or variations in their meanings. . . . These instant annotations enabled our linguistic work to progress. In this way we obtained a good supply of fresh annotations that had to be worked on when we arrived home."

Initially such annotations, revealing the special powers possessed by the whites, aroused suspicion.[17] This appears clearly in Dick Sollis's account of the missionaries' initial difficulties in learning the Wari' language:

> One afternoon, a man fresh from the jungle spotted my Coleman lantern. With a puzzled look on his face he said, *"Kain wichi nain?"* Such phrases are, to a missionary language learner, like gold nuggets to a prospector! It meant, "What is it called?" We could now move ahead by questioning [in order] to gather the names of things—except for another major difficulty.
>
> They had become very suspicious of our writing. They seemed to think we were doing some form of witchcraft and would wrestle with us to get the paper and pencils away from us. We tried leaving the pencils and paper out of sight, but by the time we could then write down a language word or phrase, as often as not, we had forgotten it. But, ever so slowly, we gained their confidence, their language, and their esteem. (Taped message from "Dick" to the mission, Language School Fall Conference, 1983, cited in Johnston 1985: 249)

It is understandable that the Wari' initially associated writing with sorcery, given that the condition for the latter to be realized was knowing the victim's name: names were very often overheard during chicha festivals held between foreigners (from other subgroups), sorcerers par excellence. I presume that the initial interest of the missionaries in the name of things included personal names, which the Wari' use freely between coresidents in everyday life, which would explain why writing aroused such suspicion. With time and closer familiarity, however, these suspicions ebbed away, though the magical character of biblical writing was preserved, taken by the Wari' to be evidence of true occurrences, including the feats of God, Jesus, and their collaborators.

We also should note that the materiality of the written word predisposes it to being taken as evidence of actions, like God's other visible creations. As Keane (2013: 13) writes, "The palpability of writing can enter into practical responses to certain problems posed by immateriality."[18] As we saw in chapter 4, the Wari' also accentuate another facet of writing's materiality when they associate God's words—read by themselves or the pastors—with food, which constitutes an important factor in their efficacy. The evidence represented by writing, in particular by its paper support, is also used in differentiating themselves and the Catholics: "The Evangelicals do not have stones or statues to look at; Jesus's double only remains on paper [*pe e' nein papel jamikon Jesus*]" (Paletó, conversation with the author, Sagarana village, 2005). People who own Bibles and lesson books, even those who cannot read, usually take them to the services, though many never open them. Likewise, the pastors always keep a book open on the pulpit, which they stare at almost constantly even when they are not reading from it.

The materiality of writing provides the Wari' with a basis for adopting the perspective of the missionaries, concerning not only the "truth" embedded in divine words but also the false character of their own words—that is, their myths, as we saw briefly in chapter 2.[19]

When the pastor Awo Kamip told me that we first came from clay, I asked him why they had been unaware of this fact before. He responded, "Had there been writing for us!" Paletó's remarks on the discrepancies between their myths and the biblical stories emphasize the same point: "Had they known how to write.... The ancient ones lied. What the whites say is correct."

On another occasion, when I asked him why they believed in what the whites said, rather than what they had heard from their parents and grandparents, he said,

The ancient ones did not know how to write. The whites [*wijam*, "enemy"], they write. The very ancient whites wrote.[20] A woman became pregnant with Jesus. We spoke in vain: *tan tan na e', oro maho, taxi tari* [myths]. We were afraid of specters [*jama*], afraid of drowning. It was only when we heard here [what the whites said] that we realized things weren't like that. That is what we thought.... The ancient ones said that we went to the subaquatic world [after death], that we turned into white-lipped peccaries, that our double turned into a white-lipped peccary, that we emerged again.... They didn't know how to write. Since we became Christians, we eat hawks, owls, coatis, all kinds of strange food, anteater. "It was I who made all the animals," [said God]. (Paletó, conversation with the author, Sagarana village, 2005)

Notably the list of errors concludes with the question of the edibility of animals previously barred from consumption, which serves as proof of the veracity of the divine words. In any event, the assertion that Bible stories are superior to native myths because they are transmitted on paper is surprising owing to the apparent acceptance by the Wari' of a notion of truth that was foreign to shamanic knowledge, forever subject to questioning and controversy, as we saw in chapter 2. Commenting on the connection made by the Amazonian Wayãpi between written words and truth, Gallois (2012: 72, 77) suggests that the idea of truth disconnected from the relational context of the production of an event constitutes a change in native knowledge practices, a new and different element of the local epistemology.[21] As Assman (2010: 3) remarks, what world religions have in common is "an emphatic concept of truth. They all rest on a distinction between true and false religion, proclaiming a truth that does not stand in a complementary relation to other truths."

Among the Wari', various testimonies make evident the concern with the question of a sole truth, such as that of Antônio, a thirty-three-year-old preacher: "The ancient ones [hwanana] did not know properly. It was the devil [kaxikon jam] who hampered them so they would not hear the speech [kapijakon] of Iri' Jam. They believed in Pinom [the mythic figure]. Where is Pinom? He's never seen. But the earth that God created, the water, the fish, all of that can be seen. That's why it is true. That of hwanana is only a story, it's not true."

Today, especially during the church sermons, as we shall see in the next chapter, people refer to biblical episodes to explain everyday situations, just as they once did with myths. This also occurs in other contexts: for example, after being searched by police officers on the river while traveling to the village, Paletó observed that what happened was like what had happened to Moses, who escaped the soldiers with God's help.

However what appears to be involved here is not an absolute notion of truth but a relational one. By making use of the fundamentalist notion of truth to delegitimize non-Christian myths and knowledge, the Wari' appear to comprehend the importance of stating aloud before God that they share his perspective in detriment to others, as we saw in the previous chapter. Just as in the family context, the relation of affiliation, since it is not given a priori, is constituted by diverse actions, one of them being public recognition of the parents either through the use of the correct kinship terminology or through acts of affection and care. As we saw in chapter 4, the relation with God cannot happen without the relations among the Wari' themselves: when people pray, and especially when they read, they always do so out loud and close to other people who can hear. The idea of a private and secret relation with God, so important to the Evangelicals, is difficult to concretize in this context. The Wari' person does not contain a space for this (although, as we shall see later, it seems to be under construction).

The relativity of the truth associated with writing is also evident when we turn to school writing. The Wari' do not produce any written religious material: all of it is supplied by the missionaries in the form of printed booklets. Some people own a Brazilian version of the Bible. Actual Wari' writing is limited to the school, therefore, which is frequented by children and adolescents who, from the start of the 1980s until the mid-1990s, worked with national textbooks in Portuguese. Following the arrival of "intercultural education" projects for indigenous peoples, some of this material began to be produced by Wari' teachers, containing among other things mythic narratives (several of them extracted directly from my books, where they are translated into Portuguese). In contrast to the biblical/missionary writing, however, the school material lacks the same status as "truth." It can be discussed and questioned. We can conclude, therefore, that the power attributed to writing can be actualized only through a particular set of factors, the most important of which is its association with powerful beings.[22]

We should also consider the possibility of a "fluctuating reading" (Rafael 1993), disconnected from paper, as further evidence of the relativity of the truth associated with words. When I returned to the Wari' land in 2005 after a year away, my siblings, Paletó's children, came to tell me that he could now read: "Our father sees the paper completely" (*kirik pin nain papel kotere*). Curious, I went to ask Paletó, then in his seventies, entirely monolingual, and having never frequented school, whether he could read something for me. He responded by opening one of the Christian lesson books translated into Wari' on a particular page and began to read. Next to him, looking at the book, I perceived that he knew the content of each phrase, but that he was not reading since he used words that differed from those written on the paper. I understood therefore that the capacity to see the paper did not depend on learning to read, but on knowing the content of the books, which derived from regular attendance of the church services, listening to readings at home and everyday coexistence with other Christians.[23] As Kulick and Strout (1990) show in relation to the Gapun of Papua New Guinea, there is no conception of knowledge that is not relational or that does not imply the establishment or transformation of relations. Hence, for example, their disinterest in textbooks and general knowledge books.[24]

Although the Wari' had no knowledge of writing before their contact with the whites, the idea of an unstable writing, developed by Rafael (1993) in his analysis of the pre-Hispanic writing of the Tagalog of the Philippines, strikes me as interesting since it allows us to draw parallels with the notion of instability that I have been developing here. The author points to the essential difference between missionary and native conceptions of writing. For the seventeenth-century Spanish Catholic missionaries, writing could be independent of the speaker, so that "the soul's thoughts could be transported in the absence of the speaker's body." Its importance was seen to derive from its "double function of representing the voice (and with it, thought) and regulating the diversity of voices" (Rafael 1993: 43). For the Tagalog, however, who already possessed their own alphabet before the arrival of the Spanish, writing was completely subsumed by reading, which had a random character, with the same characters being associated with different sounds and meanings, depending on the reader. The term for writing, *baybayin,* "means to learn the alphabet and to spell a word, but it also refers to the seacoast, or the act of coasting along a river," such that reading is associated with floating "over a streaming of sounds elicited by the characters." Consequently the Tagalog had no interest in using writing to preserve texts, using bamboo and other perishable materials as their writing surface. The lack of any fixed correspondence "between script and sound" led the Spanish to classify their writing as illegible (47, 49).

Various other ethnographies show a similar apprehension of writing, incompatible with the transparency and univocity professed by the missionaries. Among some groups, such as the Biak of Indonesia, the fascination with the written word derives precisely from its incomprehensibility, which led them to valorize copies of the Bible in English, which they could not read but which proved effective in their divinatory rites (Rutherford 2006: 259).[25] For various other Pacific peoples, the interest in the written material of the whites resides precisely in what cannot be immediately uncovered in it—in other words, the content between the lines, containing the secrets of the cargo (Kulick and Strout 1990) or the precise details concerning the end of the world.

The Tagalog also placed particular value on the foreign, untranslated words that the priests include in their sermons, and which they "fish out," "arbitrarily attaching them to their meanings . . . as if they saw other possibilities in those words" (Rafael 1993: 3, 29). These examples point to the power associated with the marks of exteriority and the capture of new perspectives, which we examined in the previous chapter. In the words of Rutherford (2006: 259) on the Biak: "The booty they obtained through their encounters with missionaries included not only foreign things, but also foreign words. . . . The very strangeness of the evangelists' words was what gave them their potency and appeal." Or as the shaman Davi Kopenawa (Kopenawa and Albert 2010: 258, my translation) puts it, faced by the Evangelical missionaries, the Yanomami "were worried to hear these unknown words. This is why everyone began repeating them." Speaking of himself, Kopenawa says, "I was more curious about these white people's new words than those of our elders" (285).

It is interesting to note too that, in contrast to the Wari' case, in certain regions of Amazonia the written text is devalued precisely because it evinces a lack of power. In these contexts, some shamans, drawing a parallel between the written message and their visions, associate the former with the deficiency in the means through which the whites acquire knowledge, though the shamans likewise accentuate writing's materiality. In the words of Davi Kopenawa (50): "Unlike white people we do not need image skins to prevent them from escaping." In contrast to what the missionaries presume about the written word's capacity to transmit "fact" and "truth," for Kopenawa writing, unlike shamanic visions, leads precisely to errors: "I didn't learn how to think about the things of the forest by fixing my eyes on paper skins. I saw them for real" (51).

This involves a confrontational posture with respect to the whites, one that predictably enough is not shared by Christianized Indians, although Kopenawa's view indicates an idea of writing's instability that echoes the peculiarities of the *baybayin* writing of the Tagalog (Philippines) described by Rafael (1993). It also points to an important distinction between images brought by the missionaries—which include films and photos—and shamanic visions. Unlike the shamans, who can relate to the spirits they see, the nonshaman Wari' cannot relate directly to the objects of their visions, which, apart from the case of dreams, remain in a relatively inaccessible world: while the Wari' can see the characters in the films and TV soap operas, they cannot talk with them.[26]

To conclude the discussion on the question of presence, the verb *howa*, chosen to translate the Christian notion of belief, does not relate to doubt about the existence of something or someone, but to the trust held in the acts and words of someone close, especially kin. The following narrative is emblematic. Hatem told me that during the first contacts with the OroMon subgroup, a Wari' man named Tem Komerem, a member of the OroNao' who had joined the whites on the expedition, persuaded them to accept the injections to avoid becoming ill. "Let's go. If you refuse, you will die." So they accepted, because they trusted Tem Komerem: *"Howa iri' kon Tem Komerem."* Moreover "belief" must be shown through actions, as made clear in the words of the late Hwerein Pe e' when I asked him once whether he still *"howa non Iri' Jam"*: his response was: *Korom korom wet ina* ("I still enter [the church]"). This is also shown in the common use of this verb preceded by the verb "to speak" (*tomi'*), as in the expression *tomi' howa na manakam* ("his wife said something that revealed her trust in her husband").

As Robbins observed, an important difference can be noted between two possible predications of the verb "to believe" (2007b: 14–15; also see Pouillon 1993: 32; and Needham 1972). *To believe that* characterizes the modern conception of belief and makes no sense for many native peoples, such as the Urapmin and the Wari', for whom existing things are those that can be seen directly or indirectly.[27] *To believe in,* on the contrary, means to trust, such as believing that someone will carry out a promise, or spoke the truth, which is precisely the meaning of the verb *howa* for the Wari'. This difference is equally recalled by Veyne (2007: 68), who writes that the pagans did not believe that the gods of others were false, but that they were merely unknown or useless. The verb "to believe" became applied in the sense of *to believe that* only with Christian exclusivism.[28]

TOO MUCH PRESENCE

There is, however, a complex problem implied in the divine incorporeality professed by the missionaries, which conflicts with a basic premise of Wari' perspectivism—namely, that everything that has a body has a limited perspective. In lesson 7 of lesson book 1, where the missionaries present the incorporeal God, this quality is associated with the divine capacities of omnipresence and omniscience. According to the book, God does not reside in one place but in all—in the sun, the moon, the stars, the waters, in the lands of foreigners, including among ourselves—which is why he sees and watches over us (*win tuku napari*') and he follows us night and day: "He does not say: it is because my body [*kwere*] is very large that I am in all places. No! God is *jam* [*Jam na Iri' Jam*]." As the pastor Wem Karamain said during a church service: "He is *jam*. He has no body. That is why he knows everything." In the words of Paletó: "In the sky God sees everything, like the sun. Everything is written on paper. When *wari'* die, they arrive in heaven, God sees the paper and knows what they did."

As we shall see in the description of the church services in the next chapter, these divine characteristics are frequently mentioned in the pastors' sermons and the congregation's prayers, as well as in the hymns sung at the beginning and end of the services, including one sung in Portuguese by the children's choir, which says, "Careful little eyes what you see, careful little mouth what you say, careful little foot where you step . . . because the Savior is looking at you."

Given the Wari' insistence on attributing a body to God, transforming incorporeality into invisibility through the adoption of the term *Iri' Jam* equivocally proposed by the missionaries, it is unsurprising that they sought to associate the divine attributes of omnipresence and omniscience with this invisibility. This is what happened, for example, in the myth of the man who became invisible, referred to simply as *jam*, and who was seen in unexpected places—that is, in all places (potentially). As we have seen above, in the myth this unusual characteristic, which arises from his resemblance to the body of a dead person, *jama*, is associated with warrior and predatory capacities. This in turn takes us back to the question of God's association with the enemy position, discussed in chapter 4. As well as being objectified in aggressive actions by God, these capacities characterize the figure of the devil, who, as we shall see below, constitutes an ex-component of the divine dividual person.

Just as the Wari' attribute a body to God, Clifford (1992: 81) mentions the Kanak translation of the idea of divine omnipresence as "stretching" by a "God who is wholly long," suggesting a similar difficulty of conceiving an incorporeal being, which in this case becomes elastic.[29] In any event, as we shall see later, despite the cognitive efforts of the Wari' to give God a body (and not only via Jesus), it was impossible to shake off the particular strangeness that makes his body different from the bodies of humans and animal spirits. An invisible body, as the Wari' first conceived of God, could not remain so forever—meaning that one day he would become visible again, whether for everyone or for particular people, like shamans. Invisibility, therefore, derives above all from a provisional state, or a visual failure.

The tension between incorporeality and invisibility remains alive for the Wari', leading them, at least until 2008, to comment exhaustively, during church services, on the chapter from lesson book 1 concerning the absence of God's body, and at the same time, to use the term *body* to express the divine way of being, as we saw above. Here we can turn to the dialogue between a Wari' pastor and the congregation that took place during a service in January 2002 in Negro River village:

> PASTOR: He is *jam*. We do not know him. Has someone ever seen God? No. We don't see him. He is *jam*. Here is his speech. This is what we know. Has anyone ever seen God?
>
> CONGREGATION: No.
>
> PASTOR: We have never seen him. Have you all seen him? Did our ancestors see him? They didn't either. There is only his speech/word. What he says came to us inexplicably. He has no body. This is what he said, this is what he said. And we believe [*howa*] in him. He is *jam*. He has no body. Does he not see us too? He sees us. He hears us. He hears the bad things we say. He is Iri' Jam. He sees us fully when we do not like our coresidents. Does he not see us fully?
>
> CONGREGATION: He sees us.

Similarly another pastor, speaking during another church service that same year, said, "God knows. God knows everything that the person thinks. If we think right, he knows. If we think wrong, he knows." In Abrão's words: "When the church ascends to heaven, everyone has their place. The list is read. If they have sinned, they don't stay there, they're sent on the path to hell. It's no use doing things hidden from others, because Iri' Jam is watching." And as another man said in a prayer at a conference meeting in 2009: "You don't speak to us, you keep looking at us."

Let's examine another component of the divine person, who, like Jesus, has a body, although this body is like that of animals and affines. As I mentioned before, the Holy Spirit has a distinct status, considered not to be a component of the divine person per se but, just like the Wari' double (*jamixi'/tamataraxi'*), to be an objectification of his perspective and agency.

As the missionary Barbara Kern explained, the choice of *Iri' Jam* to designate God was intended to contrast with the term *kaxikon jam,* which, as we saw above, refers—at least in the current narratives—to the generic animal doubles not yet identified by shamans, and which the missionaries took to refer to the devil.

Lesson 4 from lesson book 1, which follows the lesson presenting God as *jam,* focuses on the emergence of the devil, Lucifer, and his followers, his expulsion from heaven, and God's creation of the "lake of fire," or hell. According to the book, these beings, also called *jam,* were created by God to work with him in heaven. This is why God is their owner, just as we are owners of the house that we make. Angels and demons

> have no body. They have no blood. They are *jam.* That is why they go anywhere, they enter all the houses at whim. . . . It is not that we don't see them per se. If they had a body. . . . They have no body, but that is not entirely like that. They appear for no reason, they imitate [*an xiho'*] people [*wari'*], they appear with a body the same as theirs [*win kwere nonon*]. There are some who imitate animals as well, who appear with a body just like theirs. (lesson book 1, p. 13)

Another meaning of *incorporeality* and *invisibility* is introduced here, given that, unlike God, these beings can become embodied in people and animals. This enables animals to reacquire an agency with human characteristics, something that had been removed from them during the act of divine creation. The text of lesson 4 adds that the good angels knew a lot, although less than God.[30] A hierarchy between these *jam* is introduced. In the following paragraph, I summarize the narrative.

There was a *jam* who was really strong. His name was Lucifer. God made him leader of heaven (*pawin*). The other *jam* called him "my leader." He obeyed God and worked with him (*taramaja,* a corruption of the Portuguese *trabalhava*), but one day he became proud (*xek xek pin na Lúcifer*) and said he was very good (*Awi tamana ina*). So he said to himself that he would take God's place (*Tomi'ak xukun na kem, pe tain maxikon Iri' Jam ta ak xukun na*), that he would be the leader, stronger than God. "It was Lucifer who had an outburst of anger/sinned [*karakat*]. There had been no sin, Lucifer was the first to sin." Various *jam* followed (*jao jao*) Lucifer. God therefore expelled them (*wixikao',* "spat") from heaven and made (*kep*) a great fire (*kote ne xe*) for them, which he called the Lake of Fire (*xuterem nein xe*). Recently the name of Lucifer changed and he became known as Satan. Others call him by different names. "In our language [*kapijaxi*'] we call him '*jam* who dislike us a lot' [*jam ko nok tamana napari*']. That's why we call him *Kaxikon Jam*" (14–16).

Until fairly recently, when someone was sick and this sickness was associated with eating some kind of animal or with hunting, the Christian Wari' would say that the devil "had entered" inside the animal, making it act in a vengeful way. As one man said, "It is the devil who stays with the animal double" (*Wiriko kaxikon jam ko toho nain jami karawa pin na*) or "There is no animal double. It is the devil who enters it" (*Om na jamikarawa. A ni kaxikon jam ko korom mao na*). Or that "[it is] the devil who enters our mouth, our head. Not the animals" (*Wiriko ko korom mao nain kapijaxi, winaxi. Om na xijein karawa*).[31] As an animal double, the devil also assisted the shamans; and, as an animal himself, the shaman was very often referred to as a devil in the Christian context. As the shaman Orowam once said to me, "The Wari' call me a devil [*kaxikon jam na pa'wari*']." And the late Wao Tokori, referring to the devil one time, concluded that "it's him, the shaman! [*wiriko ko tuku ninim!*]."

In contradiction to the intentions of the missionaries, who, as we saw in chapter 1 and in the translation of Genesis, claim that animals are not people, and as happens in various other ethnographic contexts,[32] the figure of the devil brought back the agency of animals that, in the Wari' case at least, had ideally been desubjectivized by divine creation. The animals reverted to acting as humanized predators, their *wari*' component restored by the devil. In the words of Antônio, a thirty-three-year-old Wari' preacher, in July 2007: "It is the demons that enter the animals, which is why the shamans say they live with the animals. When God created the animals, they had no thought ['heart']."

As a consequence, the Wari' became victims, reacquiring the prey part, *karawa,* constitutive of the dividual person.[33] I sometimes heard the Wari' say that the demon breeds them like people breed chicks, feeding and caring for them until the day they eat them. The transformation of the Wari' into prey by the devil is expressed even today in their conception of hell: as we have seen, the house of the devil is a place where bodies remain in a process of eternal roasting, like game animals that never free themselves from their prey state.

As in the Christianity presented to them by the missionaries, the relation between the Wari' and God is conceived in opposition to the relation with the devil, precisely as kinship within the local group cannot be conceived outside of the dialogue with animal subjectivities. This is clear in hymn 102, in the Wari' language:

> They beat on the door of my heart.
> I want to enter you, he said to me.
> Open the door for me, said the devil.
> No! Don't enter me.
> They beat on the door of my heart.
> I want to enter you, he said to me.
> Open the door for me, said Jesus Christ.
> Stay in my heart!

For the Wari' one of God's main attributes is his capacity to combat the devil and sin, as expressed in the hymn in Portuguese that the Wari' learned in the city: "God's power is fire, it is fire to burn sin. If you join this game, my brother, you will be transformed." This battle will end at the end of the world. In Abrão's words: "At the end of the world the trumpets will arrive with the angels to summon the dead Christians, who will revive and go [in body] to heaven. The non-Christians will remain dead. Then the devil will be captured. After seven years Jesus will tell them to descend to earth. Then they will kill the devil."

The opposition God/devil is made explicit in various prayers and comments, such as the following made during a church service in the Negro River village in 2002:

> Wow! The devil really doesn't want us to escape. He doesn't like us to accompany God. He says: Stay away from God!
> He dislikes all God's things. He really doesn't like God's things. That's why God's speech becomes incomprehensible to us [when we listen to what the devil says (in many of their prayers, the Wari' ask God to make them deaf to the devil's calls)].[34]

Or as Abrão remarked during our translation of the church service from January 20, 2002, which will be discussed in chapter 7:

> There are two: God and the devil. Both of them speak to us. It is the devil who messes with the person's heart and causes him or her to do bad things. It is the devil who messes with our heart. If I believe/trust in God, I become strong and I don't hear the devil. It is the devil who calls us to run to him. When a person calls the other, like when they invited Janio [Abrão's nephew] to drink, it is not a Wari' person who calls but the devil speaking through the Wari'. (Abrão, conversation with the author, Rio de Janeiro, 2008)

The catechism booklets make this opposition very clear, as in the Epistle to the Romans (lesson book 6, pp. 7–8), where Paul's conversion is described as moving from the devil's service to God's. Some pages later, the same lesson book returns to this dispute in the following terms: "When we didn't believe in Jesus in the past, the devil worked [*taramaja*] within us. We obeyed him ["we responded to him"]. We called him leader [*taramaxikon*]" (p. 15).

In sum, the devil's presence, by reconstituting the dividual character of animals, also reconstitutes that of the Wari', enabling their relations with God to be modeled on how children are consubstantialized by their parents—specifically through the opposition to animals, who attempt to make kin of these children, either by provoking their death through diseases, or more directly by abducting them, as in the cases related in chapter 2. Kin are made "out of others": in other words, the starting point of the kinship process is the innate mixture between humans and animals, meaning that humans must be produced through differentiation or "speciation" out of this continuum (Vilaça 2002a).

However, the relation between God and the devil is more complex. As we saw above in the biblical episode of the conflict with Lucifer and his departure from heaven, the devil is conceived as part of the divine person or, we could say, as a member of his kin group. Having been created by God, the devil lived in intense proximity with him in heaven, before rebelling and moving away, just like a relative who transforms into an enemy. As one man told me, "*Kaxikon jam,* Lucifer, was created by God, until he decided that he did not want God to be *taramaxikon* [leader] and thus came to earth to teach the Wari' to disobey." In the words of the late Wao Tokori, the devil imitates (*an xiho'*) Iri' Jam.[35]

And it is not only the Wari' who conceive it this way. Other Amerindian groups, too, see God and the devil in an analogous way, as related opposite terms. According to Fausto (2007b: 90), the Apapocuva (Guarani) claim that Nhanderu, the divinity associated with the Christian God, emerged from the darkness together with his antithesis, cannibal beings called the "Eternal Bats." Santos-Granero (2007: 68n2) writes that "in the Yanesha myth of creation God and the devil appear as rival classificatory brothers, and creation itself as the result of their interpersonal competition of wills." Among the Yanomami, the shaman Davi Kopenawa identifies God with the trickster Yoase (Kopenawa and Albert 2010: 492).[36]

This reading enables us to assert that the multiple divine person, expressed in the idea of the Trinity, has a dividual character for the Wari'. Although the

Trinity itself involves a hierarchical relation between God, Jesus, and the Holy Spirit, the relation between the Trinity, represented by God, and the devil, his animal (*karawa*) component, is oppositional. When the two sides are finally dissociated following the expulsion of Lucifer from heaven, the latter will reconstitute the human pole of animals, acting as a typical trickster figure by undoing the acts of the Creator—that is, by restoring the agency to animals that had been supressed by God. In this sense, as Leite (2013: 87–88) has shown, the role of the trickster Yoase in Yanomami mythology is to provoke a return to instability, precisely because transformation is an intrinsic part of the native cosmos; indeed, as we shall see in the description of heaven in chapter 9, its complete suppression causes the paralysis of this cosmos.

In the Yanomami case, therefore, as Viveiros de Castro (pers. comm., 2010) observed in reflecting on Leite's work, we are presented by something like a "mythology and a half," rather than two mythological complexes properly speaking. In the mythology of the creation of stable forms, which puts an end to transformability, the Yoase trickster figure—an equivalent of the Christian devil—brings back the world of transformations.[37] The mythology of transformation, therefore, encompasses the mythology of stabilization, inserting itself, in the latter, in the form of the devil, who inserts himself in divine creation, penetrating it with his enemy agency. In Wagner's terms (1975), therefore, the Wari' perceive the devil as the resistance posed by their own conventions to the differentiation (Christianization) that they actively seek to achieve. The innate world, where humans and animals are mixed, imposes itself on them again, despite all their efforts to the contrary.

However, this configuration has modified over the years, especially recently. Since the shamans have ceased their activities today, the references to animal agency through the medium of the devil have become much less frequent, especially in day-to-day speculations concerning diseases, although they remain present in the narratives on the devil elicited by my questions. As a consequence of the narrower and more exclusivist notion of humanity, the devil abandoned the animals and began to enter the Wari', making them act in a morally incorrect way—that is, as sinners. We shall return to this theme in the following chapters and the conclusion.

For now, I wish to explore the relation between God and the devil in the posthumous world.

When I arrived among the Wari' for the first time in August 1986, the post-humous world was located under the water of the rivers, and the Wari' referred to it simply as *paxikom* (bottom). The exceptions to this destiny were those people who had died as result of attacks by animal spirits, including shamans as a whole, who on dying would go to accompany the species with whom they had established an alliance while alive. A specific fate was also attributed to people killed in war, who would go to live among the enemy group, becoming one of them.

With Christianity, the posthumous world has gradually shifted from the underwater realm to the sky, where both heaven and hell are located. I say *gradually* because some people, over these years, have speculated that the ancient dead lived in the subaquatic world and only those who died after the introduction of Christianity, or after the revival, had gone to heaven or hell. In 1995, I even overheard a discussion on this topic, taking place without my own involvement, where one of the men present hypothesized the existence of two doubles: one of them, *jamixi'*, would go underwater and the other, *tamataraxi'*, would go to heaven or hell. Although this duplication stems from a Christian influence, given that the Wari' used to treat the terms *jamixi'* and *tamataraxi'* as equivalent, these multiple postmortem destinies implicitly contain the idea of plurality already present in the diagnoses sur-rounding a person's death. It was common for a death to be diagnosed simul-taneously as sorcery and as an animal spirit attack: as a result one person might say that a particular dead man was now underwater, since a shaman had seen him in the guise of a white-lipped peccary, the form assumed by the subaquatic dead when they climb up to the earth surface, while another per-son would say that he was living with the animals of a certain species. Considering that their eschatology was not constituted by dogmas but by the visionary experiences of shamans, the Wari' never perceived this as a prob-lem. In fact they would very often say, perhaps to free themselves from my insistent questions, that a certain dead person was now in two different places simultaneously. The idea of the plurality of souls or posthumous bod-ies implied by this assertion did not bother them in the slightest, though I heard it formulated explicitly only in the moment narrated above, where they were reflecting on the displacement of the posthumous world with the arrival of Christianity. Over time, the Wari' ceased to think about the subaquatic world, and today the destination of the dead is confined to heaven or hell, the latter as described in the previous chapter.

Despite the other transformations, an important change should be immediately noted: in contrast to the Christian conception that a person's posthumous destiny is determined by his or her actions during life—that is, by the individual's moral behavior—in the pre-Christian Wari' world the determining factor was the cause of death. As among other Amerindian groups (see Taylor 1996), this was always external to the person, whether caused by an affine, an animal double, or an enemy.

A brief description of the posthumous pre-Christian life will help us gain a better understanding of today's heaven. In the past, the dead person's double, *jamikon/jamikam,* headed to the subaquatic world, where he or she was received by Towira Towira, a being with enormous testicles. He would offer the visitor fermented maize chicha in the manner of the hosts during the *huroroin'* and *hwitop* festivals that were exchanged—especially the former—between people from different subgroups, the prototypical affines. Drinking the chicha implied the person's definitive death. After drinking, he or she vomited and entered reclusion, as the warriors used to do (according to some, only men did so).[38]

After the end of reclusion in the subaquatic world, the dead became young and beautiful, whether they died as children or as adults. All new arrivals headed off to the geographic area of their original subgroup, even if they had inhabited different regions during their lifetime. There they would meet kin who had died already. If a man had married in life and his wife had already died, he would meet her again and resume the marriage, even having other children. If she had not died, he could marry again and establish another family.

Life there is similar to the world of the living, therefore, albeit with some important differences. First, although the dead marry, have children, and even hold festivals between subgroups, they are finally free of the ills associated with affinity, though the existence of subgroups and their territories reveals that affines also still exist. There are no more fights, rivalries, or sorcery, though, and consequently they are immortal. The Wari' often say that the dead are all kin (*ka nari wa*) to each other. The other difference concerns the question of perspective. Indeed, although the dead perceive themselves as people and, in the subaquatic world, have bodies identical to those of the Wari', they are seen by Wari'—at least the nonshamans—only as animals, more specifically as white-lipped peccaries, when they wish to come up to the earth to eat other kinds of food and see their kin. When they approach, they are killed and eaten, which is not a problem given that, as the Wari' would explain to me, the dead at that stage are "completely animals." As I have noted in my analysis elsewhere (Vilaça 1992; 2000), one of the objectives of the funerary rite and the rite bringing mourning to an end several months later was to fix the corpse in the position of animal prey, an effective way of differentiating it from the living. Killed and eaten, the doubles of the white-lipped peccaries acquire a new existence in another body, returning to the subaquatic world.

As I stated above, though, over time life in the subaquatic world became less and less evident, especially with the disappearance of the shaman's function. Called devils by their Christian coresidents, the shamans became more and more marginalized until they themselves converted, exchanging the animal doubles for the company of Jesus. I was unable to hide my disappointment when I heard that Orowam, the last shaman of the Negro River, had abandoned his animal companions, who, he said, no longer even called him to come wander with them. I asked Orowam who would cure the sick now, and he immediately responded that the Wari' should pray to their God. Paletó, who was listening to us, was perplexed by my line of argument and accused me of not considering Orowam's well-being: as a shaman he had always been sick and tired, since he spent all his time walking with the animals. Now, though, as I could see, he was strong and healthy.

As Christians, today the Wari' say that the dead go to heaven (*pawin*, high up) or hell (*xe*, fire), both located high in the sky, generically named *pawin*. According to various people, the ancient dead, those who died before the Wari' became Christians, had gone to the subaquatic world, and are still found there, although others say that these people are in hell. The Wari' tell stories with different versions of the arrival of the dead in the sky. One of them says that on arrival they find a closed door, in front of which is placed a man (usually identified as Abraham) with a list, the *relação* (inventory), as they say in Portuguese, containing the names of all sinners. If the person's name is not on the list, the door is opened and he or she enters into heaven. Other versions, closer to the biblical imagery, speak of the trail in the sky dividing into two paths, one wide and clear, the other narrow and apparently overgrown. The first, easier path, leads to hell, and the second to heaven. In any event, this list plays a significant role in the everyday life of the Wari': they try to reverse their bad actions as quickly as possible, either by apologizing directly to the person affected and ensuring their forgiveness, or by confessing, so that their name is removed from the list.[39] I return to this point in chapter 8 when discussing sin and confession.

As we have already seen, those who do not enter heaven are led to a place nearby, where there is a lake of fire, the abode of the devil. There they are forced to dance "for no reason," and the fire, apparently not hot enough to roast them, makes their flesh rot and fill with worms—in effect, a funerary antifire (Vilaça 1992; 2000), since fire is, on the contrary, what used to put an end to the rotting of the corpse. In hell, though, people become eternal prey because they are never completely roasted. One of the principal ordeals of hell is the enormous thirst experienced by its denizens, and the refusals of their kin residing nearby in heaven to respond to their pleas for water. One time, when I asked Mijain why his wife, Hatem, had been baptized (by Catholics), he immediately responded, "To drink water in heaven." Paletó, on the various occasions when he tried to convert me, attempted, as my father, to make me share his perspective, telling me that he would suffer in heaven, where he would be forced to refuse my pleas for water. Explaining why he insisted on talking to me about God, he said, "Were you not my kin [*wari' ne,* "my people"] ..." When the Wari' catechize, they do not look to convince the non-Christian about God's existence, or about his capacities, but to highlight the suffering in hell.

This seems to be, however, the only unpleasant feeling experienced in heaven—or more precisely, the only observation that refers to kinship relations, experienced there back-to-front, or in negated form. People in heaven live in isolation, as caricatures of the Christian individual contained in the missionary message. We return to this question in chapter 9.

We can now explore how the church services constitute a central moment in the production of kinship with God, and among the Wari' themselves, through the affirmation in their prayers to God that they share his perspective rather than that of the devil.

SEVEN

Christian Ritual Life

God's power is fire, it is fire to burn sin. If you join this game my
brother, you will be transformed.

Hymn

IN CHAPTER 4 WE SAW that the Wari' comprehend love, which they
translate as "to not dislike," as the outcome of a process of supressing anger,
and that God was initially associated with the position of an affine-enemy,
identified with the mythic figure Pinom, but was later perceived as a strange
and disembodied creator with whom they should become kin. Wishing to
share God's perspective, especially with respect to Creation, the Wari' today
focus their ritual life on constructing this kinship with God, which involves
the Wari' in a morality characteristic of consanguineal relations. Church
services and other Christian rites are an essential part of this construction.

According to the accounts of the Wari', the first Christian ritual contexts
involved collective prayers under canvas tents set up in clearings close to the
villages. As we have seen in chapter 4, generalized commensality, which
includes members of other Wari' subgroups, set the tone for these encounters, which were possibly similar to the conferences of today that bring
together diverse villages.

My information on the details of these first rituals is scarce, since I did not
observe them, and the Wari' seldom make comparisons between Christian
practices past and present. I can only add that, according to them, at that
time baptism by immersion was performed and was similar to the baptisms
practiced today, and that the rituals held between subgroups—the chicha
festivals—were suspended, along with funerary cannibalism and warfare.

The main Christian rites today are the church services held in each village
four times a week—once on Tuesday evenings and the remainder at the weekend, when the services are longer and attended by a large number of people.
Public confessions occur during the services, and once a month the tithe
collection and the Holy Supper take place. There are also twice-weekly prayer

days, on Monday mornings very early and on Thursday nights, when people from the village gather for spontaneous prayers, spoken aloud, and for hymn singing. Twice a year the large meetings called conferences are held, uniting people from various villages. These will be analyzed in the next chapter, juxtaposed with the traditional chicha festivals they have come to replace.

Before turning to the rites, I wish to underline the fact that Christian activities are not limited to these collective rites. The Bible is read aloud at home, as mentioned in chapter 4, and family prayers before each meal are also common, in which the family gives thanks to God for the food they are about to eat. When my children and I were guests in Paletó's house in January 2005, prayers were given before lunch and dinner, in front of the pots, before the dishes were served by his wife, To'o. In one of these prayers, To'o asked for them to always have white people's food, and for God to protect me and my children, since he was the one who had told me to go to the village. On another occasion, Paletó asked, in one of his prayers, for my youngest son, André, then aged six, to be cured of the diarrhea that had left him too listless to move about.

In 2007 and 2008, I also observed meetings of a group of men and a group of women, held separately, in which people discussed biblical themes, but also everyday questions such as the jobs to be carried out, collaborations on work, and financial problems. There were also rehearsals of the choir composed of children and adolescents, though I never saw these for myself.

Before turning to the structure of the services, I shall quickly introduce the pastors and deacons, who organize the rituals.

PASTORS AND DEACONS

All the indigenous villages have their own pastors and deacons. The pastors are responsible for teaching the word of God, visiting believers and administrative tasks. The deacons, meanwhile, help the church leaders. Today there are around 700 Wari' Christians.

"The Light Still Shines," by Maria Tereza Montovani, missionary among the Pacaas Novos people, New Tribes Mission of Brazil

There are five pastors in the Negro River settlement, each responsible for studying and preaching from one of the lesson books.[1] According to João, who is a preacher but not yet a pastor, the books are divided up as follows:

lesson book (LB) 1, Joel; LB 2, Awo Tot; LB 3, Wem Karamain; LB 4, Xijam; and LB 5, Awo Kamip (see chapter 1 for the content of each book). Every weekend (services are held on Saturday evening and on Sunday morning and evening) a pastor leads the three services using his particular lesson book, choosing a chapter or two from the book to read and comment on. Read out slowly with constant repetitions, one chapter, which is around five pages, can last over the three weekend services. In addition to the pastor in charge, other pastors may make small readings and prayers at the end of the service.

The criteria employed to select these individuals are based on a small book produced by the missionaries, titled *How to Choose Pastors and Deacons: The Lessons of 1 Timothy 3:1–13,* dating from 2003 and, as explained on the first page, based on the series Building on Firm Foundations by Trevor McIlwain (2003). In fact the booklet is a long commentary on this Bible segment in which the selection criteria are clearly specified, compiled in the direct translation of verses 1 to 7 on page 20, which I summarize here: each church leader should have just one wife, should not follow his own desires, should think and behave correctly, should welcome everyone who visits his house, should not drink, should say only good things and not speak in anger, should not spend too much money, should take care of his children and wife (if he does not, how will he care for the church?), and should not be someone who has just started to believe (in God).

The same booklet discusses deacons in lesson 3, from page 26 onward, via a translation of Acts 6:1–6. Titled "The Institution of the Deacons," it examines the selection, by the disciples of the twelve apostles, of seven men who could give food to the widows (in the Wari' translation). The booklet then shifts to 1 Timothy 3:8–13, which deals directly with the selection of the deacons, whose qualities are identified as the same as the pastors', with the addition of specific instructions for their wives, who must behave well, not speak badly of others, and not tell lies.

Both the pastors and the deacons are, I was told, chosen by the missionaries (at the time, by the missionary Thomas, who lived in the nearby village of Santo André), based on information given by people of the village concerning their activities and behavior.[2] There are also preachers, generally young literate adults, such as Abrão and the above-mentioned João, who go up to the pulpit to read and comment on excerpts from the Bible, generally toward the end of the church service. If they are successful in their activities and have good behavior, they can become pastors. In all cases, the wives of these men—pastors, deacons, and preachers—are Christians and frequent the church.

In addition to the five pastors, there are three deacons on the Negro River: Mon, Joel, and A'ain Towa. Their functions during the service include serving people coffee, waking those who have fallen asleep, hushing those who talk, and offering bread and a grape-flavored beverage during the Holy Supper. According to Abrão, they also sweep the church and look after the sealed box in which the tithe is kept, which he explained as follows: "If we have money we place five or ten reais in a box in the church, which stays there. The deacon counts it. If we need diesel or cement, we take the money."

THE CHURCH SERVICE

The current Negro River village church was constructed in 2007 and 2008 in front of the river, next to the old missionary house, which today is occupied by a Wari' couple who were very close to the missionaries who had lived there. The church has a cement floor, wood plank walls, a front door, side windows, and a fiber cement roof. Inside are two rows of wooden pews, with about ten pews per row, separated by a narrow corridor leading to the altar, where a table and a pulpit are located on a platform raised slightly off the ground. Next to and behind this table are two benches, where the pastors and older men sit facing the congregation. On the back wall behind the table is a printed calendar, each page illustrated with a biblical verse in Wari'. The back wall and the two side walls are also covered with around twenty illustrations of biblical scenes arranged in chronological order, ranging from the world's creation to Noah, to Moses and the stone tablets, and so on, and ending with the crucifixion of Christ and the resurrection. The images are in color, and each has a small caption in English below; all of them are protected with plastic lamination. In 2002, two posters were displayed on the wall of the church building then in use, featuring phrases from Genesis: 1:1 and 1:31.

The Sunday morning services, the most heavily attended (I counted around 150 people in the church in 2007), are scheduled for nine o'clock. Around half an hour earlier, people begin to arrive at church, little by little, and continue arriving after the service has already started, which generally leads the pastor to comment that people's laziness is responsible for their being late. They usually arrive in groups of nuclear families: husband, wife, grown-up children, and infants. They sit together, since men and women are

FIGURE 8. Church, Negro River village, January 2008. (Photo by Dušan Borić.)

not kept separate, as happens in some native Evangelical churches, such as those of the Amazonian Koripako (Xavier 2013) and Palikur (Capiberibe 2007). People behave much as they do at home: mothers breast-feed their infants, children run around until the service starts, and those children who are sleeping lie on a sheet placed on the ground at their parents' feet, between the pews. People wear their best clothes, and those with shoes wear them to church. In the 2002 and 2003 services that I attended in the former church (an empty family house), when there was less access to televisions with images of urban clothing, I observed peculiar outfits, such as those of young women who wore skirts paired with just colorful bras, which they raised to feed their babies. More recently, they have begun to cover themselves with blouses.

The services have a basic, predetermined structure: hymns, prayers, a reading and sermon, and more hymns and prayers. They last around two hours in the evening, a little longer on Sunday mornings. It should be emphasized that this structure already existed in the services that I attended in January 2002—that is, soon after the 2001 revival—which reveals the solid prior knowledge that the Wari' had of Christian practices, even though they had not performed them in the form of large-scale collective rites since the start of the 1980s. In other words, everything was ready for Christian life to be resumed: translations, lesson books, bibles, rules for choosing pastors and

FIGURE 9. Church service, Negro River village, July 2014. (Photo by the author.)

deacons, abandoned houses that could be used as churches, and missionaries living among them (though no longer on the Negro River).

The church service begins shortly after the scheduled time with the singing of three hymns from the hymn book, each repeated two or three times.[3] Since all the hymns in the book possess translations in Portuguese (the two versions are printed side-by-side), one of the repetitions may be in Portuguese, and these, along with the occasional reading of a Bible verse by a child or adolescent, are the only moments of the service during which Portuguese is spoken. Hence, in 2007, for example, Leila, around six years old at the time, standing alone at the front of the church, took the microphone and said, first in Portuguese and subsequently in Wari': "Matthew 24:30. Good news for you: Jesus will return."

In some of the church services the first hymns are sung by two different choirs, one of children and the other of youths. In 2007 and 2008, the songs were also sometimes led by the daughter of the pastor Awo Kamip as she stood at the pulpit with a microphone. All those present in the church sing together, since they know all the hymns by heart. In the case of the choirs of children and youths, the hymns are rehearsed during the previous week under the supervision of a preacher. During the service of January 20, 2002, which I filmed in its entirety and transcribed with the collaboration of Abrão, the choir of children sang three hymns in Wari' and then sang a hymn on divine omnipresence (mentioned in the previous chapter) in Portuguese. The latter hymn says, "Careful little eyes what you see, careful little mouth what you say, careful little foot where you step ... because the Savior is looking at you." During the 2007 and 2008 church services, the hymns were accompanied by an electronic keyboard, played by a young man, and a guitar.

Sometimes, before the hymns, one of the pastors announces everyday news concerning, for example, the number of bags of manioc flour stored and ready to be sold, or someone who is ill and could not come, or a family who went upriver to collect Brazil nuts, or even someone's successful hunting trip. Sometimes such news is given at the end of the service, as when Paletó, neither a pastor nor a preacher, went to the pulpit to announce that I had given him cartridges (ammunition) to distribute to everyone, explaining how many there were of each kind.

After the three hymns, one of the pastors goes to the table or pulpit, carrying his lesson books, which are generally kept protected in a plastic folder. His first action is to place the folder on the table, take out a book, and open it. The other pastors, even if they do not speak on the day in question, always carry plastic folders with their lesson books too. Generally the pastor summarizes what will be said in the service and then prays out loud, addressing God directly, sometimes referring to the Creation, with requests for God to share his strength with them and to allow them to hear his words well. Everyone listens to this and to the other prayers that follow, pronounced by people from the congregation, with their eyes closed and heads lowered. At the end, the name of Jesus Christ is mentioned and everyone says "Amen" in Portuguese.

At the service held on January 20, 2002, on a Sunday morning, the pastor Awo Kamip begins by explaining,

> We shall hear what Peter, with God [Iri' Jam], said in the past. God's double [*tamatarakon Iri' Jam*, "the Holy Spirit"] cured the ancient ones. He cures us today too. The Holy Spirit cures us today too. God stays with us here too. He gives us our happiness, he gives us physical well-being. So that you think of the ancient ones from long ago. The Holy Spirit exists today too. This is what God's speech says. Be good. We shall speak with God. I shall read [*noro*, "look/see"] here [the book]. I shall read a little.... We shall close our eyes [day sleep].

Below I reproduce Awo Kamip's prayer, mentioned in chapter 6, which, like the others that ensued, reveals the importance of the affirmation before God that the Wari' collectively share his perspective of Creation, testifying to the process of consubstantialization under way, as would happen between kin, especially between parents and children:

Our father God. We admire [*in ak*] you. We admire your strength. Today is the day that we admire you. My siblings know this. You who gave us the capacity to admire. Wow! We are surprised by you! When we have this capacity, then we admire you. You help us. We admire you for the animals you gave us. This is what we say to you on Sundays. It is for this, for the animals you gave us, that we admire you. For your strength a long time ago, for your speech. Your speech that remains on the earth. This is what made us happy. It also gave us kindness. . . . We see everyday how the sun is good. The night is good, we sleep. The rain is very good, the water is good, fish is good, our children are good. You gave us our children who are content with us. Wow! we say to you. Wow! I say to you. For all the animals that we see and eat. There are animals that we do not eat, others that we do eat, who live in the forest. Their sounds spread through the forest and we like to hear them. There are many fruits today. All the fruits of the forest that are good to eat, and those that are not good too, which are eaten by the animals. The animals live, we live too. Wow! we say to you for this. You are very good. Your double [*tamataram*] is good, your body is good, your son is good. Your son's blood is strong. Your speech is also very good. This is why all your things are good. Were you not the first to be good! This is why you are God. We speak with great happiness to you at night. Jesus Christ [Jesu Cristo]. Amen.

Next, another pastor, Awo Tot, prays:

Our father God, you see us when we speak your speech today. We are very content with you today. We admire you for all the animals you give us. We admire you for all the animals we eat, and for those we don't eat. So that you know that we admire you very much every day. We also admire your son, who you gave us. We admire your double [*tamataram*], which is very strong, we admire your speech, which is also very strong. . . . You also know all the other Wari' who are admiring you today.

And pastor Xin Xoi:

We are very content with you when we hear your speech today. This is your speech that we are hearing today. There is no other speech for us to hear. You are very strong. Wow! we say, for your word, about the animals that you gave us on the earth. Had our ancient ones admired you for the animals in the past! We knew nothing about this. It is you, we say, wow! for your strength. For your force in the past. Were you not the first to have strength! This is why we eat, because of the animals you made in the past. This is why there are fruits that we eat, *kapixin, tatarana*. Many fruits that we eat and that quench our thirst. We admire you for the water that you made, where we also bathe. Our siblings from Santo André, from Tanajura [other villages] are saying this too. . . . Jesus Christ is also good. Amen.

After the prayers, the pastor begins to read from one of the lesson books, interspersing repetitions, comments, and explanations. As we have seen, the Wari' do not produce any written Christian material: all of it comes from the work of the missionaries in collaboration with native translators. More recently they have begun to incorporate songs by Christian singers, taken from CDs bought in Guajará-Mirim (like the one excerpted in the epigraph at the start of this chapter), and at least one person, Abrão, has begun to compose hymns in the Wari' language that are based on biblical tracts or on hymns from the hymn book and slightly modified.[4]

At the service held on the morning of January 20, 2002, which I have been commenting on, after everyone's prayers the pastor Awo Kamip, who is already at the pulpit, begins the sermon, sections of which I reproduce here, especially to show the interspersion of reading and free speech. As I mentioned in chapter 1, the lesson books intersperse explications by the missionaries with biblical verses marked in bold. At the moment of reading, however, these are not differentiated by the pastor-speaker, so the words of the missionaries merge with the biblical text and, as we shall see, with the speech of the pastor himself.[5] As he reads, he follows the words with his fingers and continues to speak freely, his hands placed on the book so as not to lose his place in the text, which has the effect of unmarking the difference between what he reads and his own words. I also observed that, as found in Evangelical services in many other ethnographic contexts, direct parallels are drawn between the biblical episodes being read and contemporary everyday life.

READING: Avoid [resist, do not respond to] Jesus!

SPEAKING FREELY: Look at this. Let's avoid Jesus. That is what they said. Let's avoid Jesus's speech to everyone [orowari', "all people"]. Let's speak no more of him. Let's avoid Jesus, they said. Let's speak badly of him among ourselves. Stop narrating Jesus's speech! That's what they meant by avoiding him.

READING: Avoid Jesus, they said. Avoid Jesus who is so good, who worked for you before, who was chosen to be chief by our father God [kotere Iri' Jam].

SPEAKING FREELY: Avoid the one who was chosen, they said ineffectively. The one who was chosen by our father God. That's what they said to

FIGURE 10. Pastor Awo Kamip (*center*) in the new pulpit, with deacon A'ain Towa on his right (note the biblical figures on the wall and the tithe box on the floor), Negro River village, July 2014. (Photo by the author.)

them. Today there are those who also tell us to avoid him. Those who do not believe. They tell us to avoid him. Our people are resistant too. Look, they are not here [in the church]. That's what the people of the past were like too: why do you believe for no reason? [they asked the Christians]. As though being a Christian was good! they say. They talk nonsense [they talk for no reason]. The people of the past were like that too. Avoid Jesus, they say today too. This isn't good [being a Christian]. It is not good to approach Jesus, they say here too. This is what is good, this is what is good [referring to bad things]. Like the children of Cain who spread everywhere. How old was Cain? Do you think his things have been lost already?

CONGREGATION: No!

. . .

SPEAKING FREELY: That's how it is my brothers and women. If our coresidents talk to us [badly of Jesus] it is as though we do not understand what they say. No. No, Jesus is the one who is very strong, my younger brother, you women should say to him. We cannot be angry with each other. God sees us. It is he who tells us to be content with each other.

Awo Kamip preaches for another ten minutes (at which point approximately one hour has passed since the beginning of the service). Awo Tot, a younger pastor who is around thirty-five years old, climbs up to the pulpit and begins to preach from lesson book 2, item 3, page 1, which lies on the pulpit in front of him. Before starting to read from the book, however, Awo Tot speaks of the importance of what we could translate as an "examination of conscience," which, as we shall see in chapters 8 and 9, comprises "seeing one's own heart," which is opaque to other people.

> Let's look at our own hearts. If we look at our own hearts, God sees us. Aah! This is my true people [*wari'*]! [God says]. We don't see other people's hearts. Our older brother Mon [one of the deacons present] is the one who knows his own heart. We do not know what he thinks [*ka koromikat nukun*]. Look at our grandfather Paletó. We do not know his heart. We do not know how his heart is in what he thinks. We do not know the hearts of others. God knows. He is the one who knows.[6]

Awo Tot then starts to preach, reading from the lesson book:

SPEAKING FREELY: I'm going to speak just a little. I'm going to speak about how people [*wari'*] suffered. The Israelites with the pharaoh. The Israelites suffered greatly. It was good, but then a new pharaoh came and wow! Then the Israelites suffered greatly. They worked a lot. They could not sit down. . . . I shall tell the start of the history. It's like this.

READING: The pharaoh said, "There is something good to be done."

SPEAKING FREELY: This is what he thought. This is what he passed on to the bad pharaoh.

READING: Listen to this. He spoke very badly, they said bad things to God. [It was] the devil [*kaxikon jam*].

SPEAKING FREELY: Is that the way [body] of the devil today?

CONGREGATION: Yes.

SPEAKING FREELY: Were the devil not strong too. But he is not that strong, because he did not acquire life alone [it was God who gave him life].

READING: He talks a lot about the things that he wants. He lies a lot to us, he dislikes us a lot. Look at Exodus 1:8–11. "After a long time, a new chief entered, Egyptian."

The pastor continues to read and explain about the enslavement of the Jews/Israelites by the Egyptian pharaoh, until he mentions again the devil:

READING: What is happening with the pharaoh? Who is the one who whispers his thought?

SPEAKING FREELY: Who whispers the thought of the pharaoh?

CONGREGATION: The devil!

SPEAKING FREELY: It is the devil who whispers there. It is the devil who whispers to the pharaoh. He whispers a lot to the pharaoh. He is the one who gives thought to the pharaoh.

READING: He [the devil] detests [really dislikes] God, he detests the Wari' too.

SPEAKING FREELY: The devil does not like anyone [no *wari'*]. He dislikes God, he dislikes the Wari' too.

The alternation between reading and speaking freely continues as the pastor explains that the pharaoh wished to kill all the Israelites because the devil knew that the "true people of God" (*iri'wari' nukun Iri' Jam*) would be born among them, and that God had promised to save the Israelites. The figure of Moses, therefore, merges with Jesus; my brother Abrão, who helped me transcribe the discourses in this service, observed that "this is why even today Israel has earthquakes and wars. Here there are none. That is because God was born there [Iri' Jam, referring to Jesus]. And the devil is very strong."

The sermon also emphasizes the unpredictability of the end, whether through individual death or the end of the world. In the sequence of Awo Tot's discourse on the killing of the Israelites provoked by the devil via the pharaoh, he explains that the people who say, "Ah, I shall believe [*howa*] next Sunday," may be struck down by illness and die before then by the work of the devil, who has no wish to increase the number of Christians. At the end of his sermon, Awo Tot takes the calendar made by the missionaries, where each month is illustrated by a Bible verse in Wari', and observes, "God gave us 2002. Our ancient ones did not reach 2002. We reached 2002 by chance. We don't know about 2003."

Around one hour and twenty minutes after the start of the service, Awo Tot finishes his talk and hands the microphone to Valdiperes, who is a little younger than himself and still a preacher. Since it is already late and everyone looks tired, sleepy, and people are scratching their heads, Valdiperes apparently realizes that his own talk would be poorly received, even were he simply to read "a small verse," the expression used to refer to an excerpt of the lesson books. Disappointed, he uses his time on the pulpit to complain about the distribution of time during the services, suggesting that they sing fewer hymns at the start, and that the pastors be briefer. Pastor Xin Xoi follows him to the pulpit, saying that the problem is that people arrived late in the morning.

FIGURE 11. Calendar with Bible verse on the church wall, Boca village, July 2014. (Photo by the author.)

The service ends with hymns followed by prayers. The first of the hymns, number 53, sung in Wari' and later in Portuguese, is interesting, since its theme is the heart, a direct translation here of "soul," as we shall see in chapter 9.

Preacher Fernando's final prayer is also interesting, since it resumes the theme of creation and the Wari' surprise in response, but also since it asks God to give them the capacity to comprehend his words, just as children depend on their parents to teach them to understand the meaning of things. Unlike the sermons and the "historical" and moral teachings addressed to the other Wari', prayers—like hymns—are addressed directly to God (and indirectly to his son, Jesus), highlighting the Wari' interest in sharing his point of view.

Portuguese: "My Soul Is Peaceful"	Wari': "I Am Content with Him in My Heart" (*kirik te inon pain xumu ka*)
My soul is peaceful.	I am content with him in my heart.
I have a heavenly joy, a pleasure in saying.	It is him, Jesus, who stays with me.
I shall walk.	I shall follow him to heaven.
To the heavenly city.	I follow him contently.
Refrain: My soul is peaceful. I have a heavenly joy, a pleasure in saying. My soul is peaceful.	(Refrain:) I am content with him in my heart. It is him, Jesus, who stays with me. I am content with him in my heart.
I shall sing in heaven.	I shall sing in heaven.
A hymn of victory.	I shall sing the leader [God].
(Refrain).	(Refrain).

[God] give us comprehension so that we can understand your speech. You see all of us. Help those who believe [*howa*], give them comprehension. . . . Father God [*te Iri' Jam*], we admire you for all the animals that you made on earth, that you made and gave us, all the animals that we eat, all the fish that we eat, all the fruit that we eat. We know how you are strong. There is no other "invisible" [*jam*] for us to admire. Only you. They killed you, they nailed you. Water spilled, blood spilled. That is why we admire your son, who you gave to us. The son of God is very good. Amen (prayer by Fernando).

THE TITHE

On the first Sunday of each month, the service includes the offering of the tithe. A basket or box is placed along the side of the church, on the floor, in which people leave money, generally two or three reais (around one U.S. dollar) or products like flour, salt, sugar, or even meat and fish, which will be bought by other people and the money handed to the church. All the money is kept in a box with a key, for which a deacon is responsible (at the time, Joel). This money is used for repairs and improvements to the church, such as the purchase of a sound system, generator, and lights for use in the services. On a normal Sunday, the total collected tithe is around thirty reais. In the run-up to a conference due to be held at the Negro River village, however, the tithe money increased and some individuals donated ten or twenty reais. Not everyone offers money to the church every month; this only seems to become a public issue, remarked upon by the pastor during the service, when some essential job becomes necessary, such as repairing the roof.

Once a month, a nighttime Sunday service is devoted entirely to the Holy Supper, where, on an evening in July 2007, the Wari' read part of lesson 65 from lesson book 3, which contains the translation of chapter 14 of the Gospel of Mark, on the consecration of bread and wine in the Last Supper.[7] On this occasion they consume pieces of bread made by themselves and a beverage made from packets of powdered, grape-flavored drink mix bought in the city. Although they do not read it from the start, lesson 65 revolves around the actions of Judas, instructed by the devil, and how Jesus knew what was happening, since he is God and thus present everywhere.

The Holy Supper is a special service, distinct from the others, with an even more fixed structure. During the service two specific hymns are sung (numbers 73 and 16), which, like the spontaneous prayers that precede them, specifically focus on the Last Supper and Jesus's sacrifice for humankind. Usually trays with small pieces of bread, made during the day by women, are already placed on the table at the start of the church service. Other trays are laden with empty mugs or glasses, which will be filled with the grape drink once the powder has been mixed with water in a jar.

The ritual held in July 2007 begins with a prayer by the preacher Awo Serrapilha:

> Because they killed your son in the past, father. That's why we are doing this here. That's why you told us to do this on earth. You said that afterward we would do this with you in heaven. That's why we say the name of your son very often. That's why we say his name happily every day. If only we knew the day that your son will return. That's what we say to you. That you see us when we are good, you see our good heart. That's what we say to you. You are very good. If only we were good like you. Son of God. Amen.

The prayer is followed by hymn number 73, titled, in Wari', "Like True Maize Cake" and, in Portuguese, "Bread of Life."

While the hymn is still being sung, the deacons Joel and Mon begin to distribute pieces of bread to specific people, who remain seated on the benches. Those who receive the bread keep it in their hands or even in their pockets. The last to receive the bread are those who sang on the dais where the table and pulpit are located. Those who do not receive the bread continue singing without any sign of surprise, indicating that they had known beforehand that they

FIGURE 12. Preparing the bread and the small juice glasses for Holy Supper, Negro River village, 2014. (Photo by the author.)

HYMN NUMBER 73

Portuguese: "Bread of Life"	Wari': "Like True Maize Cake"
Bread of life, bread of the heavens, my Jesus is heavenly bread.	Jesus in our heart is really like the maize cake that we eat [*Ak iri' kapam' ka kao' iri'na Jesu pain ximixi' ka'*].
Bread that gives happiness, peace, and light to the heart.	Our hearts no longer ache, and we shall soon be strong.
The blood spilled by Jesus is divine, it is effective. This blood to the heart brings strength, love, and life.	That's what Jesus's blood is like, which he bled for us. The darkness/dirt of our heart ends with Jesus's blood.
Come Jesus, bless me.	Come Jesus Christ.
Fill me with You, Lord,	Stay in my heart.
Since I desire to serve You and honour You, my Savior.	I shall work [*taramaja*] with you, Jesus, and call you leader.

could not take part. Only those who had already confessed their sins could participate.

Awo then asks everyone to close their eyes, and he reads Mark 14:22: "Jesus took the bread [*kapam'*, 'maize cake'] for them to eat. 'We are happy with you, father, because you gave us bread,' Jesus said. He left and gave it to them. 'Here it is. This is my body,' he told them [*Ma' ta. Je i ka kwere ta ak kokon na*]." (In the New King James Bible, this is translated as: "And as they

Portuguese: "Sing Praise"	Wari': "His Blood Washed My Heart" (*Hohok napa' pain xumu kicon*)
Oh, come Christians [*crentes*] and sing praise to Jesus,	Sing contently for Jesus Christ, Christians.
Who was killed on a cross for our salvation.	Jesus who died for us on the wood in the past.
His blood spilled, and washed me clean.	Jesus also spilled his blood for us.
Jesus's blood washed me, washed me.	He washed our hearts.
Jesus's blood washed me, washed me.	Jesus's blood washed my heart.
Happy, I shall sing praise to my King,	I sing happily for him.
My Lord Jesus who saved me.	My heart is clean [white].
	"I shall stay with you," Jesus Christ said to me.

were eating, Jesus took bread, blessed and broke it, and gave it to them and said, 'Take, eat; this is My body'".)

Awo then says, "Eat!" and they all eat their bread in silence, their eyes still closed.

Afterward, Antônio, another preacher, asks them to close their eyes and pray about the blood of Jesus: "God our father, we are very content with you this night.... You died in our place, for our sins [*karakat*]. That's why we escaped [*witan*]. Your blood ran in the past. That's why we remember you this night. That's why we talk to Jesus Christ, son of God. Amen."

After the prayer, while the glasses of grape drink are distributed to the same people who received the bread, everyone sings hymn 16, titled "His Blood Washed My Heart" (*Hohok napa' pain xumu kikon*). According to Abrão, this hymn, along with the one that preceded the bread, are the only ones sung during this special service. On receiving the glasses, the people hold them securely in their hands without drinking.

Antônio then reads Mark 14:23–24; the version in the Wari' language is much longer and more complex than the versions in Portuguese and English. The latter simply reads: "23: Then He took the cup, and when He had given thanks He gave it to them, and they all drank from it. 24: And He said to them, 'This is My blood of the new covenant, which is shed for many'" (New King James Bible). The Wari' version is as follows: "So he took the drink recipient. 'We are content with you for having given us too this fruit juice for us to drink, father.' He gave it to them. They all drank. 'This is my blood,' he said to them. Perhaps my blood will run [future irrealis] if I die in your place, if I die in the place of everyone. In the place of many people. When my blood runs, what my father said would happen will come to pass, so that you can escape.' Drink!"

Everyone drinks and closes their eyes. Antônio concludes with a prayer telling God that they are there doing what he ordered so that they may perhaps drink in heaven. This prayer is followed by two hymns in Portuguese, not from the hymn book but learned from the whites in the city. According to Abrão, the missionaries do not like these hymns. One of them repeats the phrase "With Jesus's blood, Satan is defeated. He is defeated, Satan is defeated." The second, already mentioned in the previous chapter, repeats the following stanza: "God's power is fire, it is fire to burn sin. If you join this game my brother, you will be transformed."

In line with the nonacceptance of the dogma of transubstantiation by the Evangelical missionaries, the metaphorical quality of the relation between body/blood and bread/juice is marked in the lesson book's explanations, interspersed between the Bible verses, as well as in the questions at the end of lesson 65 from lesson book 3. Question 7 (page 173) reads, "What does the bread that Jesus broke imitate [an xiho']?" The reply follows: "It imitates my flesh, he said. That is the way the angry/sinners [oro karakat] will perhaps cut my flesh." Question 8 refers to the blood: "What does the fruit juice that runs here imitate?" Answer: "It imitates my blood, he said. Perhaps the angry/sinners, who do not like me, will make my blood spill."

The Wari' say the same when talking about the Last Supper. In the words of Paletó in 2007, "Jesus says that the juice imitates blood, it is as though you drink my blood. If you drink here, you shall drink in heaven." And the bread, I asked? "It is my body. It is like my body. I shall wash your hearts with my body and with my blood." When I asked Abrão directly whether the bread was *like* Jesus's flesh or actually his flesh, he immediately replied, "It's like flesh; it's to remember Jesus." The pastor Wem Karamain, during one church service, observed in 2005, in line with the content of the lesson book, that the similarity between bread and flesh derives from the broken, ruined state of both: "They beat Jesus, they broke his flesh [into pieces]. That's why it's like bread." It is, therefore, a rite of commensality, between the Wari' themselves and between them and God, who offers them bread and juice, which combine with his words as part of feeding the Wari' and thus producing kinship between them.

However, in the verses in Wari', and even in Portuguese, taken from the Gospel of Mark read during the service, the adverb "like" (ak), which defines comparison, is absent, suggesting metonymic continuity rather than metaphoric similarity. This undoubtedly poses a problem for the missionaries who—obliged to translate the biblical text literally on principle—must undo this continuity in their own explanatory text. As a consequence, though, a double message is maintained: a metonymic text and a metaphoric gloss, reinforcing the ambiguity of the missionary message.

While the Wari' share the metaphoric conception of the missionaries concerning the Holy Supper, they also share, as we saw in chapter 4, the idea of transformative blood, since it was precisely the blood, equally invisible, that transformed a dead enemy into a consubstantial of a killer by penetrating his body; in the same way, blood makes Jesus an important mediator in the relations between God and the Wari'. However, as I pointed out in the same chapter, these coincidences mask a crucial equivocation: the starting point of the process of consubstantialization is enmity, which makes God and Jesus originally enemies, and the Wari' a collective of killers and, therefore, of predators. The Wari' predilection for the hymn exalting the war against Satan, even though unauthorized by the missionaries, reveals the warlike aspect involved in the ritual. Placing themselves in the predator position is, as discussed earlier, one of the central objectives of the Wari' in adopting Christianity. As I already suggested, this amounts to a properly indigenous version of redemption.

One final point to mention concerning this ritual is the emphasis on the heart as the place of the transformation effected by blood, which, in the case of the killer, is distributed throughout his body. In hymn 16, the term *heart* is present only in the Wari' version, highlighting the central place that this concept began to occupy in the invention of a seat for the relation between God and the Wari', and of a notion of a person endowed with an inner self, as we shall see in chapter 9.[8]

NEW CONVERTS AND BAPTISM

In some church services, those who wish to become believers, and who have conversed previously with the pastors, climb up to the pulpit to address the congregation directly. During a service on a Sunday evening in July 2007, four adolescents, two men, and two women, rose to the dais and stood still, looking at the congregation. The oldest of them, holding the microphone, said, "I am going to believe/trust [*howa*] in God, my brothers," while another said that he was going "to believe/trust in Jesus," and another said that "there is no other *jam* [invisible] to end our sin/anger [*karakat nexi'*]."

One man amid the congregation said loudly that they must "truly believe," and another added, "All is fine with our nephews." Next, each of the adolescents took the microphone and read a prayer that had been written previously. One of the preachers then took the microphone and spoke about divine creation. Everyone began to sing and rose to walk toward the new converts to welcome them in Western style, shaking their hands. The older women hugged them.

The hymn sung on this occasion was number 39 from the hymn book, which says, "It is good to be a Christian [*crente*]. It is good. It is good on Monday, Tuesday, Wednesday, Thursday, Friday, Saturday, and Sunday [all weekdays spoken in Portuguese] too."

Baptism does not happen immediately after the declaration, since the ceremony, involving a collective meal, has to be prepared in advance. I never witnessed a baptism ceremony, and my information is based on the accounts of missionaries and the Wari'.

According to Barbara Kern, the first baptism took place in 1969, in Pitop, soon after a group of people from there had gone to the missionaries' house and said they believed/trusted (*howa*) in God. By 1971 another three baptisms had taken place there, and another three in Lage village. On the New Tribes Mission of Brazil website (www.mntb.org), the missionary Maria Tereza Montovani stated on October 2, 2011, that around twenty baptisms are performed per year.

Paletó told me about his baptism, held many years earlier. The day after he went up to the church pulpit to say that he "trusted in God," he returned to the same place to state, in front of everyone, that he would "bathe with God" (*ja' ta kom ina ta kon Deus*). The pastors Wao Xin To and Wem Parawan then sang a hymn stating, "We remember that you died for us, [we remember] that they were pitiless when they killed you in the past." Afterward they went to the river, where he entered, fully clothed, up to the waist. Two pastors, Wao Xin To and Awo Kamip, held each of his arms and pulled him backward into the water, submerging him completely. At this moment, Paletó said, a hymn was sung that speaks of the death of the old double (*jamixi'*) and the birth of a new one. The person, just before entering the water, repeats that he or she will "bathe with God." Afterward everyone went to the church and sang. Paletó's eyes were closed. They said to him: "May you always have something to eat. . . . Amen." He then opened his eyes. Xin Narao made food, and before eating they prayed for help for all their "siblings." That night, they returned to church for the service. Another time, Paletó told me that the baptism had occurred about three years back, and that the person who had submerged him had been the pastor Joel. In any event, according to him, people are baptized only once in life, and those who have already undergone the rite just watch and sing during the other baptisms.

Pijim told me about a baptism performed in 2003, in Piranha, a village on the middle Negro River, involving various people, including the young adults José and his wife, Maria Luisa; Samuel and his wife; Ronaldo and his wife, Orowao Kawara; Tarcísio; André and Janaína (daughter of the pastor Awo Kamip); other single young people, all of them residents of Piranha, or of the Negro River village, downriver, or of Ocaia village, situated upriver. This was when Pijim's daughter Maisa, aged around twenty, married with children, was baptized. The ceremony took place on a Sunday morning soon after the church service. As in Paletó's account, two men held the arms of each person, all of them clothed, and submerged them one by one. They returned to the church soaked, and the congregation greeted each one, saying, "Be strong with God" (*Hwara' opa' kon Iri' Jam*). Afterward the pastor spoke a little; everyone sang and then left for a collective meal. On this occasion, Pijim said, they killed a chicken.

The bodily transformation involved in this bathing became evident in an observation made by Paletó, when we were talking one day about conjugal betrayal. According to him, the reason why two women we knew had engaged in extramarital sex was incomplete baptism: when they were immersed, the tops of their heads had been left exposed (their hair was dry).

Two other important Christian rituals, confession and conference, are examined in the next chapter, which deals with ritual transformations and their moral effects.

EIGHT

Moral Changes

My father God, help me control the evil gaze of my eyes. Give me
the capacity to not have evil eyes, help me.

Prayer

IN THE PREVIOUS CHAPTER we examined the structure of the church
services, the main and most frequent Christian ritual activity of the Wari'.
There we observed the recurrence of themes examined over the course of the
book, such as the importance of divine creation for the Wari', the construction of generalized consanguinity out of affinity, and the establishment of
kinship with God, mediated by the commensality of the Holy Supper's words
and food and by Jesus's blood. This new relation must be made explicit in
their prayers spoken out loud to God, showing that they share his perspective
(rather than the devil's), similar to what happens within the relation between
children and their parents. As we saw with jaguar abductions, the fact that
animals, like the devil, are involved in an eternal dispute with parents for the
Wari' implies that sharing perspectives must always be made explicit to ward
off any suspicion of metamorphosis taking place.

Simultaneously we can observe comments that indicate an interiorized
version of the self focused on the notion of an invisible heart hidden from
everyone else. Likewise, there is another type of action undertaken by the
devil, one focused less on the subjectivization of animals and more on the
affinization of the Wari'—that is, on exposing the failures in the process of
generalized consanguinization, which correspond to their activities as sinners. We shall return to this topic in the next chapter when we examine the
emergence of an alternative notion of self among the Wari', one that approxi-
mates the inner self present in diverse analyses of Christianization.

The analysis of the religious services also reveals the importance of these
rituals in the constitution of Christian morality, and we could note the
centrality of the moral discourse in the sermons.[1] Abrão's reply when I asked
why they read the Bible is revealing: "So we can know what you can and

cannot do, because there are so many things we can't do. They read: you cannot steal, you cannot be proud with new clothes. It places a barrier to thought [*Tao' kaho nain ka oro ka koromikat ak wa*]. Lula [then the president of Brazil] does not walk alone, his security guards make a barrier to protect him from thieves. [It is the same for the Wari'.] They just think of good things."

Abrão gave the example of Tiago, a resident from the Negro River, who went to hit those who had beaten his brother, José Carlos, at a football match. The pastor Awo Kamip stopped him, saying that Tiago did not know how to see the Bible, because one cannot become angry. They had to understand that if this happened, God wanted it so.[2]

During one service, the pastor Xijam, talking about divine omniscience, listed some of the condemned behaviors: "He sees us completely, he hears us completely. Hadn't he known us in our hearts. It is good that we stay content, siblings. Don't dislike each other, he told us. It is the word of God, siblings. He doesn't like you to be angry with each other. . . . He doesn't like us to steal, either. That is what it is like, the body/way of God's word." In the moralizing discourse of a pastor in another service, sins were once again listed: "With God, you respect [*respeita-se,* in Portuguese] everyone. You respect other people's things. You respect the things from our swiddens. If they plant potatoes, papaya, maize, pineapple, respect them. But this is not done any longer. Lately it is improved a little. Before they were stealing petrol from other people's tanks."

MORALITIES

While the profound difference between Pagan and Christian ritual lives seems clear, the same does not apply when we compare Pagan and Christian moral codes. According to Rivière (1981), in one of the pioneering studies on Christianization in Amazonia, morality was for the Trio one of the points of agreement between the different "symbolic systems": "The sins against which the missionaries preached are those listed in numerous passages in the New Testament, and include such things as adultery, fornication, uncleanness, lasciviousness, strife, sedition, idolatry, witchcraft, sorcery, hatred, anger, murder, drunkenness, revelling, orgies, and so on. All of these are features of Trio life, and even if they did not regard them as sins they did recognise most of them as potential sources of disharmony" (Rivière 1981: 8).[3]

The same is found among the Koripako of northwestern Amazonia. The book of catechism in the Koripako language, elaborated by a missionary from the New Tribes Mission, Sophie Muller, lists the following sins under item 36: "Do not deceive, steal, drink alcohol, kill people, prostitute oneself, say bad things, desire another man's wife, desire another woman's husband, worship idols or shamans" (Xavier 2013: 553, my translation). The similarity between the acts in this list and acts traditionally condemned by the Koripako is evident when we compare the list provided by Xavier: selfishness, avarice, sloth, envy, lack of self-control, curiosity, and excessive sexuality; these were held responsible for diseases within the "logic of the ancient shamanic traditions" (407).

In some cases this seems to be the viewpoint of the natives themselves, who, like the Wari', as we discussed in chapter 4, see Christianity as an instrument of pacification, capable of eliminating anger and the rivalries responsible for internal ruptures. According to Capiberibe (2009), the Palikur conceive religious conversion as the start of civilized life. In the words of one man: "We were the wildest Indians of the region, nobody could tame us. At that time there was a lot of disunity, much fighting, the Palikur lived scattered, nobody could unite us, not even the SPI, or the army, the only one to succeed was the gospel" (Nilo Martiniano, Kumenê village, 1997, in Capiberibe 2009: ch. 5, p. 8, my translation).

Gallois (2012: 73, my translation) comments on the perspective of a Wayãpi man concerning the similarities between native and Christian moral codes. According to the author, A. observes that in both cases one must "speak well, calmly, unaggressively, only saying words that can help the other, strengthen the other." A. also insisted on explaining that only those who had not stolen, murdered anyone, or struck their wives would reach heaven.

In most of the cases studied, the continuities tend to relate exclusively to what we could call moral codes, which, as Foucault (1990: 266) argues, may remain very similar in the context of ethical transformations, such as happened in the transition from Greek to Christian morality. Robbins (2004: 216–219) provides an excellent summary of Foucault's discussion of the components of any moral system, which served as a guide for my formulations below. According to Foucault, a moral system is composed of two basic elements: codes of behavior and "forms of subjectivation" (Foucault 1990: 29) or "ethics" (Foucault 1997: 266). The moral codes are lists of prescribed and prohibited behaviors, like those for the Wari', Trio, and Koripako, noted above, while forms of subjectivation are more complex, related to how "one ought to form oneself as an ethical subject" (Foucault 1990: 26). The formation of the ethical subject, for its part, is determined by four components: (1) "ethical substance," the part of the person that primarily determines his or her moral conduct: intentions, desire, behavior, and so on, (2) the "mode of subjection," which makes the person recognize his or her moral obligations: divine law, reason, and so on, (3) "ethical work," the work that one must do to constitute oneself as an ethical subject, through "technologies of the self," and (4) the "telos," "the kind of being one aims to become by acting in a moral way": pure, immortal, and so on (Foucault 1990: 26–29). Citing Foucault, Robbins (2004: 217) recalls that as distinct elements of the moral system, the code and the forms of subjection "may develop in relative independence from one another" (Foucault 1990: 29), also noting that some systems are focused more on the code and others more on the forms of subjection (also see Laidlaw 2013).

Robbins (2004: 218) writes that, in terms of codes, the Urapmin maintained a "legal code" similar to the Christian code, though they abandoned the two "taboo codes." In relation to the components of the other part of the moral system, the changes there, too, were significant. In terms of ethical substance, however, the author recognizes that the focus on the person's inner self already existed among the Urapmin, and that, unlike what occurs among the Wari', as we shall see, "Christianity did not need to invent the subject in Urapmin."[4]

The transformations relate above all to the other components: ethical work and telos. In relation to telos, the failures to constitute oneself as a good person assumed unusual dimensions in Christian life, determining not one's punishments during life, like those meted out for breaking taboos and laws, but one's entire posthumous fate (Robbins 2004: 219).

But it is in relation to ethical work that the most serious problems exist. Robbins suggests that, in the traditional Urapmin system, although the "will" was dangerous it had an important place in the constitution of social relations and was, ideally, balanced with obedience to rules ("law"). In the Christian world, however, the will was clearly condemned, making it impossible for the Urapmin to constitute themselves as ethical people in the traditional way, placing them in a constant state of conflict, which they associate with sin.

Central to understanding this conflict is the fact of different cultures— Urapmin and Christian—being governed by distinct and opposed values: the former by relationalism and the latter by individualism, especially relevant when we consider the central concern of the Urapmin with salvation, which, in the Christian world, is strictly individual. Robbins (2007a: 300) argues that the coexistence of opposite values creates a notion of moral life focused on freedom of choice, when "people become aware of choosing their own fates." With Christianity, the Urapmin began to live in constant moral conflict, forever examining and reflecting on their actions, even the most quotidian, to know whether they had sinned or not (305). The solution, always partial and provisional, has been sought in new rites offered by Christianity for constituting the ethical subjects, especially through possession by the Holy Spirit, which depends on one's leading a good Christian life, one that includes confession and participation in church services (304).

As we shall see below in discussing the traditional moral system, among the Wari' too the moral code was relatively well preserved under Christianity, with an emphasis on the condemnation of anger, adultery, and theft. Forms of subjection became transformed, as in the case of the Urapmin, in particular the ethical work accomplished through the adoption of new technologies of the self, especially the Christian rituals of confession, prayer, and Bible reading, enacted in church services and beyond.

PRE-CHRISTIAN RITUAL AND MORAL LIFE

Given that the sphere of morality coincides with humanity, in the pre-Christian world the Wari' constituted themselves as moral people through the establishment of appropriate relations with animals and with other Wari'. The importance of the procedures related to hunting and diet show the imbrication between the morality internal to the Wari' and the morality linked to their relations with other humans. In other words, although the morally correct action was essential to the stabilization of a properly Wari' humanity, it did not exclude relations with animals.

In the case of animals, a set of food taboos and table manners had the effect of preventing predation, in this case involving the revenge of the animals against Wari' hunters or members of their families. Animals had to be treated with respect in general: there could be no messing about with their corpses or speaking ill of them. It was also essential for prey to be roasted and eaten quickly. Immortal, the animals would return to their houses after being eaten completely, and would even ignore the predation, telling their own relatives that the injuries to their bodies (caused by the arrows) had come from getting scratched in the forest. When, in 1987, fifty white-lipped peccaries were killed at one time on the Negro River, various people became sick with diarrhea. The shamans diagnosed the problem, saying that some peccary heads had remained for days on the smoking grills, provoking the peccaries to exact revenge by shooting the Wari' with arrows.

Generally speaking, before being roasted, prey (only those species with a potential double and who thus are human) had to be examined by shamans, who would remove annatto dye, babassu palm straw, and other body adorn-ments from their corpses, as well as the remains of food. This practice was intended to avert the danger of eating the animal in its human, decorated version or, in the case of removing the foodstuffs, of becoming a commensal of the animal, which would imply identifying with it.

Even with animals that were still living, care needed to be taken. Shamans would admonish children who played in the river, saying that although they saw that as water, it was actually the house of some animals (fish and pecca-ries, the latter being the dead Wari'), who might become annoyed, causing them to surface and attack people with arrows.

However, when we specifically consider the food taboos, we can conclude that they referred less to direct relations with animals than to the relations between the Wari' themselves. Parents with small children were prohibited from eating armadillos, anteaters, and birds of prey, among other animals, because these animals would attack their children, causing urinary retention and constipation, in the case of the mammals; or they would squeeze the head of a newborn with their claws, in the case of the birds. Given that no parent of a newborn would eat these species, a baby's sickness immediately revealed marital betrayal, since the sexual partners of the father and mother would not remember to respect the taboos, and their actions equally affected the children. In the diverse curing sessions that I saw during my initial field research, the shamans, usually working in pairs, would make long moralizing discourses to all those present, saying that people could not eat such and such an animal during particular phases of their lives (in the case of some animals, this meant throughout infancy, while menstruating, after childbirth, and in warfare reclusion). A shaman worked to remove traces of the animal from a sick person, including fur, adornments, and food, while at the same time his double negotiated with the animals of the forest for the return of the sick person's double (*jamixi'*), which had already gone to join the group of ani-mals, taking them to be kin. It was also said that the shaman, himself an animal, would prey on the animal causing the sickness, which was why the jaguar-shamans were particularly effective curers. Since illnesses are usually manifested through fever, the verb for shamanic cure is *kep xio,* literally "make-cool."

As counterpredation and the consequences of violating food taboos suggest, animal aggression was also conceived as a reaction to a failure to care properly for kin, as if the animals acted as guardians of a typically human morality. A common effect of this animal "supervision" is abduction, described in chapter 2, frequently attributed to a prior family conflict or the abandonment of a child by the parents, after which the child is attracted by the animals to live with them. Adequate care by parents involves, of course, commensality, provided by the sharing of food: meanness and usury are heavily condemned, both internally and by the animals themselves. All large game was partly distributed by the hunter and his wife to close kin. Any failure in this procedure could provoke the revenge of the animal and the consequent sickening of the hunter or his close kin.

Here we can identify an important dimension of morality—namely, the interdependence between internal and external relations, with the predatory powers of animals governing the behavior between people. As I remarked earlier, the kinship between humans was situated amid a dispute with animals, such that a failure in intrahuman attitudes would lead to the relations of identity with animals. Moral deviations are a route to dehumanization, replicated in the Christian world through relations with the devil.

However, in addition to the control exerted by animals through their predatory power, there were internal forms of control over deviant attitudes, the most serious of which was aggression between kin.

RITES OF MORAL CONTROL

Along with the shaming and gossip that are commonplace forms of moral control among indigenous peoples, specific rituals exist for the resolution of internal conflicts, including club fights and "death" by excess of fermented chicha, the latter of which usually takes, place in the festivals held between subgroups.

The chicha festivals and club fights mark the clear separation between affines and enemies. Although both are groups with which an a priori rivalry exists, only enemies can actually be killed, with arrows, while affines are the target of milder forms of aggression and symbolic death through chicha.

People say that it was the red macaw who taught a man getting ready to shoot a coresident how to use the war club, explaining that arrows should be shot only at enemies. The relation between the club and the bow reproduces the relation between affines and enemies: the first is a pre-bow, not yet ready for a string to be attached, just as affines may become enemies. Killing another Wari' with arrows is considered an immoral act, and accounts of its occurrence always observe that the attacker tried to hide the fact.

There is the well-known case of a man who, in the past, along with his lover, killed the latter's husband, after which they disposed of the corpse on a mountain. Enraged, the dead man's kin made the man shoot his lover dead with arrows, before shooting him. By treating a Wari' as an enemy, they (the lovers) made themselves into enemies and were treated as such. Another case of this type of killing is recounted, in which the men responsible secretly tried to eat the dead man's body (just as enemies are eaten), and the smell of roasted Wari' flesh, which Wari' perceive as unmistakable, revealed the crime.

Another well-known case is that of a man who killed the child of a single mother with arrows, since the boy, starving, never stopped crying. The man was not berated, since the children of single mothers were not considered properly human. However, when he became Christian many years later he was forced to confess the act as a sin, accepting his guilt out loud in front of everyone, the way in which confessions were made at the start of the Christian experience.

CLUB FIGHTS

An example of internal relations, the club fight is an event involving a group of both men and women, though only the former fight while wielding their clubs, which should strike the head of the adversaries, provoking light bleeding but no serious injuries. Generally, the starting point is an accusation of adultery, followed by the husband's aggression against the wife.

Sometimes this accusation begins with the illness of a child of the couple, arising from the infraction of a food taboo. Since it is easy to prove that neither the father nor the mother has eaten the animal in question, the infraction is inevitably blamed on a lover of the wife, who, as mentioned earlier, would have the power to affect the child (although in theory a lover of the husband has the same capacity). After striking his wife, the husband may choose to go to the lover's house and strike him on the head with his club.

In both cases the kin of those attacked—fathers, uncles, brothers—take their clubs and strike the assailant. Then the kin of the latter arrive, sometimes coming from other villages, gathering before leaving to attack the group of men who beat their kinsman. The women stand next to their kin, trying to separate those fighting, and treating any wounds. I never observed a fight, although they still happened during the initial period of my fieldwork: indeed all the houses had, stored in their roofs, one or more clubs for the explicit purpose, as one young man told me, of "striking people on the head." The impression one would get of such fights, judging by the photos shown by Von Graeve (1989: 71–72), is one of general confusion, with clubs raised in all directions and various people with bloodied heads.

The Wari' recount that after this kind of fight, they would talk rapidly to extinguish whatever anger might have remained. This is the *tomi' xio,* literally "talk-cool," although the fight itself is the crucial moment of cooling down. The Wari' typically say, "He struck, didn't he? So it ended [the anger]." In the words of Abrão: "Before, when someone was angry, his heart would writhe, he would strike with a club and it ended. The person became calm" (the verb used here refers to an animal's lowering of its raised fur). This is a moment in which, as happens in funerary cannibalism (Vilaça 1992; 2000), the affines become differentiated within an ideally consanguine group, revealing the instability of the consanguinization produced through the masking of affinity or, in other words, the constitutive incompleteness of this process. As we saw in chapter 4, participation in these fights is the reason given in most cases of having abandoned Christian life in the past.

MURDER BY CHICHA: THE FESTIVALS

Like the club fights, any acts of meanness, theft of women, and other immoral acts could be punished by a ritual "death" by fermented chicha (maize beer, *tokwa*). The myth of the invisible man, narrated in chapter 6 in discussing the term *jam,* begins, as we have seen, with an act of meanness on the part of a "grandfather" who, having killed a tapir, did not invite his grandchildren who lived in a nearby village to share it. Knowing that they were enraged by his attitude, the grandfather invited them to a chicha festival, in which they were punished with excess drink. Here we can note that this did not constitute a punishment for being mean, but was instead a punishment for the grandchildren's explicit hostility to a kinsperson. The grandfather then killed the people made unconscious by chicha and used the bones of their arms as drumsticks. Witnessing this, the survivors organized an armed expedition to the man's village. His stinginess provoked a war, and this evinces the constant risk of enemization of kin, defining the limits and reversibility of the process of producing kinship, a risk that is also revealed in the acts of sorcery and poisoning.

In the usual festivals this type of killing did not occur; only a symbolic or temporary death took place, since falling unconscious is also referred to as a death. In these festivals, people from distinct subgroups would divide up and take the positions of hosts and guests. I did get to witness some of these festivals in 1986 and 1987, and it seems that they were the last held by the Wari', which shows that their social life was already undergoing change, even if they were not Christians at that point.

In the most elaborate of those festivals, the *huroroin'* (the only type I did not see), a man from the host subgroup would go to one of the villages of the guests to summon them to the festival. There he might be subjected to some forms of punishment, such as being covered in clay or forced to drink maize beer in excess, if the residents had any available. Subsequently the women from the host village would begin to make large quantities of maize beer, deposited in a large container made from a hollow trunk stuck in the earth. There the beer fermented for two or three months, with the guests counting the number of moons to calculate when the beer would be ready. They arrived without warning, via the forest. The men blew the long flutes called *huroroin'* while hidden behind a screen of leaves. The women would sit on the ground and, one after the other, play a small clay-and-rubber drum, the *towa*, performing songs learned from the ancestors that tell of mythical events and themes related to animals, such as the songs of a particular bird. Meanwhile pairs of male hosts would take turns playing a drum made from two sections of a tree trunk and suspended from a tree.

The male guests would enter the village, still hidden behind leaves, and destroy houses, breaking stakes and roofs. They would display sexual desire for their hosts' wives, behaving as animals, predators (as was already evident in their jaguar or snake body paintings), crawling and sniffing the women's legs. Although these acts provoked laughter, the visitors would be punished (the Wari' use the verb "make the same") by the offering of excessive amounts of maize beer, which would make them vomit and, after a time, collapse unconscious on the ground. The hosts would express their joy, saying, whenever a guest collapsed: "I killed him." At regular intervals, the male hosts

FIGURE 13. Guests dancing at a *tamara'* festival in 1986. (Photo by the author.)

would go to the forest and approach the guest women, carrying the sticks they had used to play the drum, and simulate the sexual act by inserting them between the crossed legs of the women.

At the end of the festival, there would be an inversion of roles, and the male guests, by now awake, would offer what remained of the beer to the hosts with aggressive gestures of explicit revenge. However, the main inversion, or revenge, would occur not in this festival but in the next one, when the guests would assume the role of hosts.

An important point to mark in these festivals is that hosts and guests avoided using consanguine kinship terms between themselves, even when some of them were effectively kin. Instead they used terms of affinity, especially "wife-taking brother-in-law" (*nem*), which they avoided using on an everyday basis, when the affinity internal to the local group is masked. The foreigners (members of other subgroups, kin or not) are prototypical affines,[5] which is why they act ritually in an aggressive way, and why they are legitimately punished with excess beer, provoking their "deaths." As becomes clear in the treatment of the person chosen to announce the festival in the other village, revenge does not depend only on acts that occur during the festival, because the relation between affines is marked by a latent rivalry that justifies the punishments administered without provocation.

FIGURE 14. Hosts offering chicha and food to guests at a *tamara'* festival in 1986. (Photo by the author.)

One myth makes clear that the offering of fermented chicha connotes punishment. A man, Hwijin, had sex with his older brother's wife. The older brother, enraged, invites him to drink chicha in his village. Confronting Hwijin face-to-face, he says, "I was just angry with you. I didn't hit you over the head because of what you did with my wife. I'm merely filling you with beer" (see Vilaça 2010: 146–163).

The festivals also played an important role in marking time for the Wari'. Festivals held in specific, named villages, permeated life histories as a way to

FIGURE 15. Hosts dancing at the end of a *tamara'* festival, Tanajura village, 1986. (Photo by the author.)

situate moments of a person's life. Another important temporal guideline was the alternation between the part of the year when they lived in the villages and the part when they trekked through the forest, hunting and gathering fruits while they waited for the planted maize to sprout. During this period, they calculated the time through the fructification of particular plants.

Returning to the question of assuaging anger, we can conclude that this depends on its collective display through acts rather than words, although the latter could succeed the acts, as in the case of the talk-cool after a war club fight. Moreover, nobody would ever assume responsibility for performing an illicit act suggested by others, but would instead blame an external agent, such as a lover, who for his part would seldom assume the responsibility attributed to him. With Christianity this role was taken up by the devil, who, interiorized, led people to inappropriate actions. I also note that a person was never denounced in public, as occurred at the start of Christian life. In the words of Paletó: "In the forest we never told the husband that the woman had betrayed him."

Although obeying moral codes and performing rituals for assuaging anger offered clear paths to the constitution of ethical subjects, these acts were no guarantee against metamorphosis and death. Animals could act unpredict-

FIGURE 16. Jimon Pan Tokwe and Xijam playing the log drum at a *hwitop* festival, Negro River village, 1993. (Photo by the author.)

ability, wishing to make new kin among the Wari', just as club fights and chicha festivals could worsen tensions rather than resolving them. The Wari' feared sorcery, as well as collective poisonings, all of them caused by foreigners, often perpetrated after a festival. By putting their victims in the position of prey, these aggressors were considered just as immoral as those who killed with bows and arrows.

It is important to note that the rituals are actions that have not only a moral effect but also an ontological effect, constituting a key means of inverting quotidian action—that is, of producing the innate world of alterity and difference (Wagner 1975: 93). The innate world produced by means of the new Christian rituals is the world of identity and fraternity, as we saw in the previous chapter, and as we shall see next while examining the conferences.

NEW FESTIVALS: CHRISTIAN CONFERENCES

As I mentioned in chapter 4, the beer festivals of the past, where affinity was made explicit, and where anger and revenge were performed, were replaced by the biannual three-day "conferences" that reunited foreigners from several subgroups, who are then made into brothers and sisters through sharing and commensality and through prayers to God.

In July 2005, I spent a day at a conference in Lage Novo. Gathered there were representatives from different villages. Most of those coming from the water villages—to use the Wari' expression for the inhabitants of the shores of the Pacaás Novos and Negro Rivers, most of them OroNao', OroEo, and OroAt—slept in hammocks and on mats in the school classrooms. Those who had close kin among the hosts, most of whom were OroWaram, OroWaramXijein, and OroMon—as was the case of To'o, Paletó's wife, who is OroMon—slept with their families in their relatives' homes. This also applied to the majority of the inhabitants from Ribeirão, the village closest to Lage.

According to what Abrão told me when we talked about another conference, also held in Lage Novo village, in 2009, the hosts sent an invitation by letter via boat or car to each village. The letter made clear that the invitation was limited to "two pastors, two deacons and their wives, two teachers of children [catechists] and two singers per village." The limit, Abrão explained, was due to food availability since it had to be provided by the hosts, although they asked for donations in money from the guests on the first day, which enabled them to buy chickens and even cattle.[6] Predictably, restrictions in numbers are not respected, and it is common for many more people than expected to arrive, which generates veiled complaints among the guests themselves about the lack of food. Sometimes the subject is broached publicly, but indirectly, like when one guest, Jimon, in his speech from the pulpit at the 2009 conference, observed that they had come to Lage not to eat but to learn. The same applies to the prayer spoken out loud by the pastor Awo Kamip from the Negro River village on the same occasion: "We don't know what we're going to eat. We're not worried about that. It's you [God] who gives us food. We have no idea where the food will come from. Help our siblings not to worry or feel sorry for us. We admire your word [and not the food]." The words of the New Tribes missionary Valmir on this topic, supporting the local inhabitants, channel the question to the equation between the food and the word of God discussed in chapter 4: "What kills the hunger of our soul [*tamataraxi'*] is the word of God."

Along with the Wari', all the missionaries available at the time, and sometimes one or two visitors, who are introduced to the Wari' on this occasion, attend the conferences. Present in 2005 along with Valmir, who lived in Lage with his wife, Fátima, were the couples Thomas and Claudeliz (from Santo André) and Apolônio and Seila, who had lived in Tanajura and were now retired. Attending the July 2009 conference in Lage were Valmir and Fátima, Thomas and Claudeliz, and Tereza (who was then living in Lage), as well as the visitors Hélio and Felipe (from Manaus) and Pedro Paulo, married to Fátima's sister.

In 2005 there were about a hundred people at the church in the morning, including many children. I did not see many elders. When I arrived, the Brazilian missionary Valmir was preaching at the pulpit, speaking in faltering Wari' owing to the small amount of time he had spent living there. As a reference text he used a booklet called *Curso nexi pain Rio Negro* (Our course on the Negro River), dated 2004, which describes the history of Israel and the different times since the creation of the world, up until the "time of the church," when people began getting ready for the coming of Jesus, which, according to him, will happen soon. In speaking of Abraham, chosen by God as "the first Israelite," Valmir added, to my surprise, a lesson drawn from international politics: the Americans help the Israelites, and so God helps the Americans, who are very powerful. He then spoke of Jesus, who was *wari'*, and thus ate, drank, and slept. But he had no anger, which was why his body did not perish after his death.

During the sermon, people talked among themselves and a deacon circulated between the rows of seats trying to keep order. Two men, probably deacons too, walked about with flasks of coffee and two mugs, serving the people present. Around midday, they started passing around a bucket of unfermented maize chicha, also served in mugs, alternating the chicha with the coffee. Later, lunch was served in large pans under a roofed area close to the church. Each person took his or her plate and received rice, beans, spaghetti, manioc flour, and a piece of cooked meat.

The missionaries ate separately in the house of the missionary Tereza. They invited me to eat with them, but I could not accept, since the abundance of their food compared to that of the Wari' made me uncomfortable: chicken stew and various other dishes laid out on the table. When I mentioned this to the pastor Awo Kamip, my friend from the Negro River, he told me that the missionaries always ate separately. This separation was not limited to food, since all the visiting missionaries, as well as Thomas and Claudeliz, would return to the city to sleep at the mission headquarters, requiring a journey of around an hour in Thomas's car. Whatever the case, in church they and the Wari' referred to each other as "siblings" (*xere*).

The 2009 conference, held July 8–11 in Lage, and which I was able to study with the help of Abrão's report and the five audiotapes he recorded, was very carefully organized. The guests from each village arrived on July 8, Thursday evening, when they introduced themselves as a group to everyone else: at this point the pastor from each village spoke for "seven minutes," timed by the people from Lage, and each choir sang one song. The days were structured as follows: three hymns were sung in the church, followed by a sermon; a twenty-minute interval at 9:30 A.M. to allow participants to drink chicha; another sermon; and lunch at 11:30 A.M. According to Abrão, not only peccary meat was served there but also paca, since seventeen had been killed in the hunt before the meeting. At 2 P.M. the activities recommenced, stopping again at 3 P.M. so attendees could drink chicha. As far as I could tell, this break continued until 7:30 P.M., when they returned to the church to read verses and sing, stopping again at 9:30 P.M. for dinner. According to Abrão, this schedule referred only to the activities in the church; there were also a number of parallel activities going on, including a meeting of married women, in which the hosts taught participants about housekeeping. Unlike the conferences held among the Koripako of northwestern Amazonia (Xavier 2013), the Wari' events are not necessarily an occasion for baptisms, although they do all include a Holy Supper like the one described in the previous chapter.

The precise organization of time based on the clock, at a Wari' event, was a novelty for me, as was the forming of female groups to discuss gender-related topics—although I cannot say whether things actually functioned in this way. The presence of a large number of missionaries is certainly an important factor differentiating the conferences from the everyday Christian activities of the village, which collaborated in organizing the conference in this specific way.

The fact that this is a ritual in which the different subgroups meet exposes a series of transformations in relation to the pre-Christian chicha festivals. The act of making explicit the relations of affinity and of anger, which culminated in symbolic killing with fermented chicha, is replaced by the production of generalized kinship through commensality, in which the Wari' seek to include the missionaries, even though the latter's behavior sets limits on this incorporation. In the Christian world, anger ceases to have a place where it can be enacted, becoming completely banned from social life. However, like affinity, and indeed intrinsically associated with it, anger continues to exist, and making it explicit generates the need for confession, a ritual that directly regulates internal relations and implies the shift from acts of anger to talk-cooling.[7] This ends up involving an idea of personal guilt, previously unknown, with the naming of those involved in the disputes. Just like the pre-Christian rituals of moral regulation, confession fails sometimes; and sorcery continues to exist among the Wari', today perceived as constituting the main cause of death, given the weakening of the devil's actions among animals.

Given these clear differences, it is important to identify some of the continuities between the moral systems. One of these is the fact that internal relations between kin are encompassed in relations with the outside in terms of motivation: in other words, one acts properly with one's own family primarily to ensure that the latter are not attacked/captured by animals or the devil. The key difference between the two systems resides, as among the Urapmin, in the forms of subjection involved in the formation of ethical subjects. Turning to the system's "telos," we can observe that although the outcome of infractions has also become more long-lasting in terms of personal destiny, there is an important continuity: both in the past as today, its objective is to constitute human persons.

We can turn now to examine confession, the main Christian ritual of moral regulation.

CONFESSION

During the church services, at a moment designated by the officiating pastor, the confessions (*tomi' hwet,* "speak out" or "release by speaking") take place. In the Christian past, as I have already commented, people confessed by saying explicitly what they had done wrong, naming persons and places. Most cases involved adultery, but according to the Wari', internal killings have also been confessed, especially cases of men killed by their wives' lovers. This ended up generating many conflicts, including club fights and sorcery.[8]

In any event, the public account of the act was replaced over time by a brief speech in front of the church followers in which the person can simply say, "I fell in with the devil" (*pan' mao ina kon kaxikon jam*), "I acted badly" (*em' ina,* "I failed"), "I sinned" (*karakat ina,* "I was angry"), "I did wrong" (*pan' tem ina*), or even: "Everyone, I want to return to God. I was very naughty (literally, 'a bad child') in the past. I shall stop this." Here the congregation usually manifests itself, asking questions like: "Is that true? Don't lie."

On one occasion, during a church service in February 2008, a young man of eighteen went to the front of the church and said, "I did wrong." The pastor told him that he should "deny the devil [*nain ho' non kaxikon jam*], and that it was God who made our body, because the devil does not know how to make people." Another pastor, who sat on the pew placed on the raised dais, remarked aloud that the congregation had seen on the DVD the previous night that the son of God had been severely beaten. The pastor asked the young man to state out loud that he had said yes to the devil, and he spoke into the microphone: "I said yes to the devil [literally, 'I replied to the devil's call']." The congregation then began to make simultaneous observations out loud, and the pastor then asked the congregation: "Are you okay with that?"

At no point was the sin itself specified, although it was clear that everyone had heard about it through the informal circulation of information and gossip. After the young man's confession, I asked the woman by my side in the church what had happened, and she immediately replied that he had become drunk while his parents, with whom he lived, were away fishing.

On another occasion, a young man rose to the dais with his wife and announced into the microphone that he had "played" (in the sense of "not taking seriously," *waraju*) with God four times and that he would not do so again. After a long silence he said that we must believe ("to trust," *howa*) in God and his son Jesus. The man asked the Wari' to close their eyes, and he prayed, saying that God was happy that he had returned like a sheep. His wife then prayed: "My father God, I am content for beginning to believe, and this ended my anger." She became embarrassed speaking in front of everyone, and the congregation started to laugh.

According to Abrão, who is a preacher, the sinner, after confessing, remains for a time in a kind of limbo in which he or she cannot sing in the choir, for example. Pastors and deacons who commit sins must relinquish their functions for a long period—two years, according to Abrão—while they are reassessed.

However, what I have described here is only the final moment of the confession, which begins sometime before with the participation of pastors and the congregation in general. Direct confession in church is not conceivable without this prior mediation. In the following section, I reproduce some excerpts from a July 2007 interview with the pastor Awo Kamip, where the stages of confession, and the moral infractions associated with the notion of sin, are specified.

PREPARING FOR CONFESSION

Everything begins with what we could call gossip (*tomi' na mi:* "speak-denounce"; *tomi' xirak/morat:* "speak badly"; *tomi' hwet:* "speak out"), which is not conceived negatively in the Christian context. Someone tells the pastor that a certain person, necessarily someone who claims to be a Christian, did something wrong. The pastor then goes to the other local pastors (a deacon may also be told) and invites them to go with him to the sinner's house. On finding him or her, they ask directly: "What have you been doing?" The answer might be: "I was angry" (*mana' ina*), "I was worried" ("I was trembling through my heart": *toron na pa' xumu*). "What is worrying you?" they ask. "My wife said bad things. She was angry with me, and I with her too. That's what happened!" To which the pastors retort, "Didn't you hear God's word properly? Look at what he says: it is not good to become furious ['to have an outburst of anger'/'to break things'/'to sin,' *karakat*], it is not good to be angry with your wife, or steal, or talk nonsense [*tomi'ximao*], or dislike other people, this is not good, that is not good. That's it. Finished? Are you okay with that?" The sinner may reply, "Yes, I'm okay with that. I am content." Later the sinner goes to the church service and confesses: "I sinned [*karakat ina*], I was very angry. Then our brothers [referring to the pastors] arrived and spoke out loud [*tomi' hwet,* 'speak-out,' the same term used to confess] the word of God. I heard and became content. That's what happened."[9]

In some cases the denounced person resists when the pastors come to his or her house to say, "We heard something about your name, that you did something bad." The person denies the accusation, saying repeatedly "no," until one of the pastors observes, "You are lying to me, and God is watching you." The person may admit to committing an error, or may say that he or she wants to think and will look for them later. A young woman, whose story was told to me, said, "I fell in with the devil" (*Pan' mao ina kon kaxikon jam*). "I did it" (*Ara inain ta*). According to the narrator, she thereby admitted that she was having sex with some young men.

On other occasions, though, the sinner may take the initiative of going to the pastor Awo Kamip, saying, "I acted angrily. I want to return to God" (literally, "I shall appear/go back to God," *in hwet ma ton ina Iri' Jam ta*). Or: "I am trembling through my heart." When asked by the pastor why he or she was worried, the sinner may reply, "I acted angrily/I sinned" (*karakat ina*). Responding to another question from the pastor, the person may explicitly describe his action: "I messed with something bad. I had sex with that woman." The pastor would then reply, "Why do you act like that?" Awo Kamip adds, "That's what I say to people. If there is something that makes your heart angry [*ka karakat na ximihu*] at night, during the day, talk to each other directly. If a wife is angry with her husband, or if he is angry with her, they should talk to each other. Forgive each other [*perdoar*, in Portuguese] for each other's anger. That's what God says."

This kind of talk is called "talk-cool" (*tomi' xio*) by the Wari' which, as we have seen, is the same expression used for the conciliatory speech sometimes following a club fight. Although a direct comparison between the pastor and shaman makes no sense to the Wari' today, given that the latter is an incarnation of the devil, we can observe that the Wari' also refer to shamanic curing as an act of cooling, specifically "make/touch-cool" (*kep xio*). While the verb is different—since the shaman's activity, though it might include a moralizing speech at the end, would have focused on the manipulation of the patient's body—there is an equation between rage and sickness: both are associated with warming the body. The comparison becomes clear in the question that, according to Abrão, is sometimes posed to the sinner: "What did you eat?" referring to the fact of not eating God's word, exactly the same question posed by a shaman to the parents of a sick child.

After such a conversation with a pastor, the pastor announces to the congregation during the church service: "Perhaps there is someone here who wishes to return to God" or "There is someone here who fell in [*pan' mao*] with the devil." That person rises, proceeds to the dais, and while remaining standing, confesses.

In any event, the idea of effective speech was alien to the pre-Christian world, where anger was resolved through the act of beating and, at a collective level, through club fights.[10] In the Christian world, the war club ceased to be an appropriate means of resolving anger and became anger properly speaking, a sin. As we saw in chapter 4, both anger and sin relate to a perceived failure in the process of generalized consanguinization, which is central to Wari' understanding of Christian life. The idea that exchanging words through conversation would resolve the question presumes, however, the notion of a secret, a heart whose content is not necessarily expressed in the person's body and actions, which, as we shall see in the next chapter, contrasts with the pre-Christian conceptions.[11]

I once observed a woman heading to the house of another, whose son had got her daughter pregnant and refused to marry her, in order to tell her that she was no longer angry and, thereby, to free herself of sin and be able to participate actively in the church service. As Abrão explained, the first thing one must do is try to resolve the conflict personally, either by talking to or offering a present to the other person. The person offended must forgive the sinner in order for the name of the latter to be taken off the list of names made by God to identify the sinners: this list will be consulted at the time of the person's death in order to allow or refuse his or her entry to heaven.[12]

Moreover, sin does not necessarily involve an explicit conflict—that is, one previously expressed in acts or words. Christianity brought the Wari' the idea of a wrong "thinking" (*koromikat*) and, consequently, of an examination of conscience. As Abrão explained to me: "Someone who thinks aimlessly, thinks wrongly." He would say (or would think), "My thinking does not seem good to me. I catch myself thinking of the woman I saw with my eyes. It's as though I had sex with her." The sinner can pray to God, privately, saying aloud: "My father God, help me control the evil gaze of my eyes. Give me the capacity to not have evil eyes, help me."

This is an important change in the conception of the person, who begins to have a secret interior. Concomitantly the ethical substance is also transformed, since intentions grow in importance relative to behavior.

A notion of inner self seems to emerge here, which is commonly associated in the literature with the development of a notion of the individual among Christians, but which was unknown to the Wari'. Before turning to this question in the next chapter, though, I wish to examine the relations between Christian and traditional morality from a broader perspective—that is, the contrast between Western and indigenous moralities—which allows us to glimpse again the idea of a duality or an alternation in opposition to the idea of substitution, the topic of the next chapter.

The comparison between Amerindian and Euro-American moralities is a theme explored by Overing, one of the first Americanist authors to be concerned with defining and analyzing the central characteristics of Amazonian moral systems. According to Overing (1999: 81–84; 1985b; Overing and Passes 2000: 1–2), Amazonian peoples' moral systems are based on interpersonal trust, focused on the domain of the domestic and quotidian, in clear opposition to the coercion through laws and institutions that characterizes Western morality.[13] Another important point raised by the author, which I examine in the next chapter, is the fact that individual autonomy, although valued by Amazonian peoples, is subsumed by the interdependence between persons (a category that, as we saw, includes other beings).

Overing and Passes (2000: 6) point to an important paradox in these moral systems: though they emphasize tranquillity and living well—with an emphasis on the domestic relations of kinship, which involve mutual affect and care—they conceive that all "forces for life . . . have their origin in the dangerous, violent, potentially cannibalistic, exterior domains beyond the social," which must be transformed in order for this much-desired peaceful sociality to be constituted.

Viveiros de Castro (2000; 2001: 28–32) indicates the same dichotomy, organizing it diagrammatically in two parallel lines that travel in opposite directions: a descending line, that of the production of peaceful sociality through the gradual extraction of difference in the process of constituting kin, and an ascending line, where alterity is reinserted in the system through war, shamanism, and ritual. There are two essential points in the author's scheme. First of all, alterity is the starting point: in other words, it constitutes the innate world, an idea that converges with Overing's view of the outside world as the source of life (1985b: 157). The second point concerns the importance of a coexistence, in the form of an alternation, between the two movements, showing that alteration is not always involuntary and undesired, but is sometimes essential and actively sought. It does not, therefore, involve only an emphasis on peaceful sociality and the work of domesticating exterior alterity; sometimes it also involves the active production of this otherness, as I have been showing in relation to the Wari' and their desire to preserve the alterity of the whites.

If we consider that, as stated above, morality is that which is conceived to be the correct direction of human action, it would therefore have two directions among the Wari' and other Amazonian groups: one is the differentiation of a group of kin from an innate alterity/affinity, and the other is controlled alteration through ritual action.[14] In Wagner's terms (1975: 93, 99), we could say that the former constitutes the meaning of everyday social action, and the latter the intentional inversion of this meaning—limited to ritual action, which is characterized precisely as an inversion of the quotidian model—by creating new conventions (reinventing the alterity that forms part of the conventional world). Differentiating systems of the Wari' type involve precisely this dialectic between differentiating and conventionalizing, or—as we saw in chapter 5, in exploring Leite's analysis of Yanomami mythology (2013)—the oscillation between stabilization and alteration. Each of these intentional movements, however, produces an unintentional movement in the opposite direction, perceived as resistance. Hence the dehumanization of people caused by animal attacks (or those of the devil) as the countereffectuation of everyday differentiation/humanization. These contrary movements are understood as something that happens independently of the actions and interest of persons, who do not see the acts that lead to dehumanization as their own responsibility, attributing them always to external agents. As we saw in chapter 6, the Wari' today attribute to the devil each and every process of dehumanization of people, whether those involved in the capture by animal subjectivities possessed by the devil, or by morally wrong acts encouraged by the devil. Listening to the devil is what makes them act wrongly, such that this being personifies countereffectuation or resistance (Wagner 1975: 41–50) to the process of differentiation that they seek with Christianity: they return to the innate state of enmity, animality, and rage. This becomes clear when we examine the confessions, which, generally speaking, amount today to a public affirmation, during a church service, that "I fell in with the devil."

The conventionalizing systems that, according to Wagner (1975: 46), characterize the Euro-American urban world oppose this model by focusing on everyday moral action in the production of conventions, rules, or "culture" in order to domesticate "nature," an innate world of differences and individual particularities. It is precisely these new rules and conventions—the law of God, taught by him through the Bible—that the missionaries, over the centuries, have wished to imprint on the natives. This is a movement in the opposite direction from that pursued by Amazonian peoples in their everyday actions, given that the latter comprehend transformation not as the adoption of conventions but as the bodily differentiation enabled by kinship and mimesis.

If we compare the chicha festivals with today's conferences, we can observe that the ritual has ceased to be a moment of inversion of the everyday actions of producing kinship and of the reinsertion of difference in the system. Instead, it has become continuous with the daily activities, implying, in Wagner's terms (1975: 145–146), the end of the dialectics between conventionalization and differentiation that characterizes Amazonian symbolic systems, making them similar to our own. Likewise, ritual temporality ceases to contain an important difference in relation to quotidian time, establishing a continuity with it instead and, thus, exacerbating the adoption of clock-based linear time, which begins to take up everyday life. Hence the function of the chicha festivals as markers of time in individual life histories is lost, giving way instead to an annual calendar, reinforced by the introduction of birthdays and anniversaries, which have recently begun to be commemorated, as well as the monthly dates fixed by the government for receiving financial welfare benefits.

In conclusion, affinity and anger are still produced through counterinvention, but the active production of difference ceases to exist, and it is as though its "benign" characteristic, once objectified in the existence of shamanism, warfare, and the chicha rituals, has been completely repressed in order to turn difference into pure resistance. This strikes me as an important transformation, although, as we shall see, the Wari' work of translating Christian concepts reveals an explicit intention to maintain the alterity and alternation that we have been discussing. It is as though ritual inversion has been replaced by a complexification of concepts related to the person, which is facilitated by the paradoxical characters of the concepts and figures of the Christian pantheon.

NINE

Personhood and Its Translations

I do not see in dual organization a universal phenomenon resulting from the binary nature of human thought. I only note that
certain peoples, occupying an immense though bounded geo-
graphical area, have chosen to explain the world on the model of
a dualism in perpetual disequilibrium, whose successive states
are embedded into one another.

LÉVI-STRAUSS, *The Story of Lynx*

IN THE PREVIOUS CHAPTERS we examined the Christian ritual life of
the Wari', including the continuities and ruptures with the traditional way
of constituting ethical subjects. I suggested that these changes have been
accompanied by transformations in the notion of personhood, indicating a
process of individualization involving an inner and secret self.

As we know, the relation between Christianity and the emergence of a
notion of the individual is widely observed in anthropological works, especially those inspired by Mauss and Dumont. In his essay on the notion of
the person, Mauss ([1950] 1999) analyzes the transition over the course of the
West's history from the notion of a person as a multiple (the persona) to the
individual, associating the final moments of this transition with Christianity.
Mauss's essay was later reworked by Dumont (1983) in his analysis of the
genesis of the individual as a cardinal value in modern societies. A notion of
the individual before Christianity, he argues, can be found in ancient Greece,
especially among the Stoics (36–39, 48), though in the latter case the notion
contained otherworldly characteristics also typical of the ideas of the first
Christians. It was following the institution of the church and its political
stabilization, and especially after the Reformation, that the mundane antago-
nistic element characteristic of Christianity—namely, the opposition
between the believer's relations to God (individual) and his or her relation to
the world (holistic, collective)—eventually disappeared. The final blow was
landed by Calvin, who established the importance of the worldly action of
the individual devoted to God as the only evidence of his or her choice and

salvation. The individual is thereby inserted completely in the world, and individualism becomes the dominant, unrestricted value (70–73).[1]

Dumont (56, 60) highlights the correlation between the invention of an idea of nature and the genesis of the individual, which resonates with the Wari' adoption of the biblical Genesis as an origin myth. The author argues that the historical process through which the Christian individual became stabilized in the world coincided with the separation of humans from non-humans:[2] the identity established between human and divine will in Calvinism consolidated the separation between man and nature already present in the thought of Saint Augustine as man became the master and owner of nature (76; see also Latour 1993: 139, and Descola 2005: 103).[3]

The missionary and ethnologist Maurice Leenhardt suggests a clear relation between cosmological transformations and individualization. Inspired by Mauss—to whom he was closely linked—and his essay on the historical evolution of the notion of the person, Leenhardt in chapter 11 of *Do Kamo*, embarks on an in-depth analysis of personhood among the Kanak of New Caledonia, exploring how this concept began to transform following contact with Europeans and the Christian message in particular. According to Leenhardt ([1947] 1971: 249–250, my translation), before contact the Kanak saw themselves as distributed among their relations, including relations of "mythic participation" involving the mixture between persons and their totems.[4] Leenhardt argues that the Kanak previously conceived their own bodies as dispersed in various directions or relations without any possibility of synthesis or unification. As his informant Boesou explained, the arrival of the missionary and the Christian message gave them "a body," which Leenhardt associates with the idea of a properly human body, disconnected from mythic participation (263). In his words, the person "detaches itself finally from the socio-mythic domain where it had been trapped. . . . The psychological self that had been seen wandering everywhere, far from the body, is finally fixed" (264). However, Leenhardt has a complex vision of this "detachment" from the mythic world of participation. He suggests a selection of participative relations inspired by the Christian message (the "new religion"; 269)—from among those conceived (by Leenhardt) as real (that is, as properly human)—that must be maintained, and other relations, with their totems, that "no longer inspire trust" (268) and which must be severed, "freeing [one] of mythic thought" (272). Clifford (1992: 78) in his biography of Leenhardt writes that the latter saw the Kanak undergoing the transition "from a diffuse, participatory consciousness toward self-consciousness. . . .

Conversion was the emergence of an internalized moral conscience based on an intimate communion with Christ." He adds, "Attaining the conception of a sole God thus involves a long process of mental and cultural change. . . . An immanent but also overarching deity, would require further changes in modes of thought and in the definition of the human person" (175–176).

My interest in Leenhardt's analysis of Kanak Christian transformation does not reside with the "rationalization" of native thought proposed in his text. Unlike various authors who focus on this point (Horton 1975, Weber 1956, Bellah 1964, Geertz 1973), Leenhardt—following Mauss and making use of an enormous wealth of ethnographic and linguistic detail—concentrates on the passage from plurality ("personas"; Leenhardt [1947] 1971: 262) to the unity conceived as the "psychological self." He attributes this transition to a change in the conception of the body brought by the rupture of the mutual constitution of the Kanak with the beings inhabiting their mythic universe. This clearly reflects a shrinking in the notion of humanity, yet one that preserves a form of participation—namely, the participation among persons. For Leenhardt, the disappearance of these relations implies the "unwelcome" processes of individuation arising from schooling, employment, and other practices linked to contact with the West. The emergence of the "psychological self" is an outcome, therefore, of this ontological reduction (267).

As Strathern (1988: 268–271) points out, there is, however, a problem in Leenhardt's argument. Like Mauss before him and Dumont after, Leenhardt conceived that the individual emerging from these transformations already potentially existed. Here we can recall Mauss's argument ([1950] 1999: 337, 348–354) that this new concept of the self formed over historical time from a germinal existence among many different peoples, including the Zuni, but above all the Hindus, Chinese, and Romans. Mauss's idea was appropriated and amplified by Dumont in a more detailed historical study, showing how the genesis of the individual was associated with questions of value and hierarchy: a preexistent notion of the individual, objectified in the figure of the religious ascetic, became stabilized in the world (Dumont 1983: 76), especially with the advent of Calvinism. Leenhardt ([1947] 1971: 250) claimed that the place of the "self" among the Kanak was "empty," that "no member of the group showed themselves capable of subscribing to this, of naming themselves, of saying, 'I am,' 'I act.'" Strathern (1988: 268–269), though, analyzing the diagram of the Kanak person provided by Leenhardt (249), detects a mistake: some of his "more subtle discursive observations" reveal that

Leenhardt had conceived of a center (Strathern 1988: 378n1, 269)—that is, the (albeit virtual) possibility of the totalization of this person. For Strathern, "Leenhardt's star shaped configuration carries the one and same presumption: living within, guided by, driving, functioning as, or knowing through these structures of relationships must be the individual subject" (271). The model of the person proposed by Strathern for Melanesia, which grounds her critique of Leenhardt, focuses on the notion of the essentially divided, or dividual, person who contains the perspective of the other within herself, determining his thought and action (272).

I turn now to what seems to be an analogous movement of the internalization of the person among the Wari', showing its relation to the adoption of Genesis (and the separation between humans and animals) and to the effects of the notions of omnipresence and omniscience, which started to become part of their world with the introduction of the Christian God. Similarly, we can observe that the ritual transformations have brought to light another notion of humanity and the innate world. My intention here is to show that the notion of inner self brought by Christianity is completely new to the Wari', who conceived the self to be determined from the outside, by the perspective of the other, as we shall see. We shall also see that we are not dealing with a linear process in which a notion of the self replaces another and comes to regulate everyday life, since the same Christian message brought to them allows the reproduction of the traditional notion of personhood. We can begin by returning to the notion of body and double, and the introduction of the notion of the heart.

HUMANITY AND THE OUTER SELF

> One's truth is known to no one, and frequently—as in Delphine's very own case—to oneself least of all.
>
> PHILIP ROTH, *The Human Stain*

As we have seen already in chapter 2, the Wari' have a complex definition of the body (*kwerexi'*, "our [inclusive] body"), encompassing not only the idea of flesh, or matter, but also that of personality, or way of being. The Wari' say that a person has a particular way of behaving or being because his or her body is like that. This body not only differentiates individuals through their particularities but also differentiates the Wari' as a whole from other indigenous peoples, whites, and other kinds of beings. They often say that "the

Wari' body is like that" (*je kwerexi' pain ka wari' nexi*) when referring to their collective practices and habits. Everything that exists, animals and objects alike, also has a body, the seat of its capacities and affects.

As part of the body, the heart—*ximixi'* (our [inclusive] heart)—is a central organ, responsible for the most vital physiological functions and, in turn, associated with cognitive and emotional capacities and dispositions. Used more generally, the term *heart* simply designates the inside or core of something, like the hearts of some fruits. More specifically, *heart* refers to intellectual capacity and understanding and is associated with vitality and agency. Hence when people say that active living beings have a heart, they mean that such beings know how to act, what to do, and what to eat. As with the body, possession of a heart is not limited to those beings conceived to be human. All animals know how to search for food, find a shelter, and so on. Just like the body, the heart differentiates "kinds" of beings. An incident involving my Wari' father, Paletó, on a visit to Rio de Janeiro in 2009 helps explain the dissociation of this notion of understanding from humanity: observing the automatic door of the garage open as we were driving out, and unaware of the remote control in my hand, Paletó asked me whether the door "had a heart." Just as the Wari' might say that the door can have a heart by acting appropriately, they also say that beings that act inappropriately "lack a heart," such as an animal that fails to perceive its predator and allows itself to be killed.

When it comes to the Wari' themselves, the notion of heart acquires a complexity absent from their discourse on other beings: as well as understanding, it also refers to thinking and moral attitudes, attributed here to specific physiological processes controlled by the heart.[5] The heart is responsible for producing blood and distributing it to the rest of the body. Vitality is associated with the quantity of blood, which increases in proportion to its rate of circulation. A slow, shrunken heart leads to physical and emotional weaknesses. At the same time, sadness, especially yearning for dead kin, can cause the heart to malfunction, leading to physical debility, illness, and even death (see Conklin 2001a: 139–145). When worried or anxious, the Wari' often say, "My heart makes me moan" (*Toron na pa' xumu*), or "Our heart isn't breathing well, it's panting" (*Wereme xi na ximixi'*). By contrast, being well implies that one's heart is well settled. "Now you will all rest" (*Xao to warawa ak hwein tara xumuhu;* literally, "Now you will all seat and suspend/relax your hearts").

Other examples include: "I am in doubt, wavering" (*I ina na pa' xumu*); "My heart is making me bitter" (*Jom' na pa' xumu*); "I am sad" (*Mija na ka xite pin kapa' xumu;* literally, "My heart is much too heavy"); "He is immature" or "He acts like a child" (*Ximikon pije' na;* literally, "He is a child heart"); "I was shocked" (*Xat na pa' xumu;* literally, "My heart stopped me"); "You only bother about your own things" (*Win xumu e' ma' hwein karamaxuhu';* literally, "You only really have a heart for your things"); "I want you to be mature, to act like adults" (*Ximikokon hwanana pin' ho' xirara na inuhu'*); "Your hearts are divided" (*Tokwan na xumuhu;* literally, "Your hearts are several").[6]

Emotional state and moral behavior are likewise inseparable from cognitive thought processes (see Conklin 2001a: 140–144; also Overing Kaplan 1985b). For the Wari', being emotionally well means thinking well, understanding things properly. An intelligent person who quickly understands what is explained to him or her, who learns a skill quickly, "has a heart," just as a sensible person does things correctly, such as avoiding extramarital sex and stealing, and not becoming excessively sad because of a death. As the pastor Rubens/Jimon Maram said, "The ancestors acted correctly, they did not play around, wives did not speak nonsense to their husbands. The ancestors really had a heart [*iri' ximikakam hwanana*]." Like the body, the heart has a collective aspect typical to the kind of beings, and an individual aspect, singularizing a person through his or her appearance and way of acting and feeling, although, as we have seen, this particular way of acting is thought to result from a specific relational context. In the Christian context, "having a heart" is one way of saying that the person behaves like a good Christian, as demonstrated in the Wari' version of a hymn originally sung in Portuguese, which also illustrates the perception of love as a transformation of anger, as discussed in chapter 4: the stanza repeating "I am happy, Christ saved me" was transformed into "You're angry, Jesus said to us long ago. You have no heart, Jesus said to us long ago. I shall give you a heart, Jesus said to us long ago, so you will no longer be angry" (hymn 37).

Returning to the more general Wari' idea of the body, we can observe that it evokes a notion very similar to that of the "mindful body" or "embodied mind" used to reformulate the Euro-American notion of the body previously based on the Cartesian paradigm and its strict differentiation of mind and body, a separation alien to people's everyday experience (Lock and Scheper-Hughes 1987; Vilaça 2005, 2009a). However the Wari' notion of the body involves an additional level of complexity insofar as it is based on a distinct conception of humanity predicated on its instability.

As we saw in chapter 2, although everything has a body and a heart, only those entities possessing a double, *jamixi'* (or *tamataraxi'*), are considered human. These include not only the Wari', other indigenous groups, and white people but also diverse species of animals. *Jamixi'* is not an immaterial component of the person located in some part of the body: it is a capacity to transform, the ability to assume the form of other bodies, a characteristic of every human being. Hence, when a person becomes sick after being shot with an arrow by a capuchin monkey, the Wari' say that it is the monkey's *jamikon* (-*kon*, male suffix) that caused the illness by acting as a person rather than as an animal. Simultaneously the Wari', through the shaman's vision, know that the victim's double (*jamikam/jamikon*) is transforming into a monkey because it is living among the monkeys as though they were kin, eating their food. Consequently the sick person acquires a monkey subjectivity/understanding, which the Wari' translate as the loss of a Wari' heart. A man once told me that during the disease process, "the animal enters us and starts to eat our heart." If not rescued by the shaman, the victim would turn into a monkey completely, ceasing to have a body visible to the Wari' as human.

Hence, while *jamixi'* is a capacity for transformation, it could only be objectified as a body, a different kind of body because of its links to other relations. The bodily constitution of the double becomes clear in the feeling expressed by Paletó after the rare episode of the account of a dream, in which his daughter had died: "My double's heart moaned" (*Toron na ximikon jamu*). The fact that the double has a heart necessarily implies its possession of a body.

The status of a person, whether human or animal, did not traditionally depend on self-perception—since different kinds of beings saw themselves as human—but instead depended on who saw the person *as* a person. In the above example, the Wari' see the victim as a monkey, while the monkeys see him or her as a person. As noted earlier, this kind of undesired transformation was not a rare event dissociated from everyday life. People with nobody to look after them were always vulnerable to turning into an animal, or going to live among the dead, since these other humans were always interested in attracting Wari' and transforming them into their own kin. To become vulnerable, it sufficed to answer their call, talk to them, and above all, eat their food or have sex: such actions could lead to the victim's perspective being completely subsumed by the other. By losing their Wari' body/understanding, the person began to see the animals as humans and to be seen by the other Wari' as an animal, a process that from the Wari' point of view translated as disease and death or as abduction.[7]

To avoid being seen as prey in the eyes of others, both animals and affines, the Wari' looked to obey a series of rules and procedures, which included the relations between themselves and with animals, as we saw in the previous chapter. In their internal relations the Wari' looked to avoid stirring anger, an anger that, as expressed by the verb "not to dislike," constitutes the starting point to their actions. Therefore, they shunned meanness, adultery, abductions of women, and any outward expression of aggressiveness, aside from ritually sanctioned forms—the club fights and getting affines drunk with chicha. The failure to realize these "modes of subjectivization" (Foucault 1990: 26–29; Robbins 2004: 216–217) could lead to sorcery in which the victim (his or her double), usually an affine, is killed like animal prey, just like the killings with arrows and poisonings, all of them considered immoral within the context of internal relations.[8]

The vitality attributed to the proper functioning of the heart was traditionally conceived to be a sign or guarantee of nontransformation, registering the person's stability. People who lacked an appetite, were lazy, and above all were sad might be suffering from a process of transformation that needed to be reversed. This explains the constant monitoring of the signs of vitality/morality in everyone else, especially close kin, expressed not only in bodily form (fat, movement) but also in speech and the capacity to listen. Children who begin to speak properly display signs of being able to comprehend what is said to them, showing that they are becoming Wari' children.[9] People undergoing transformation, including the victims of sorcery, are unable to hear: they are deaf precisely because they hear only the voices of others, who call these victims to join them. They are also unable to say anything comprehensible. Another important sign is the refusal of food, which reveals that the person sees the food of other beings as true food, mistaking blood for chicha, for example. Isolation, silence, and lack of appetite are, therefore, considered not personal singularities but relational equivocations.

From this we can gather that the Wari' conceive secrets to be highly dangerous. The threat posed by equivocation means that people must give clear proof of their humanity, their *wari'* way of being—thereby showing that their "hearts" are open and exposed.[10] This is expressed by the fact that the Wari' commonly use the verb "to speak" (*tomi'*) to designate actions with a moral connotation, even those that do not involve verbal action, as though the expression of what one is feeling or thinking to others, implicit in the notion of speaking, is the starting point, the default action: to be jealous is "to speak jealously" (*tomi' naroin*); to be greedy is "to speak-deny" (*tomi' narain ho*); to point with a finger is "to speak close by" (*tomi' mi'*).[11] Hence, the secret, properly speaking, is a denial of speech, an act of remaining silent concerning something that one knows—literally, "to not speak or say anything" (*tomi' om*), "to speak-deny" (*tomi' jok xim*), or "to speak-hide" (*tomi' kaho'*). The antonym of these is "to speak out" (*tomi' hwet*), the term used in the Christian context to designate confession. The container of the unspoken is the heart. People say, for example, "It is well settled in his [or her] heart; he [or she] does not speak it" (*An pe xo' tain pain ximikam. Om ka tomi' hwet kamain ta*).

Intense relations between people are essential because they fill the place otherwise occupied by relations with other kinds of people. There are no people without relations, only those with the wrong relations. In this sense morality for the Wari', as we have seen, is subordinate to relations with the outside. People became like one another, constituting a moral community, in order to avoid turning into others by being seduced or captured by these other subjectivities.

Hence, if humanity, for the Wari', was indissociable from morality, it was not because other humans had other moral standards, as found among the Piro/Yine (Opas 2008: 331–340), but because adequate morality not only produced but also made evident a stable humanity. Deviating from standards of affability, generosity, food sharing, and child care led to a loss of humanity, conceived in relative rather than absolute terms. Those who became dehumanized in the eyes of the Wari' became human in the eyes of animals. There was nothing like a "self" identity to be possessed, since this identity was contextual, produced on the basis of a relation determined from the outside.

A CHANGE OF HEART

This absence of an intimate inner self was sensed by the missionaries, who indeed blamed it for the deconversion of the Wari', as Royal Taylor made clear in a moment of frustration in 1994, when the Wari' had fully returned to pagan life: "They were not converted through the spirit, only through mental persuasion. Believing for them only meant changing their life, and believing is an intimate relation with God, which they had not known. . . . However much I explain that it is Christ's spirit that brings salvation, they still link salvation to their conduct" (Royal Taylor, pers. comm., 1994, my translation). The interiorized person, whom Royal sought, is clearly described in the translation into Wari' of the Epistle to the Romans, in which the notions of the secret and the inner self appear frequently.[12]

As an example we can take the translation of Romans 2:16 from lesson book 6, page 61, which reads in English: "In the day when God will judge the secrets of men by Jesus Christ, according to my gospel" (New King James Bible). And in Wari':

> Perhaps this is what will happen [future irrealis] on the day of the end of the world, when Jesus Christ will speak to God. He will tell [*tomi' kut hwere-hwet;* literally, "gather and speak out in words"] everything that the Wari' have done wrong [*oro ka pan' teretem;* literally, "take the wrong path, enter wrongly"], what is found in their thought [*ka koromikat nukukun*] and what they hide [*ka jok xim kaka ma'*]. This is what Jesus Christ will say perhaps [future irrealis]. It is what God says to Jesus. It is what he ordered to be said too.

As we saw in the analysis of church services and confession, this interiorization, and the accompanying secrecy, is starting to be conceived among the Wari', at least in the context of the Christian rituals. The concept of heart, related to personal singularity, has undergone a kind of hypertrophy, rendering it more internal and less visible. Though mostly concentrated in the speech of the Christians during the church services and prayers, expressions have emerged that were seldom used during my first years of fieldwork, such as "Let's look at our own hearts" (*Kirik wet pan xin ximixi'*), "He sees his own heart" (*Kirik pin pan xijein ximikon*), "My heart detests you" (*Nok tamana nem xumu*), and "You see me through my heart" (*Kirik pin ma pa' pain xumu*), indicating a shift toward the singularization of the person through the constitution of an inner self. Just as pastor Awo Tot stated in his speech translated in chapter 7, on the "examination of conscience," another pastor said while reading from Romans in a church service: "Each one sees his/her own heart. We cannot see the hearts of our coresidents." Likewise people often say that those wanting to take part in the Holy Supper should first let out (*hwet*) what is in their heart (the confession). Some of the hymns are also revealing, such as hymn 53, which declares, "I am happy in my heart. It is he, Jesus Christ, who is with me." And hymn 33, titled "Jesus Entered into My Heart," begins with: "Cristo Jesu made me into another person [*wari'*] as he entered into my heart."

While the inner self is not necessarily accompanied by the Euro-American view of the person as a self-contained individual, we should note that the quotidian practices of the missionaries are also associated with individuality. The works of Pollock (1993: 189) and Taylor (1981: 652), comparing the activities of

Catholic and Evangelical (SIL) missionaries among the Amazonian Culina and Achuar. respectively, show that both groups base their work on clearly individualist conceptions, recognized as such by the indigenous people themselves, whether they adopt or reject them. The most important difference according to the authors is that the individualizing premises are made explicit by the Evangelicals while they remain implicit in Catholic practice. Among the Achuar, the Evangelicals extol routinized physical work and relate success in accumulating capital to divine assistance, while the Catholics created a cooperative system governed by a notion of property alien to the Achuar (Taylor 1981: 669).[13] The cooperative created among the Culina is also cited by Pollock (1993) to illustrate what seems to be a significant equivocation made by the Catholics. The produce removed for sale was linked to a notion of individual productivity, which, as in the case of the Sagarana Catholic cooperative I witnessed operating among the Wari' in the 1990s, was not traditionally valued. According to Pollock, the system—based on the idea that social relations could be measured by individually owned goods—violated the Culina view of sociability, leading them to reject the missionary projects and thus Christianity itself (183). Taylor (1981: 671) concludes that, for the Achuar, although it had been their "own ideological system," especially the equation between ritual control of the supernatural and material wealth, that had made them vulnerable to the ideology of the missionaries, the transformations resulting from the "missionary ideological penetration" cannot be overstressed, especially the Christian technologies of the production of the self, such as economic practices, school education, dwelling habits, and behavior (659–664), which lead to a growing individualization.[14]

Among the Wari', the Evangelical missionaries also enact an explicit individualism in their everyday practices. They encourage individual exchanges according to the market economy model, demanding that each item offered by them to the Wari' is paid with an item of equivalent value. So, for example, a hook would be equal to one hen's egg, while two hooks would have to be repaid with two eggs. They also encourage the execution of services, such as cleaning the house yards, very often paid directly in money.[15] The situation is more complex, however, and an examination of the data, especially the translation into Wari' of some of the key concepts of Christianity, reveals that the latter, while offering an alternative model of personhood, also allowed them to reproduce their own. Moreover, as we shall see below in reexamining their view of heaven, the Wari' associate the idea of the bounded individual with a paralysis of social life.

Before turning to this question, I wish to examine what Americanists have said about individualism in Amazonia.

(IN)DIVIDUALITY IN AMAZONIA

The question of individualism in Amazonian societies has been discussed for some decades, especially in the wake of the pioneering work by Rivière (1984: 94–95). Starting from an observation common among the region's ethnographers, who have characterized the members of these societies as "individualistic," Rivière looks to specify "the nature of this individualism." He rejects the notion's psychological dimension and relates it instead to characteristics of Guianese social organizations, which are inherently cognatic and exclude corporate groups that organize wider social contexts. In highlighting the centrality of corporal participations ("sharing in a common substance") among persons from the same group, Rivière suggests the existence here of something very distinct from the modern individual.[16]

Overing (1975) was one of the first authors to call attention to this peculiarity of Amerindian societies, in her monograph on the Piaroa and, particularly, in her later attempt to develop a positive conceptualization of the region's native groups (Overing Kaplan 1976), which until the 1970s were described through a "litany of negations and lack[:] . . . no lineages, no corporate groups, no land-holding groups, no authority structure." (Overing and Passes 2000: 1). This effort culminated in the articles by Seeger (1980) and Seeger, Da Matta, and Viveiros de Castro (1979), where the notion of corporate groups was replaced by that of corporal groups, pointing to the centrality of the body for constituting identity in Amazonian collectives, defined not by genealogical structures but by sharing substances over the course of life.

In her more recent work, Overing returned to the theme of the individualistic aspect of these societies, reinforcing precisely the paradox of this conception when applied to the Amazonian world. Overing and Passes (2000: 2) remark on the idea found throughout indigenous Amazonia that the self constituting the collective is independent and autonomous, accompanied by a general antipathy to rules and coercitive constraints.[17] The authors point out, however, that this impression of independence and freedom is complicated by the "embodiment of self and community" described in various chapters of their edited book, and by the fact that "at the same time, the moral gaze is other-directed, where the autonomous I is ever implicated within and joined with an intersubjectivity" (2).[18]

The Melanesian notion of the dividual, whose close approximation to the Wari' model of relationality was briefly mentioned in chapters 5 and 6, seems to me to correspond more faithfully to the aspects of the Amazonian person described above. Inspired by Marriot's reference to South Asian theories of the person as "'dividual' or divisible" (1976: 111), Strathern (1988: 13) claims that Melanesian persons "contain a generalized sociality within. . . . The singular person can be imagined as a social microcosm." As the terms used synonymously by Marriot make clear, this dividual is above all a multiple person formed by relations that can be detached and incorporated by others.

However, turning to relations between persons or groups (taken as equivalent insofar as each person contains the set of relations characterizing the group), the notion of dividual refers not simply to the idea of a divisibility or multiplicity but to a duality, such that the source and outcome of action are "dyadically conceived relationships" in which "each party is irreducibly differentiated from the other" (Strathern 1988: 14).

In sum, the notion of dividual simultaneously contains the idea of multiplicity, emphasizing the person as a composite of multiple relations and above all the capacity for decomposition, and the idea of duality, insofar as different multiplicities relate to each other in the form of pairs, whether internally (as the dividual) or externally, in the form of two individuals (as decomposed dividuals) different from each other but together reconstituting the pair. It is in the presence of the other, experienced as an opposite, that the person is individualized through the eclipsing of one of its two aspects—precisely the aspect represented by this other.[19]

As I already mentioned in the introduction, the application of the Melanesian model of the dividual to the Amazonian context is particularly productive given its resonance with a concept elaborated by Lévi-Strauss (1991) in the context of Americanist ethnology—namely, the idea of dualism in perpetual disequilibrium, a logical principle that implies an ordering of the world into stable pairs that become successively differentiated.[20] Lévi-Strauss argues that Native American peoples ascribe a negative value to identity and its potential to paralyze the society's system of reproduction. Thus each position or category demands its opposite, such that the notion of compatriot, for example, is unthinkable without the notion of foreigner or enemy. As Viveiros de Castro (2001: 19) has shown in a work exploring the Lévi-Straussian concept of dualism and relating it explicitly to this Melanesian model of the person, this dichotomy is reproduced at all levels of the system, from the collective to the individual, following a fractal model (see Kelly 2001; 2005a). Thus compatriots are themselves differentiated into affines and consanguines, the latter into same-sex or cross-sex (or younger and older) siblings, until we arrive at the individual, who, as Viveiros de Castro (2001: 25) shows, is not so much an "individual" as a "dividual" (33), comprising a body and a soul, the former constituting the compatriot or consanguine pole, and the latter the enemy or affine pole. In the process of kinship production analyzed here by Viveiros de Castro, the "affine" pole is systematically eclipsed—but never eliminated—at the different levels of the fractal model. It is the persistence of affinity that explains the instability of this dualism, producing new pairs in a continuous (and infinite) movement of extracting affinity.

In Amazonia—as the authors cited above have shown, and as I have suggested for the Wari'—in contrast to Melanesia, where gender categories constitute one of the main principles of differentiation (Strathern 1988: 14–15, 275; 1998: 117, 135n10), the pairs of opposites are constituted at different levels through configurations of the human/nonhuman opposition (which includes the compatriot/enemy and consanguine/affine contrasts).[21]

The concepts of dividual, or dual, person elaborated in the two regions share an essential feature of their dynamics: the fact that relations are based on difference. The words of Viveiros de Castro on Amazonia resonate with those of Strathern (1988:14) cited above: "So the cardinal rule of this ontology is: no relation without differentiation. In socio-practical terms, this means that the parties to any relationship are related insofar as they are different from one another. They are related through their difference, and become different as they engage in their relationship" (2001: 25–26). As we shall see in the conclusion, this fractal schema of opposing poles undergoes a transformation in its dynamic when we remove its outer extreme—that is, the most radical form of alterity, in the Wari' case represented by the humanized animals. This transformation, as I look to show there, seems to be directly implicated in the constitution of what is defined above as an inner self. Before turning to this question, let's see how the Wari', through the translation of Christian terms into their own language, succeed in maintaining the central aspects of their perspectivist and dual conception of personhood.

TRANSLATION AND ITS EFFECTS

Translation *is* the ethnographic object.

FRED MEYERS, "Culture-Making"

As we saw in chapter 6, the two names used by the Wari' as synonyms for the double became differentiated in the Christian translation: *tamataraxi'* came to designate the incorporeal soul, equated with the heart (*ximixi'*) as the seat of thought, while *jamixi'* retained its original meaning, associated with the body and transformation.

As the soul and heart became equivalent, animals lost the attributes of agency that once characterized them: animals have no soul and, therefore, also have no reflexivity or thought. When I asked Abrão—who had explained to me that it was the heart of animals that led them to search for food and shelter—whether God therefore spoke in the heart of the capuchin monkey, I received an apparently contradictory answer: "No. It's not *wari'!* It has no heart. It doesn't know how to think properly." Having a soul/heart has become an attribute of the new humanity, no longer equated with animality but with the divine. God has his own soul (*tamatarakon*), namely the Holy Spirit. As Paletó said in 2008: "It is *tamatarakon* who speaks in our heart."

Although "body" is translated in Christian writings by the Wari' term *kwerexi'*, whose meaning partly overlaps the term for "body" (*corpo*) in Portuguese, it loses its central attributes as the seat of the will and personality and becomes a mere envelope, a "skin" (*taparixi'*). In the words of one man: "The things of our body are not good. Only our soul [*tamataraxi'*]. Those who do not believe ['to trust,' *howa*] only like the things of the body." The words of the pastor Awo Kamip during a church service in July 2007, when he read from the Epistle to the Romans, show the clear dissonance between the traditional and Christian acceptations: "It is Jesus Christ who helps our soul [*tamataraxi'*]. . . . It is our soul that believes in God, not our body."

In conversation with me in 2008, André, a young pastor from Piranha village, using a mixture of Portuguese and Wari', associated God's lack of a body with the absence of the evil embodied in the idea of a double, *jamixi'*: "God was not born. He has no mother or father. He exists out of nothing. That's why God has no *jamikon*, only *tamatarakon*. *Jamikon wari'* only exists because of *kaxikon jam* [the devil]. We have a body [*kwerexi'*]."

Like *jamixi'*, the body is associated with evil and sin, translated into the Wari' language by a variety of terms, including *ka karakat wa,* where, as we have already seen, *karakat* is an emphatic duplication of the verb *kat,* "to break," meaning the act per se, something visible through the body. As Awo Kamip explained in one service in 2007: "God's *tamatarakon* stays in our heart. We do not delight [*param*] in sin [*ka karakat wa*]. Our body [*kwerexi'*] delights in sin. We speak with God through our soul [*tamataraxi'*]. Our skin [*taparixi'*] does not speak to him."

While the heart/soul is the locus for communication with God, the devil makes use of our body as well as our soul, as lesson book 6 makes clear (page 15): "[The devil] speaks to us through our heart, ordering us to do things that are not good. He stays malignantly in our soul [*tamataraxi'*], he stays malignantly in our body [*kwerexi'*] too."

In the missionary version of the creation of man, contained in lesson book 1, God created Adam with his hands. He makes each part of his body with a lump of earth:

> He had a head, arms, legs, eyes, nose. He had all his body parts. He just lacked life. He was someone dead. He did not breath, his body did not breath.... He wasn't thinking yet, he still lacked a heart. He didn't know how to think [*koromikat*], he didn't know how to want, he didn't have a soul yet [*tamatara-kon*]. [God] breathed life into him, he lived, finally he had a soul. He finally knew how to think, he finally had a heart, he knew how to want, too. (lesson book 1, page 36)

Later the text adds: "He became strong, he was good. He wasn't a bad person. He was very good" (37).

Some pages earlier, the lesson book had described God's thoughts at the moment of creating man. It explains that God, speaking in the name of the Trinity, wanted man "to appear like us," but here he was not referring to the body: "Had he [God] a body." The text continues: "He was not referring to our body. He was referring to something else. He was talking about our soul [*tamataraxi'*]. He was talking about our heart, from where our will comes, our thought, it comes from our heart, it comes from our soul.... He did not talk about our body. Our body is like a house, our skin is like a house. Our soul [*tamataraxi'*] is only lodged in our body. Our thought is only lodged in our body. Our will is only lodged in our body" (lesson book 1: 32).

The divergence between the Amazonian and missionary conceptions of the soul, and its relation to the body, which is evident here, have been remarked by Taylor and Viveiros de Castro (2007: 159, my translation): "Deceived by the superficial resemblance between their own dualism, namely between flesh and spirit, the missionaries (and in turn very often ethnologists) quickly assimilated the latter with the soul. In reality the indigenous terms refer to something entirely different to the inner spiritual principle, opposed to the body, implied by our notion of soul. . . . In short, the Indian 'soul' is formed by the other's perspective."

The Wari' case allows us to complexify the equivocation identified by the authors, showing that the Wari' and Christian perspectives intersect with each other in different ways. The demonization of the term *jamixi'* shows that the missionaries had some idea of its transformative potential and its role in the definition of the duality of the Wari' person, which they sought to unify through the divine perspective. They therefore turned to the term *tamataraxi'*, less imbued with the sense of transformation, as the solution for the literal translation they sought. But why did the Wari' accept (or even propose) this solution?

Bearing in mind the perspectivist notion of translation we have been examining, it seems to me plausible that, with the aim of preserving the alterity that interested them, the Wari' made use of the distinction between *jamixi'* and *tamataraxi'* proposed by the missionaries as a way of maintaining the double perspective that characterizes shamanic transformations. Double in two senses. First, it maintains the Wari' perspective of the relation between the double (*jamixi'*) and transformation at the same time that it distinguishes the latter from the Christian perspective, which proposes a bodiless and nonmetamorphic soul, exclusive to the Wari' in contrast to animals. And second, it preserves an essential characteristic of the double through the Christian meaning of the soul—namely, the embodiment of the other's perspective, God's in this case, which was precisely the perspective that the Wari' wished to adopt. *Tamataraxi'* became precisely God's gaze over the Wari', arising, just like among shamans and animals, from their kinship to him. In this sense *soul,* in its two acceptations, has become a "twisted word" (Townsley 1993), pointing to two simultaneous worlds; unlike the vocabulary used by shamans, however, it has become part of the public domain, allowing the Wari' to circulate through these two distinct universes. It therefore involves a conception of translation that does not contain the notion of mediation, with the establishment over time of "passages between discontinuities," as suggested by Almeida (2002: 155–156), Montero (2006: 25–26), and Hanks (2014: 29).

The implications of the translation of the term *body* seem to me even more complex, insofar as it makes evident the continuity between the duality embraced by the Wari' and the ambiguity intrinsic to the Western Christian tradition, which oscillates between demonizing the body and sanctifying it (Schmitt 1998: 344).

For the missionaries, while the body is the seat of evil, as we have seen in the above translations, it is also the seat of the Holy Spirit, and it was by making himself human, in bodily form, that God revealed himself to men. The Christian ambiguity provides the space for the duality sought by the Wari', although this duality does not refer to the same notions of good and evil. Hence, the body maintains its original meaning, as an objectification of a relation, since the visible result is given by a relation, which can be established with either God or the devil. As Paletó observed (in July 2009): "God asks for the person to give him all the parts of his body to leave none to give to the devil. If he gives [part] to the devil, he drinks, he goes with women."

The Christian idea that the body does not belong to the person finds an echo in what I earlier called the Wari' outer self, determined by the other's perspective. Is it not precisely the idea of an outer self that we find in 1 Corinthians 6:19, used to illustrate a page from the calendar produced by the missionaries in the Wari' language? The Bible verse in English (New King James Bible) reads as follows: "Or do you not know that your body is the temple of the Holy Spirit who is in you, whom you have from God, and you are not your own?" The translation into Wari' in the calendar states as follows: "You must all already know that your body is like the house of the Holy Spirit [*Tamatarakon Iri'Jam*]. He enters and remains in you. [The body] was given to you by God. You cannot say that 'it is mine' among you [*Om ka mene pan xujuhu'*]." As Abrão explained, "The Holy Spirit enters inside our body. It is what gives thought, what makes us hungry." Pastor Awo Kamip's prayer during a conference meeting in 2009 likewise states, "It is your spirit [*tamataram*] that makes us believe in what you say. . . . Were it not for your spirit, we wouldn't know." Or as another pastor said during a service: "We don't like to do our things [but rather God's things]" (Estevão, Santo André church service, July 2002).[22]

In other words, just as the self was constituted relationally in the pre-Christian world, determined from the outside either by the perspective of kin or that of animal spirits, in the Christian world the self is determined by God or by the devil, who, as we saw in the previous chapter, vie with each other for the perspective of the Wari'.

While this may be true, we must remember also that, unlike the Wari' animals of the past, God is not perspectivist.[23] On the contrary, as we saw in chapter 6, his existence, omniscient and omnipresent, produces a flattening of perspectives and an interiorization of the person, who acquires a heart constantly scrutinized by God, though secret to everyone else. His perspective also implies a drastic reduction in the scope of humanity, supressing the perspective of animals, objectified since Genesis. According to Dumont (1983), Latour (1993), and other authors, as we saw above, there is a close relation between the production of an idea of nature, via the objectification of animals, and the genesis of the "psychological self" of Leenhardt, as a person who perceives himself or herself separate from the properly "cosmological" relations, although he or she continues to form part of a strictly human relational world.

One of my objectives for the conclusion is to identify this relation as the Wari' see it—that is, to explain the process through which the reduction in the scope of humanity implies an interiorization of the person. The latter, as we shall see, is not in any sense equivalent to the notion of the bounded individual so often associated with Christianity. This becomes clear when we examine another angle of the invention of heaven by the Wari', which reveals that they very clearly understood the individualist discourse of the missionaries. However, given the incompatibility between this individualist discourse and the Wari' conception of social life, they opted to exile it to a distant place in which, as we shall discover, the Wari' show very little interest.

HEAVEN AND THE OUTCAST INDIVIDUAL

In chapter 6 we saw that the posthumous destiny of the Wari' is today limited to heaven and hell. They say that heaven contains a house for each person, where they spend all their time writing the words of God, dictated by him, who, however, never makes himself visible.[24] They unanimously claim that in heaven everyone is a sibling to everyone else, as an example pointing to the fact that a dead man does not call his wife "wife," or treat her as a wife, when meeting her in heaven but instead treats her as a younger or older sister. As in the underwater world, everyone in heaven is young, beautiful, and healthy, with the difference being that in heaven they use footwear and clothing. They finally learn to read and write like white people.[25] They hold no festivals, never marry, never exchange food, and never live with each other. The most frequent response to my insistent questions on what people eat in the sky was, as mentioned earlier, the "word of God." Some said that they eat

FIGURE 17. Orowao Xik Waije and author, Negro River village, 1987. (Photo by Beto Barcellos.)

bread, like white people, and drink water, which the Wari' dislike and for which they usually substitute unfermented chicha or, today, soft drinks and a beverage made with packets of powdered, grape-flavored drink mix.

Orowao Xik Waije, a woman of around eighty, provided in 2008 a rich and peculiar description of heaven: "I shall leave behind my old clothes. The clothes I shall wear will be white. . . . My white hair will disappear, I shall have teeth again. I shall see the paper completely. God will give it [the paper] to me and I shall see. I shall sing and pray night and day. . . . I shall only eat cake with God. Sweets too." According to Paletó, the elder woman Wem Parawan visited heaven before she died, and told the Wari' that heaven was good, with good, well-made houses.[26]

Given that everything the Wari' most value in their everyday life is absent from heaven—that is, living with kin and caring for them daily, which includes making and offering chicha, along with good food, consisting of

FIGURE 18. Orowao Xik Waije and her daughter Dina, Negro River village, July 2014. (Photo by the author.)

game, fish, and maize—I asked them various times why they actually wanted to go to heaven. Everyone, without exception immediately replied: to avoid going to the fire. Heaven is not a posthumous destiny for which they yearn, therefore, but a counterpoint to hell, which is markedly undesired. In fact, in contrast to hell, heaven is seldom present in the discourse of the Christians, and I heard it mentioned only in response to my own questions. As one man told me once: "I believe ['to trust,' *howa*] in God so that my double [*jamu*] will escape [*witan*]."[27]

I should also observe that there is a way of reaching heaven before death, should death not occur before Jesus's return. Although there are variations on the idea of the end of the world, as we have seen, people usually say that Christians will rise to heaven with Jesus still "raw"—that is, alive (in opposition to the dead, traditionally roasted)—and will remain there. On earth only the sinners will remain, who will become the game of predatory animals, jaguars in most versions, though Paletó mentioned a giant cricket and even dragons (TV had already arrived among the Wari').

It is important to remember, too, that heaven as a posthumous destiny is, a number of people reminded me (a minority, I should say), just temporary. With the coming of Christ and after the final battle with the devil, heaven's inhabitants will once again occupy the earth, having now become "leaders" (*taramaxikon*). According to Abrão: "After ten to fifteen years in heaven, God will order them to descend to be leaders.... The Christians will turn into leaders, rich [*oro rico*], authorities [*oro autoridade*].... When they return, all sins will end."

In any event, a question clearly arises here: why, based on diffuse biblical imagery (see, for example, Isaiah 35:56, Isaiah 66:1, Matthew 5:34, Matthew 6:20–21, 1 Corinthians 2:9, 2 Corinthians 12:1–4, and Revelation 21:3–4), did they construct a heaven with such particular details?[28]

It is as though, in my view, heaven is constituted as the place where the process of constant transformation in which the Wari' live finally reaches a conclusion. As happens in other groups (see Kulick and Strout 1990 on the Kapun of Papua New Guinea, and Meyer 1998 on the Ewe of Ghana), they see themselves, in heaven, turning completely into whites, wearing clothing and shoes (which, owing to their expense, constitute an important sign of the difference of white people), and writing and reading fluently.[29] A direct equivalence emerges, therefore, between turning white and turning completely Christian, with turning white related principally to bodily transformation through food, clothing, and habits, especially writing.

Making themselves completely Christian requires the end of affinity, which occurs in heaven with the suppression of enacted kinship and the end of the spatialization of subgroups, which, we can recall, still existed in the underwater world with the distribution of the dead across different territories. Here the extension of consanguine kinship to everyone has the strange outcome of complete isolation, as if the absence of affinity, though desired, made relations as a whole meaningless. It also seems that consanguinity given a priori, rather than as an outcome of daily acts of caring, which transform "dislike" into "like," is not properly a relation.

The isolation of each person in his or her own house in this heaven is what most draws our attention, since it is precisely something detested by the Wari' in their everyday life. When I lived in an empty storeroom in the village for a while, they were worried about leaving me alone at home and would send their daughters to keep me company at night. They are always together, close, touching each other, sharing food, talking. The isolation in heaven seems to me like a Wari' caricature of the Christian individualist discourse, which they show they have comprehended, although its incorporation into their lived world has been difficult and, even today, partial, given the existence of the devil and, especially, affines.[30]

The final passage to becoming individual is necessarily accompanied by the end of transformation, and has, from the Wari' perspective, precisely the outcome predicted by Lévi-Strauss (1991: 90): the paralysis of the world. They do not speak, do not marry, do not have children, and do not hold festivals. The position of full humanity acquired in heaven, free from the attacks by animals and affines, contrasting with the position of pure prey in hell, leads to stagnation and the appearance of a dead world.[31] The image of heaven offered by Abrão in 2009 seems to me a clear caricature of what happens when difference is eliminated: "In heaven everyone has the same face, as though they were angels [jami pawin]. And they use the same clothing, the same color. There is no difference between people, you don't recognize them as different." This seems to have been why the Wari', in their elaborations, delegated the completion of their process of transforming into white people and Christianization to posthumous life. Experiencing this completeness on earth would imply death in life.

Conclusion

WHAT HAS ALWAYS SURPRISED ME about the Wari' during my thirty years of knowing them closely is their enormous capacity to deal with changes, with the obvious exception of those that cause suffering and death. If young people want to hear Brazilian music on the radio instead of learning the *tamara'* songs of the elders, or if they reveal that they don't know the myths, all their parents and grandparents do is laugh and remark that they are now completely white. Once I saw youths carrying enormous tape decks on their shoulders with Brazilian music playing loudly while they danced in a line of men singing traditional music, the *tamara'* songs. My perturbation over the music, which made it difficult to hear what the adults were singing, and which seemed disrespectful of the traditions (always the culture!) was not shared by the elders in the least. *Je kwerekukun,* that's what their body is like, it's their way, the elders said. The same kind of perturbation, when verbalized by myself to the pastor Awo Kamip, who had told me that he no longer remembered the myths, was answered, as I already mentioned, by the simple observation that his head was now full of the words of God.

This does not mean that the Wari' perceive themselves to be on a linear path of transformation, turning white, as a result of conditions external to themselves or even by choice. They do not see themselves through the lens of culture. If there is something that characterizes them, it is the capacity to alternate, and undoubtedly the successive movements of conversion and deconversion in the past provide a clear example of this. They seem to live with this alternation with few problems, without thinking of it negatively, just as they often assert either that they are completely Wari', different from white people, or completely white (*wijam,* "enemy"). As one young woman told me when explaining how even on the Day of the Indian, April 19, they

FIGURE 19. Paletó and Abrão in Itacoatiara, Niterói, December 2012. (Photo by the author.)

did not sing traditional music anymore, only Christian hymns: "We are completely white. We have ID papers, clothing, we eat rice and pasta." Or as Paletó said when explaining the end of the food taboos: "The animals' doubles have vanished. We are completely white [*wijam*]." When I asked him why they no longer hold the *huroroin'* festival, he replied, "The Wari' who are white do not answer our call" (*Om ka tomi' ha' ka wari' ko wijam na*). The same Paletó, at another moment, defended his *wari'* position when rebuking me for having commented, jokingly, that they were turning white: "You keep saying that we shall turn white [*wijam*], we are *wari'*, we are still completely *wari'* [*wari' wari' wet pin urut*]." He was right. Could there be anything more *wari'* than this kind of alternation between these two positions?

I was able to observe this alternation during visits by Paletó and Abrão to my house in Rio de Janeiro in recent years. On their last visit, in December 2012, when I decided to resume my study of funerary cannibalism with them, I never once heard them use the terms for body and soul with the Christian connotation and rarely heard them mention sin. I perceived a clear change in language, though, when they talked via Skype with the missionary Barbara Kern, addressing her by the term *older sister,* concentrating on the moral aspects of recent events, and using their vocabulary with the Christian meanings.

It is as though the Wari', like the shamans who inhabited the world of animals and spoke to them, were able to talk to the missionaries in their own language, aware that the shared words pointed to distinct referents. Back in their traditional relational contexts, such as family conversations about children or topics unrelated to Christianity, the former referents of the same terms used in the discourse of the church service come to the fore again.

I should also note that the narrative on abduction by jaguars and the questions posed by the listeners, described in chapter 2, involved Christian people, as was the case of To'o Xak Wa and Paletó, my Wari' parents. While listening to the narrative of the abducted woman, and when recalling what had happened to the mother of To'o, who was also captured, they never once remarked that it was a trick of the devil or attributable to the ignorance of the ancestors who did not know how to read. Not only was the narrative taken as fact, but also remarks were made about how the risk of jaguar abduction still exists today. To my eyes, it was as if the Wari' of the past were talking. Later, when we went to the house where I was staying with To'o and Paletó, they resumed their routine of praying in the morning, before meals, and before going to sleep.

PARADOX, CONTRADICTION, AND HYBRIDITY

While these questions refer us to the notion of the dual, or dividual, personhood, which contains different identities or perspectives within itself, each of which is displayed alternately, they also refer us to the notions of paradox, contradiction, and hybridity attributed to native peoples by different authors across different periods of time. One of the most well-known authors to take this line of argument, Lévy-Bruhl, observes the following about the thought of so-called primitive peoples:

> By designating it "prelogical" I merely wish to state that it does not bind itself down, as our thought does, to avoiding contradiction. It obeys the law of participation first and foremost. Thus oriented, it does not expressly delight in what is contradictory (which would make it merely absurd in our eyes), but

neither does it take pains to avoid it. It is often wholly indifferent to it, and that makes it so hard to follow.... They take but little account of the logical law of contradiction. (Lévy-Bruhl [1926] 1985: 78, 361; see also Viveiros de Castro 2002: 215; 2011: 41)

As we saw, Wagner (1975), analyzing the inventiveness of native peoples, arrives at a similar conclusion, observing an important distinction between societies that consciously conventionalize and those that differentiate. While the former stress "the avoidance of paradox and contradiction"), groups that differentiate "play out" the contradictions (116). Reflecting on the encounter between native and Western peoples, Wagner concludes that what the urban middle class perceives as strange or paradoxical in the natives is not their primitivism but a "quality of brilliance" typical of those who conceive life as "inventive improvisation" (88–89).[1]

As we saw in chapter 5, the conception of humanity as a continuum with markedly distant poles, as found among several Amazonian groups, illustrates perfectly this type of dialectical relation in Wagner's terms (1975: 116–124). In his inaugural article on Amerindian perspectivism, Viveiros de Castro (1996; 1998: 474–477) proposed, drawing from observations by a range of Amazonist ethnographers, that the region's natives appear to oscillate between very distinct conceptions of humanity, ranging from an unrestricted humanism, where all beings are human, to an exacerbated ethnocentrism in which humanity is attributed solely to coresidents or even just close kin. According to Viveiros de Castro (1998: 476), these antinomies stem from the shifts of focus typical to perspectivism, as well as from the opposite and correlated movements of fabricating (stabilizing) kinship and metamorphosis.[2]

This takes us back to the discussion, presented in chapter 5, of the double, and apparently contradictory, origin mythology of the Yanomami: one set of myths referring to the simultaneous creation of humans and animals, the other telling of the creation of a humanity, properly speaking, by the demiurge Omama. Leite (2010, 2013) suggests that the two Yanomami mythologies are related precisely to the dialectic between differentiation and conventionalization that Wagner describes, while extending them to the notions of metamorphosis and stabilization commonly found in Amazonian ethnology, as discussed above. According to Leite (2010, 2013), the first group of myths, in which humans and animals are created simultaneously, is one "of metamorphosis and differentiation," in the sense that human action is defined as a production of differentiated (somatic) collectives, counterinvented as interspecific metamorphosis. The second, which predefines a differentiated humanity, is the "mythology of stabilization and conventionalization" (2013: 87), and is thus a deliberate inversion of the salient inventive process. However, as we saw in chapter 6, this does not involve a symmetric opposition, since even the mythology of stabilization indicates the return to metamorphosis through the action of the trickster Yoase, whom we saw acting in a way equivalent to that of the devil among the Wari'. Hence, as observed in the earlier discussion, we are faced with something like a mythology and a half, in the sense that both end up referring to the world of primordial mixture.

Whether in the figure of the devil or that of other hybrids, including the simultaneously single and multiple divine and human persons, it is Christianity itself, therefore, that offers them the means to enact the alternation characteristic of their mode of reproduction. As we have seen, this is combined with the paradoxical actions of the fundamentalist missionaries, who introduce individualizing practices at the same time that they are forced to translate literally Bible stories imbued with a kind of participation that has parallels with the kind animating the Wari' world.

GOD'S EFFECTS: SEPARATION
AND INTERIORIZATION

We have seen, though, that the Christian experience of the Wari' involves significant transformations, which allow the emergence of notions that were once entirely foreign to them, like that of a world inhabited by a narrow humanity that excludes animals, constituted by people endowed with an inner self, kept secret from other people but visible to God. It is clear, therefore, that even though a hollow space already existed in Wari' thought for the adoption of the Genesis myth, given its equivalence to the mythology of stabilization present in other groups (as we saw in chapter 5), and even though they have maintained the perspectivist principle of the determination of the self through what is external to it (as we saw in chapter 9), God has revealed himself to be an other of a very special kind.

First, his invisibility is not provisional and contextual, as implied in the concept of *jam,* and so far he has remained invisible even to shamans, who, in the beginning went searching for him in the sky and were surprised to be unable to see him or even his house. Moreover, God's omnipresence, his totalizing gaze, as we have seen, renders the notion of perspective paradoxical. By definition, in the perspectivist world there can be no all-encompassing perspective.

Therefore, while the messages contained in the two creation myths analyzed in chapter 5 are similar (that of the Yanomami, and that of the Wari' interpretation of Genesis), an important difference exists between them, determined by the figure of the demiurge and his relation to humans. Omama lived among the Yanomami as one of them. But God is not a Wari', and even his son, despite having had a body and therefore having acted as an important mediator in the relations with God, can be seen only in dreams, remaining inaccessible to the gaze of shamans.

It seems that the difference between these two demiurges is essential, in the precise sense that divine transcendence (and omnipresence) is a guarantee of the "constitution" of the moderns—that is, it is crucial to the success of the human/nonhuman separation. According to Latour (1993: 98–99), a totally natural nature emerges only among moderns, who work to purify nature from culture. The true success of this separation, Latour argues, stems from the emergence of a God who, becoming transcendent while, at the same time, coming to exist in intimate space, turns into a "remote referee" who guarantees the efficacy of purification, maintaining "as much distance as possible between two symmetrical entities, Nature and Society" (127).[3]

Descola (2005), in a book dedicated to the categorization and analysis of ontologies, identifies Christianity, and more specifically the Christian Creation, as the key event in the constitution of the moderns, who are taken as paradigmatic examples of the naturalist mode of identification "founded on an apartheid regime" between humans and nonhumans (540). He argues,

> In order for the nature of the Moderns to acquire existence, a second operation of purification would be necessary [the first concerns the Greek concept of *phusis* and its development by Hippocrates and Aristotle; 99–100], it would be necessary for men to become exterior and superior to nature. It is Christianity to which we owe this second perturbation with its double idea of a transcendence of man and a universe created out of nothing by divine will. . . . From this supernatural origin, man assumes the right and the mission to administer the Earth, God having made him on the last day of genesis in order for him to exert his control over Creation. (103, my translation)

The success of the divine purifying act—in turn arising from the growing success of the Wari' attempt to make God into kin—implies a transformation in the devil's spectrum of action. Previously the devil's actions among the Wari' focused on animal agency; today, as the separation of humans and animals is becoming clear, the devil's actions are shifting toward a more narrowly defined universe of humanity, being deemed responsible for the morally inappropriate actions of Wari' themselves. In other words, today the attacks of animals—which, qua humans, preyed on the Wari'—have ceased to serve as the primary explanation for sicknesses; and the shamans, who had acted as mediators between humans and animals precisely because they could occupy the two positions simultaneously, are gradually disappearing. The place of animal attacks as *causa mortis* has been overtaken by the alternative preexisting explanation, sorcery practiced by affines who are motivated by the anger provoked in them as victims of avarice and adultery. These are the moral defects most widely condemned by the Wari' and associated with the Christian notion of sin. Such actions are attributed to the agency of the devil, who is said to seduce people and lead them to act sinfully. Public confession, as we have seen in chapter 8, basically consists of a declaration made before other believers that the person "fell in with the devil."

Once a mediator between humans and animals, the devil has therefore become an agent that exposes affinity, a relation the Wari' consider a constant source of tension. As I have already observed, both myth and social practice show that, for the Wari', an affine is a kind of internal enemy, partly domesticated but retaining the potential for alterity characteristic of both enemies and animals. The danger posed by affines becomes more acute with the demise of the traditional rituals geared toward resolving internal conflicts, such as the chicha festivals and the club fights. The new rituals, which consanguinize affines through generalized commensality and collective filiation to God, paradoxically exacerbate the negative aspects of the same affinity the Wari' wish to eclipse, since they have suppressed the means to control the aggressive acts of affines. While humanized animals may cease to exist, affines are, as we know, a necessary evil for the course of social life.

The passage from animality as a general condition of metamorphosis, to affinity as an expression of alterity, implies, however, a reduction in the scope of humanity and, as a consequence, an interruption of the characteristic Amerindian dialectic between its wider and narrower ranges of application mentioned above. As soon as humanity ceases to be a position constituted through the human action of differentiating from animals, humans appear to become distinct, as though affinity as a site of alterity were insufficient to maintain the relational dynamic characteristic of the dividual person (see Vilaça 2013b, 2015b).

It is as though this separation unleashes a process of internalization in chain reaction. This could be related to what Viveiros de Castro, in his analysis of the relation between horizontal and vertical (sacerdotal) shamanism in northwestern Amazonia (see Hugh-Jones 1994), calls the "political cooling" of mixed shamanic systems (meaning that shamanism is subsumed by power relations), related to the eclipsing of the horizontal shamanism based on nonhierarchical relations with alterity and the featuring of a well-defined sacerdotal shamanism, associated with ancestrality and hierarchy. In his words: "Sacerdotal transformation, its differentiation from the underlying shamanic function, is associated with a process of constituting a social interiority of a substantive kind" (Viveiros de Castro 2002: 471, my translation).

This would seem to involve what Taylor (1996: 211), exploring cultural changes among the Achuar Jivaro arising from contact with the West, defines as a narrowing of experience. In her words: "Acculturation begins in a condition of being locked into a state of undefined or unmarked normality by no longer engaging in the situations of interaction characteristic of the extreme states: thus an acculturated, or potentially acculturated, Jivaro is simply an ordinary being, what the Achuar themselves aptly call a *nangami shuar*, a 'just-so-person'" (see also Gallois 2007: 106).

As we know, voluntary metamorphosis has an important function in the constitution of the innate world through which the human action of differentiation makes sense, such that this narrowing does not constitute simply a gain. A "just-so-person" is freed from predation by animals and from the risk of being transformed into one of them but also loses the traditional means of producing difference. The two are indissociable.

It remains to determine, therefore, whether we can trace any parallel between the restricted notion of humanity described here and the emergence of the inner self. The Wari' experience, as well as that of the Kanak according to Leenhardt, appears to suggest that this "social interiority" can be linked to a kind of personal interiority, which, as I observed, has been developing with the transformation of the notion of the heart.[4]

In the previous chapter, in exploring the theories of Mauss ([1950] 1999), Dumont (1983), and Leenhardt ([1947] 1971) on the relation between Christianity and the emergence of the notion of the individual, I observed, inspired by the observations of Strathern (1988: 268–271) concerning Leenhardt, that one of the problems with the application of the models of these authors to the Wari' case was the supposition of the prior existence of an inner self, a psychological self, or an individual ready to emerge with the ontological changes brought by Christianity.

The Wari', as we have seen, did not have this notion of an inner self that could emerge with the ontological transformations, and in this sense they differed not only from the Kanak (according to Strathern's reading) but also from other groups of the Pacific, such as the Urapmin (Robbins 2008) and the Bosavi (Schieffelin 2008a) of Papua New Guinea. We therefore need to understand how the notion of an inner self begins to make sense among the Wari'—although, as we saw in chapter 9, its stabilization there is hindered not only by the dualist and perspectivist principles that continue to govern their thought but also by the ambiguity of the Christian message in relation to the question of the person's univocality.

Wagner's reflections in *The Invention of Culture* (1975: 124, 145–146) on the transformation of tribal societies toward urban Euro-American forms is of particular interest here, for they allow us to conceive of the birth of a notion of individuality without having to suppose its innate existence. According to Wagner, this transformation arises from two indissociable movements. The first is the inversion in the direction of the inventive process from differentiation to collectivization, while the other involves the aversion to paradoxes that is constitutive of conventionalizing systems. A brief exploration of this observation will bring us closer to understanding the Wari' case.

Considering the transition of tribal societies, whose preferential mode is differentiation, to modernity, which is characterized instead by the conventionalization of individualities conceived as innate, Wagner (1975: 116) argues that in crisis situations a change in the inventive movement can imply the end of the dialectic between convention and differentiation. Here I recall that this dialectic primarily takes place through the episodic inversion of the direction of action, a context we call ritual, in which the innate is produced, thereby giving meaning to the movement of everyday differentiation. In the Wari' case, as we have seen, the traditional rituals that produced the innate world of mixture between humans and animals were abandoned with the decline of shamanism, just like those, such as the chicha festivals, that unmasked affines and made the control of rivalries possible.

What happened was not just the suppression of the traditional rituals. As we saw in chapter 8, instead of inverting the direction of everyday action, focused on the production of a specific humanity equated with a group of kin, the new rituals introduced with Christianity run in the same direction as the everyday action, producing generalized fraternity and the separation of animals.[5] This implies not only the end of the Wagnerian dialectic between convention and invention but also the production of a very distinct innate world, constituted by beings similar in principle who will be conventionalized by divine rules.

According to Wagner (1975: 145–146), in this type of transformation the cultural codes or controls cease to form the basis for inventive improvisation and become a set of rules to be followed. We shift from a view of action as a continual adventure in "unpredicting" the world, and of life as an "inventive sequence," to an attempt to conform to the code.

CONCOMITANT CHANGES

As we saw at the start of this conclusion, though, and over the course of the book as a whole, especially in the analysis of the translations of Christian terms into the Wari' language, this new ritually produced innate world does not eliminate the original Wari' world founded on difference. Hence, as we have seen, even in the absence of the traditional rituals the Wari' knew how to preserve their innate world of the "dislike" through the careful choice of terms in the Wari' language to designate Christian concepts that allow the inhabiting of two worlds simultaneously, despite the fact that the Christian meanings, like omniscience and omnipresence associated with invisibility, led them to a world not only unknown but also inconceivable. In any event, in speaking of a process of individualization, I am not referring to the self-contained Euro-American individual, which would be the extreme of a complex continuum, and which the Wari' exile to heaven.

However, the other changes that have been occurring over the last few decades, especially in the economic context of the Wari', lead me to think that the contemporary Christian experience not only is different from that of the past but also may be different in the near future. Since the 1990s the Wari' have been led to an increased immersion in the market economy and the world of white people as a whole. During this period, energy generators were installed in the larger villages adjacent to the FUNAI posts, with electrical outlets and lighting supplied in the house of the FUNAI officer, the school, and the infirmary, as well as in an open-sided shed, where, in 2001, a television was connected. Seven years later, in 2008, around half the houses had generators, frequently accompanied by televisions, which people use to access free-to-air satellite channels, watching news, soap operas, and other programs. Expressions used by TV actors, including the heavily repeated "thanks to God" and "go with God," highlight the Christian makeup of the Brazilian people as a whole and are used by some of the younger Wari' whenever they speak in Portuguese with outsiders. Words in Portuguese have begun to form part of everyday life, something absent twenty years ago.

An intercultural education project has also begun, the Açai Project, which entails the training of indigenous teachers, the production of textbooks in the Wari' language, and the adaptation of school content to what the project calls the local "reality." Indigenous health agents have also been trained, who, along with the teachers, replaced almost all the whites performing these functions in the villages, receiving a monthly salary that in 2015 was comparable to around two hundred U.S. dollars. In 2009, a few young people began enrolling in a university course of study designed exclusively for indigenous people and aimed at training high school teachers. There they take course modules lasting two months, during which time groups of students share houses in the city. Their curriculum includes linguistics, anthropology, Brazilian legislation concerning education and indigenous peoples, history, science, geography, mathematics, and Portuguese.

Money entered not only in the form of payments to these new professionals but also through government benefits paid to retired rural workers,[6] as well as to women during the four months of maternity leave, along with the Family Allowance (*Bolsa Família*), a benefit available to all those with children below the age of eighteen. These income sources had a significant impact on the local lifestyle, especially in relation to the consumption of industrially produced food and objects, bought on the monthly trips they made to the city to receive their payments. Those with wages built brick houses (previously made from straw and paxiúba palm, *Socratea exorrhiza*), which they covered with asbestos roofing and furnished with tables, chairs, beds, and mattresses. They began to stock industrial food, becoming differentiated people to whom others, even non-kin, would go in order to ask for a tin of oil, sugar, or coffee, paid for with local produce such as manioc flour and Brazil nuts or even with money. Since 2001, one of the teachers has hired an orphaned young woman as a domestic maid, paying for her services with food and clothing.

In the 1980s, when I started my research, the money that circulated among the Wari' came entirely from the sale of Brazil nuts and manioc flour and was used to buy ammunition, sugar, coffee, oil, and tobacco from the *marretões,* nonindigenous traders who visited the villages in their boats piled high with merchandise, or during the sporadic journeys to the city. Industrialized foods were limited to those listed above, the Wari' staple diet comprising swidden produce (especially maize), fruits, honey, fish, and game.

In 2001, after five years' absence, I observed a clear change in food habits. Meals were now composed of rice, beans, and pasta, which had taken the place of maize as an accompaniment to meat and fish, both of which were now rarer and obtained from more distant places owing to the exhaustion of resources caused by years of fixed residence in the same location. To these foods were gradually added soft drinks, sweets, and other sugar-rich products, which worsened the dental problems already present since the first contacts. Cases of high blood pressure, cholesterol, and glucose levels began to be recorded, associated with an increase in cardiovascular diseases and diabetes.

Besides the missionaries, other whites, including me, established long-term relations with the Wari'. More than once, I brought Paletó and Abrão to Rio de Janeiro to visit me and meet members of my family, with whom they came to forge very close relationships.

We need to bear in mind, therefore, that the Wari' now find themselves in a different phase of their Christian experience, implying various kinds of transformations that have been analyzed in relation to other native groups. Maxwell (2007) draws attention to generational differences, suggesting that those who have grown up since childhood within a Christian environment do not share the same conceptions as people who entered into contact with Christianity as adults. As Keane (2007: 139) observes, "The story of conversion, whether in the colonial world or after, needs an account of subsequent generations, as much as one of 'first contact.'"[7] Among the Wari', the fact that two generations have been born since the first Christian phase combines with the death of those who lived as adults before contact with white people and who today would be around eighty years old. As one man explained to me in Portuguese: "Now it's another people, it's no longer the people of the forest."

Although the insertion of the Wari' into the market economy is still very limited, we may presume that the increase of this insertion will allow them to better understand the meanings of the individualizing practices of the missionaries and the notion of inner self, today associated with the heart. We know that one of Leenhardt's fears was that the growing involvement of the

Kanak in Western economic activities would lead to the complete end of not only participation of the type that is considered mystic, whose end was desired by the missionary-ethnologist, but also internal participation, between kin, which he saw as positive ([1947] 1971: 267).

Along the same lines, Robbins (2004: 311) concludes his monographic book this way: "It would, I think, take the dominance among the Urapmin of those social forms through which Westerns individuals succeed in inhabiting *this* world, especially the capitalist market, for individualism finally to be completely at home there."

I stress that it is not a question of backing the theories of authors like Weber (1956, 1987), Bellah (1964), and Horton (1975), who associate the interest in Christianity with these prior transformations. In the Urapmin case, such changes had still not occurred at the time of Robbins's research, and, in the case of the Wari', as we saw, the interest in Christianity preceded the economic changes. In both cases, rather than preceding the Christian experience, the other changes emerged in parallel to it, in the sense of producing a transformation in the same direction.

A TAPIR AND THE UNIVERSITY

Once again, I emphasize that the changes do not move in an inexorable direction, and that the Wari' always continue to surprise me, as in 2005, when a man killed a tapir. To my surprise, after distributing some of the meat to his close kin, he sold the rest at his house, using some scales to weigh the cuts and charging a fixed price per kilo, which the buyer could pay in either money or produce. My reflections on the mercantile and individualizing character of this practice were cut short when I saw people's elation at being able to obtain meat that previously would have been limited to close kin and thus unavailable to them. The possibility of buying meat had the effect of extending the ties of commensality and, therefore, kinship with the local group as a whole, recalling the analyses of Sahlins (1997a, 1997b) on anthropologists' "sentimental pessimism," in which he shows that diverse native groups worldwide use the new resources to extend their network of kin, minimizing the individualizing character of these practices. Even the notion of "culture" adopted by them, Sahlins shows, ends up enabling a resumption of old practices, albeit inevitably recontextualized.

Very recently I learned via a telephone call from my brother Abrão that "culture" has just emerged as an issue for the Evangelical Wari'.[8] Abrão is a student in the Basic Intercultural Teacher Training Degree course at the Federal University of Rondônia, on the Ji-Paraná campus, which is where he called me from. Since the university is labeled "intercultural," the question of indigenous culture is central, which led Abrão, an enthusiastic Christian, to ask me: "Our professor says that we are losing our culture. Can you help us, older sister?"

NOTES

INTRODUCTION

1. For a critique of those models based on the metaphor of mixture, see Robbins (2004: 5, 313–333), as well as Friedman (1999) and Amselle (1998), whom he cites.

2. See Hanks (2013: 388, 391) on the "ongoing cycles of renunciation and affirmation" of the Maya of Yucatan regarding Christianity.

3. See Sahlins (2011a, 2011b, 2013) for a recent discussion.

4. See Vargas 2010 and Strathern 2012. The term *Alter-a[c]tion* comes from the latter.

5. It is worth noting here that the Wari' material was, along with the Araweté and Yudjá/Juruna cases, the ethnographic inspiration for developing the notion of perspectivism (Viveiros de Castro 1996: 36n5), constituting one of the prototypical examples of this ontology.

6. As Viveiros de Castro (2002: 215; 2011: 41) observed in analyzing the problem posed by the conversion of the Tupinambá to the missionaries, these are cultures for whom "the notion of dogma is completely foreign."

7. The orthography used in this book is based on the phonetic transcription system for Wari' developed by the New Tribes Mission, the only difference being that I use the letter *k* instead of *c* or *qu* to represent the phoneme /k/. The symbol ' indicates a glottal stop (see Everett and Kern 1997 and Vilaça 2010). All Wari' narratives and conversations were recorded in the Wari' language and translated by myself, except on the rare occasions, specified in the text, when a person spoke to me in Portuguese. The book was originally written in Portuguese and translated into English by David Rodgers.

CHAPTER I. THE NEW TRIBES MISSION

1. See Cloutier (1988: 42–56) for a brief history of the NTM aimed at understanding their work among the Zoró, an indigenous Amazonian people.

2. After the first friendly contact, they also learned that the killing had been "almost by accident," provoked by one man's uncontrolled desire for presents, since from the outset the missionaries had actually been classified positively as descendants of a light-skinned mythic figure (Johnston 1966: 64).

3. For details on the contact with the Ayoré, see Bessire 2014.

4. For an account of everyday life on a training course, see Dawson (2000, ch. 5). Also see Scharf (2010) for an account of his time living among the Wari'.

5. Nowadays, Almeida (2002: 53) writes, the training of NTM missionaries in Brazil involves the following curriculum "structured in three levels: 'Theological' lasting three years; as well as theological materials, courses are given in Cultural Anthropology, Introduction to Pedagogy and Foreign Languages. The second level lasts a year and the main courses are Transcultural Communication, Basic Notions of Mechanics and Nursing (First Aid, Notions of Clinical Diagnostics, Vital Signs, Prevention in Healthcare, Notions of Tropical Diseases). Finally the third level, 'Cultural Linguistics,' lasts one year and includes the courses Introduction to Pedagogy and Principles of Didactics, Introduction to Cultural Anthropology, Bilingual Literacy, Production of Bilingual Material, the Universal Phonetic Code for Codification and Transcription, and General Principles of Translation."

6. On conversion as "the most individual point of one's life," see Stolz (1999: 11).

7. See Stoll (1982: 5) for statements on the doctrine of the Wycliffe Bible Translators / Summer Institute of Linguistics, which also emphasizes the literal nature of the biblical text, the fall of man, and salvation in Christ. See Harding (2001) on the emergence of fundamentalism from the debate in the United States concerning the book of Genesis. See Crapanzano (2000).

8. Cited in Gallois (2012: 69). See Schieffelin (2007: 143) on the Unevangelized Field Mission.

9. See Johnston (1985: 250–251).

10. For an update, see the untitled interview with missionary Barbara Louise Kern in *Revista Confins da Terra* 42, no. 138 (July–September 2009): 11–12, http://issuu.com/digital-anapolis/docs/138_-_revista_confins_da_terra_-_tribo_pacaas_novos, accessed on May 9, 2014. The magazine is a publication of Missão Novas Tribos do Brasil.

11. See Barros (1994: 71) and Gallois (2012: 71).

12. See Stoll (1982: 22) on Wycliffe Bible Translators / Summer Institute of Linguistics: "Bible translation will hasten the Second Coming."

13. In the latest version of the "Statement of Faith" by the missionaries of New Tribes Mission, they affirm that they believe in the "pretribulational, premillennial return of Christ for the church" (statement 10). "What We Believe," New Tribes Mission, n.d., https://usa.ntm.org/about/what-we-believe, accessed November 6, 2015. See Oliveira (2010) on the Missão Evangélica da Amazônia (MEVA). Naomi Haynes (pers. comm., 2015) called my attention to the peculiarity—when compared to other missionary translations—of the fact that the letters of Paul to the Thessalonians were, according to Barbara Kern's information, one of the first biblical books to be translated: this is precisely where the end of the world and the unannounced

return of Christ are foretold, emphasizing the importance of this eschatological conception for the NTM missionaries.

14. My thanks to Naomi Haynes (pers. comm., 2015) for highlighting this point.

15. During the service of January 27, 2002, the pastor Awo Kamip named as enemies "communists," who, fortunately, had not arrived there, he said, but had tried to enter churches in other places.

16. The NTM site observes, "Missionary training teaches you about the complex concepts involved in tribal church planting, such as understanding *culture* and learning *language* so you can effectively communicate cross-culturally." "Training," New Tribes Mission, n.d., https://usa.ntm.org/training (accessed November 6, 2015).

17. For a discussion of this theme, see Gallois and Grupioni (1999: 106).

18. In an interesting text titled "Anthropologists and Missionaries: Brothers under the Skin," Van der Geest (1990: 592) calls attention to the fact that anthropologists, unlike missionaries, do not take the native religion seriously, instead rationalizing it and taking its premises as metaphors.

19. Far from being exclusive to the NTM, the view of native culture as a "regime of terror" is shared by other faith missions. In the words of Taylor (1981: 66) on SIL missionaries among the Amazonian Achuar: "They consider Achuar culture to be an oppressive system that maintains the natives themselves in a state of permanent spiritual terror."

20. See Cloutier (1988: 56) on the Amazonian Zoró, and Dawson (2000).

21. In a certain sense we could say that for the missionaries, Christianity, the biblical reality, and its values are all equated with "nature" as a universal given and are independent from culture, as shown by Engelke (2014: S300) in relation to African apostolics in Zimbabwe: "The truth of Christianity is universal, and this puts it beyond any bounds of culture." I thank Naomi Haynes (pers. comm., 2015) for pointing me to this work and to this connection.

CHAPTER 2. VERSIONS VERSUS BODIES

1. I should make clear that is not my intention to explore the intense philosophical, theological, and anthropological discussions concerning the concept of translation per se, since not only are these outside my field of competence, but also such an exploration would lead us away from the central objective of this chapter, which is to contrast the concept of translation of a specific group of missionaries with that of the Wari' and other Amazonian peoples. For a recent study of indigenous Christianity focused on translation, see Handman 2015.

2. Also see Clifford (1992: 79). The same kind of premise can be identified in the decree *Ad Gentes,* section no. 26, on Catholic missionary activity, issued in 1965 by the Second Vatican Council.

3. See Durston (2007: 79) on the need for sixteenth-century Catholic priests to understand Quechua, and Hanks (2010, 2013, 2014) on the Yucatan Maya. In the

case of Peru, the language was a dialect of Quechua spoken in Cuzco: see Durston (2007: 2, 187–189).

4. The site of the Wycliffe Bible Translators (www.wycliffe.org/, accessed May 25, 2012) states, "In 1999, Wycliffe committed to the mission of seeing a Bible translation program started in every language still needing one by the year 2025." According to the organization, there are 943 native languages in the Americas, 81 of which have not received any translation of scripture into the idiom "of their heart."

5. Previously found on www.ntm.org, accessed May 2010; the article that this quote was drawn from is no longer posted, and its title and the author's name are not available. In the words of the fundamentalist missionaries of the Unevangelized Fields Mission, in their work among the Bosavi of Papua New Guinea, the native language (in this case Tok Pisin, the local lingua franca into which the Bible was translated) is "the shrine of a people's soul" (Schieffelin 2007: 144). See also Handman (2015: 19, 64–89) on the SIL concept of translation.

6. On the influence of Nida's work on missionary translations in Papua New Guinea, see Handman (2015: 66–67; 90). Regarding Africa (Ghana), see Meyer (1999: 80). On the impersonality of language, assumed by the missionaries to exist independently of the community of speakers, see Rafael (1993: 36); and see Durston (2007: 228) on the debate among sixteenth- and seventeenth-century Christians between *ad verbum* and *ad sensum* translations, the former based on equivalences between each word (word for word) and the latter on the observation of the syntactic form of the original text, which made the resulting texts difficult to understand.

7. See Durston (2007: 84) on Quechua. Also see Robbins (2004: 128; 2007c: 128), Schieffelin (2007: 145), Handman (2015), and Stasch (2007: 113–114) on Papua New Guinea, and Clifford (1992: 80) on New Caledonia.

8. On the African context, see also Lienhardt (1982) and James (2013). For various equivocations in the translation of Christian texts into Quechua, see Durston (2007: 96, 208–209, 211).

9. See also Hanks (2013: 397) on similar reasons for keeping *God* as *Dios* among the Yucatan Maya. The hierarchy of languages becomes clear in the notion of the "original Bible text" cited above from Schieffelin (2007: 147).

10. According to Paletó, the Wari' idiom was the language spoken in the Tower, whites included. White people's language came to existence after the differentiation.

11. See Cesarino (2011: 185) on the human component of books among the Marubo.

12. See Segal (2003: 217–218).

13. It can be seen, therefore, that theories of language may vary enormously between Amazonian groups.

14. Among the lexical differences, we can highlight a number relating to kinship terms. It is worth noting that a young Christian man once compared the different dialects to the division into many languages with the fall of the Tower of Babel. On the different versions of some myths, see Vilaça 2010.

15. See Vilaça (1992, 2000). On the difference between real and potential affines, see Viveiros de Castro (1993).

16. Also see Gow (1997) on the Piro/Yine.

17. A Wari' boy told me in 1992 that when he went hunting with his father and they separated, he would look first at his father's feet and hands when they met up again and would also check to see whether he had a tail.

18. As a current example of the same type of perspectivist translation, a woman once told me that people in hell suffer from a terrible thirst because the devil does not drink water, since water is blood for him.

19. On the opposition between this concept of translation and Benjaminian theory, see Cesarino (2011: 133).

20. Combined with a possessive suffix: male *jamikon*, female, *jamikam*, neutral *jaminain/jami*, collective *jamixi'*, and so on. The term *tamataraxi'* is used as a synonym of *jamixi'* in most contexts. I return to this point in chapter 6.

21. See similar interpretations of the Ge *karō* by Coelho de Souza (2002: 534, 536), the Candoshi (Jivaro) *vani* by Surrallès (2003: 46), and the Marubo *vaká* by Cesarino (2011: 34–35).

22. According to some people, however, the shaman's animal body is active only when his Wari' body is inert, generally during sleep.

23. See Opas (2008: 127) on sexual relations with nonhuman beings as a motor of definitive translations of perspective among the Piro/Yine.

24. See Cesarino (2011: 97–99) on this type of parallelism.

25. See Lima (2002: 12) on the development of this idea in relation to the Yudjá; also see Vilaça (2005).

26. In the words of Cesarino (2011: 134, my translation): "Here it is as though the limit towards which translation *tends* is not one determined by convergence but by the *divergence* between radically distinct conceptual systems (Western, Amerindian)."

27. See Queiroz (1999: 262) on the Waiwai, for instance.

28. See Lloyd (2012: 73–77) for a discussion on the metaphorical/literal dichotomy.

29. She goes on to say that while we may think "our informants are being poetic and ambiguous, though untruthful or ignorant or unconcerned with truth about the world[,] . . . the confusion is often ours: it is we who assume this image of a single, unified world, and not they" (605). See also Overing Kaplan (1985b: 158–159).

30. Neglect by kin, or conflicts with them, are very often cited as factors facilitating abduction, which confirms the idea of the dispute of kinship between humans and animals, which is explored in chapter 5. On some occasions, a particular death may be explained as having been caused by God for the same motive, as happened with the pastor Xin Xoi, an OroAt man. According to Paletó, Xin Xoi had been called by God because his kin did not care for him.

31. Today in 2015, Google Translate is considered an important translation tool. One of the book's reviewers pointed out the similarity between the translative acts of the woman-jaguar and those of Jesus, who, among other miracles, transmuted

water into wine. Although the Wari' have never made this analogy explicit to me, its pertinence can be observed in the fact that the Wari' consider Jesus the translator par excellence of the divine word, as we shall see in chapter 6.

32. Also see Kopenawa and Albert (2010: 292, 340) on the Yanomami; Fausto (2007b: 82) on the Guarani; Fausto and De Vienne (2014) on a recent prophetic movement in the Upper Xingu, analyzed through the concept of "acting translation"; and Laugrand (1997) on shamans and priests among the Inuit, including the inverse mimetism of shamans by priests. On Bible translation as an enacted ritual among the Reformed Guhu-Samane, see Handman (2015).

33. See also Reichel-Dolmatoff (1975: 55, 58, 99, 115, 120, 124, 125) and Wright (1996: 79).

34. Clifford (1992: 76), in his biographical study of Leenhardt, notes that for him, conversion "can be a method of 'observation' of the white." See Gell (1998: 99–101) for an interesting discussion of mimesis, and Zoppi (2012) on the Cashinahua in Brazil.

35. See Santos-Granero (2009: 118–119) and Sahlins (1985: 153).

36. On the Guarani forgetting the appropriation of various aspects of Christianity, see Fausto (2007b: 89–92).

37. According to Taylor (2007: 154), by imitating the whites the Jivaro did not wish to "become the other." They wanted to preserve a clear Jivaro "identity": the adoption of white people's objects, for example, was a means for them to become better than the whites, not like them. For a concept of mimetism that involves imitation without a loss of the previous identity, see Willerslev (2004) on the Siberian Yukaghirs, for whom mimetism is not metamorphosis but the experience of a double point of view.

CHAPTER 3. THE ENCOUNTER WITH THE MISSIONARIES

Maria Tereza Montovani, "The Light Still Shines," New Tribes Mission of Brazil, n.d., www.novastribosdobrasil.org.br, accessed October 17, 2015.

1. The Wari' did not keep pets.

2. For a similar myth among the Ge, see Auké, in Da Matta (1970).

3. For a complete version of this myth, see Vilaça (2010: ch. 6).

4. See Kelly (2001, 2005) and Fausto (2007a, 2012).

5. See Vilaça (2010: 112–115).

6. It is important to note that the Wari' were unfamiliar with river navigation and lived close to small rivers and streams, avoiding the shores of larger rivers and crossing the latter only during the dry season, when they could be traversed on foot.

7. See Souza Lima (1995) on the activities of the SPI.

8. Recall that the NTM was founded in 1942, and that its first expedition was to Bolivia, where the missionaries were killed by the Ayoré. This explains why Guajará-Mirim, on the border with Bolivia, was one of the first Brazilian destinations for these missionaries. On the NTM among the Yanomami since the end of the 1950s, see Kopenawa and Albert (2010: 255–277, 713–715).

9. Today a widow, Delores lives in the mission house in Sanford, Florida. In 2007 I tried to organize a trip to Florida to interview Delores and other missionaries (LeRoy Smith and Richard Sollis were still alive at the time, though the latter had Alzheimer's disease), sending a letter in which I explained my intentions. The reply to this letter was sent not to me but to Barbara Kern, who sent me an email with Delores's refusal. However it was Delores who provided Barbara, in 2011, with data on the chronology of the missionary presence among the Wari', for which I had asked her (Barbara) by email.

10. Royal was not present during these first stages, which, he said, took place in 1956 while he was on holiday. Friedrich Scharf (2010: 83), who took part in later expeditions to the Laje and Negro Rivers, describes some interesting organizational details, such as the use of colored ribbons for identification purposes, tied to the presents left on the trails for the Indians and to the missionaries' clothes so that they would be associated with the items. They also all used the same kind of tennis shoes, which made footprints different from those left by rubber tappers and hunters.

11. Microfilms 41 to 45, Museu do Indio, FUNAI, Rio de Janeiro.

12. Personal communication to Barbara Kern, 2011.

13. Personal communication, 1994. The information on the arrival dates of the missionaries varies from informant to informant (see Friedrich Scharf 2010: 80–81).

14. Friedrich Scharf (2010: 82) states that the expeditions included himself, Abraham, Joe, and Richard. Royal, LeRoy, and Assis "continued the work already begun."

15. For a while in the 1960s, the missionaries were "expelled" from the area by the army, but a short time later they were recalled to support the SPI's contact attempts. The conflicts between the missionaries and the SPI were usually related to suspicions concerning overseas interest in Brazilian territory. In the words of one OroEo man: "People talked nonsense, saying that missionaries took gold and diamonds from the river shore here."

16. She was the daughter of NTM missionaries (see "Entrevista," *Revista Confins da Terra* 42, no. 138 (July–September 2009): 11–12.

17. This relocation was organized by FUNAI, which decided to reestablish the post on the shores of the Pacaás Novos River to facilitate the transportation of goods and people. As part of the same process, the Dois Irmãos Post was transferred to the locality of Santo André, also on the west shore of the Pacaás Novos, a few kilometers upriver from Tanajura.

18. Barbara is the coauthor, with linguist Dan Everett, of the only academic linguistic study of the Wari' language (Everett and Kern 1997).

19. For a short biography of this couple, see Maria Eli de Oliveira e Silva, "Biografia: Um dos nossos pioneiros entre os Pacaas Novos," *Revista Confins da Terra* 42, no. 138 (July–September 2009): 13–14.

20. See Kelly (2011b: 65) on the Yanomami.

21. The conflicts among the whites, who, owing to circumstances beyond their control, were obliged to live together, were numerous, beginning with the dispute

over the Indians between the Protestant missionaries and those linked to the Catholic Church, which continues even today.

22. Conklin (2001a: 47–50); Vilaça (2010: 229–300).

23. The Wari' do not have a word for a community of believers, so they use the word *crentes* in Portuguese. This term is translated throughout the book as "Christians."

24. Recorded by Abrão, tape 5, side A.

25. See Von Graeve (1989) on the epidemics among the Wari'.

26. For a similar episode narrated by a SIL missionary working among the Palikur, see Capiberibe (2007: 175). See Rivière (1981: 9) on the Trio.

27. See Fienup-Riordan (1991), Laugrand (1997), Burch (1994: 92), Hugh-Jones (1994), Taylor (1981), Viveiros de Castro (2002), Wright (1999: 187–188, 200, 207), Queiroz (1999: 268), and Capiberibe (2007: 161; 174–176). On the introduction of new pathogenic agents by missionaries, see Pollock (1993: 166).

28. See Queiroz (1999: 275). Gow (2006: 225) concludes: "It would suggest that Piro people understood the Adventist message as a potential collective shaman-becoming, and the Adventists as powerful shamans."

29. See Andrello (1999: 292) on the Taurepang shamans' appropriation of Christian booklets to perform their cures; also see Amaral (2014: ch. 3) for a broader analysis of the circum-Caribbean region. See Capiberibe (2007: 161; 2009: 51) on the Palikur, Santos-Granero (2009: 118) on the Yanesha, and Carneiro da Cunha (1998: 11) on the Cashinahua.

30. See Fausto (2002) on the Tupian Parakanã and the curing of diseases; see also Queiroz (1999: 272–274).

31. It should be noted that part of the Yanomami population was Christianized and remained so.

32. See Chamorro (1998: 65).

CHAPTER 4. EATING GOD'S WORDS

1. See Queiroz (1999), Oliveira (2010), Grotti (2007, 2009), and Amaral (2014).

2. According to Robbins 2004, missionaries are often the only people who bother to clearly explain to the natives about the creation of the world and how it functions, the moral rules of the whites, and so on (see also Lasmar 2005).

3. Gow (1997) defines the state of abandonment as the motor of relations among the Piro/Yine.

4. Lucindo, along with the rubber bosses Nazozeno and Manussakis, had ordered several of the previous massacres suffered by the Wari'.

5. Note that the Wari' term that I translate as "language," *kapijakon wari'*, refers not only to the lexicon but also to the oral tradition as a whole.

6. It is important to remember that the Wari' did not have chiefs who could persuade others to convert, as occurred among some other groups, especially in the Pacific.

7. One young man, for example, declared his belief to the community gathered in the church as follows: "My father believes, my mother believes, I too believe." See also Gow (2006: 219), quoting Artemio: "To be an evangelista, you have to live in a village of Piro evangelista people" (see also Gow 2006: 234; and Grotti 2009: 120, regarding the Trio). It is worth noting the striking difference between the motives given here for converting to Christianity and the classic accounts of conversion to Christianity, founded on individual experience, as in, for example, the conversion of Paul on the road to Damascus (described in lesson book 6: 7–8). I should make clear, however, that although conversion is comprehended and experienced as a collective undertaking, not all people in the community say they became Christian at the same time.

8. For a Christian version of a life story of another Wari' man (collected and published by the missionaries), see Wem Karamain quoted in "A Voz do Índio," *Revista Confins da Terra* 42, no. 138 (July–September 2009): 6.

9. See Rivière (1981: 10) on the Trio.

10. See Vilaça (1996, 1997, 1999).

11. On the transformative power of anger, see Belaunde (2000: 209–211). The conversion to Christianity as a means to suppress anger and sorcery is common in the ethnographies (see Wright 1999; Grotti 2009: 120). On the equation between anger and sin, see Robbins (2007a: 309) on the Urapmin.

12. Conversion is very often expressed in the language of the sharing and companionship that characterizes kinship. People say that one "accompanies Jesus" or "abandoned God," the same expression used to leave a spouse (but an act inconceivable in the context of the parent-child relation).

13. The end of the world constitutes a threat above all because of its unpredictability, as made clear in the words of the pastor Awo Kamip in a church service (2007): "We do not know the day when he [God] will arrive. It may be tomorrow, it may be in the middle of the night." Or, in the words of Paletó: "Nobody knows. It's not when FUNAI advises us that you [the anthropologist] are going to arrive. It's God who is going to tell Jesus the day that he is going to descend." As we saw in chapter 1, Christians prophesize that this event will be preceded by the coming of the antichrist, who will incite widespread wars. Considering that the whites have better access to information than them (see the same observation in Robbins 2004), it is understandable that the Wari' had reacted with concern to news of a war of the size announced against the Taliban, desiring more precise information from me on what was happening in a big city like Rio de Janeiro (Vilaça 2014a).

14. As we shall see in chapter 6, other versions of heaven list other foods, typically alien to the precontact Wari' universe, such as breads, biscuits, and cakes.

15. See also Robbins (2004: 266); on the relation between words and materiality, see chapter 6; also see Keane (2013: 13) and Coleman (2006: 165).

16. The Wari' often say that people in the time of Moses adored statues because they ate stone powder (see Vilaça 2014a).

17. See Mosko (2010) on blood and the partible person. See also Kelly (2001, 2005a).

18. For a complete version, see Vilaça (1992: 237–245; 2010: 175–194).

19. On the punitive action of God among the Trio, see Rivière (1981: 10); on the Gavião, see Cloutier (1988: 63).

20. Jesus is sometimes associated with the mythic figure Hwijin, a man who had sex with his brother's wife, was "killed" by maize beer as punishment, and became part human, part dead. Other Wari' mythic figures are related to Christian figures as protagonists of situations that, to them, appear similar to biblical episodes, whether through localization or through the events in themselves, as in the case of Noah, associated with the protagonist of the Wari' flood myth, Nanananana (see Vilaça 2010: 146–174).

21. See Lévi-Strauss (1991: 299–320) and Overing Kaplan (1985b: 157) on the centrality of difference for Amerindians.

22. Abrão's use of the letter C to replace the K, used by myself to represent the same phoneme, reflects the writing system taught by the missionaries and still used today by the Wari'.

23. The idea of Christianity as a religion of love is explored by Veyne (2007: 42–43) in his study of the Christianization of the West: he argues that God's boundless love for all the faithful, whether royalty or vassals, and irrespective of any offerings made, was the great innovation of Christianity, and one of the important factors in its success. Also see Fausto (2007b) on the "de-jaguarification" of Guarani cosmology with the advent of Christianity, and Santos-Granero 2009 on the Amuesha. We can note, however, in the Wari' lesson book 1, the biblical episodes on divine rage, such as Isaiah 25:15–38 and especially Hosea 13:7–8 on God's anger against the people of Israel and his jealousness of the worship of idols. The image of animal predation, so dear to the Wari', is also central here: "So I will be to them like a lion; Like a leopard by the road I will lurk; I will meet them like a bear deprived *of her cubs;* I will tear open their rib cage; And there I will devour them like a lion. The wild beast shall tear them." Also see Isaiah 9:9–20: "Through the wrath of the Lord of hosts the land is burned up, and the people shall be as fuel for the fire; no man shall spare his brother. And he shall snatch on the right hand and be hungry; he shall devour on the left hand and not be satisfied; every man shall eat the flesh of his own arm" (an image of consanguine cannibalism that would horrify the Wari'; citations from the New King James Bible).

24. See also Chamorro (1998: 49), who says that the first feeling experienced by a Guarani baby is anger, and that nonbaptized children become sad and enraged; see Cadogan (1959: 19). See also Grotti (2009: 120) on the Trio. On the Korowai from Papua New Guinea, see Stasch 2009: ch. 2.

CHAPTER 5. PRAYING AND PREYING

1. Affines are related to but not equivalent to enemies and animals: as we shall see in chapter 9, affinity proved to be more resistant to the Wari' masking strategies than the humanity of animals.

2. The expression found in the subhead at the start of this section, "no innocents to the experience of conversion," is taken from Gershon (2007: 147).

3. Here I use the term *conversion* in a very narrow sense. The concept is complex and the topic of numerous studies, which I cannot examine here. For an interesting analysis of the concept's shift from ancient Greece to Christianity, see Foucault (2001: 197–219).

4. This is an abridged version. For the complete myth, see Vilaça (2008) and (2009b).

5. See Leite (2013: 77–78, 82) for a similar but inverted myth among the Yanomami.

6. Based on the ethnography of the Piro/Yine, Opas (2008: 134) differentiates two different types of perspectival change, though these are not distinguished terminologically by the Yine themselves. Abrupt change is termed *metamorphosis,* while change arising from a lengthy process is termed *transformation,* both equally related to corporeality. This difference in the time scale of the processes does not seem to me relevant in the Wari' case.

7. See also Gow (2006: 217–218) on conversion among the Amazonian Piro/Yine not being related to an inner-state change.

8. This is an important difference between perspectivism and animism (see Viveiros de Castro 1998: 474).

9. According to Opas (2008: 272), the Piro/Yine situate the difference between animals and humans in morality: to be human is to be properly moral, a condition separating humans from nonhumans.

10. See Ewart (2008: 518; 2013: 184).

11. It should be noted the body is not indefinite or neutral but has an animal potency that must be neutralized—work that indeed continues throughout the person's life.

12. See Da Matta (1976: 85–88), Lima (1995: 187; 2005), Schaden (1962: 85–94), Viveiros de Castro (1986: 474; 1992a), and Opas (2008).

13. In several Amazonian groups, gender distinctions tend to be conceived as human/animal or predator/prey oppositions. See Taylor (2000: 314–316; pers. comm., 2004), Descola (2001: 108), Strathern (1999: 252–253), Viveiros de Castro (2000: 45n39; 2002: 444n7), Hugh-Jones (2001), and Vilaça (1992; 2000).

14. New King James Bible. The Bible used as the source for the translations is in Portuguese. The version usually kept by Wari' pastors is *A Bíblia na Linguagem de Hoje,* published by the Brazilian Biblical Society.

15. On the subjugation of animals, also see Genesis 9:2–3, where God speaks to Noah: "And the fear of you and the dread of you shall be on every beast of the earth, on every bird of the air, on all that move on the earth, and on all the fish of the sea. They are given into your hand. Every moving thing that lives shall be food for you. I have given you all things, even as the green herbs" (New King James Bible). This passage is translated into Wari' in lesson book 1, p. 123.

16. The term used in the translation of the verb "create/make" to Wari' is *kep,* meaning to make something by hand, to manufacture, like a basket or pot.

However, in their present-day comments about Creation, both in church services and in conversation with me, the Wari' emphasize that God created with his talk (the verb *tomi'*, "to talk"). People say, for example, that God *tomi'ma'na karawa*, "speak-exist-the-animals." Moreover, an important point to remember is that the Christian mythology differs from the Wari' mythology not only through its exclusivist notion of truth but also through the very idea of creation ex nihilo, which is foreign to the Wari' universe. See footnote 18.

17. See Kopenawa and Albert (2010: 426) on the equation made by the shaman Davi Kopenawa between the words of God (Teosi) and the objectification of spirits as animals to be eaten.

18. Here it is important to note Cesarino's reservation concerning the comparison between Amerindian "geneses" and this notion in Greek-Christian thought: "The first stages of the cosmos and the formation of their first inhabitants occur however through processes of 'emergence' or 'appearance' or 'derivation' and not *ab ovo,* as in the case of Orphic cosmogonies" (2011: 168, my translation). Also see Gell (1995: 23) on the same difference between Polynesian and Judeo-Christian creationism, and Tedlock (1983: 136, 261–271) on similar distinctions between Popol Vuh, the Quechua-Mayan creation narrative, and Genesis (see Cesarino 2011: 169).

19. In passing we can also note a duality in the biblical Genesis, where the first two chapters to some extent overlap, though this duality is different from the kind observed in Amazonia. Hence, although a clear separation between humans and animals/plants is found in both chapters, in the first the universe antecedes man, who is clearly separated from the world (as a predator); while in the second, humanity is newly created in the figures of Adam and Eve, who antecede the world insofar as they are given the power to create it by naming its creatures. In contrast to Amerindian peoples, who have no problem with such duality, this is a constant topic of discussion among Evangelicals, who try to resolve the implied contradiction (see the conclusion for a further discussion). See Lloyd (2011: 831) for a discussion of the biblical Genesis and the question of humanity.

20. Similarly Overing analyzes the creation of current time as a process of differentiation from the "before time" among the Piaroa: "Speciation also took place: beings who once could mate no longer could (usually) do so; animals, fish, and plants, autochthonously human in form, received their form of today" (Overing Kaplan 1990: 608; see also Kelly 2011a: 16). For an analysis of this kind of transformation, see Viveiros de Castro 2007. Among the Piro/Yine, the mythic time of transformation is associated with the Old Testament, while the present is associated with the New Testament: "Humans and most animals lost their ability to metamorphose, animals were separated from humans" (Opas 2008: 249–250, see also 246–264).

21. *Oro Tamara': Hinos e coros em Pacaas Novos e Português,* ed. Missão Novas Tribos do Brasil, n.d. Cloutier's observation suggests that the NTM missionaries were aware of the importance of this question for the Indians. According to the author, they told the Gavião Indians in the 1980s that "if they refused to believe, they [the missionaries] would ask God to make all the game vanish from their territory" (1988: 63, my translation).

22. As we can see, this primarily involved experiments: it was the fact they did not become sick after breaking the food taboos that caused them to observe the power of God proclaimed by the missionaries. See Queiroz (1999) on the same procedure among the Amazonian Waiwai, and see Robbins (2004: 219) on the Urapmin perception of the end of taboos as a liberation; see also Fausto (2002).

23. One man drew a direct equivalence between the shaman's de-animalization through fumigation with maize smoke and conversion to Christianity. Answering my question about a certain shaman who had been smoked (and was therefore no longer performing cures), he stated, "He believes in God." The shaman Wem Karamai told me that for a while he ceased to "accompany" the animals in order to accompany God: "After I began walking with Jesus, I didn't see animals as people." The shaman Orowam once told me that he had stopped being a believer ("speaking in church") because the jaguars would not leave him: "They became my companions completely."

24. For a similar kind of prayer among the Yanomami, see Kopenawa and Albert (2010: 260).

25. Interestingly, in these books the verbs are always in the first person plural inclusive, which turns the speech of the missionaries into Wari' speech at the moment when the text is being read. It is also worth remarking on the insertion of the word *probably*, which is one way of translating the VIC marker of the Wari' irrealis future tense verbs (Everett and Kern 1997: 321–322); but the word is not part of the Christian message. On fire for the Christianized Yanomami, see Kopenawa and Albert (2010: 261).

26. See Oliveira (2010: 52) on the Waiwai and Viveiros de Castro (2002: 199; 2011: 22) on the Tupinambá.

27. See Bonilla (2009: 136) on the location of the Paumari hell next to the House of God, and Opas (2008: 275) on the same situation among the Piro/Yine.

28. See Cesarino (2011: 109) on the initiation of Marubo shamans. See also Déléage (2006: 320, 328, and 332) on the Sharanawa.

29. See also Rafael (1993: 12), Cannell (2006: 138), and Handman (2015: 208).

30. See Robbins (2004: 319) on the Urapmin.

31. I thank one of the anonymous reviewers for pointing this out.

32. See also Overing and Passes (2000: 20–22).

33. See Rafael (1993) on the same phenomenon among the Tagalog.

CHAPTER 6. STRANGE CREATOR

1. See Clifford (1992: 83) for an analogous description of the work of translation by Leenhardt. Given the evident limitations of the linguistic analysis presented in this chapter, I emphasize that the associations made here are primarily based on ethnographic data.

2. The Wari' language possesses three genders: male, female, and neuter. The three corresponding suffixes are *kon/kun, kam,* and *nain,* respectively; the latter,

neuter, which can also be marked by the absence of any suffix, refers exclusively to animals, plants, and objects (the male gender is also used for some animals).

3. On a worldview based on binary oppositions as a characteristic of conservative Christian missionaries, see Schieffelin (2014: S230).

4. I should add that *jam* is also the term by which the Wari' refer to lightning bolts. For a direct association between God and lightning bolts, see Paletó's observation below concerning the threat of death if one sees God.

5. I refer the reader to chapter 8 for the symbolic equivalence between traditional festivals and warfare, here taken literally.

6. The term *jama* refers both to the corpse (a still-visible dead Wari' person, generally in a process of decomposition) and to the specter of a dead person, which may appear to a living relative in a frightening guise, such as a decomposing corpse (bulging eyes, body parts dropping off, hairless). In addition, the Wari' use the collectivizing prefix *oro* (people of, group of) along with the term *jama* to refer to the collective of the dead as a whole, the *orojama* or *orojima*.

7. In its wider context of application, no longer linked to the notion of agency, *jamixi'* also refers to shadows, images, or any other trace of the person or object. A footprint is *jaminain* or *jami kaximaxi'* (our foot's double) and the shadow of a person is *jamikon/jamikam*. The Wari' refer both to the voice of God heard by the Old Testament prophets and to the recorded voice of a person as *jami kapijakon/kan* (the double/image of his or her voice). Documents like ID cards are called *jamixi'*, perhaps owing to the photo, which, like any image, is called *jamixi'*.

8. The translative equivocity objectified in this neologism, whose invention clearly escaped the control of the missionaries, as well as in the translation of the term for *spirit/soul*, contrasts with the control that—according to Hanks (2010: 158–160; 2013: 398–400), who based his analysis on the notion of commensurability—the Catholic missionaries seemed to possess when proposing neologisms in the Maya language. The interesting thing to observe here is not that the neologisms in the Wari' language constitute "a medium of semantic exchange in which to commensurate between the two languages" (Hanks 2014: 29), but that they point to ontologically distinct universes.

9. I should make clear that, according to the missionary Barbara Kern (email to the author, April 12, 2011), *jamu* means simply "to act wickedly" or in a bad way.

10. On the difficulties encountered by the Bosavi from Papua New Guinea in translating certain Christian ideas, see Schieffelin (2007: 149–154; 2008b).

11. The preceding subhead, "A Problem of Presence," is also the title of Engelke's 2007 book. See comments on this topic in Meyer (2013: 314).

12. This problem was also crucial to the Palikur (Capiberibe 2007: 201–203), the Piro/Yine (Gow 2006: 221), the Paumari (Bonilla 2009: 139), the Yanomami (Kopenawa and Albert 2010: 281), and the Jivaro Achuar (Taylor 2002). In Indonesia, the same kind of question emerges clearly in the words of a Biak shaman rejecting God's transcendence: "God may be great, but he is not here" (Rutherford 2006: 260; see also Clifford 1992: 81, on the Kanak from New Caledonia).

13. See Douglas (1995) on the role of history in these ambiguities. On the "real" presence of God for urban North American Evangelicals, see Luhrmann 2012. For the idea of Christianity as an essentially anthropomorphic religion, see Mayblin (2014), Keane (2014), and Schmitt (1998: 346–347).

14. See Robbins (2004: 343n12) on the relatively minor role of Jesus among the Urapmin.

15. The same seems to have happened among the Yanomami, as attested by the outbreak of conversions after the screening of a film on Noah (Kopenawa and Albert 2010: 715n22). See also Capiberibe (2009: ch. 5; 2007: 201) on the equation made by the Palikur between "to see" and "to know."

16. With the popularization of television sets over recent years, now found in various houses, the situation can change fast.

17. See Lévi-Strauss (1955: 349–350) for a beautiful description of a similar surprised reaction among the Nambikwara, and Viveiros de Castro (1986: 79–80) on the Araweté, both mentioned in Capiberibe (2007: 195).

18. See also Keane (2007: 68–69) and Engelke (2007: 49).

19. See Silverstein (2003). See Robbins (2004: 219) on the notion of falsehood among the Urapmin. On the association between the missionaries' power and material goods and writing from an African perspective, see Comaroff and Comaroff (1991: 188–197).

20. According to Paletó, Moses wrote on stone and was the person who invented writing, "which is why you know how to write."

21. See Viveiros de Castro (2002: 216); see Capiberibe (2007: 197) on this association among the Christian Palikur.

22. Franchetto (2008: 42) observes that since the introduction of writing among various Amazonian peoples was generally undertaken by Evangelical and Catholic missionaries, there is a tendency for the native myths to be written in a simplistic and banalized form, like "children's stories" (48), which contrasts with the carefully reproduced "great myths of the whites." For an analysis of the relation between reading and writing in church services and schools, see Vilaça (2012).

23. The late Ko'um once observed that he knew how to read, but that he had already wept for his dead so much that he could no longer see properly. Here it should be recalled that mourning and sadness are important factors in the Wari' distancing themselves from the church. On the place of memorization in Bosavi cults and its relation to difficulties in reading, see Schieffelin (2007: 145).

24. The same point is observed by Hornborg (2006: 27) in contrasting animist and "modern" epistemologies, showing that objectivism presumes the possibility of knowledge existing outside a relationship. See also Wagner (1975: ch. 2). Taylor (1981: 663), discussing schooling among the Achuar, argues that we should question whether traditional contents can really be transmitted by nontraditional means. Traditional ideologies, transmitted by traditional means, are much more dynamic and manipulable. An interesting parallel can also be made with the notion of copyright associated with the New Ireland sculptures called Malanggan. Following Strathern's analysis (2001a: 13–14), we are faced with something very different from

the Euro-American issue of "the identical text." For New Irelanders, copyright relates primarily to the rights to reproduce the object, which is always different from the original, a unique combination of memory, skills, and magic.

25. Compare the same apprehension among the Tukano of northwestern Amazonia (Hugh-Jones 2009: 51) and the Yanesha of Peru (Santos-Granero 2009: 118).

26. Lloyd (2012: 80n9) observes that for Plato the problem of books lay precisely in the fact they do not allow effective interaction with the reader: "Books cannot answer questions." Writing in the form of dialogues was a way Plato found to get round this problem. For a different view, focused on the properly material aspects of writing (which can be ingested, for example), see Keane 2013. Limitations of this kind are intrinsically associated with the valorization of the experience of possession by the Holy Spirit among Pentecostals, as shown in the works of Robbins (2004), Engelke (2007: 50–51), Austin-Broos (1997), Meyer (1999), Daswani (2011), and Capiberibe (2007), among others.

27. On the distinction between belief and experience, see Lévy-Bruhl (1938: 125) and Needham (1972: 31–50).

28. See Tooker (1992) and Viveiros de Castro (2002: 215; 2011: 40).

29. See Hanks (2013: 400) on the association, in the translation of Christian ideas into the Maya language, between divine omnipotence and the image of a body with open arms "fully extended and embracing."

30. It is worth noting that the Christian texts also refer to the angels as *jami pawin,* the "doubles of heaven," analogous to the way in which the Wari' designate unidentified animal spirits that arrive with the wind as *jami hotowa* or *jami nahwarak* ("double of the wind" or "double of the forest"). Unlike Lucifer, the angels have no role in the Christian discourse of the Wari'.

31. See Opas (2008: 141, 159, 202n30) and Gow (1991: 236n7) on similar characteristics of the devil among the Piro/Yine.

32. See Burch (1994: 96) on the Inupiat of Alaska and Meyer (1996: 218–219; 1998; 1999) on the Ewe of Ghana.

33. See Strathern (1988: 14, 275–276) on the inherently oppositional quality of the notion of the dividual. See chapter 9.

34. Mosko's observation concerning the devil among the North Mekeo suggests a point of comparison: "Villagers accordingly understand sin as adding to one's person some bit or taint of Diabolo, which simultaneously closes oneself off from receiving Deo's gifts" (2010: 230). See Kopenawa and Albert (2010: 261) on the Yanomami.

35. Paletó's observation concerning the cause of death of the pastor Xin Xoi clearly indicates the identity between God and the devil by associating the former with the animal spirits who abducted the Wari': "Come my son, [said God]. He called him because his [Xin Xoi] sons were rough with him. God's double [the Holy Spirit] took him."

36. See too Rivière (1981: 8) on the Trio. Evens (1997: 212), in an analysis of the biblical episode of Adam and Eve, suggests the equivalence between the serpent and

God: "The serpent is peculiarly identifiable with the absolute, with God." See Lévi-Strauss (1991: 74) on the equivalence between Adam's fall and the fall of the Amerindian mythological tricksters.

37. See Xavier (2013: 411) on an analogous opposition between the Koripako/Baniwa creator, Ñapirikoli, and the trickster, the "great hybrid Kowai."

38. In the recent past, some people associated Towira Towira with the Christian devil. Awo Kamip once told me that, as a "leader of water," he sent fish to cause disease and kill the Wari' as a way of augmenting the aquatic population (in other words, making kin for himself).

39. The same idea of a list is found among the Urapmin (Robbins 2004: 278).

CHAPTER 7. CHRISTIAN RITUAL LIFE

1. The section epigraph comes from an article by Maria Tereza Montovani, "A luz continua brilhando" [The light still shines], *Revista Confins da Terra* 42, no. 138 (July–September 2009): 7, my translation.

2. On the selection of pastors among the Zoró by the NTM missionaries in 1985, see Cloutier (1988: 77–80).

3. On the format of the services among the Zoró in 1984 and 1985, see Cloutier (1988: 68–77).

4. Unlike the Wari', the Zoró compose their own hymns, learned through dreams (Cloutier 1988: 91–92).

5. This differentiates this narrative from myths, for example, which clearly mark who is speaking.

6. Shortly before, Awo Kamip had said in the middle of his sermon: "If you speak through your mouth only, [God] sees in your heart that you do not like him." On the opacity of mind, see Robbins and Rumsey (2008), Robbins (2008), Schieffelin (2008a), and Stasch (2008).

7. During the Holy Supper that I attended in 2002, 1 Corinthians 11:25–26 was read.

8. On the concentration of more general bodily processes in the heart after Christianization, see Robbins, Schieffelin, and Vilaça 2014.

CHAPTER 8. MORAL CHANGES

1. See Cloutier (1988: 94) on the Amazonian Zoró.

2. Abrão also recounted that one of the missionaries had told him there are no thieves in the United States, because when you steal the first time, one of your fingers is cut off, the second time, another finger, the third time, one more, and after that you are killed. That is why you can leave a R$100 banknote in the street in the United States and nobody will take it.

3. It is important to add that, for Rivière (1981: 13), the similarity between the codes cannot explain by itself the adoption of Christianity. See Capiberibe (2009: ch. 5, p. 9) on the Amazonian Palikur and Robbins (2004: 216) on the Urapmin.

4. See also Barker (2003: 285) on the idea, among the Maisin, of "a sharing of one's innermost self."

5. As I observed earlier, marriages with them were avoided, but they occurred with a certain frequency.

6. For an ethnographic study of Bible conferences among the Koripako of the Upper Içana (northwestern Amazonia), see Xavier (2013: 453–492). There too we find the letter invitation, the problem of feeding the guests, and the generalized siblingship.

7. See Keane (2002: 73–74) on the change of focus to words as intentions after Christianization: "Sincere speech makes that interior state transparent."

8. On confession among the Zoró, see Cloutier (1988: 90–91).

9. Here I note the difference between the Wari' view of anger as an act and that of the Urapmin, whose view, according to Robbins (2007a: 311), is based on an internal and personal feeling: "Feeling anger is the most common sin the Urapmin commit and its regular presence in their hearts stands for them as proof of their sinful nature."

10. On the encompassment of action by speech and its importance in mediating native Christian life, see Robbins (2001a: 904), who associates Christianization with the encounter with "modern linguistic ideology."

11. On Christianity and the belief in the reality of something hidden, see Robbins (2004: 224), Cannell (2006: 15, 19), Lambek (1998: 122n20), and Foucault (1978: 61–70).

12. See Keane (2002: 78) for the same idea in Sumba.

13. See C. Taylor (1989: 11).

14. See Kelly (2011a); see also Howell (1997: 11), Gershon (2007: 148), and Robbins (2004: ch. 5) on two moral discourses coexisting in one society.

CHAPTER 9. PERSONHOOD AND ITS TRANSLATIONS

1. See also Tillich (1968: ch. 1).

2. In the words of Keane (2002: 67, 73): "The transformation of the subject would seem inseparable from the redefining of its distinction from the world of objects"; "the shift in the understanding of material goods reinforces the shift in focus to the individual." See also Gallois (2012: 75).

3. Howell (1997: 16), commenting on the chapter by Evens (1997), concludes that the biblical Genesis informs readers that they, as humans, are "those creatures who are especially given to giving themselves their own identity." Howell goes on to say, "If this interpretation is correct, it certainly helps to explain the old and persistent value placed on individualism in these religions."

4. The category "mythic participation" is taken directly from Lévy-Bruhl, of whom Leenhardt was an admirer and personal friend (Clifford 1992: 151–152).

5. See Conklin (2001a: 141) on the Wari' and Opas (2008: 120) on the heart as the seat of thought among the Piro/Yine; see also Belaunde (2000: 211).

6. I thank Barbara Kern (pers. comm., 2011) for providing some of these examples along with their literal translations.

7. See Cohn (2004: 97) on the problem of soul loss among the Xikrin and the need for constant conversation with others in order for children to remain in the world of the living.

8. On the relation between anger, sorcery, and the transformation of kin into prey among the Peruvian Airo-Pai, see Belaunde (2000: 209–214).

9. See Gow (1997) for the Piro/Yine.

10. According to Taylor (2002: 462) on the Amazonian Achuar: "Insofar as they are made up of their reciprocal gazes, people who live together are assumed to be entirely transparent to each other." For an opposite conception in Melanesia, see Robbins (2008) and Schieffelin (2008a). For a case of an Amazonian heart that remains "partially hidden to others," see Yvinec (2014: 25).

11. We can add other expressions that involve the verb "to speak," but which, unlike the others, involve speech per se: lying is "to speak lies" (*tomi'xina*); to obey is "to speak-answer" (*tomi' ha'*); to be amused by something one has heard is "to speak-laugh" (*tomi' tatam*).

12. Recently this translation was revised, and as a result lesson book 6, titled *Romans,* began to be read more often during church services. See Schieffelin (2007 and 2008b) for the problems with the translation of inner thoughts among the Bosavi.

13. On the Calvinist and Lutheran sanctification of work through the worship of God and self-discipline, see Troeltsch (1976: 641)

14. Here I note the interesting association made by Comaroff and Comaroff (1991: 187–188) between the emergence of mirrors, both in the Western world and among native peoples, African and otherwise, and the invention of self that characterizes the Christian subject.

15. See Fienup-Riordan (1991: 110–113) on the conflict between Yup'ik "holism" and the missionaries' individualistic practices. As we shall see in the conclusion, over the last decade the Wari' have begun to have direct access to manufactured goods with more frequent trips to the town of Guajará-Mirim.

16. See also Burridge (1979) and Morris ([1972] 1987).

17. See Robbins (2004) for an analogous conception of the pre-Christian individual among the Melanesian Urapmin. On the difference between Tswana individualism and Western individualism, based on "fundamentally different ontological roots," see Comaroff and Comaroff (1991: 144).

18. The coexistence of apparently contradictory premises in these societies, as observed by the book's authors, is an important point mentioned in the previous chapter and to which I return in the conclusion.

19. See Strathern (1988: 275–276) and Gell (1997: 43), for whom eclipsing "implies that the prior set of relations are still implicit, though latent." See also Hirsch (1994: 694–695), Mosko (2010), and Vilaça (2011, 2015a).

20. This concept is a development of the notion of concentric dualism elaborated in Lévi-Strauss ([1958] 1991).

21. See Descola (2001) and Strathern (1999) for specific comments on this difference.

22. As a Palikur man said to Capiberibe (2007: 194, my translation): "It was God who cared for him, who was making him breathe, who was making him walk, it was God who did that. It was God, were God not to do that, then you would be like a statue that doesn't speak, that doesn't do anything." See Handman (2015: 203–208) on the body as an offering to God among the Guhu-Samane of Papua New Guinea.

23. One reviewer astutely suggested that this phrase could have been the title of the book.

24. According to Vanda, God is not seen in heaven, because he is "like the wind" (for the Wari', as we saw, the wind also has a body).

25. See Opas (2008: 175) for an analogous heaven among the Piro/Yine, and Xavier (2013: 446) for the same among the Koripako.

26. Paletó, speaking in 1992 about the horror of the fire of hell, observed, "In heaven it is different: you pick up a plate and eat." On the importance of food in the Zoró heaven, see Cloutier (1988: 96).

27. See Xavier (2013: 450, my translation) for an opposite vision among the Koripako, for whom, "ultimately, it is heaven that matters, not this world." Also see Robbins (2004) on heaven as a desired destination among the Urapmin.

28. For biblical comments on the fire (and worms) of hell, see especially Mark 9:42–48. Lesson book 1, lesson 8, p. 48, describes hell as an enormous fire that is the abode of the devil, where the Wari' are struck in the face and moan.

29. According to Paletó, in heaven people speak only the language (*kapijakon*) of the whites (enemies): "Our language ended."

30. The Piro/Yine of Peruvian Amazonia describe a similar image of heaven. According to Opas (2008: 275, and n. 47), the possibility of a lack of family life there (the lack of relationality) concerns them, since they believe that a relation with God alone would not be enough.

31. On the relation between the absence of affinity and the static aspect of the posthumous Kraho world, in opposition to the dynamic aspect of the lived world, see Carneiro da Cunha (1978: 122, 128). Also see Overing (1985b: 157), who notes that heaven among the Piaroa comprises a place without affines, a place of "asocial safety." See, too, the essay by Viveiros de Castro (2002: 207; 2011: 32) on the interest of the Tupinambá in the missionaries and Christianity, "an alterity without which the world would sink to indifference and paralysis."

CONCLUSION

1. Also see Overing Kaplan (1976). It is important to note that the use of the term *contradiction* by these two authors refers, by opposition, to the paradigms of the philosophy of science dominant in the first half of the twentieth century

(Carneiro da Cunha 2012: 457) rather than being determined by the debates between Aristotle and Heraclitus on the Law of Contradiction. In the latter case, attributes said to be contradictory must be "predicated of the same subject at the same time, in the same respect and in the same relation" (Lloyd 1966: 87; see also 86–102). An interesting comparison can be made between this type of characteristic and the absence of our sense of whole among Melanesian peoples according to the analysis by Hirsch (2008). On the unsuitability of the Dumontian concept of "totality" in relation to Amazonia, see Viveiros de Castro (2001: 27).

2. See also Viveiros de Castro (2001), Taylor (1996: 206–207, 213n10), and Descola (2005: 460–461) for another formulation of this opposition.

3. See Viveiros de Castro (2012b: 40); see Keane (2007) for a critical view of Christian purification.

4. See Durkheim (1963: 5) on the moral aspects of this kind of interiorization related to Christianity.

5. On the importance of new semiotic forms in the emergence of the inner self, especially the notion of sincere speech that is the foundation of confession, see chapter 8. In deciding not to give particular emphasis to these semiotic practices as the contextual basis for these changes in the notion of personhood, a strategy critically noted by one reviewer, I intended to stress the complex and peculiar relationship between morality and humanity in Amazonia, situating the narrowing of the notion of humanity and the new rituals that transmit new ideologies of language on the same plane and in dialectical relation.

6. Available to the Wari' who were over sixty years old, although they had never worked as paid employees.

7. Also see Durston (2007: 83) and Hanks (2013: 390) on the difference between initial and subsequent evangelization in Peru and Yucatan, as well as Eriksen (2008) and Barker (2010: 248) on the "cumulative impact of Christianity."

8. In the case of the Catholic Wari' village of Sagarana, under the influence of progressive missionaries, "culture" has already been a theme for some years, although this discussion has had no repercussions on the Evangelical villages until very recently (see Vilaça 2014a).

REFERENCES

BOOKS AND ARTICLES

ALBERT, Bruce. 1985. "Temps du sang, temps des cendres: Représentation de la maladie, système rituel et espace politique chez les Yanomami du sud-est (amazonie brésilienne)." PhD diss., Université de Paris X Nanterre, Paris.

ALBERT, Bruce, and KOPENAWA, Davi. 2003. "Les ancêtres animaux." In *Yanomami—l'esprit de la forêt,* edited by Bruce Albert and Hèrves Chandès, 67–87. Paris: Foudation Cartier/Actes Sud.

ALMEIDA, Ronaldo. 2002. "Traduções do fundamentalismo evangélico." PhD diss., IFLCH, Universidade de São Paulo.

AMARAL, Virginia. 2014. "A Caminho do Mundo-Luz Celestial: O Areruya e os profetismos Kapon e Pemon." Master's thesis, PPGAS, Museu Nacional, Universidade Federal do Rio de Janeiro.

AMSELLE, Jean-Loup. 1998. *Mestizo Logics: Anthropology of Identity in Africa and Elsewhere.* Translated by Claudia Royal. Stanford, CA: Stanford University Press.

ANDRELLO, Geraldo. 1999. "Profetas e pregadores: A conversão taurepáng à religião do Sétimo Dia." In *Transformando os Deuses: Os múltiplos sentidos da conversão entre os povos indígenas no Brasil,* edited by Robin Wright, 285–308. Campinas, Brazil: Editora da Unicamp.

———. 2006. *Cidade do índio: Transformações e cotidiano em Iauaretê.* São Paulo: Universidade do Estado de São Paulo and Instituto Socioambiental; Rio de Janeiro: Nuti.

ÅRHEM, Kaj. 1993. "Ecosofía Makuna." In *La Selva Humanizada: Ecología Alternativa en el Trópico Húmedo Colombiano,* edited by François Correa, 105–122. Bogotá: Instituto Colombiano de Antropología.

ASSMAN, Jan. 2010. *The Price of Monotheism.* Stanford, CA: Stanford University Press.

AUSTIN-BROOS, Diane. 1997. *Jamaica Genesis: Religion and the Politics of Moral Orders.* Chicago: University of Chicago Press.

BARKER, John. 1992. "Christianity in Western Melanesian Ethnography." In *History and Tradition in Melanesian Anthropology*, edited by James G. Carrier, 145–173. Berkeley: University of California Press.

———. 1993. "'We Are Ekelesia': Conversion in Uiaku, Papua New Guinea." In *Conversion to Christianity: Historical and Anthropological Perspectives on a Great Transformation*, edited by Robert W. Hefner, 199–230. Berkeley: University of California Press.

———. 2003. "Christian Bodies: The Dialetics of Sickness and Salvation among the Maisin of Papua New Guinea." *Journal of Religion History* 27: 272–292.

———. 2010. "The Varieties of Melanesian Christian Experience: A Comment on Mosko's 'Partible Penitents.'" *Journal of the Royal Anthropological Institute*, n.s., 16: 247–249.

BARROS, M. C. D. M. 1994. "Uma modalidade de pergunta missionária." *Cadernos de Estudos Linguísticos* (Campinas, Brazil) 27: 5–25.

BELLAH, Robert. 1964. "Religious Evolution." *American Sociological Review* 29(3): 358–374.

BELAUNDE, Luisa E. 2000. "The Convivial Self and the Fear of Anger among the Airo-Pai of Amazonian Peru." In *The Anthropology of Love and Anger: The Aesthetics of Conviviality in Native Amazonia*, edited by Joanna Overing and Alan Passes, 209–220. London: Routledge.

BESSIRE, Lucas. 2014. *Behold the Black Caiman: A Chronicle of Ayoreo Life*. Chicago: University of Chicago Press.

BONILLA, Oiara. 2009. "The Skin of History: Paumari Perspectives on Conversion and Transformation." In *Native Christians: Modes and Effects of Christianity among Indigenous Peoples of the Americas*, edited by Aparecida Vilaça and Robin Wright, 127–145. Hampshire, U.K.: Ashgate.

BRIGHTMAN, Marc, GROTTI, Vanessa, and ULTURGASHEVA, Olga, eds. 2012. *Animism in Rainforest and Tundra: Personhood, Animals, Plants and Things in Contemporary Amazonia and Siberia*. New York: Berghahn.

BROWN, Peter. 1988. *The Body and Society: Men, Women and Sexual Renunciation in Early Christianity*. New York: Columbia University Press.

BURCH, Ernest, Jr. 1994. "The Inupiat and the Christianization of Arctic Alaska." *Études/Inuit/Studies* 18(1–2): 81–108.

BURRIDGE, Kenelm. 1979. *Someone, No One: An Essay on Individuality*. Princeton, NJ: Princeton University Press.

CADOGAN, Léon. 1959. "*Ayvu rapyta* (o fundamento do dizer): Textos míticos de los Mbyá-Guarani del Guairá." *Boletim* (São Paulo, USP, Faculdade de Filosofia, Ciências e Letras), 227(1): 1–227.

CANNELL, Fenella, ed. 2006. *The Anthropology of Christianity*. Durham, NC: Duke University Press.

CAPIBERIBE, Artionka. 2007. *Batismo de fogo: Os Palikur e o Cristianismo*. São Paulo: Annablume and Fapesp; Rio de Janeiro: Nuti.

————. 2009. "Nas duas margens do rio: Alteridade e transformações entre os Palikur na fronteira Brasil/Guiana francesa." PhD diss., PPGAS, Museu Nacional, Universidade Federal do Rio de Janeiro.

CARNEIRO DA CUNHA, Manuela. 1978. *Os mortos e os outros: Uma análise do sistema funerário e da noção de pessoa entre os índios Krahó.* São Paulo: Hucitec.

————. 1998. "Pontos de Vista sobre a Floresta Amazônica: Xamanismo e Tradução." *Mana: Estudos de Antropologia Social* 4(1): 7–22.

————. 2012. "Questões suscitadas pelo conhecimento tradicional." *Revista de Antropologia* 55(1): 439–464.

CARNEIRO DA CUNHA, Manuela, and VIVEIROS DE CASTRO, Eduardo. 1985. "Vingança e temporalidade: Os Tupinambás." *Journal de la Société des Américanistes* 71: 191–208.

CESARINO, Pedro de Niemeyer. 2011. *Oniska: Poética do Xamanismo na Amazônia.* São Paulo: Editora Perspectiva/Fapesp.

CHAMORRO, Graciela. 1998. *A espiritualidade guarani: Uma teologia ameríndia da palavra.* São Leopoldo: IEPG and Editora Sinodal.

CHAUMEIL, Jean-Pierre. 1983. *Voir, savoir, pouvoir: Le chamamisme chez les Yagua du Nord-Est péruvien.* Paris: Éditions de L'École des Hautes Études en Sciences Sociales.

CLASTRES, Pierre. 1972. *Chronique des Indiens Guayaki.* Paris: Plon.

CLIFFORD, James. 1988. *The Predicament of Culture: Twentieth-Century Ethnography, Literature and Art.* Cambridge, MA: Harvard University Press.

————. 1992. *Person and Myth: Maurice Leenhardt in the Melanesian World.* Durham, NC: Duke University Press.

CLIFFORD, James, and MARCUS, George, eds. 1986. *Writing Culture: The Poetics and Politics of Ethnography.* Berkeley: University of California Press.

CLOUTIER, Sophie. 1988. "Une nouvelle étique en rupture avec la tradition: La conversion des indiens Zoró à l'evangélisme de la Mission Nouvelles Tribus." Master's thesis in Anthropology, Université de Montréal.

COELHO DE SOUZA, Marcela. 2002. "O traço e o círculo: Os Jê e seus antropólogos." PhD diss., PPGAS, Museu Nacional, Universidade Federal do Rio de Janeiro.

COHN, Clarice. 2004. "Os processos próprios de ensino e aprendizagem e a criança indígena." In *Cadernos de Educação Escolar Indígena,* 94–111. Barra do Bugres, Brazil: UNEMAT.

COLEMAN, Simon. 2006. "Materializing the Self: Words and Gifts in the Constitution of Charismatic Protestant Identity." In *The Anthropology of Christianity,* edited by Fenella Cannell, 163–184. Durham, NC: Duke University Press.

COMAROFF, Jean, and COMAROFF, John. 1991. *Of Revelation and Revolution: Christianity, Colonialism and Consciousness in South Africa.* Vol. 1. Chicago: University of Chicago Press.

CONKLIN, Beth-Ann. 2001a. *Consuming Grief: Compassionate Cannibalism in an Amazonian Society.* Austin: University of Texas Press.

———. 2001b. "Women's Blood, Warriors' Blood, and the Conquest of Vitality in Amazonia." In *Gender in Amazonia and Melanesia: An Exploration of the Comparative Method,* edited by Thomas Gregor and Donald Tuzin, 141–174. Berkeley: University of California Press.

COSTA, Luiz, and FAUSTO, Carlos. 2010. "The Return of the Animists: Recent Studies of Amazonian Ontologies." *Religion and Society: Advances in Research* 1: 89–109.

CRAPANZANO, Vincent. 2000. *Serving the Word: Literalism in America from the Pulpit to the Bench.* New York: New Press.

CSORDAS, Thomas. 1990. "Embodiment as a Paradigm for Anthropology." *Ethos* 18: 5–47.

Da MATTA, Roberto. 1970. "Mito e Anti-mito entre os Timbira." In *Mito e Linguagem Social,* edited by Roberto da Matta, 77–106. Rio de Janeiro: Tempo Brasileiro.

———. 1976. *Um mundo dividido: A estrutura social dos índios Apinayé.* Petrópolis, Rio de Janeiro: Vozes.

DASWANI, Girish. 2011. "(In-)Dividual Pentecostals in Ghana." *Journal of Religion in Africa* 41: 256–279.

DAWSON, Millie. 2000. *All the Day Long: Missionaries Reaching Tribes in the Amazon.* Enumclaw, WA: WinePress.

De CIVRIEUX, Marc. 1980. *Watunna: An Orinoco Creation Style.* San Francisco: North Point.

DÉLÉAGE, Pierre. 2006. "Le Chamanisme Sharanahua: Enquête sur l'apprentissage et l'épistemologie d'un rituel." PhD diss., École des Hautes Études en Sciences Sociales, Paris.

DESCOLA, Philippe. 1992. "Societies of Nature and the Nature of Society." In *Conceptualizing Society,* edited by Adam Kuper, 107–126. London: Routledge.

———. 2001. "The Genres of Gender: Local Models and Global Paradigms in the Comparison of Amazonia and Melanesia." In *Gender in Amazonia and Melanesia: An Exploration of the Comparative Method,* edited by Tomas Gregor and Donald Tuzin, 91–114. Berkeley: University of California Press.

———. 2005. *Par delà nature et culture.* Paris: Gallimard.

DOUGLAS, Mary. 1995. "Forgotten Knowledge." In *Shifting Contexts: Transformations in Anthropological Knowledge,* edited by Marilyn Strathern, 13–29. London: Routledge.

DUMONT, Louis. 1983. *Essais sur l'individualisme: Une perspective anthropologique sur l'idéologie moderne.* Paris. Éditions du Seuil.

DURKHEIM, Émile. 1963. *L'éducation morale.* New ed. Paris: Presses Universitaires de France.

DURSTON, Alan. 2007. *Pastoral Quechua: The History of Christian Translation in Colonial Peru, 1550–1650.* Notre Dame, IN: University of Notre Dame Press.

ECLÉSIA: Portal Evangélico de Notícias. 2000. www.eclesia.com.br. The article has since been removed from the website, and its title and the author's name are not available.

ENGELKE, Matthew. 2007. *A Problem of Presence: Beyond Scripture in an African Church*. Berkeley: University of California Press.

———. 2014. "Christianity and the Anthropology of Secular Humanism." *Current Anthropology* 55(S10): S292–S301.

ERIKSEN, Annelin. 2008. *Gender, Christianity and Change in Vanuatu*. Aldershot, U.K.: Ashgate.

EVANS-PRITCHARD, Edward E. 1969. "The Perils of Translation." *New Blackfriars* 50: 813–815.

EVENS, T. M. S. 1997. "Eve: Ethics and the Feminine Principle in the Second and the Third Chapters of Genesis. In *The Ethnography of Moralities*, edited by Signe Howell, 203–228. London: Routledge.

EVERETT, Daniel L., and KERN, Barbara. 1997. *Wari': The Pacaas Novos Language of Western Brazil*. New York: Routledge.

EWART, Elizabeth. 2008. "Hearing, Seeing and Speaking: Morality and Sense among the Panará in Central Brazil." *Ethnos* 73(4): 505–522.

———. 2013. *Space and Society in Central Brazil: A Panará Ethnography*. London School of Economics Monographs in Social Anthropology, vol. 80. London: Bloomsbury.

FAUSTO, Carlos. 2001. *Inimigos Fiéis: História, Guerra e Xamanismo na Amazônia*. São Paulo: EDUSP.

———. 2002. "The Bones Affair: Indigenous Knowledge Practices in Contact Situations Seen from an Amazonian Case." *Journal of Royal Anthropology Institute*, n.s., 8: 669–690.

———. 2007a. "Feasting on People: Eating Animals and Humans in Amazonia." *Current Anthropology* 48(4): 497–530.

———. 2007b. "If God Were a Jaguar: Cannibalism and Christianity among the Guarani (16th–20th Centuries)." In *Time and Memory in Indigenous Amazonia: Anthropological Perspectives*, edited by Carlos Fausto and Michael Heckenberger, 74–105. Gainesville: University Press of Florida.

———. 2012. *Warfare and Shamanism in Amazonia*. Cambridge: Cambridge University Press.

FAUSTO, Carlos, and DE VIENNE, Emmanuel. 2014. "Acting Translation: Ritual and Prophetism in Twenty-First-Century Indigenous Amazonia." *HAU: Journal of Ethnographic Theory* 4(2): 161–191.

FERNANDES, Rubem César. 1980. "Um exército de anjos: As razões da Missão Novas Tribos." *Religião e Sociedade* 6: 129–166.

FIENUP-RIORDAN, Ann. 1991. *The Real People and the Children of Thunder: The Yup'ik Eskimo Encounter with Moravian Missionaries John and Edith Kilbuck*. Norman: University of Oklahoma Press.

FOUCAULT, Michel. 1978. *The History of Sexuality I: An Introduction*. Translated by Robert Hurley. New York: Vintage/Random House.

———. 1990. *The Use of Pleasure*. Translated by Robert Hurley. New York: Vintage Books.

———. 1997. *Ethics: Subjectivity and Truth*. Vol. 1. New York: New Press.

‑‑‑‑‑‑. 2001. *L'Herménéutique du sujet: Cours au Collège de France (1981–1982)*. Paris: Gallimard Seuil.

FRANCHETTO, Bruna. 2008. "A guerra dos alfabetos: Os povos indígenas na fronteira entre o oral e o escrito." *Mana: Estudos de Antropologia Social* 14(1): 31–59.

FRANCHETTO, Bruna, and HECKENBERGER, Michael. 2001. *Os povos do Alto Xingu: História e Cultura*. Rio de Janeiro: Editora UFRJ.

FRIEDMAN, Jonathan. 1999. "The Hybridization of Roots and the Abhorrence of the Bush." In *Spaces of Culture: City, Nation, World*, edited by M. Feathersone and S. Lash, 230–256. London: Sage.

GALLOIS, Dominique. 2007. "Materializando saberes imateriais: Experiências indígenas na Amazônia Oriental." *Revista de Estudos e Pesquisas* 4(2): 95–116.

‑‑‑‑‑‑. 2012. "Traduções e aproximações indígenas à mensagem cristã." *Cadernos de Tradução* 30(2): 63–82.

GALLOIS, Dominique, and GRUPIONI, Luís D. 1999. "O índio na Missão Novas Tribos." In: *Transformando os deuses: Os múltiplos sentidos da conversão entre os povos indígenas no Brasil*, edited by Robin Wright, 77–129. Campinas, Brazil: Editora da Unicamp.

GEERTZ, Clifford. 1973. "Internal Conversion in Contemporary Bali." In *The Interpretation of Cultures*, 170–189. New York: Basic Books.

GELL, Alfred. 1995. "Closure and Multiplication: An Essay on Polynesian Cosmology and Ritual." In *Cosmos and Society in Oceania*, edited by Daniel de Coppet and Andre Iteanu, 21–56. Oxford: Berg.

‑‑‑‑‑‑. 1997. "Strathernograms, or the Semiotics of Mixed Metaphors." In *The Art of Anthropology: Essays and Diagrams*, 29–75. London: Athlone.

‑‑‑‑‑‑. 1998. *Art and Agency: An Anthropological Theory*. Oxford: Clarendon.

GERNET, Jacques. 1982. *Chine et Christianisme: La première confrontation*. Paris: Gallimard.

GERSHON, Ilana. 2007. "Converting Meanings and the Meanings of Conversion in Samoan Moral Economies." In *The Limits of Meaning*, edited by Matthew Engelke and Matt Tomlinson, 147–164. New York: Berghahn.

GOW, Peter. 1991. *Of Mixed Blood: Kinship and History in Peruvian Amazonia*. Oxford: Clarendon.

‑‑‑‑‑‑. 1997. "O parentesco como consciência humana: O caso dos Piro." *Mana: Estudos de Antropologia Social* 3(2): 39–66.

‑‑‑‑‑‑. 2001. *An Amazonian Myth and Its History*. Oxford: Oxford University Press.

‑‑‑‑‑‑. 2006. "Forgetting Conversion. The Summer Institute of Linguistic Mission in the Piro Lived World." In *The Anthropology of Christianity*, edited by Fenella Cannell, 211–239. Durham, NC: Duke University Press.

‑‑‑‑‑‑. 2009. "Christians: A Transforming Concept in Peruvian Amazonia." In *Native Christians: Modes and Effects of Christianity among Indigenous Peoples of the Americas*, edited by Aparecida Vilaça and Robin Wright, 33–52. Hampshire, U.K.: Ashgate.

284 · REFERENCES

GROTTI, Vanessa. 2007. "Nurturing the Other: Wellbeing, Social Body and Transformability in Northeastern Amazonia." PhD diss., Trinity College and Department of Social Anthropology, University of Cambridge, U.K.

———. 2009. "Protestant Evangelism and the Transformability of Amerindian Bodies in Northeastern Amazonia." In *Native Christians: Modes and Effects of Christianity among Indigenous Peoples of the Americas,* edited by Aparecida Vilaça and Robin Wright, 109–125. Hampshire, U.K.: Ashgate.

HANDMAN, Courtney. 2015. *Critical Christianity: Translation and Denominational Conflict in Papua New Guinea.* Berkeley: University of California Press.

HANKS, William. 2010. *Converting Words: Maya in the Age of the Cross.* Berkeley: University of California Press.

———. 2013. "Language in Christian Conversion." In *Companion to the Anthropology of Religion,* edited by Janice Boddy and Michael Lambek, 387–406. Oxford: Wiley-Blackwell.

———. 2014. "The Space of Translation." *HAU: Journal of Ethnographic Theory* 4(2): 17–39.

HARDING, Susan. 1987. "Convicted by the Holy Spirit: The Rhetoric of Fundamentalist Baptist Conversion." *American Ethnologist* 14: 167–182.

———. 1991. "Representing Fundamentalism: The Problem of the Repugnant Other." *Social Research* 58(2): 373–393.

———. 2001. *The Book of Jerry Falwell: Fundamentalist Language and Politics.* Princeton, NJ: Princeton University Press.

HAWKINS, Robert E. 1954. *Bob's Diary: Four Months in the Forests of North Brazil.* Dallas: Radio Revival.

HEFNER, Robert. 1993. "World Building and the Rationality of Conversion." In *Conversion to Christianity: Historical and Anthropological Perspectives on a Great Transformation,* edited by Robert Hefner, 3–44. Berkeley: University of California Press.

HILL, Jonathan. 1993. *Keepers of the Sacred Chants: The Poetics of Ritual Power in an Amazonian Society.* Tucson: University of Arizona Press.

HIRSCH, Eric. 1994. "Between Mission and Market: Events and Images in a Melanesian Society." *Man,* n.s., 29: 689–711.

———. 2008. "God or *Tidibe?* Melanesian Christianity and the Problem of Wholes." *Ethnos* 73(2): 141–162.

HOLBRAAD, Martin. 2010. "Ontology Is Just Another Word for Culture: Against the Motion." *Critique of Anthropology* 30(2): 179–185.

HORNBORG, Alf. 2006. "Animism, Fetishism, and Objectivism as Strategies for Knowing (or Not Knowing) the World." *Ethnos* 71(1): 21–32.

HORTON, Robin. 1975. "On the Rationality of Conversion." *Africa* 45: 373–399.

HOWARD, Catherine. 2001. "Wrought Identities: The Waiwai Expeditions in Search of the "Unseen Tribes" of Northern Amazonia." PhD diss., University of Chicago.

HOWELL, Signe, ed. 1997. *The Ethnography of Moralities.* London: Routledge.

HUGH-JONES, Christine. 1979. *From the Milk River: Spatial and Temporal Processes in Northwest Amazonia.* Cambridge: Cambridge University Press.

HUGH-JONES, Stephen. 1979. *The Palm and the Pleiades: Initiation and Cosmology in Northwest Amazonia.* Cambridge: Cambridge University Press.

———. 1994. "Shamans, Prophets, Priests and Pastors." In *Shamanism, History and the State,* edited by Nicholas Thomas and Caroline Humphrey, 32–75. Ann Arbor: University of Michigan Press.

———. 1997. "Education et culture: Réflexions sur certains développements dans la région colombienne du Pira-Paraná." *Cahier des Amériques Latines* 23: 95–121.

———. 2001. "The Gender of Some Amazonian Gifts: An Experiment with an Experiment." In *Gender in Amazonia and Melanesia: An Exploration of the Comparative Method,* edited by Thomas Gregor and Donald Tuzin, 245–278. Berkeley: University of California Press.

———. 2009. "The Fabricated Body: Objects and Ancestors in Northwest Amazonia." In *The Occult Life of Things: Native Amazonia Theories of Materialities and Personhood,* edited by Fernando Santos-Granero, 33–59. Tucson: University of Arizona Press.

———. 2010. "Entre l'image et l'écrit: La politique tukano de en Amazonie." *Cahiers des Amériques latines* 63–64: 195–227.

JACKSON, Jean. 1975. "Recent Ethnography of Indigenous Northern Lowland South America." *Annual Review of Anthropology* 4: 307–340.

———. 1984. "Traducciones competitivas del Evangelio en el Vaupés, Colombia." *America Indígena* 44: 49–94.

JAMES, Wendy. 2013. "Translating God's Words." In *Companion to the Anthropology of Religion,* edited by Janice Boddy and Michael Lambek, 329–343. London: Wiley-Blackwell.

JOHNSTON, Jean Dye. 1966. *God Planted Five Seeds.* New York: Harper and Row.

JOHNSTON, Kenneth. 1985. *The Story of the New Tribes Mission.* Sanford, FL: New Tribes Mission.

JORDAN, David. 1993. "The Glyphomancy Factor: Observations on Chinese Conversion". In *Conversion to Christianity: Historical and Anthropological Perspectives on a Great Transformation*, edited by Robert Hefner, 285–303. Berkeley and Los Angeles: The University of California Press.

JOURNET, Nicolas. 1995. "La paix des jardins: Structures sociales des Indiens Curripaco du haut Rio Negro, Colombie." In *Memoires de l'Institut d'Ethnologie,* 31. Paris: Institut d'Ethnologie, Musée de l'Lomme.

KAHN, Marina. 1999. "Levantamento preliminar das organizações religiosas em áreas indígenas." In *Transformando os deuses: Os múltiplos sentidos da conversão entre os povos indígenas no Brasil,* edited by Robin Wright, 19–76. Campinas, Brazil: Editora da Unicamp.

KEANE, Webb. 2002. "Sincerity, 'Modernity,' and the Protestants." *Cultural Anthropology* 17(1): 65–92.

———. 2007. *Christian Moderns: Freedom and Fetish in the Mission Encounter.* Berkeley: University of California Press.

—. 2013. "On Spirit Writing: Materialities of Language and the Religion Work of Transduction." *Journal of the Royal Anthropological Institute*, n.s., 19(1): 1–17.

—. 2014. "Rotting Bodies: The Clash of Stances toward Materiality and Its Ethical Affordances." *Current Anthropology* 55(S10): S312–S321.

KEE, Howard. 1993. "From the Jesus Movement toward the Institutional Church." In *Conversion to Christianity: Historical and Anthropological Perspectives on a Great Transformation,* edited by Robert W. Hefner, 47–63. Berkeley: University of California Press.

KEESING, Roger. 1982. "Kastom in Melanesia: An Overview." In "Reinventing Traditional Culture: The Politics of Kastom in Island Melanesia," edited by Roger Keesing and Robert Tonkinson, special issue, *Mankind* 13(4): 297–301.

KELLY, José Antonio. 2001. "Fractalidade e troca de perspectivas." *Mana: Estudos de Antropologia Social* 7(2): 95–132.

—. 2005a. "Fractality and the Exchange of Perspectives." In *On the Order of Chaos: Social Anthropology and the Science of Chaos,* edited by Mark Mosko and Frederick Damon, 108–135. New York: Berghahn.

—. 2005b. "Notas para uma teoria do 'virar branco.'" *Mana: Estudos de Antropologia Social* 11(1): 201–234.

—. 2011a. "Dialética de figura e fundo na mitologia Yanomami, Piaroa e Yekuana." Unpublished manuscript.

—. 2011b. *State Healthcare and Yanomami Transformations: A Symmetrical Ethnography.* Tucson: University of Arizona Press.

KOPENAWA, Davi, and ALBERT, Bruce. 2010. *La chute du ciel: Paroles d'un chaman yanomami.* Paris: Plon.

KULICK, Don, and STROUT, Christopher. 1990. "Christianity, Cargo and Ideas of Self: Patterns of Literacy in a Papua New Guinea Village." *Man* 25(2): 286–304.

LAIDLAW, James. 2013. "Ethics." In *Companion to the Anthropology of Religion,* edited by Janice Boddy and Michael Lambek, 171–188. Oxford: Wiley-Blackwell.

LAMBEK, Michael. 1998. "Body and Mind in Mind, Body and Mind in Body: Some Anthropological Interventions in a Long Conversation." In *Bodies and Persons: Comparative Perspectives from Africa and Melanesia,* edited by Michael Lambeck and Andrew Strathern, 103–123. Cambridge: Cambridge University Press.

—. 2013. "What Is 'Religion' for Anthropology and What Has Anthropology Brought to 'Religion'?" In *Companion to the Anthropology of Religion,* edited by Janice Boddy and Michael Lambek, 1–32. London: Wiley-Blackwell.

LASMAR, Cristiane. 2005. *De Volta ao Lago de Leite: Gênero e Transformação no Alto Rio Negro.* Rio de Janeiro: Nuti.

LATOUR, Bruno. 1993. *We Have Never Been Modern.* Translated by Catherine Porter. Cambridge, MA: Harvard University Press.

LATTAS, Andrew. 1998. *Cultures of Secrecy: Reinventing Race in Bush Kaliai Cargo Cults.* Madison: University of Wisconsin Press.

LAUGRAND, Fédéric. 1997. "'Ni vanqueurs, ni vaincus': Les premières rencontres entre les chamanes inuit (*angakkuit*) et les missionaires dans trois régions de l'Artique canadien." *Anthropologie et Sociétés* 21(2–3): 99–123.

REFERENCES · 287

———. 1999. "Le mythe comme instrument de la mémoire: Rémemoration et inter-prétation d'un extrait de la Genèse par un aîne inuit de la Terre de Baffin." *Études /Inuit/Studies* 23(1–2): 91–115.

LAUGRAND, Fédéric, and OOSTEN, Jarich. 2009. "Shamans and Missionaries: Transitions and Transformations in the Kivalliq Coastal Area." In *Native Christians: Modes and Effects of Christianity among Indigenous Peoples of the Americas,* edited by Aparecida Vilaça and Robin Wright, 167–186. Hampshire, U.K.: Ashgate.

LEENHARDT, Maurice. [1947] 1971. *Do Kamo: La personne et le mythe dans le monde Mélanésien.* Paris: Gallimard.

LEIGUE CASTEDO, Luis. 1957. *El Itenez Salvaje.* La Paz: Ministerio de Edu-cación y Bellas Artes.

LEITE, Serafim. 1954. *Cartas dos primeiros jesuítas do Brasil.* Vol. 1. São Paulo: Comissão do IV Centenário da cidade de São Paulo.

LEITE, Tainah. 2010. "Pessoa e humanidade nas etnografias yanomami." Master's thesis, PPGAS, Museu Nacional, Universidade Federal do Rio de Janeiro.

———. 2013. "Imagens da humanidade: Metamorfose e moralidade na mitologia Yanomami." *Mana: Estudos de Antropologia Social* 19(1): 69–97.

LÉVI-STRAUSS, Claude. 1955. *Tristes tropiques.* Paris: Plon.

———. [1958] 1991. "Les organizations dualistes existent-elles?" In *Anthropologie Structurale.* Paris: Plon.

———. 1964. *Mythologiques: Le cru et le cuit.* Paris: Plon.

———. 1966. *Mythologiques: Du miel aux cendres.* Paris: Plon.

———. 1968. *Mythologiques: L'órigine des manières de table.* Paris: Plon.

———. 1971. *Mythologiques: L'homme nu.* Paris: Plon.

———. 1991. *Histoire de Lynx.* Paris: Plon.

———. 1995. *The Story of Lynx.* Translated by Catherine Tihanyi. Chicago: Uni-versity of Chicago Press.

LÉVI-STRAUSS, Claude, and ERIBON, Didier. 1988. *De près et de loin.* Paris: Éditions Odile Jacob.

LÉVY-BRUHL, Lucien. [1926] 1985. *How Natives Think.* Princeton, NJ: Princeton University Press.

———. 1938. *L'experience mystique et les symboles chez les primitifs.* Paris: Alcan.

LIENHARDT, R. G. 1982. "The Dinka and Catholicism." In *Religious Organiza-tion and Religious Experience,* edited by J. Davis, 81–95. London: Academic Press.

LIMA, Tânia. 1995. "A Parte do Cauim: Etnografia Juruna." PhD diss., PPGAS, Museu Nacional, Universidade Federal do Rio de Janeiro.

———. 1996. "O dois e o seu múltiplo: Reflexões sobre o perspectivismo em uma cosmologia tupi." *Mana: Estudos de Antropologia Social* 2(2): 21–47.

———. 1999. "The Two and Its Many: Reflection on Perspectivism in a Tupi Cos-mology." *Ethnos* 64(1): 107–131.

———. 2002. "O que é um corpo?" *Religião e Sociedade* 22: 9–19.

———. 2005. *Um peixe olhou para mim: O povo Yudjá e a perspectiva.* São Paulo: Universidade do Estado de São Paulo and Instituto Socioambiental; Rio de Janeiro: Nuti.

LINDORO, Ronaldo. 2011. *Introdução à antropologia missionária.* São Paulo: Vida Nova.

LLOYD, Geoffrey. 1966. *Polarity and Analogy: Two Types of Argumentation in Early Greek Thought.* Cambridge: Cambridge University Press.

———. 2011. "Humanity between Gods and Beasts? Ontologies in Question." *Journal of the Royal Anthropological Institute* 17(4): 829–845.

———. 2012. *Being, Humanity, and Understanding.* Oxford: Oxford University Press.

LOCK, Margaret, and SCHEPER-HUGHES, Nancy. 1987. "The Mindful Body." *Medical Anthropology Quarterly* 1: 6–41.

LOWIE, Robert. 1948. "The Tropical Forest: An Introduction." In *Handbook of South American Indians.* Vol. 3, ed. Julian Steward, 1–56. Washington, DC: Smithsonian Institution.

LURHMANN, Tanya. 2012. *When God Talks Back: Understanding the American Evangelical Relationship with God.* New York: Vintage books.

LYON, Patricia. 1974. *Native South Americans: Ethnology of the Least Known Continent.* Boston: Little, Brown.

MARRIOT, McKim. 1976. "Hindu Transactions: Diversity without Dualism." In *Transaction and Meaning,* edited by B. Kapferer, 109–142. Philadelphia: ISHI Publications.

MAUSS, Marcel. [1950] 1999. "Une catégorie de l'esprit humain: La notion de personne, celle de 'moi.'" In *Sociologie et Anthropologie,* 332–362. Paris: PUF.

MAXWELL, David. 2007. "Comments to Robbins' 'Continuity Thinking and the Problem of Christian Culture.'" *Current Anthropology* 48(1): 25–26.

MAYBLIN, Maya. 2014. "People Like Us: Intimacy, Distance, and the Androgyny of Saints. *Current Anthropology* 55(S10): S271–S280.

MAYBURY-LEWIS, David. 1967. *Akwe-Shavante Society.* Oxford: Clarendon Press.

McCALLUM, Cecilia. 1996. "The Body That Knows: From Cashinahua Epistemology to a Medical Anthropology of Lowland South America." *Medical Anthropology Quarterly* 10: 347–72.

McILWAIN, Trevor. 2003. *Alicerces Firmes: Da criação até Cristo.* 2nd ed. Translated by Adriana Lima Colaço Melgarejo. Anápolis, Brazil: Missão Novas Tribos do Brasil.

MENDES, Rafael. 2013. "Mbya-Guarani." In "O Cristianismo na Amazônia Indígena," edited by Aparecida Vilaça et al., 34–43. Unpublished manuscript, report to CNPq.

MEYER, Birgit. 1996. "Modernity and Enchantment: The Image of the Devil in Popular African Christianity." In *Conversion to Modernities: The Globalization of Christianity,* edited by Peter van der Veer, 199–230. London: Routledge.

———. 1998. "'Make a Complete Break with the Past': Memory and Postcolonial Modernity in Ghanaian Pentecostal Discourse." In *Memory and the Postcolony: African Anthropology and the Critique of Power,* edited by Richard Werbner, 182–208. London: Zed Books.

———. 1999. *Translating the Devil: Religion and Modernity among the Ewe in Ghana.* London: Edinburgh University Press, for the International African Institute.

————. 2013. "Mediation and Immediacy: Sensational Forms, Semiotic Ideologies, and the Question of the Medium." In *Companion to the Anthropology of Religion*, edited by Janice Boddy and Michael Lambek, 307–326. London: Wiley-Blackwell.

MEYERS, Fred. 1994. "Culture-Making: Performing Aboriginality in the Asia Society Gallery." *American Ethnologist* 21(4): 679–699.

MONTERO, Paula. 2006. "Introdução." In *Deus na aldeia: Missionários, índios e mediação cultural*, edited by Paula Montero, 9–29. São Paulo: Editora Globo.

MONTOYA, Antonio Ruiz. 1985. *Conquista espiritual feita pelos religiosos da Companhia de Jesus nas províncias do Paraguai, Paraná, Uruguai e Tape*. Porto Alegre, Brazil: Martins Livreiro.

MORRIS, Colin. [1972] 1987. *The Discovery of the Individual, 1050–1200*. Toronto: University of Toronto Press.

MOSKO, Mark. 2010. "Partible Penitents: Dividual Personhood and Christian Practice in Melanesia and the West." *Journal of the Royal Anthropological Institute*, n.s., 16: 215–240.

NEEDHAM, Rodney. 1972. *Belief, Language, and Experience*. Oxford: Basil Blackwell.

OLIVEIRA, Leonor Valentino de. 2010. "O cristianismo evangélico entre os Waiwai: Alteridade e transformações entre as décadas de 1950 e 1980." Master's thesis, PPGAS, Museu Nacional, Universidade Federal do Rio de Janeiro.

OPAS, Minna. 2008. "Different but the Same: Negotiation of Personhoods and Christianities in Western Amazonia." PhD diss., Department of Comparative Religion, University of Turku, Finland.

ORTA, Andrew. 2004. *Catechizing Culture: Missionaries, Aymara, and the "New Evangelization."* New York: Columbia University Press.

OVERING KAPLAN, Joanna. 1975. *The Piaroa: A People of the Orinoco Basin*. Oxford: Clarendon Press.

————. 1976. "Comments to *Social Time and Social Space in Lowland South American Societies*." *Actes du XLIIe Congrès International des Américanistes* (Paris), 2: 387–394.

————. 1985a. "There Is No End of Evil: The Guilty Innocents and Their Fallible God." In *The Anthropology of Evil*, edited by David Parkin, 244–278. Oxford: Basil Blackwell.

————. 1985b. "Today I Shall Call Him 'Mummy': Multiple Worlds and Classificatory Confusion." In *Reason and Morality*, edited by Joanna Overing, 153–179. London: Tavistock.

————. 1986. "Images of Cannibalism, Death and Domination in a Non-violent Society." *Journal de la Société des Américanistes* 72: 133–156.

————. 1990. "The Shaman as a Maker of Worlds: Nelson Goodman in Amazonia." *Man*, n.s., 25: 601–619.

————. 1999. "Elogio do cotidiano: A confiança e a arte da vida social em uma comunidade amazônica." *Mana: Estudos de Antropologia Social* 5(1): 81–107.

OVERING, Joanna, and PASSES, Alan. 2000, eds. *The Anthropology of Love and Anger: The Aesthetics of Conviviality in Native Amazonia.* London: Routledge.

POLLOCK, Donald. K. 1993. "Conversion and 'Community' in Amazonia." In *Conversion to Christianity: Historical and Anthropological Perspectives on a Great Transformation,* edited by Robert Hefner, 165–197. Berkeley: University of California Press.

POUILLON, Jean. 1993. *Le cru et le su.* Paris: Seuil.

QUEIROZ, Rubem Caixeta. 1999. "A saga de Ewká: Epidemias e evangelização entre os Waiwai." In *Transformando os Deuses: Os múltiplos sentidos da conversão entre os povos indígenas no Brasil,* edited by Robin Wright, 255–284. Campinas, Brazil: Editora da Unicamp.

RAFAEL, Vicente. 1993. *Contracting Colonialism: Translation and Christian Conversion in Tagalog Society under Early Spanish Rule.* Durham, NC: Duke University Press.

REICHEL-DOLMATOFF, Gerard. 1975. *The Shaman and the Jaguar.* Philadelphia, PA: Temple University Press.

RIVIÈRE, Peter. 1969. *Marriage among the Trio: A Principle of Social Organization.* Oxford: Oxford University Press.

———. 1981. "'The Wages of Sin Is Death': Some Aspects of Evangelisation among the Trio Indians." *Journal of the Anthropological Society of Oxford* 12: 1–13.

———. 1984. *Individual and Society in Guiana: A Comparative Study of Amerindian Social Organization.* Cambridge Studies in Social Anthropology. Cambridge: Cambridge University Press.

———. 1993. "The Amerindianization of Descent and Affinity." *L'Homme* 33(2–4): 507–516.

ROBBINS, Joel. 1994. "Equality as Value: Ideology in Dumont, Melanesia and the West." *Social Analysis* 36: 21–70.

———. 2001a. "God Is Nothing but Talk: Modernity, Language, and Prayer in a Papua New Guinea Society." *American Anthropologist* 103(4): 901–912.

———. 2001b. "'This Profound Differentiation of Mankind': On 'The Uninvited Guest' and 'The Invention of Culture.'" *Suomen Antropologi* (journal of the Finnish Anthropological Society) 26(1): 29–34.

———. 2002. "On the Critical Uses of Difference: 'The Uninvited Guest' and 'The Invention of Culture'" *Social Analysis* 46(1): 4–9.

———. 2004. *Becoming Sinners: Christianity and Moral Torment in a Papua New Guinea Society.* Berkeley: University of California Press.

———. 2007a. "Between Reproduction and Freedom: Morality, Value and Radical Cultural Change." *Ethnos* 72(3): 293–314.

———. 2007b. "Continuity Thinking and Christian Culture." *Current Anthropology* 48(1): 5–38.

———. 2007c. "You Can't Talk behind the Holy Spirit's Back: Christianity and Changing Language Ideologies in a Papua New Guinea Society." In *Consequences of Contact: Language Ideologies and Sociocultural Transformations in Pacific Societies,* edited by Miki Makihara and Bambi B. Schieffelin, 125–159. Oxford: Oxford University Press.

———. 2008. "On Not Knowing Others' Minds: Confession, Intention and Linguistic Exchange in a Papua New Guinea Community." *Anthropological Quarterly* 81(2): 421–430.

———. 2009. Afterword to *Native Christians: Modes and Effects of Christianity among Indigenous Peoples of the Americas,* edited by Aparecida Vilaça and Robin Wright, 229–238. Hampshire, U.K.: Ashgate.

———. 2015. "Dumont's Hierarchical Dynamism: Christianity and Individualism Revisited." *HAU: Journal of Ethnographic Theory* 5(1): 173–195.

ROBBINS, Joel, and RUMSEY, Alan. 2008. "Introduction: Cultural and Linguistic Anthropology and the Opacity of Other Minds." *Anthropological Quarterly* 81(2): 407–420.

ROBBINS, Joel, SCHIEFFELIN, Bambi, and VILAÇA, Aparecida. 2014. "Evangelical Conversion and the Transformation of the Self in Amazonia and Melanesia: Christianity and New Forms of Anthropological Comparison." *Comparative Studies in Society and History* 56(3): 1–32.

RUTHERFORD, Danilyn. 2006. "The Bible Meets the Idol: Writing and Conversion in Biak, Irian Jaya, Indonesia." In *The Anthropology of Christianity,* edited by Fenella Cannell, 240–272. Durham, NC: Duke University Press.

SAHLINS, Marshall. 1981. *Historical Metaphors and Mythical Realities: Structure in the Early History of the Sandwich Islands Kingdom.* Ann Arbor: University of Michigan Press.

———. 1985. *Islands of History.* Chicago: University of Chicago Press.

———. [1992] 2005. "The Economics of the Develop-Man in the Pacific." In *The Making of Global and Local Modernities in Melanesia: Humiliation, Transformation and the Nature of Cultural Change,* edited by Joel Robbins and Holly Wardlow, 23–42. Hampshire, U.K.: Ashgate.

———. [1996] 2005. "The Sadness of Sweetness: The Native Anthropology of Western Cosmology." In *Culture in Practice,* 527–584, New York: Zone Books.

———. 1997a. "O 'Pessimismo sentimental' e a experiência etnográfica: Por que a cultura não é um 'objeto' em via de extinção (Parte I)" *Mana: Estudos de Antropologia Social* 3(1): 41–73.

———. 1997b. "O 'Pessimismo sentimental' e a experiência etnográfica: Por que a cultura não é um 'objeto' em via de extinção (Parte II)." *Mana: Estudos de Antropologia Social* 3(2): 103–150.

———. 2010. "The Whole Is a Part: Intercultural Politics of Order and Change." In *Experiments in Holism: Theory and Practice in Contemporary Anthropology,* edited by Ton Otto and Nils Bubant, 102–126. Sussex: Blackwell.

———. 2011a. "What Kinship Is (Part One)." *Journal of the Royal Anthropological Institute,* n.s., 17(1): 2–19.

———. 2011b. "What Kinship Is (Part Two)." *Journal of the Royal Anthropological Institute,* n.s., 17(2): 227–242.

———. 2013. *What Kinship Is—and Is Not.* Chicago: University of Chicago Press.

SANDOR, A. 1986. "Metaphor and Belief." *Journal of Anthropological Research* 42: 101–122.

SANTOS-GRANERO, Fernando. 2007. "Time Is Disease, Suffering, and Oblivion: Yanesha Historicity and the Struggle against Temporality." In *Time and Memory in Indigenous Amazonia: Anthropological Perspectives,* edited by Carlos Fausto and Michael Heckenberger, 47–73. Gainesville: University Press of Florida.

———. 2009. "Hybrid Bodyscapes. A Visual History of Yanesha Patterns of Cultural Change." *Current Anthropology* 50(4): 477–512.

SCHADEN, E. 1962. *Aspectos Fundamentais da Cultura Guarani.* São Paulo: Difusão Européia do Livro.

SCHARF, Friedrich. 2010. "Sim Deus é fiel: Um relato de como Deus cumpriu as promessas dadas a mim." Unpublished manuscript.

SCHIEFFELIN, Bambi B. 2007. "Found in Translating." In *Consequences of Contact: Language Ideologies and Sociocultural Transformations in Pacific Societies,* edited by Miki Makihara and Bambi B. Schieffelin, 40–165. Oxford: Oxford University Press.

———. 2008a. "Speaking Only Your Own Mind: Reflections on Talk, Gossip and Intentionality in Bosavi (PNG)." *Anthropological Quarterly* 81(2): 431–441.

———. 2008b. "Tok bokis, tok piksa: Translating Parables in Papua New Guinea." In *Social Lives in Language: Sociolinguistics and Multilingual Speech Communities,* edited by Miriam Meyrhoff and Naomi Nagi, 111–134. Amsterdam: John Benjamins.

———. 2014. "Christianizing Language and the Dis-placement of Culture in Bosavi, Papua New Guinea." *Current Anthropology* 55(S10): S226–S237.

SCHIEFFELIN, Edward, and CRITTENDEN, Robert, eds. 1991. *Like People You See in a Dream.* Stanford, CA: Stanford University Press.

SCHMITT, Jean-Claude. 1998. "Les corps en Chrétienté." In *La production du corps: Approches anthropologiques et historiques,* edited by Maurice Godelier and Michel Panoff, 339–356. Paris: Éditions des archives contemporaines.

SCHNEIDER, David. [1968] 1980. *American Kinship: A Cultural Account.* 2nd ed. Chicago: University of Chicago Press.

———. 1984. *A Critique of the Study of Kinship.* Ann Arbor: University of Michigan Press.

SEEGER, Anthony. 1980. *Os índios e nós: Estudos sobre sociedades tribais brasileiras.* Rio de Janeiro: Campus.

———. 1981. *Nature and Society in Central Brazil: The Suya Indians of Mato Grosso.* Cambridge, MA: Harvard University Press.

SEEGER, Anthony, DA MATTA, Roberto, and VIVEIROS DE CASTRO, Eduardo. 1979. "A Construção da Pessoa nas Sociedades Indígenas Brasileiras." *Boletim do Museu Nacional* 32: 2–19.

SEGAL, Alan. 2003. "Text Translation as a Prelude for Soul Translation." In *Translating Cultures: Perspectives on Translation and Anthropology,* edited by Paula Rubel and Abraham Rosman, 213–248. Oxford, New York: Berg.

SHAPIRO, Judith. 1981. "Ideologies of Catholic Missionary Practice in a Postcolonial Era." *Comparative Studies in Society and History* 23(1): 130–149.

SILVERSTEIN, Michael. 2003. "Translation, Transduction, Transformation: Skating 'Glossando' on Thin Semiotic Ice." In *Translating Cultures: Perspectives on Translation and Anthropology,* edited by Paula Rubel and Abraham Rosman, 75–107. Oxford: Berg.

SOUZA LIMA, Antônio Carlos. 1995. *Um grande cerco de paz: Poder tutelar, indianidade e formação do Estado no Brasil.* Rio de Janeiro: Editora Vozes.

STASCH, Rupert. 2007. "Demon Language: The Otherness of Indonesian in a Papuan Community." In *Consequences of Contact: Language Ideologies and Sociocultural Transformations in Pacific Societies,* edited by Miki Makihara and Bambi Schieffelin, 96–124. New York: Oxford University Press.

———. 2008. "Knowing Minds Is a Matter of Authority: Political Dimensions of Opacity Statements in Korowai Moral Psychology." *Anthropological Quarterly* 81(2): 443–454.

———. 2009. *Society of Others: Kinship and Mourning in a West Papuan Place.* Berkeley: University of California Press.

STOLL, David. 1982. *Fishers of Men or Founders of Empire? The Wycliffe Bible Translators in Latin America.* London: Zed Press.

STOLZ Franz. 1999. "From the Paradigm of Lament and Hearing to the Conversion Paradigm." In *Transformations of the Inner Self in Ancient Religions,* edited by Jan Assman and Guy G. Stroumsa, 9–30. Leiden, Netherlands: Brill.

STRATHERN, Marilyn. 1988. *The Gender of the Gift: Problems with Women and Problems with Society in Melanesia.* Berkeley: University of California Press.

———. 1995. Foreword to *Shifting Contexts: Transformations on Anthropological Knowledge,* edited by Marilyn Strathern, 1–11. London: Routledge.

———. 1998. "Novas formas econômicas: Um relato das terras altas da Papua Nova Guiné." *Mana: Estudos de Antropologia Social* 4(1): 109–139.

———. 1999. *Property, Substance and Effect: Anthropological Essays on Persons and Things.* London: Athlone Press.

———. 2001a. "The Patent and the Malanggan." In *Beyond Aesthetics: Art and the Technologies of Enchantment,* edited by C. Pinney and Nicolas Thomas, 259–286. Oxford: Berg.

———. 2001b. "Same-Sex and Cross-Sex Relations: Some Internal Comparisons." In *Gender in Amazonia and Melanesia: An Exploration of the Comparative Method,* edited by Thomas Gregor and Donald Tuzin, 221–244. Berkeley: University of California Press.

———. 2012. "Eating (and Feeding)." *Cambridge Anthropology* 30(2): 1–14.

SURRALLÈS, Alexandre. 2003. *Au coeur du sens: Perception, affectivité, action chez les Candoshi.* Paris: CNRS/Maison des sciences de l'Homme.

TARIRI and WALLIS, Ethel. 1965. *Tariri: My Story; from Jungle Killer to Christian Missionary; as Told to Ethel Emily Wallis.* New York: Harper and Row.

TAUSSIG, Michael. 1993. *Mimesis and Alterity: A Particular History of the Senses.* New York: Routledge.

TAYLOR, Anne-Christine. 1981. "God-Wealth: The Achuar and the Missions." In *Cultural Transformations and Ethnicity in Modern Ecuador,* edited by Norman Whitten Jr., 647–676. Urbana: University of Illinois Press.

———. 1996. "The Soul's Body and Its States: An Amazonian Perspective on the Nature of Being Human." *Journal of the Royal Anthropological Institute,* n.s., 2: 201–215.

———. 2000. "Le sexe de la proie: Répresentations Jivaro du lien de parenté." *L'Homme* 154–155: 309–334.

———. 2002. "The Face of Indian Souls: A Problem of Conversion." In *Iconoclash: Beyond the Image Wars in Science, Religion and Art,* edited by Bruno Latour and Peter Weibel, 462–464. Cambridge, MA: MIT Press.

———. 2007. "Sick of History: Contrasting Regimes of Historicity in Upper Amazon." In *Time and Memory in Indigenous Amazonia: Anthropological Perspectives,* edited by Carlos Fausto and Michael Heckenberger, 133–168. Gainesville: University Press of Florida.

TAYLOR, Anne-Christine, and VIVEIROS DE CASTRO, Eduardo. 2007. "Un corps fait des regards." In *Qu'est-ce qu'un corps?* eds, S. Breton, J.-M. Schaeffer, M. Houseman, A-C. Taylor, and E. Viveiros de Castro, 148–199. Paris: Flammarion/ Museé du Quai-Branly.

TAYLOR, Charles. 1989. *Sources of the Self: The Making of the Modern Identity.* Cambridge, MA: Harvard University Press.

TEDLOCK, Dennis. 1983. *The Spoken Word and the Work of Interpretation.* Philadelphia: University of Pennsylvania Press.

———. 1985. *Popol Vuh.* New York: Simon and Schuster.

TILLICH, Paul. 1968. *A History of Christian Thought: From Its Judaic and Hellenistic Origins to Existentialism,* edited by Carl E. Braaten. New York: Touchstone.

TOOKER, Deborah. 1992. "Identity Systems in Highland Burma: 'Belief,' Akha Zan and a Critique of Interiorized Notions of Ethno-Religious Identity." *Man* 27: 799–819.

TOWNSLEY, Graham. 1993. "Song Paths: The Ways and Means of Shamanic Knowledge." *L'Homme* 33(2–4): 449–468.

TROELTSCH, Ernst. 1976. *The Social Teaching of the Christian Churches.* Vol. 2. Translated by Olive Wyon. Chicago: University of Chicago Press.

TURNER, Terence. 1995. "Social Body and Embodied Subject: Bodiliness, Subjectivity and Sociality among the Kayapo." *Cultural Anthropology* 10: 143–170.

VAN DER GEEST, Sjaak. 1990. "Anthropologists and Missionaries: Brothers under the Skin." *Man,* n.s., 25: 588–601.

VARGAS, Eduardo Viana. 2010. "Tarde on Drugs, or Measures against Suicide." In *The Social after Gabriel Tarde: Debates and Assessments,* edited by M. Candea, 208–229. London: Routledge.

VENKATESAN, Soumhya, ed. 2010. "Ontology Is Just Another Word for Culture." *Critique of Anthropology* 30: 152–200. Motion tabled at the 2008 meeting of the Group for Debates in Anthropological Theory.

VEYNE, Paul. 2007. *Quand notre monde est devenu chrétien (312–394)*. Paris: Albin Michel.

VILAÇA, Aparecida. 1992. *Comendo como gente: Formas do canibalismo wari'*. Rio de Janeiro: Editora UFRJ/Anpocs.

———. 1996. "Cristãos sem fé: Alguns aspectos da conversão dos Wari' (Pakaa-Nova)." *Mana: Estudos de Antropologia Social* 2(1): 109–137. Republished in *Transformando os deuses: Os múltiplos sentidos da conversão entre os povos indígenas no Brasil,* edited by Robin Wright, 131–154. Campinas, Brazil: Editora da Unicamp.

———. 1997. "Christians without Faith: Some Aspects of the Conversion of the Wari' (Pakaa Nova)." *Ethnos* 62(1–2): 91–115.

———. 1998. "Fazendo corpos: Reflexões sobre morte e canibalismo entre os Wari' à luz do perspectivismo." *Revista de Antropologia* 41(1): 9–67.

———. 1999. "Devenir autre: Chamanisme et contacte interethnique en Amazonie brésilienne." *Journal de la Société des Américanistes* 85: 239–260.

———. 2000. "Relations between Funerary Cannibalism and Warfare Cannibalism: The Question of Predation." *Ethnos* 65(1): 84–106.

———. 2002a. "Making Kin out of Others in Amazonia." *Journal of the Royal Anthropological Institute*, n.s., 8: 347–365.

———. 2002b. "Missions et conversions chez les Wari': Entre protestantisme et catholicisme." *L'Homme* 164: 57–79.

———. 2005. "Chronically Unstable Bodies: Reflections on Amazonian Corporalities." *Journal of the Royal Anthropological Institute*, n.s., 11(3): 445–464.

———. 2006. *Quem Somos nós: Os Wari' Encontram os Brancos*. Rio de Janeiro: Editora UFRJ.

———. 2007. "Cultural Change as Body Metamorphosis." In *Time and Memory in Indigenous Amazonia: Anthropological Perspectives,* edited by Carlos Fausto and Michael Heckenberger, 169–193. Gainesville: University Press of Florida.

———. 2008. "Conversão, predação e perspectiva." *Mana: Estudos de Antropologia Social* 14(1): 173–204.

———. 2009a. "Bodies in Perspective: A Critique of the Embodiment Paradigm from the Point of View of Amazonian Ethnography." In *Social Bodies,* edited by Helen Lambert and Maryon McDonald, 129–147. New York: Berghahn.

———. 2009b. "Conversion, Predation and Perspective." In *Native Christians: Modes and Effects of Christianity among Indigenous Peoples of the Americas,* edited by Aparecida Vilaça and Robin Wright, 147–166. Hampshire, U.K.: Ashgate.

———. 2010. *Strange Enemies: Indigenous Agency and Scenes of Encounters in Amazonia*. Translated by David Rodgers. Durham, NC: Duke University Press.

———. 2011. "Dividuality in Amazonia: God, the Devil and the Constitution of Personhood in Wari' Christianity." *Journal of the Royal Anthropological Institute*, n.s., 17(2): 243–262.

———. 2012. "Manger la parole de Dieu: La Bible lue par les Wari'." *Journal de la Société des Américanistes* 98(1): 81–100.

———. 2013a. "Communicating through Difference: Comments on Lloyd's Book *Being, Humanity and Understanding.*" *HAU: Journal of Ethnographic Theory* 3: 174–178.

———. 2013b. "Reconfiguring Humanity in Amazonia: Christianity and Change." In *Companion to the Anthropology of Religion,* edited by Janice Boddy and Michael Lambek, 363–386. London: Wiley-Blackwell.

———. 2014a. "Culture and Self: The Different 'Gifts' Amerindians Receive from Catholics and Evangelicals." *Current Anthropology* 55(S10): S322–S332.

———. 2014b. "'What If a Religion Is Not Made to Last?' Reply to Joel Robbins's 'How Do Religions End? Theorizing Religious Traditions from the Point of View of How They Disappear.'" *Cambridge Anthropology* 32(2): 16–18.

———. 2015a. "Dividualism and Individualism in Indigenous Christianity: A Debate Seen from Amazonia." *HAU: Journal of Ethnographic Theory* 5(1): 45–73.

———. 2015b. "Do Animists Become Naturalists When Converting to Christianity? Discussing an Ontological Turn." *Cambridge Anthropology* 33(2): 3–19.

VILAÇA, Aparecida, and WRIGHT, Robin, eds. 2009. *Native Christians: Modes and Effects of Christianity among Indigenous Peoples of the Americas.* Hampshire, U.K.: Ashgate.

VIVEIROS DE CASTRO, Eduardo. [1977] 1987. "A Fabricação do Corpo na Sociedade Xinguana." In *Sociedades Indígenas e Indigenismo no Brasil,* edited by João P. Oliveira Filho, 31–41. Rio de Janeiro: UFRJ/Marco Zero.

———. 1986. *Araweté: Os deuses canibais.* Rio de Janeiro: ANPOCS/Jorge Zahar Editor.

———. 1992a. *From the Enemy's Point of View: Humanity and Divinity in an Amazonian Society.* Translated by Catherine Howard. Chicago: University of Chicago Press.

———. 1992b. "O mármore e a murta: Sobre a inconstância da alma selvagem." *Revista de Antropologia* 35: 21–74.

———. 1993. "Alguns aspectos da afinidade no dravidianato amazônico." In *Amazônia: Etnologia e história indígena,* edited by Manuela Carneiro da Cunha and Eduardo Viveiros de Castro, 149–210. São Paulo: Núcleo de História Indígena e do Indigenismo da USP/ FAPESP.

———. 1996. "Os pronomes cosmológicos e o perspectivismo ameríndio." *Mana: Estudos de Antropologia Social* 2(2): 115–143.

———. 1998. "Cosmological Deixis and Amerindian Perspectivism." *Journal of the Royal Anthropological Institute* 4(3): 469–488.

———. 2000. "Atualização e contra-efetuação do virtual na socialidade amazônica: O processo de parentesco." *Ilha* 2(1): 5–46.

———. 2001. "GUT Feelings about Amazonia: Potential Affinity and the Construction of Sociality." In *Beyond the Visible and the Material: The Amerindianization of Society in the Work of Peter Rivière,* edited by Laura Rival and Neil Whitehead, 19–43. Oxford: University Press.

———. 2002. *A inconstância da alma selvagem.* São Paulo: Cosac and Naify.

———. 2004. "Perspectival Anthropology and the Method of Controlled Equivocation." *Tipití: Journal of the Society for the Anthropology of Lowland South America* 2(1): 3–22.

———. 2007. "The Crystal Forest: Notes on the Ontology of Amazonian Spirits." *Inner Asia* 9: 153–172.

———. 2011. *The Inconstancy of the Indian Soul: The Encounter of Catholics and Cannibals in 16th-Century Brazil.* Translated by Gregory Duff Morton. Chicago: Prickly Paradigm Press.

———. 2012a. "Cosmological Perspectivism in Amazonia and Elsewhere." *HAU: Journal of Ethnographic Theory.* Masterclasses Series 1.

———. 2012b. Immanence and Fear: Stranger-Events and Subjects in Amazonia. *HAU: Journal of Ethnographic Theory* 2(1): 27–43.

VON GRAEVE, Bernard. 1989. *The Pacaa Nova: Clash of Cultures in the Brazilian Frontier.* Ontario: Broadview Press.

WAGNER, Roy. 1975. *The Invention of Culture.* Englewood Cliffs, NJ: Prentice-Hall.

WEBER, Max. 1956. *The Sociology of Religion.* Translated by Ephraim Fischoff. Boston: Beacon Press.

———. 1987. *A ética protestante e o espírito do capitalismo.* São Paulo: Livraria Pioneira Editora.

WERBNER, Richard. 2011. "The Charismatic Dividual and the Sacred Self." *Journal of Religion in Africa* 41: 180–205.

WILBERT, Johannes, and SIMONEAU, Karin, eds. 1990. *Folk Literature of the Yanomami Indians.* Los Angeles: UCLA Latin American Publications.

WILLERSLEV, Rane. 2004. "Not Animal, Not Not-Animal: Hunting, Imitation, and Empathetic Knowledge among the Siberian Yukaghirs." *Journal of the Royal Anthropological Institute* 10: 629–652.

WILLERSLEV, Rane, and PEDERSEN, Morten Axel. 2009. "The Soul of the Soul Is the Body: Rethinking the Soul through North Asian Ethnographies." In *Identities under Construction: Translocal Connections and the Transformation of Bodies, Persons and Social Entities,* edited by E. Halbmayer, P. Schwitzer, and E. Mader. Oxford: Berghahn.

WISE, M.R., LOOS, E.E. and Davis, P. 1977. "Filosofia y métodos del Instituto Lingüístico de Verano. *Actes du XLIIe Congrès des Américanistes* (Paris), 2: 499–525.

WOOD, Peter. 1993. "Afterword: Boundaries and Horizons." In *Conversion to Christianity: Historical and Anthropological Perspectives on a Great Transformation,* edited by Robert W. Hefner, 305–321. Berkeley: University of California Press.

WRIGHT, Robin. 1996. "Os guardiões do cosmos: Pajés e profetas entre os Baniwa." In *Xamanismo no Brasil: Novas Perspectivas,* edited by Jean Langdon, 75–115. Florianópolis, Brazil: UFSC.

———. 1999. "O tempo de Sophie: História e cosmologia da conversão Baniwa." In *Transformando os deuses: Os múltiplos sentidos da conversão entre os povos indígenas do Brasil,* edited by Robin Wright, 155–216. São Paulo: Editora da Unicamp.

————, ed. 1999. *Transformando os deuses: Os múltiplos sentidos da conversão entre os povos indígenas no Brasil.* Campinas, Brazil: Editora da Unicamp.

————, ed. 2004. *Transformando os Deuses, v. II: Igrejas evangélicas, pentecostais e neo-pentecostais entre os povos indígenas no Brasil.* Campinas, Brazil: Editora da Unicamp.

XAVIER, Carlos César. 2013. "Os Koripako do Alto Içana: Etnografia de um grupo evangélico." PhD diss., PPGAS, Museu Nacional, Universidade Federal do Rio de Janeiro.

YVINEC, Cédric. 2014. "Temporal Dimensions of Selfhood: Theories of Person among the Suruí of Rondônia (Brazilian Amazon)." *Journal of Royal Anthropologic Institute* 20(1): 20–37.

ZOPPI, Miranda. 2012. "O índio político a partir dos Kaxinawá do Alto Purus." Master's thesis. PPGAS, Museu Nacional, Universidade Federal do Rio de Janeiro.

BIBLES

A Bíblia na linguagem de hoje. Sociedade Bíblica Brasileira (SBB).
New King James Bible.

MICROFILM

FUNAI, Museu do Indio, Rio de Janeiro.

INDEX

animal *(continued)*
  perspective of, 67, 237; as predators, 79,
    97, 217, 240, 249, 266n23; shaman's
    animal body, 261n22; spirits, 5, 45, 149,
    162, 236, 272n30,35; transformation
    into, 73
animality, 138, 217, 233
animism, 18, 267n8, 271n24
anthropology of Christianity, 9, 21
anthropophagy. *See* cannibalism
antichrist, 40, 265n13
Araweté, 80, 127, 142, 257n5, 271n17
Århem, Kaj, 19
Arruda, Dom Roberto, 90
Assembly of God (Church), 41, 42
Assman, Jan, 16, 157
Austin-Broos, Diane, 272 n 26
Aymara, 55
Ayoré, 32, 87, 258n3, 262n8
Aztecs, 48, 81

Baniwa, 132, 273n37
baptism, 2, 4, 28, 191–93, 210; and epidem-
    ics, 95; by immersion, 173
Baptists, 42
Barker, John, 8, 13, 274n4, 277n7
Barros, M. 258n11
beer, 63, 202–205, 208, 266n20; festivals, 7.
    See also chicha
behavior, 20, 72–73, 104, 116, 140, 170, 175,
    197, 200, 211, 215, 224, 229; codes of, 35,
    196; condemned, 195; fraternal, 106
belief, 4, 11, 16, 38, 41–43, 52, 93, 95, 104–5,
    114, 119,136–38, 161, 182, 184, 192, 212,
    233, 258n13, 265n7, 268n21, 269n23,
    272n27, 274n11; indigenous, 42, 138, 157;
    Christian notion of, 161. *See also howa;
    see also* trust
Belaunde, Luisa E., 265n11, 275nn5,8
believer (Christian), 10, 34, 38, 40–41,
    102–3, 107, 112, 117, 136, 138, 174, 191, 219,
    248, 264n23, 269n23
Bellah, Robert, 10, 221, 254
Bessire, Lucas, 258n3
Biak, 140, 159, 160, 270n12
Bible, 5, 16, 28, 35–36, 38, 42, 50–55, 61, 72,
    110–11, 140, 152–59, 174, 175, 177, 178,
    184, 185, 190, 194, 195, 198, 217, 236;

course books, 36; Hebrew, 16; literal
    reading of, 47; stories, 8, 154, 156–57,
    176, 181, 246, 266n20,23; translation of,
    22, 33, 49, 112, 191, 258n7,12,13 260n4,5,9,
    262n32, 267n14, 274n6
Bible books: Acts, 36–38, 55, 175; Corinthi-
    ans, 36, 43, 236, 240, 273n7; Ephesians,
    36, 38; Exodus, 36, 38, 183; Genesis, 20,
    28, 35, 36, 38, 39, 52, 114, 122, 128, 129–
    132, 138, 165, 176, 220, 222, 237, 246, 247,
    258n7, 267n15, 268n18,19, 274n3; Hosea
    266n23; Isaiah, 240, 266n23; John, 36,
    38, 110; Mark, 36, 40, 153, 187–190,
    276n28; Matthew, 36, 38, 40, 47, 110,
    178, 240; New Testament, 36–38, 49,
    54, 150, 195, 268n20; Numbers, 38; Old
    Testament, 5, 35, 36, 117, 268n20, 270n7;
    Revelation, 40, 240; Romans, 36–38,
    42, 151, 167, 227–28, 233, 275n12
biblical; concepts, translating, 148; films,
    154; imagery, 154, 171, 182, 240; key-
    words, 50, 52; literalism, 34–40, 41,
    258n7; themes, 77, 174; traditions, 53
blood, 17, 24, 69–70, 80–82, 127, 150, 164,
    191, 223, 226, 261n18, 265n17; of dead
    enemy, 80, 111–12; double, 79; of Jesus,
    111, 152, 180, 186, 188–90, 194
body, 21, 27, 40, 54–55, 57, 59–60, 63, 66,
    68, 70, 74–75, 79–80, 112–13, 128,
    131–32, 145, 147–50, 153, 161–63, 165,
    169–71, 183, 195, 199, 212, 214–15, 220,
    223–26, 230, 233–36, 242, 247, 261n22,
    267n11, 276n22,24; of Jesus Christ,
    188–91, 209; definition of, 19; demoniz-
    ing the, 236; differentiation, 58, 217, 222;
    as double, 66, 68, 222; duality of, 71; as
    envelope, 233; ex-, 147; fabrication of, 19;
    instability of, 17–20, 126–128; invisible,
    71, 147, 149, 163; language, 28; notion/
    concept of, 18, 149, 221, 224; paintings,
    155, 203; and perspectives, 20; and soul,
    16, 26, 29, 143, 232, 243; substances, 19;
    resurrection of, 34, 137; transformation/
    metamorphosis of, 19, 20, 27, 59, 61–64,
    69, 75, 102, 193, 240; translation via, 24,
    67, 69, 71, 73, 152. *See also* embodiment
bodiless, 149, 151, 164, 235
Bolivia, 30–32, 37, 58, 83, 85, 87, 262n8

Bonilla, Oiara, 51, 269n27, 270n12

books, 264n29, 272n26; catechism, 7, 150, 152, 196; course, 22, 36, 41–42, 136, 209; feather, 72; hymn, 116, 178–79, 181, 190, 192; lesson, 22, 27, 28, 35, 37–39, 53, 110, 114, 116, 119, 149–51, 156, 158, 161, 163–64, 167, 174–75, 177, 181, 183–84, 190, 228, 234, 265n7, 266n23, 267n15, 275n12, 276n28; reading, 55

Bosavi, 50, 250, 260n5, 270n10, 271n23, 275n12

Botswana, 14

Brightman, Marc, 18

brother-in-law, 78, 95, 100, 114–117, 204

Brown, Peter, 16

Burch, Ernest, 264n27, 272n32

Burridge, Kenelm, 275n16

Cadogan, Léon, 266n24

Calvin, 219

Calvinism, 220, 221, 275n13

Canada, 94

Cannel, Fenella, 107, 269n29, 274n11

cannibalism, 3, 4, 6, 47, 75, 81, 87, 167, 216, 266n23; funerary, 44, 64, 112, 114, 173, 202, 243; symbolic, 106

Capiberibe, Artionka, 177, 196, 264nn26,27,29, 270n12, 271n15,17,21, 272n26, 274n3, 276n22

Carib, 99

Carneiro da Cunha, Manuela, 19, 67, 264n29, 276n31, 277n1

Cashinahua, 116, 262n34,29

catechism, 5, 21–23, 27, 33, 54, 55, 72, 92, 105, 130, 132, 150, 152, 167, 172, 196, 208; teaching manual, 35

Catholic, 49, 55, 156, 172, 229, 270n8; Church, 27, 90, 104–105, 264n21; liturgy, 72; missionaries, 4, 27, 48, 55, 159, 229, 259n2, 270n8, 271n22; orders, 49; priests, 26, 46, 104, 150, 259n3

Cesarino, Pedro, 51, 68, 260n11, 261n19,21,24,26, 268n18, 269n28

Chamorro, Graciela, 72, 264n32, 266n24

Charismatics, 16, 34; neo-, 41; Apostolic, 14

Chaumeil, Jean-Pierre, 73

chicha, 24, 59, 70, 124, 210; fermented (sour), 78, 106, 146–47, 170, 200, 211, 226; festivals/rituals, 5, 74, 78, 141, 155, 173–74, 200, 202–8, 211, 218, 248, 250; peach-palm, 71; unfermented maize chicha, 209, 238. See also beer

Chimane, 37

China, 2, 3, 221

choirs, 162, 174, 178–79, 210, 212

Christ, 2, 6, 31, 34–35, 42, 94, 111, 119, 153, 166, 179–81, 188–89, 221, 224, 227–28, 233, 258nn7,13; resurrection/ascension of, 154, 176; death of, 112; love of, 32, 75; Second Coming of, 34, 40, 240. See also Jesus

Christian, 5–10, 21, 26, 28, 42, 71, 93–95, 103–6, 108–9, 119–121, 143, 137–138, 148, 157, 159, 161, 165–66, 171–72, 176, 181–82, 189, 192, 201, 214–15, 224, 239–240, 244, 264n23, 265nn7,8; activities/practices, 7, 173–74, 177, 210; ambiguity, 236; association, 41; becoming, 8, 94, 108, 191; concepts, translation of, 50–51, 112, 142–43, 218, 232–33, 235, 251, 270n10, 272n29; conferences, 93, 208–211; cosmology, 45, 51, 268n16; experience, 12, 14, 22, 26, 29, 51, 201, 246, 251, 253; God, 51, 95, 113, 132, 167, 222; hymns, 7, 116, 243; individualism, 15, 220; life, 177, 202, 206, 274n10; message, 6, 11–12, 15–16, 20, 23, 35, 37, 98–99, 102, 122, 144, 150–51, 220, 250, 269n25; missionaries, 20, 48, 270n3; morality, 170, 194–98, 211, 248; perspective, 235; phases, non-, 13; rice, 98; ritual/rites, 118, 173, 193–95, 198, 208, 228; soul, 25; symbols, 2, 95–96; teaching, 102; technologies of the production of the self, 229; theology, 16; values, 13, 47, 107

Christianity; abandonment of, 6, 104, 106; adoption of, 10, 135, 191, 274n3; continuities of, 10; plasticity of, 10

chronological; lessons, 36–37; principle, 36, 40, 176; teaching of the Bible, 35

church, 2, 5, 7–8, 31, 35, 41–42, 54, 138, 154, 175, 209–10, 258n13, 259n15, 265n7, 269n23, 271n23; envoys, 2; formation, 38, 219; leader, 174–75; sermons, 157; services, 4, 7–8, 13, 28, 39, 108–111, 129, 134–35, 150–154, 158, 162–63, 166, 172–

INDEX · 305

Dumont, Louis, 11–14, 219–221, 237, 249, 277n1
Durkheim, Émile, 277n4
Durston, Alan, 259n3, 260nn6–8

economic context, 251
ecumenical, 34, 41
edible, 63, 124, 130, 145, 157
embodiment, 224, 233, 235; of self and community, 230
encounters, first. See contact
end of the world, 7, 34, 40, 107–108, 135, 137–38, 153, 159, 166, 184, 228, 240, 258n13, 265n13
enemies, 4, 19, 25, 53, 59, 64, 75–80, 82–83, 86, 89–90, 97, 106, 115, 122, 124–27, 144, 200–201, 259n15, 266n1, 276n29; end of; new, 140; origin of, 77; powerful, 144; traditional, 79, 126
enemization, 203
enemy, 80–82, 111–12, 132, 139–143, 146, 151, 156, 167–68, 191; adopted, 89, 124, 232, 242; captured; children, 80; group, 90, 111–12, 125, 169; internal, 248; position, 80, 162; -affine, 112–13, 144, 173
Engelke, Matthew, 16, 259n21, 270n11, 271n18, 272n26
England, 10
epidemics, 4, 86, 92, 95, 97, 122, 264n25
equivocal homonyms, 64, 67
equivocation, 21–28, 51, 63, 74, 116, 118, 125, 162, 191, 226, 229, 235, 260n8; translatable, 116
equivocity, 120, 270
Eribon, Didier, 20
Eriksen, Annelin, 277n7
eschatology, 34, 40–41, 136, 169, 259n13
ethics, 7, 196–98, 215; subjects, 206, 211, 219
ethnocentrism, 56, 245
evangelical, 26, 46, 92, 156, 158, 177, 181, 255, 268n19, 271nn13,22, 277n8; missionaries, 3–4, 48, 50, 90–91, 104, 125, 160, 190, 229; programs, 26; neo-, 34, 41
Eve, 3, 36, 119, 154, 268n19, 272n36
Evens, T.M.S., 272n36, 274n3
Everett, Daniel, 257n7, 263n18, 269n25
evil, 44, 50, 119, 148, 194, 216, 233; spirit, 145; seat of, 236

Ewart, Elizabeth, 127, 267n10
Ewe, 51–52, 140, 240, 272n32
expeditions; contact, 27, 86–90, 92–93, 161, 262n8, 263nn10,14; hunting and gathering, 83; war, 146, 203
extermination, 79

faith, 30, 35, 44–45; inconstancy of, 5; in God, 33; mission, 31, 41, 49, 259n19; new; predominant, 9; statement of, 33–34, 41, 258n13
Fausto, Carlos, 18, 127, 167, 262n32,36,4, 264n30, 266n23, 269n22
Fernandes, Rubem César, 31, 32
festivals, 7, 69, 74, 90, 146, 170, 200, 237, 241, 243, 270n5; chicha, 5, 141, 155, 173, 200, 202–208, 218, 248, 250; pre-Christian chicha, 106, 174, 211. See also rituals
Fienup-Riordan, Ann, 264n27, 275n15
fights, 5, 6, 59, 100, 106–107, 109, 113, 139, 170, 196, 200–202, 206–7, 212, 214–15, 226, 248
fire, 32, 53, 55, 62, 80, 100, 166, 171–72, 190, 266n23, 269n25, 276n28; origin of, 112–14; eternal, 117, 136–38, 239, 276n26; lake of, 164–65, 172
Fleming, Paul, 30–32
flesh, 58, 75, 80, 137, 149, 172, 190, 201, 222, 235, 266n23
food taboos, 4, 198–201, 243, 269n22
foreigners, 43, 53, 57, 59, 76–78, 82, 89–90, 92, 104, 106, 122, 140–41, 144, 155, 162, 204, 207–208, 231
Foucault, Michel, 25, 28, 196–97, 226, 267n3, 274n11
Franchetto, Bruna, 57, 271n22
fraternity, 121, 138, 208; generalized, 29, 105–6, 251
Friedman, Jonathan, 257n1
FUNAI, 90–92, 139, 141, 251, 263n17, 265n13
fundamentalist, 16, 34, 42, 49, 56, 157, 246, 260n5; Christian message, 23; doctrine, 33
funeral, 44, 59, 64, 92, 112, 114, 171–73, 202, 243; fire, 138

Gallois, Dominique, 22, 44, 45, 52, 157, 196, 249, 258n8,11, 259n17, 274n2

game (animals), 6–7, 39, 70, 86, 101, 108, 113, 121–24, 126, 135, 139, 165, 200, 239, 240, 253, 268n21
Geertz, Clifford, 10, 221
gender, 14–15, 128, 210, 232, 267n13, 269n2, 270n2
Germany, 53, 140
Gernet, Jacques, 2–3, 24
Gershon, Ilana, 16, 125, 267n2, 274n14
Ghana, 15–16, 51, 140, 240, 260n6, 272n32
ghost, 118
God, 3–4, 7, 10–11, 16, 21, 25–26, 28–39, 44–47, 50–54, 68, 75, 93–95, 99, 104–6, 108, 111–12, 114–15, 117–19, 121, 124–25, 127, 133–39, 144–154, 156–58, 162–68, 171–74, 179–187, 189–195, 208, 212–15, 217, 219, 221–22, 227–28, 233–40, 246–48, 252, 260n9, 261n30, 265n13, 266nn19,23, 267n15, 268n21, 269nn22,23,27, 270n4,7,12, 271n13, 272n35, 273nn36,6, 275n13, 276nn22,24,30; abandoned, 5, 265n12; the Creator, 74, 119, 126, 129–32, 167, 268n16; double of, 114; faith in, 33; gift from, 34; incorporeal, 149, 161; kinship with, 172–73; language of, 53; and Pinom, 114–15; spirit of, 38–39; way of being of, 150; word of, 34, 38, 41–43, 45, 52, 54–55, 104, 110, 112, 135–36, 141, 174, 195, 209, 213–14, 237, 242, 268n17. *See also* Iri'Jam
gods, 19, 81–82, 142, 161
gospel, 31, 35–36, 38, 40, 45, 50, 107, 135, 187, 190, 196, 228
government, 3, 30, 32, 45, 86, 218, 252; agents, 46, 99, 104, 141
Gow, Peter, 9, 31, 54, 57, 127, 261n16, 264nn28,3, 265n7, 267n7, 270n12, 272n31, 275n9
Grotti, Vanessa, 18, 127, 264n1, 265n7,11, 266n24
Grupioni, Luís, 22, 44, 45, 52, 259n17
Guajará-Mirim, xiv, 5, 42–43, 85–88, 90–92, 101–2, 105, 118, 124, 181, 262n8, 275n15
Guaporé River, 85, 87, 104
Guarani, 55, 72, 94–95, 167, 262n32,36, 266nn23,24

Guayaki, 127
guilt, 44, 120, 201, 211

Hagen, 10, 13, 16
Handman, Courtney, 259n1, 260n5,7, 262n32, 269n29, 276n22
Hanks, William 257n2, 260n9, 270n8, 272n29, 277n7
Harding, Susan, 8, 9, 258n7
hate, 119
Hawaiians, 81
Haynes, Naomi, 258n13, 259n14
heart, 7, 31, 38, 49, 53, 62, 111, 115–16, 118, 146, 150, 153, 165–66, 178, 183, 185–91, 195, 202, 213–15, 227–28, 233–34, 237, 253, 260n4, 273nn6,8, 274n9, 275nn5,10; concept of, 26, 29, 222–27, 249; invisible, 194
heaven, 8, 29, 40, 52, 94, 104, 108–110, 117, 199, 129, 136–38, 152–53, 162–64, 166–72, 186–88, 190, 196, 215, 229, 237–241, 251, 265n14, 272n30, 276nn24–27, 29–31
Heckenberger, Michael, 57
Hefner, Robert, 2, 9–10
hell, 7–8, 32, 40, 107, 109, 119, 136–39, 163–65, 169–72, 237, 239, 241, 261n18, 269n27, 276nn26,28; fear of, 135
hierarchical encompassment, 13
hierarchy, 1, 44, 152, 164, 168, 221, 249; of languages, 52, 75, 260n9
Hill, Jonathan, 132
Hirsch, Eric, 275n19, 277n1
Holbraad, Martin, 18
holism, 14, 275n15
Holy; Scriptures, 34; Spirit, 16, 34, 38, 110, 114, 148, 152–53, 163, 168, 179, 198, 233, 236, 272nn26,35; Supper, 28, 111, 173, 176, 187–191, 194, 210, 228, 273n7; Trinity, 38, 51, 152
homonym, 64, 67, 69, 148
Hornborg, Alf, 271n24
Horton, Robin, 10, 221, 254
howa, 4, 38, 41, 103, 109, 144, 161, 163, 184, 186, 191–92, 212, 233, 239. *See also* believe; trust
Howell, Signe, 274n3,14
Hugh-Jones, Christine, 17, 57

Hugh-Jones, Stephen, 17, 57, 94, 132, 249, 264n27, 267n13, 272n25

human, 15, 18, 20–21, 27–29, 44, 59–61, 63–66, 68, 75, 77, 79–82, 120, 127–28, 130, 132, 142, 145, 150, 162, 164, 167–68, 187, 199–201, 211, 219–221, 224–225, 236, 245–48, 250, 260n11, 261n30, 266n20, 267nn9,13, 268nn19,20, 274n3; agency, 28, 54, 118–19, 148, 216, 248–49; appearance, 62, 113, 120, 148; different types of, 47, 66; identity; -ized, 20, 60, 165, 232, 248; non-, 15, 59, 76, 126, 128, 220, 232, 247, 261n23; person, 16; position of, 20, 98, 109, 112, 138. *See also* dehumanization

humanity, 15, 63, 98, 122, 198, 217, 222–27, 233, 241, 248, 266n1, 268n19, 277n5; conception of, 26, 29, 34–35, 56, 138, 222, 224, 245; differentiated, 246; extended notion of, 18, 25, 126; origin of, 131, 245; position of, 79; restricted notion of, 56, 168, 249; shrinking notion of, 221, 237; stabilization of, 198, 227; universe of, 248; instability of, 20, 81, 86, 122, 126, 132

humiliation, 12

hybridity, 11–12, 15, 244–46, 273n37

hymn, 7, 22, 72, 97, 116, 133–134, 151, 154, 162, 166, 173–74, 177–79, 181, 184–92, 224, 228, 243, 273n4

identity, 10, 17, 67–68, 73, 76, 81, 94, 112, 115, 125, 127, 142, 199–200, 208, 220, 227, 230–31, 244, 247, 262n37, 274n3; double, 70, 74; human, 128

ideology, 16, 26, 33, 136, 229, 271n24, 274n10, 277n5

illness, 128, 184, 200–201, 223, 225. *See also* disease

imitation, 4, 27, 53, 72–74, 92, 100, 102, 113–14, 149, 151, 164, 167, 190, 262n37, 269n1. *See also* mimetism

immateriality, 156, 225

immoral, 106, 144, 201–2, 207, 226

immortality, 114, 119, 148, 170, 197–98

Inca, 48, 81

inconstancy, 5, 20

incorporeality, 25, 149, 161–64, 233; divine, 38, 161

Indian Protection Service (SPI), 45–46, 86–88, 90, 93, 196, 262n7, 263n15

individual, 15, 33, 219–22, 224, 229–32, 241, 250–51, 274n2, 275n17; autonomy, 216; bounded, 29, 116, 229, 237; conversion, 34, 258n6; Euro-American, 217, 228, 254; genesis of the, 221; inner, 11; notion of the, 215, 249; self-contained, 15, 228; salvation, 198; subject, 222

individualism,14–16, 197, 220, 229–30, 237, 254, 274n3, 275nn15,17; Christian, 15, 172, 241, 265n7

individuality, 228; notion of, 250

individualization, 11, 14, 219–20, 229, 231, 246, 251, 253–54

individuation, 14, 221

Indonesia, 140, 159, 270n12

initiation, 128, 269n28

innate', 142, 167, 217, 250; universe, 25, 118; world, 25, 29, 118–20, 142–43, 168, 208, 216–17, 222, 249–51

innovation, radical, 24, 266n23

instability, 17–21, 81, 86, 122, 126–28, 131–32, 159–60, 168, 202, 224, 232

interiorization, 194, 206, 227–28, 237, 246–251, 277n4

Inuit, 94, 130, 262n32

invisibility, 50, 71, 144, 147–50, 162–64, 186, 191, 194, 202, 246, 251; constitutive, 148; problem of, 154

Iri' Jam, 38, 51, 104, 112, 115, 145–46, 148–53, 157, 161–64, 167, 179, 181, 184, 186, 193, 214, 236. *See also* God

Israel, 53, 184, 209, 266n23

Israelites, 183–84, 209

Jackson, Jean, 17

jaguar, 19, 21, 24, 40, 59, 61–71, 80, 108, 113–14, 117, 123–25, 127, 133–34, 138, 146, 194, 200, 203, 240, 244, 261n31, 266n23, 269n23

James, Wendy, 260n8

jamixi', 25, 66, 145–49, 163, 169, 192, 199, 224–25, 233, 235, 261n20, 270n7. *See also* double

jamu, 64, 66, 100, 127, 148, 239, 270n9. *See also* transform

Jesuits, 3–4, 47

literacy, 33, 49, 52–55, 258n5; il-, 44; non-,
52
literalism (biblical), 34–41, 47
Lloyd, Geoffrey, 23, 261n28, 268n19,
272n26, 277n1
Lord, 30, 32–33, 36, 54, 75, 93–94, 136, 188,
266n23. *See also* God
love, 32, 75, 115–16, 118, 134–36, 143, 150, 173,
188, 224, 266n23. *See also* dislike, not
Lowie, Robert, 17
Lucifer, 119, 164–65, 167–68, 272n30. *See
also* devil
Luther, 49; -an, 10, 275n13
Lyon, Patricia, 17

Madeira-Mamoré railway, 84, 147
Madeira river, 83, 85
Maisin, 13, 274n4
maize, 24, 61, 65, 72, 83, 93, 123, 195, 206,
239, 253; beer, 7, 202–3, 266n20; cake,
89, 187–88; chicha, 70, 78, 124, 170,
209; smoke, 62, 65, 70, 269n23
Malay, 31
Malaysia, 31, 84, 86
Mamoré river, 83, 85, 91
Marcus, George, 9
Marriot, McKim, 14, 128, 231
Marubo, 51, 68, 260n11, 261n21, 269n28
mass, 3, 4, 71–72, 86, 105
massacre, 122, 264
materiality, 156, 160, 265n15
Mauss, Marcel, 10–11, 219–221, 249
Maxwell, David, 26, 253
Mayblin, Maya, 271n13
Mayans, 81, 268n18
Maybury-Lewis, David, 17
McCallum, Cecilia, 19
McIlwain, Trevor, 24, 35–38, 42, 50, 149,
175
meals (collective), 4, 80, 174, 192–93
medicine, 4, 93–96, 154
Melanesian, 15, 28, 222, 231, 275n10,17;
cargo cults, 73; ethnography, 128; eth-
nology, 14; model, 128, 231–32; persons,
231–32, 277n1; social worlds, 128
Mesoamerica, 48
metal tools, 80, 86–87
metamorphosis, 21, 27, 61–63, 71, 73, 75, 98,

100, 109, 121, 126–27, 138, 194, 206,
245–46, 248, 262n37, 267n6; involuntary,
132, 142; voluntary, 249; world of, 145
metaphor, 56, 67–68, 110–11, 190–91, 257n1,
259n18, 261n28; conception of, 191;
similarity, 190
metaphysics, 68, 73, 75
metonymic continuity, 190
Meyer, Birgit, 9, 15, 51–52, 55, 140, 233, 240,
260n6, 270n11, 272n26,32
mimesis, 73, 217, 262n34
mimetic; behavior, 20, 72–73; fever, 92
mimetism, 24, 27, 71–74, 95–96, 98, 121,
142, 262nn32,37
mimicry, 71
miracle, 38, 54, 261n31
Missão Novas Tribos do Brasil (MNTB),
47, 75, 97, 116, 192, 258n10, 268n21
mission, 30–34, 41, 44, 46, 49–50, 72,
87–88, 98, 100–102, 136, 155, 210; field,
31; station, 13; basic principles of, 31
missionaries, 1–7, 9–13, 16–17, 21–28,
30–52, 54–57, 61, 71–72, 74–75, 77,
86–102, 104–114, 116–121, 125, 128, 130,
132–33, 135–41, 144–45, 147–56, 158–62,
164–65, 172, 174–76, 178, 181, 184,
190–92, 195–96, 209–211, 217, 220,
227–29, 234–37, 244, 254, 258n10,13;
power of the, 92–93; expansion, 1;
training, 44, 49, 91, 259nn16,2, 260n6,
263n9, 264n26, 270n9; translation, 64,
145; work, 5, 7, 24, 31, 34, 48, 94, 99;
writing, 158
misunderstanding, 1, 22, 120
modernity, 25, 250
moderns, 11, 247
monotheism, 16
moral, 10, 13, 35, 43, 104, 144, 168, 185, 193,
198, 217, 231, 277n4; action, 119; attitudes, 223; behavior, 170, 224; codes,
195–98, 206, 264n2; community, 227;
conduct, 197; conflict, 15, 198; conscience, 148, 221; control, 200–201;
defects, 248; deviations, 200; discourse,
194, 274n14; domain, 12; infractions,
213; life, 198; obligations, 197; principles,
34; regulation, 211; system, 196–98, 211,
216; transformations, 28

morality, 11, 13–15, 61, 106, 118, 135, 173, 194–96, 198, 200, 215–16, 226–27, 267n9, 277n5; Western, 216
moralization, 195, 199, 214
Moré, 87, 99
Morris, Colin, 275n16
Moses, 1, 41, 93, 134, 157, 176, 184, 265n16, 271n20
Mosko, Mark, 14, 16, 265n17, 272n34, 275n19
mourning, 80, 124, 171, 271n23
multinaturalism, 75
music, 26, 44, 58, 95, 105–6, 108, 138, 242–43
myth, 19–20, 57, 77, 112–15, 121–25, 130–31, 134, 141, 145–47, 149, 156–57, 162, 167, 202, 205, 242, 245, 247–48, 260n14, 262n2,3, 273n5; flood, 90, 266n20, 267n4,5; Genesis, 132, 220, 246; lizard, 122, 140; origin, 58, 77, 113, 132, 220
mythic, 28, 52–53, 58, 60, 80, 89, 147, 203, 268n20, 271n22; continuity, 132; figure, 51, 53, 112, 114, 144–45, 157–58, 173, 258n2, 266n20; origin, 82; participation, 220, 274n4; thought, 220; world, 20; universe, 221
mythology, 6, 19–20, 56, 81–82, 97, 131–32, 139, 168, 217, 245, 268n16, 273n36; of stabilization, 168, 246; stabilization and conventionalization, 246; of transformation, 168

National Indian Foundation. See FUNAI
naturalism, Western, 18
naturalist; mode of identification, 247; ontologies, 19
nature, idea of, 220, 237
Negro River, 5–6, 21, 60, 85, 89–94, 99–111, 124, 135, 137–39, 150, 152–54, 163, 166, 171, 174, 176–78, 182, 186, 188, 193, 195, 199, 207–210, 238–39, 263n10
New Caledonia, 220, 260n7, 270n12
New Tribes Mission (NTM), 3, 5, 21, 26, 30–31, 33, 35, 46, 49–50, 55, 86, 95, 98, 196, 257n7, 258n13, 259n16, 259n16,19, 262n8; missionaries, 22–23, 26–27, 30, 35, 42, 47, 49, 89–90, 101, 209, 258n5,13,

259n13, 263n16,21, 273n2; history, 30, 54, 257n1; ideology, 33, 136
Noah, 36, 52, 93, 176, 266n20, 267n15, 271n15
Nóbrega, Father Manuel da, 3, 71
North America, 16, 44, 49, 271n13
NTM. See New Tribes Mission

Ocaia river, 85, 90, 193
Oliveira, Leonor, 258n13, 264n1, 269n26
omnipresence, 25, 28, 144, 161–62, 179, 222, 237, 246–47, 251
omniscience, 25, 161–62, 195, 222, 237, 251
ontological, 68, 82, 130, 270n8, 275n17; changes, 250; effect, 207; multiplicity, 51; reduction, 221; transformations, 250
ontology, 18, 48, 232, 247, 257n5; naturalist, 19; perspectivist, 22, 25–27
Oosten, Jarich, 94
Opas, Minna, 51, 227, 261n23, 267n6,9,12, 268n20, 269n27, 272n31, 275n5, 276n25,30
orality, 52–53
Orta, Andrew, 16, 55
oscillation, 12–13, 15, 29, 64, 73, 79, 217, 236, 245
other; becoming, 13, 20, 25, 131; opening to the, 15, 19, 28, 81, 140; repugnant, 8–9; perspective of the, 28, 222, 235–36
otherness, 216
Overing [Kaplan], Joanna, 17, 19, 67–68, 132, 142, 216, 224, 230, 261n29, 266n21, 268n20, 269n32, 276n31,1

Pacific, 2, 17, 81, 159, 250, 264n6
pagan, 26, 43, 107–108, 137, 161, 195, 227
Palikur, 177, 196, 264n26,29, 270n12, 271n15,21, 274n3, 276n22
Panará, 127
Pano, 67–68
paper, 54, 110, 117, 154–58, 160, 162, 238, 243; power of, 54
Papua New Guinea, 10, 12–13, 40, 46, 50, 61, 81, 110, 140, 159, 240, 250, 260nn5,6,7, 266n24, 270n10, 276n22
paradise, 119
paradox, 11, 16, 23, 142, 144, 216, 218, 230, 244–246, 248, 250

Paraguay, 72

Parakanã, 127, 264n30

Passes, Alan, 19, 216, 230, 269n32

pastor, 7–8, 10, 28, 30, 36, 39–40, 42, 46, 55,
93, 99, 100–101, 103, 107–111, 114, 125,
129–30, 149–53, 156, 162–63, 174–84,
186, 190–93, 195, 208, 210–14, 224, 228,
233, 236, 242, 259n15, 261n30, 265n13,
267n14, 272n35, 273n2

Paul, apostle, 9, 34, 36, 42, 50, 167, 258n13,
265n7

Paumari, 51, 269n27, 270n12

Pedersen, Morten, 18

Pentecost, 55, 57

pentecostal, 15, 41, 110, 140, 272n26; neo-,
41

person, 14–15, 19, 21, 25–26, 34, 36, 56,
58–61, 64–69, 71, 76, 118, 128, 133, 136,
138, 140, 142, 144–45, 147–48, 150–51,
163, 165–67, 169, 216–17, 220–22, 224–
26, 228, 231–32, 234–37, 241, 248–50,
265n17, 270n7; complex, 151, 158; composite, 14; conception of the, 11, 14, 29,
191, 197, 199, 211, 215, 218–20; configuration of the; deceased, 124, 128, 146, 162,
169–70, 215, 270n6; human; interiorized, 227; interiorization of the, 222,
237, 249; multiple, 15–16, 219, 231;
multiple divine, 162, 167, 246; singularization of the, 228

personhood, 13–14, 128, 229, 244; alternating, 14; and its transformations, 29;
conception of, 11, 14, 28, 118–19, 219–20,
222, 232, 277n5

perspectival epistemology, 24

perspective, 14, 20–23, 28, 58, 66–67, 73,
122, 125–26, 141, 161, 163, 170, 172, 194,
196, 215, 225, 237, 241; of Creation, 141,
179; of the missionaries, 100, 125, 156; of
the other, 28, 222, 235–36; divine, 28, 35,
134, 157, 173, 235; double, 65, 235; notion
of, 246; change of, 121, 125, 139, 267n6

perspectives, 118, 140; capture of new, 160;
difference between, 19, 22, 26, 117, 125,
235, 244; flattening of, 237; translator
of, 65, 261n23

perspectivism, 11, 14, 18–19, 23–24, 63, 68,
73, 161, 245, 257n5, 267n8

perspectivist, 18, 24, 232, 236; equivocation,
116; notion of conversion, 28; notion of
translation, 235; ontology, 22, 25–27;
principle, 246, 250; translation, 63, 71,
144, 261n18; universe, 144; world, 247

Peru, 51, 54, 72, 136, 260n3, 272n25, 275n8,
276n30, 277n7

Philippines, 35, 48, 159–60

Piaroa, 67–68, 132, 142, 230, 268n20,
276n31

Piro/Yine, 51, 54, 127, 227, 261nn16,23,
264nn28,3, 265n7, 267nn6,7,9, 268n20,
269n27, 270n12, 272n31, 275n5,9,
276nn25,30

Pollock, Donald, 3, 10–11, 26, 51, 228–29,
264n27

Portuguese (nation), 2, 48, 81

posthumous; destiny, 107, 109, 128, 136,
169–70, 197, 237, 239–40; life, 106, 148,
170, 241; world, 80, 168–69, 276n31

postmortem destinies, multiple, 169

prayer, 3, 31–33, 35, 56, 93, 95, 99, 108, 111,
121, 129–30, 133, 135, 152–53, 162–63, 166,
172–75, 177, 179, 181, 185, 187, 189–90,
192, 194, 198, 208, 228, 236, 269n24

praying, 3, 5, 7, 20, 35, 72, 94, 118, 150, 158,
171, 179–80, 189, 192, 212, 215, 238, 244

preach, 4, 37, 41–42, 49, 54–55, 174, 182–83,
195, 209

preacher, 28, 133, 152–53, 157, 165, 174–76,
178–79, 184, 189, 192, 212

predation, 79, 126, 134, 138–39, 198, 249,
266n23; counter-, 200

predator, 20, 59, 68, 79, 81, 97, 114, 122, 126,
128, 132, 134, 138, 165, 191, 203, 223,
267n13, 268n19; -y action of animals, 79,
240; -y capacities, 162, 200

premillennialist, 40

pretribulationist, 40

prey, 20, 59–60, 64, 70, 76, 78–80, 97, 108,
124, 126, 130, 132, 134, 138, 141, 165, 171,
198–99, 225–26, 241, 275n8; position,
40, 59, 79, 82, 128, 137, 207, 267n13;
eternal, 138, 172. See also game

priest, 26, 46, 55, 72, 104–5, 150, 160, 259n3,
262n32

prophesy, 81–82, 262n32

prophet, 35, 94, 153, 270n7

proselytize, 136
Protestant Reform, 11, 49
pulpit, 134, 156, 175–76, 178–79, 181–84,
187, 191–92, 208–9
punishment, 52, 95, 114, 119, 136, 197, 202–5,
266n20
purification, 247, 277n3

Queiroz, Rubem, 261n27, 264n1,27,28,30,
269n22

Rafael, Vicente, 48–49, 51–52, 55, 158–60,
260n6, 269n29,33
rage, 114, 146, 201–2, 205, 214, 217,
266n23,24
reading, 5, 7, 12, 28, 33, 36, 39–40, 54–55,
71–72, 101–7, 111, 118, 121, 156, 158–59,
163, 167, 174–75, 177–79, 181, 183–84,
187–89, 192, 194, 198, 210, 228, 233, 237,
240, 244, 269n25, 271nn22,23, 273n7,
275n12; fluctuating, 158
reclusion, 80, 111, 128, 147, 170, 199
reconversion, 108
redemption, 112, 191
Reichel-Dolmatoff, Gerard, 262n33
relational, 10–11, 15, 18–19, 64, 68, 78–79,
142, 149, 157, 159, 224, 226, 231, 236,
244, 248, 276n30; world, 26, 237; universe, 11, 59, 66; -ism, 14–15, 197
resurrection, 34–35, 38, 154, 176
revenge, 46, 66, 146, 198–200, 204, 208
reversibility, 23, 203
reversible, 13, 20, 138; non-, 107, 141
revival, 7, 12, 49, 169, 177
Ribeirão, 42, 91, 107, 136, 208; Ribeirão
river, 85, 89, 108
rite, 80, 159, 171, 173–74, 193, 198; collective,
174, 177; of commensality, 190; traditional, 25, 122
ritual, 1, 4, 6, 11, 14, 24, 29, 55–58, 72, 78,
86, 89, 95, 111, 118, 142, 173–74, 187, 191,
193–94, 198, 200, 202, 211, 216, 218, 226,
228–29, 262n32; abstinence, 127; action,
71–72, 95, 194, 204, 206–7, 217; affines,
98; of commensality, 106, 122; efficacy,
73, 95, 98; end of traditional; inversion,
218; life, 7, 28, 173, 195, 219; new, 6,
15, 25, 28, 208, 248, 250–51, 277n5;

paraphernalia, 73; partners, 97; traditional, 7, 55, 248, 250–51; transformations, 193, 222
rivalry, 9, 78, 167, 170, 196, 200, 204, 250
Rivière, Peter, 11, 17, 51, 78, 195, 230,
264n26, 265n9, 266n19, 272n36, 274n3
Robbins, Joel, 9, 11–15, 27–28, 40, 98, 110,
122, 161, 196–98, 226, 250, 254, 257n1,
260n7, 264n2, 265nn11,13,15, 269n22,30,
271n14,19, 272n26, 273nn6,8, 274n3,
274nn9,10,11,14, 275nn10,17, 276n27
Roman Empire, 1–2
Rondônia, 3, 5, 83, 100, 137–38, 255
rubber, 84, 86, 99, 203; boom, 83, 86; boss,
101–2, 264n4; tappers, 3, 82, 84, 86–87,
97, 139, 263n10
Rumsey, Alan, 11, 273n6
Rutherford, Danilyn, 140, 159–60, 270n12

sacrifice, 34, 43, 45, 119, 187
sadness, 150, 223, 271n23
Sagarana village, 61, 69–70, 85, 104–5, 108,
138, 150, 156–57, 229, 277n8
Sahlins, Marshall, 9, 12–13, 16, 22–24, 81,
119, 254, 257n3, 262n35
saint, 94, 220
salvation, 6, 34, 119–20, 189, 198, 220, 227,
258n7; through faith, 34
Santo André, 91, 101, 107, 111, 136, 175, 181,
209, 236, 263n17; river, 69
Santos-Granero, Fernando, 72–73, 167,
262n35, 264n29, 266n23, 272n25
Satan, 42, 51, 165, 190–91. See also devil
save, 34, 40, 119, 189, 224. See also salvation
Schaden, Egon, 267n12
Scharf, Friedrich, 22, 43, 45, 72, 88, 91,
93–94, 100, 155, 258n4, 263nn10,13,14
Schieffelin, Bambi, 9, 11, 27, 50, 250, 258n8,
260nn5,7,9, 270nn3,10, 271n23,
273nn6,8, 275nn10,12
Schieffelin, Edward, 81
Schneider, David, 9
school, 13, 44, 158, 208, 221, 229, 251–52,
271nn22,24; school writing, 158
Second World War, 86
secrecy, 73, 158–59, 201, 215, 226–28, 237,
246
secret interior, 15, 215

Seeger, Anthony, 17, 19, 128, 230

Segal, Alan, 260n12

self, 29, 194, 221, 274n4, 275n14; -control, 196; -discipline, 275n13; inner, 26, 29, 191, 194, 197, 215, 222, 227–28, 230, 232, 236, 246, 249–50, 253, 277n5; inner secret, 219; interior, 15; outer, 236; psychological, 220–21, 237, 250; technologies of the, 25, 28, 197–98, 229

self-contained individual, 15, 228, 251

sermon, 30, 36, 93, 102, 110–12, 117, 129, 157, 160, 162, 177, 181, 184–85, 194, 209–10, 273n6

service. *See* church services

seventeenth century, 49, 55, 94, 159, 260n6; seventeenth-century Franciscan, 48

shaman, 5, 43, 51, 55, 59, 63–69, 71–74, 77, 80, 82, 94–96, 125, 139, 140, 143, 144, 147–50, 152, 160, 163–65, 167–69, 171, 196, 199–200, 214, 225, 235, 244, 246–48, 261n22, 262n32, 264nn28,29, 268n17, 269nn23,28, 270n12

shamanic; auxiliaries, 51, 94; curing, 4–5, 7, 65, 146, 200, 214; dictionary, 27; knowledge, 157; language, 95; powers, 54; practices, 150; systems, 249; traditions, ancient, 196; transformations, 20, 74, 235; vision, 55, 160, 225

shamanism, 7, 25, 67, 73, 96, 142, 216, 218, 249–250; and translation, 27, 64, 67; horizontal, 249

Shapiro, Judith, 50

siblinghood, 28, 107, 118; generalized, 107, 274n6

siblings, 92, 105–106, 116, 124, 139, 158, 180–81, 192, 195, 209–210, 232, 237

sickness, 59, 64, 66–67, 71, 93–95, 99–100, 123, 134, 165, 171, 199–200, 214, 225, 248, 269n22. *See also* illness; *see also* disease

SIL. *See* Summer Institute of Linguistics

Silverstein, Michael, 271n19

sin, 5–6, 34, 50–51, 54, 75, 107, 111–12, 117, 119, 152, 163–64, 166, 172–73, 188–91, 195–98, 201, 212–15, 233–34, 240, 244, 248, 265n11, 272n34, 274n9; notion of, 213, 248; original, 119–20

sincerity, 11, 274n7, 277n5

sinner, 15, 168, 171, 190, 194, 212–15, 240

sixteenth century, 2–3, 47, 259n3; missionary, 4, 17; Tupinambá, 19

sorcery, 4, 6, 43, 59, 68, 79, 86, 94, 97, 106, 114, 121–22, 155, 169–70, 195, 203, 207, 211–12, 226, 248, 265n11, 275n8

Sotério, 37, 91; Sotério river, 91

soul, 16, 21, 25–26, 28–29, 31, 34, 51, 132, 141, 143, 148, 159, 169, 185–86, 209, 232–35, 243, 260n5, 270n8, 275n7; incorporeal, 233. *See also tamataraxi'*

Souza Lima, Antônio Carlos, 262n7

Spanish, 2, 48, 50–52, 81, 159

SPI. *See* Indian Protection Service

spirits, 5, 19, 43, 45, 64, 68, 77, 94–95, 104, 112, 138, 142, 145, 148–49, 151, 153, 160, 163, 169, 236, 268n17, 270n8, 272nn30,35; auxiliary, 94; native, 51

stability, 9, 226. *See also* instability

stabilization, 109, 122, 198, 217, 219–21, 245–46, 250; of bodies, 20; of humanity, 131; mythology of, 168

Stasch, Rupert, 260n7, 266n24, 273n6

Stoll, David, 31, 47, 258n7,12

Stolz, Franz, 258n6

Strathern, Marilyn, 9–10, 13–14, 16, 18–19, 81, 128, 221–22, 231–32, 249–250, 257n4, 267n13, 271n24, 272n33, 275n19, 276n21

Strout, Christopher, 159, 240

subaquatic world of the dead, 5, 66, 138, 147, 156, 169–71

subgroups, 5, 44, 57–59, 77–78, 83, 86–87, 89–90, 104, 124, 132, 141, 155, 161, 170, 173, 200, 203–4, 208, 211, 240

subjection, mode of, 197–98, 211

subjectivation, forms of, 196

Sumbanese, 55

Summer Institute of Linguistics (SIL), 31, 33, 44, 47, 136, 229, 259n19, 260n5, 264n26

Surrallès, Alexandre, 261n21

Suyá, 128

syncretism, 12

Tagalog, 48, 51–52, 159–60, 269n33

tamatarakon Iri' Jam, 38, 148, 179, 236. *See also* Holy Spirit

Milton Keynes UK
Ingram Content Group UK Ltd.
UKHW020621120424
441015UK00004B/250

9 780520 289147